SCUBA

Other Books by Jimmy Olsen

- Things In Ditches
- Poison Makers
- The Hero of Blind Pig Island and Other Island Stories

SCUBA
A Novel

by Jimmy Olsen

Hoffman House
PRESS

Hoffman House
PRESS

505 Fourth Street South
P.O. Box 161
Hoffman, MN 56339

Contact Hoffman House Press: www.hoffmanhousepress.com
or Email hoffmanhousepress@cloudnet.com
Jimmy Olsen: www.jimmyolsen.net

ISBN 978-0-9801835-9-7

For Camille

My lifetime dive buddy

Author's Note

This novel is fiction with one exception - the battle between warships of Britain and France is historically correct, including the names of sea captains and admirals involved. I researched the naval archives of both nations, and though they differ slightly in perspective, the 1806 battle in which the world's largest warship was destroyed, is reported as it happened, according to those who fought on both sides. The shipwreck is described as I found and dove it in 1973. The actual wreck site is near Punta Palenque, Dominican Republic. Several years after its discovery an American salvage company in search of gold destroyed the wreck, just as Warren Wilson feared. The small amount of gold recovered barely paid the expense of salvage.

Reggie Wilson and his family are fictional characters. However, the "pressing" of American sailors by the British in the 1800s is well documented.

Charming Island is fictional also, and I altered Caribbean geography to create it. However, scattered remains of *Imperial* can no doubt still be seen by divers in the Dominican Republic.

SCUBA

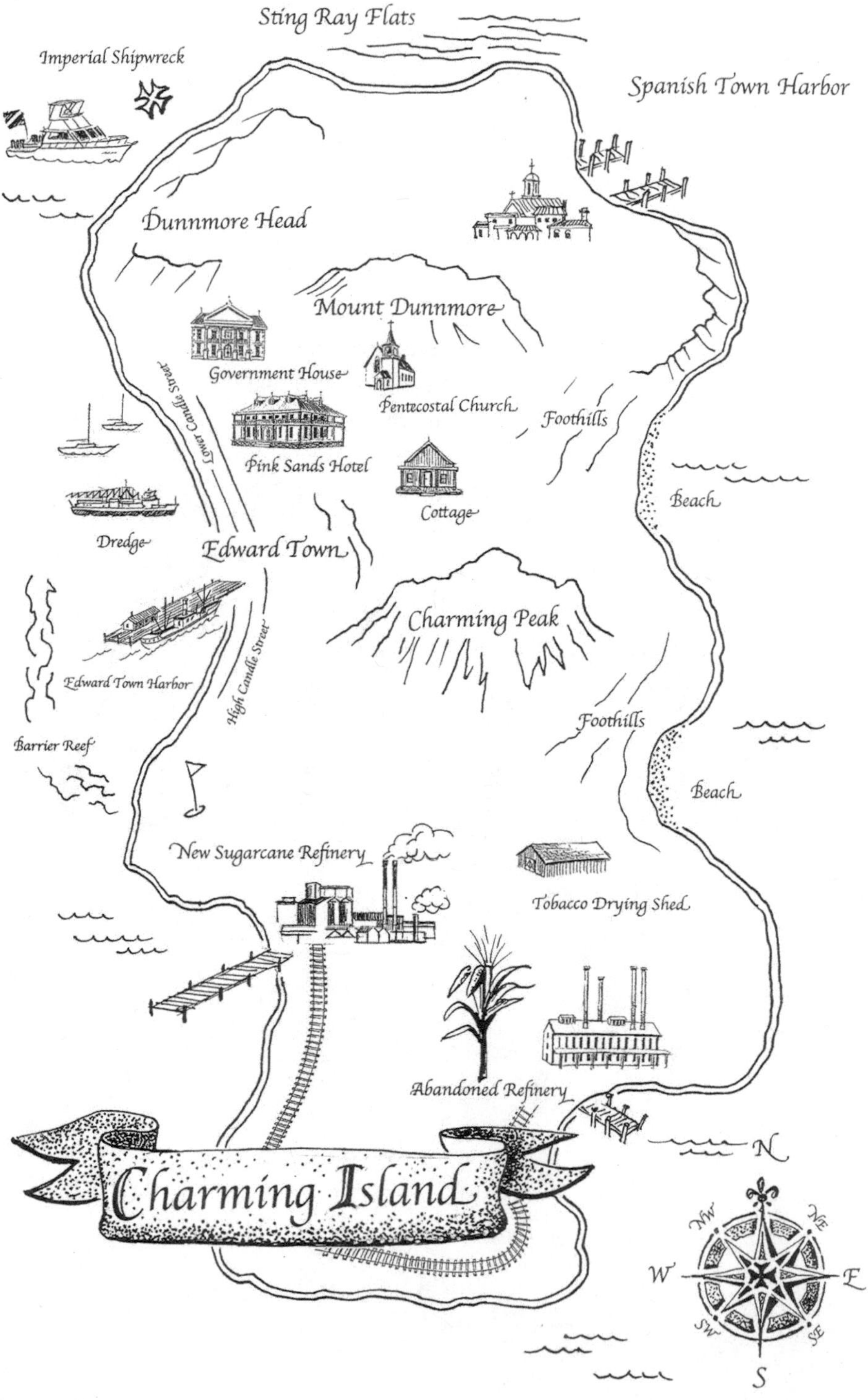

Sketch by: R.C. McCoy
www.rcmccoyartist.com

Yonder is the sea, great and wide, which teems with things innumerable, living things both small and great. There go the ships, and Leviathan which thou didst form to sport in it.

- Psalm 104

Sailors

February 6, 1806

CHAPTER ONE

THE BRITISH

February 6, 1806
Morning watch. Surprised French fleet at anchor near Charming Island. In pursuit. Fine West Indies day. Blue sky, light northeasterly breezes and moderate seas. Main topgallants set. Hope to engage the enemy within the hour. Gulls have come out to dive in our wake and we smell the land.

Tossing the logbook onto an overturned bucket, Vice Admiral Sir John Duckworth closes his eyes, listening to the straining hemp and slapping canvas of captured breezes pulling them across the water. Bowing his neck to the sun's soothing warmth he yearns to rest on the quarterdeck awhile. The surprised Frenchys are running to gain sea room and gather their wits. Soon they'll turn and fight, this fleet he's chased all the way from the European blockade at Brest.

High in the yards, a seaman tallies the enemy's strength. "Four ships of the line! Two frigates and a first-rater, heavily armed!" cries the young lookout, unable to hide his awe at sighting a first-rater. "Forming two battle lines!"

The first-rater, of course, is *Imperial*, one of the largest warships in the world. Three decks of heavy cannon. One hundred and twenty guns.

Seamanship wins more battles than cannon, Sir John nervously reminds himself. Nevertheless, *Superb* and the other seven vessels under his command are all third-raters or less. *Imperial* is a match for any two.

Battle drums roll above the deck like jungle thunder. Sir John comes to his feet. It's out of his hands now. The violent storm about to engulf them even he cannot order quiet. There's thunder below too, as six hundred men swarm on deck, hoarse battle cries masking their fear.

"What signal to the fleet?" Captain Richard Goodwin Keats, a soft-spoken man, intrudes reluctantly on his admiral's thoughts.

"*Superb* shall lead the weather line," he orders, planning a course to cross ahead of the French lines. "Followed by *Northumberland*, *Spencer*, and *Agamemnon*. To larboard, *Canopus*, *Donegal*, and *Atlas*. Signal the smaller ships to stand windward."

At 58, nearing the end of his naval career, Sir John can't afford mistakes. The Admiralty, always fond of court-martials, has little pity for officers who lose battles, even if they face a world menace like *Imperial*, which he's dogged all the way to the Caribbean.

Spotting the admiral's personal log, Captain Keats asks, "Would you like that taken below, Sir?"

Duckworth nods and a uniformed aide is dispatched with the heavy book. "The letters are in place," Keats continues, referring to personal documents detailing their final wishes.

The admiral nods disdainfully. "Once again we're worth more dead than alive," he says, grinning enough to lift his jowls and form a jaw line. Combat brings out the best in him.

Duckworth snatches his telescope and strides to the rail. No mistakes this time. He had his fill of court-martials last year with that *Acasta* mess at Jamaica. Even his acquittal - he'd been charged with using HMS *Acasta* to haul cargo for profit - couldn't put a stop to the endless rumors. Defeating *Imperial* will balance the scales nicely, perhaps earn him a peerage and funds to live his remaining years in comfort.

Falling in beside him, Captain Keats dispatches another aide with signaling instructions. "This time we have them, Sir John," he predicts.

"Yes," Duckworth agrees. "We shan't turn aside until *Imperial* is destroyed. On that you have my word."

"She'll make a glorious prize if we take her intact."

"To hell with prize money! Her keel on the sand or let every man aboard perish in the effort." Ignoring Keats, he swings the glass leeward toward the rugged coast of Charming Island. Dick Keats is one of his best captains, but a judicious fellow. Floggings almost unheard of aboard *Superb* since Keats took command. Though ridiculed by his peers, the man's crew fight like demons to please him. Wisely, Duckworth hasn't interfered, but no appeasement today, Dick. Before this morning is done, we'll sow the sea with blood and bones until it yields up a victory. Inwardly, he smiles at the thought. Quite profound for a sailor. Must make note of it for his diary.

Sir John braces himself against the irregular heaving of the deck, steadying the telescope with both hands. A high, black coastline dances inside the glass. Charming Island's sparsely inhabited, he recalls. Perhaps fifty leagues lengthwise. All of it contended by the major powers for two centuries. First Spain, then Britain, France, Spain, and Britain again.

"Who in hell owns the place now?" he asks the captain.

Keats shrugs. "No idea, Admiral. Might be Spanish, even Portuguese."

"Cliffs are sharpened stone. Forty feet above the water, swells smashing against them." He sighs and lowers the glass. "Make every effort to pick our men out of the water. Can't have them cut to bits climbing up there, only to be lanced through the gizzard by some tallow-eyed Spaniard."

"Yes, Sir John," Keats agrees. Admirals issue such orders to make themselves feel better. During battle there's no time to row about picking up men in the water, and after it's over, two kinds are left in the sea - floaters and sinkers.

Keats signals to his first lieutenant, waiting several yards away. Time to inspect combat preparations and swagger a bit on the gun decks. The men expect it. "By your leave, Admiral." Keats bows.

Duckworth nods.

"The long-range guns first I believe, Mr. Norton," Keats tells the First Lieutenant striding after him. Away from the Admiral he's relieved, back where he belongs. Above all, Keats is a sailor. "I'm tired of watching men die," he says, louder than intended. "Though dead men are easier to forget then those I face now."

"Sir?"

"Nothing. Nothing at all."

Deck cannon, unlike the more portable carronade, stand always in one of three positions: run-out, recoiled, or secured on the gun deck. Ordinary seaman Reginald V. Wilson squats beside his gun, Number Seven, smoking a clay pipe. Number Seven is still secured.

"This time they'll kill us sure."

Reggy peers though the smoke. It's Ian Stuart speaking in a hoarse whisper.

"Proper lot of murdering scum, these gentlemen," the Irishman continues, jerking a thumb at Keats and Norton. "And Old Ducky up there waddling about on the quarterdeck, quacking orders. Bloody hell! Get his peerage too one day, don't you worry. Not that a one of us'll be alive to see it."

"Pipe down," Reggy warns.

"Afraid they'll hear me?"

"No," the American grins. "Afraid I'll have to listen to it all again. Anyway, they're your officers, not mine."

"Bloody hell!"

Stuart, Wilson, and gun captain Richard Kempenfelt are crewmen on Number Seven, a well-worn 24-pounder. They specialize in waterline shots, and they're good at it. They hadn't started as friends. Reggy Wilson was pressed, dragged aboard from an American merchantman the previous year. He'd resisted so violently a bo's'n and several of *Superb's* crew, including Stuart, beat him senseless, indulging England's right to press any so-called American seaman found aboard a vessel trading with France. Stuart hadn't changed that opinion, but he knew courage when he saw it, and if the rest of these American sailors were anything like Reggy, there'd be a lot more trouble with them before long. "I'll say this for you Yankee, and I don't much care who hears it, you're a good man in a fight."

Reggy knocks a glowing ember of tobacco onto the deck, brushing it in between the cracks. "I've got an ill feeling about this one, Ian," the American confides. "Last night I dreamed of the Chesapeake. Sunday. Mary with her hair tied up under a white scarf, drifting along Bloodsworth Island fishing skipjack. Not catching any. Not caring." Reggy's face grew dark. "She's had the child by now."

"It's Satan," Stuart explains. "The French are a devil-worshiping race. This close to 'em you're bound to dream. Old Beelzebub be after me as well, if it weren't for this." He yanks a leather pouch from beneath his shirt. "Amulet," he boasts. "Jamaican witch give it to me."

"Sold it to you, you mean." It was Dickey Kempenfelt, a thin-lipped, bony-faced man with paper skin. "And no witch. Kingston whore."

Dickey is a mystery to Reggy. He shows little interest in anything but the gun. Even food bores him. "These holes," Reggy asks, pointing with his pipe stem. "For larger pins?"

"No," Dickey says. "New tackle positions. Safeguard on recoil. Greater traverse-firing capability too, I hope." Yesterday he drilled two new bulkhead holes for breeching ropes and recoil tackle pins, one on each side of the gunport. When a 24-pounder fires, the recoil is so violent tackle is easily jammed, spinning the massive gun around or even flipping it. Inexperienced gunners face more danger from their own cannon than anything fired at them from an enemy's barrel.

Unlike Reggy and Ian, who provide guts and muscle, Dickey understands the geometry of accurately flinging 24-pound balls into an enemy vessel. And the French are his enemy. This past winter they butchered his older brother, George, at Trafalgar. For such things there's a price.

Bored with Dickey's gunnery, Ian slaps Reggy's knee. "What say you, Mate? Our friend Dickey paling just a mite at the thought of aiming his great gun on the likes of *Imperial*?"

Without a hint of irony Dickey answers, "She's nothing to me but an easy target."

"Aye, my pale friend," Ian teases. "And what do you suppose all those Frenchys will be doing while you're so calmly making an easy target of them?"

"Putting their heads between their knees if they know what's good for them."

Reggy can't suppress a grin. Englishmen. Easy to love. Easy to hate. The United States won its independence two decades ago. They pay no attention. If he dies here - a common seaman, an American - who cares? Any midshipman's dog is more highly regarded and would undoubtedly receive a more Christian burial. The officers, gentlemen all, deem it a privilege for the lower classes to generously shed their common blood for England. Better to die swimming for the American vessels reported inshore. They'd certainly take him aboard. A week and he might be back in Baltimore, Mary in his arms. Why then, this hollowness in his stomach? These pangs of guilt?

Frustrated, Reggy leans against the bulkhead and stretches his cramped legs, wiggling his toes. Like the others, he's barefoot, a precaution against slipping.

A powder monkey, one of many small boys snatched from London's poverty-ridden streets, spreads sand on the gun deck.

"Hey, boy! What're you about there?" taunts one of the new men, a brutish fellow they'd picked up a month ago in Kingston.

The boy, too frightened to answer, freezes in his tracks. "You deaf, boy?" The man snatches his thin arm and pinches it white.

Reggy sees pain on the urchin's face. "Let him be," he commands.

The man sneers. "I take no orders from Yankee scum."

The American at first ignores the insult, then in the blink of an eye leaps across and grasps the man's wrist, painfully breaking his grip on the boy's arm. With his free hand, Reggy locks hard fingers onto the man's left ear, twisting until he howls in pain. "Be a good little limey now and leave the boy be."

Desperate, the new man whines for help. "He's tearing it off!"

Agile, brooding for a fight, Ian Stuart hops onto Number Seven's back and squats there like a great pelican. "Only a damn fool asks a question like that," he tells the man. Other heads nod. "You've bragged a bit loudly on your exploits since coming aboard, but no one here needs ask the boy what he's about. Only you. You've never sailed on a fightin' ship, I'm thinkin', and a weak sister you'll be here today."

Suspicious murmurs from the gun crews. There's no room for a man who can't pull his weight. Their lives depend on each other, and a bit of luck.

Reggy releases the man's ear but remains close. "The boy spreads sand on the deck," he explains, "to soak up the blood."

The man's round face blanches. Ian smiles at him. "We'll be ever so busy loading our gun, you see. Wouldn't do to slip on the juice of your guts and bang a shin, now would it?" A round of laughter.

Reggy shoves the man back against the bulkhead. If it was dark, he'd swim for it right now.

"You men there," the Bo's'n growls. "Turn to." A short distance behind him Captain Keats strolls the gun deck, white breeches gleaming in the morning sun. Keats isn't so bad, for an officer. Before he took command, Reggy got flogged twice for minor offenses.

"How are you, Wilson?" the Captain inquires, pausing near the secured cannon. Reggy has no idea Keats knows his name.

"Fine, thank you, Sir."

The Captain glides his thin fingers lightly along Number Seven's rough surface. "In the little harbor just there - Edward Town - are two American merchantmen. Would you like to go aboard one of them?"

Reggy held his breath. Could Keats know even his thoughts?

"Speak up, man," the Bo's'n orders.

"Well...yes Sir."

"Do your duty here today," the Captain smiles, "as you have done, and I'll see to it. We'll have done with the French before noon. I plan to take *Superb* inshore for water this evening. I'll have you sent over. Your services here are laudable. Time now to return you to your family."

Keats continues his inspection. Reggy should thank him. Say something. But his mind is choked with thoughts of home, Mary, a baby he's never seen. Fishing the Chesapeake again. Seems impossible. One more fight and he's free.

Reggy's anger at the new man evaporates, replaced by something deeper, more compelling. He leans out the gunport, hugging Number Seven for balance. The French sails are clearly visible, all in line, ready to fight. He's ready now too. Those ships, those men are all that stand between him and home.

THE FRENCH

Across the ever narrowing expanse of blue water, Francois Javert has his own ideas about freedom. A small, dark Frenchman, Javert loathes his service in the French Navy every bit as ardently as Reggy Wilson strains against the leash of England. His bare feet curled, gripping the high yard rigging, Javert ponders his escape plan. From this dizzying height, officers appear as miniature penguins capering about the deck. A sight to warm your heart, these men of property and influence waddling far below. Today, he puts an end to them.

A topman, Javert works aloft in the sheets. A trained monkey 120 feet above *Imperial's* polished teakwood decks hopping and swinging to make sail. Among the first to sight the British fleet, he has strength and dexterity that will be pushed to the limit now, rigging the sparse combat sail.

Though it's a fine day, Javert shivers in the February sun. He can see for miles. The rich Caribbean rolls before him, thick with life. With its burdensome rules and arrogant enforcers, the Navy is contemptible, but the sea, that's another matter. The sea can take you anywhere. Looking aft, the penguins are playing into his hands. Captain Bigot has ordered two boats put over, one loaded with livestock and the other filled to its gunwales with officer's furniture.

The boats, towed astern out of harm's way during the fight, fit into Javert's escape plan. "Escape," not desertion. He's no coward, after all, resolving to remain aboard until the hated British are defeated, then slip into the sea, swim to the furniture boat and row ashore. Stealing the livestock boat hardly seemed right. If the goats, chickens, and hogs survive the battle, the remaining crewmen will butcher them for a feast. He won't deny them that. Making off with the officer's furniture and goods on the other hand, promises a grand exit from Emperor Napoleon's stinking navy.

"Attention aloft!" shouts the First Lieutenant into his speaking trumpet. "Bear a hand with that swivel gun."

A group of struggling topmen and sharpshooters drag a half-pounder through the lubber's hole where it can be platform mounted to fire a swath of grape across at the enemy topmen. Javert is glad for once to be out on the yard ready for the command to take in sail. Lugging canvas bags of heavy grape shot is backbreaking work. Theory holds that if you fire enough grape and get enough sharpshooters up, the enemy vessel can't keep men aloft to maneuver. Such strategy gives a first-rater like *Imperial* the advantage. More than two hundred feet long and crewed by almost 1,500 men (about 1,200 aboard now) it has few equals. Javert guesses the approaching *Superb* carries 600 men or fewer, and as sea battles are often fights of attrition, the larger crew has better odds.

The half-pounder is followed up by four grenade throwers, shoulder bags filled to overflowing. Javert knows them all. Hopeless drunkards, and not one yet twenty. High atop the mizzen platform, they'll fling lighted grenades into the enemy's sails, setting them ablaze. Doubtful any will survive the first few minutes of close combat once British marines get a bead on them. Grenade throwers don't last long.

Naval engagements aren't the tender affairs of romantic stories. Nothing romantic in missiles of chain or multiple bar shot hurling at your skull. Designed to shred sail and rigging, chain is heated to glowing red by enemy gunners and unfolds as it flies, whirling and hissing across the water. Multiple bar is worse. One popular British version, a ring with three metal bars attached and hammerheads on the ends, spins through the air like an iron mosquito. Nothing survives its bloodlust. The spinning hammers chew a man's flesh into small chunks, spraying it onto the canvas in ghastly red shapes. Javert lost his own ear from multiple bar. The ear lobe, and his head, miraculously remained attached. He covers it now with a green bandana. A whore gave him an earring for the lobe.

Surviving the fight earns you what? Low pay, spoiled grub, the cat put to your back if you don't scramble topside fast enough to suit some dandy in tight britches? The right to boast of your bravery to waterfront whores?

The seaman clinging to the spar closest to him is a menacing individual of few words known simply as Marti. Ordinarily, Javert wouldn't address him, but today, who cares? "Did you see that little packet sail in awhile back?"

Marti ignores his shipmate, probing with his tongue the vacant gums where his two top front teeth were once anchored.

Javert feels like talking. "I saw Leissegues on board," he persists. "Hair standing up on his head."

Marti sneers in disbelief. "Are you an idiot? Why would the Admiral be coming aboard on some packet boat after the squadron has already deployed for battle?"

"Because he was in bed with the Governor's wife," Javert answers. "Or his daughter. I don't know. He was ashore when we sailed. That I know."

"Incredible."

"Why do you think we are running now? So Leissegues has time to figure something," Javert says. "And that isn't the worst of it."

Afraid Javert might be telling the truth, Marti slips his feet along the standing line closing the distance between them while maintaining a firm grip on the yard, swaying high above the deck. He'd like a whiff of Javert's breath. Some seamen drink heavily before battle. Especially cowards. "Tell me the worst of it," he demands.

"The sharpshooters," Javert smiles. "These few here are all we've got."

Marti leans closer. Javert's eyes seem clear and his breath garlic not rum. "Why do you say this?"

"Because I am an idiot," Javert says. "Unlike you, I pay attention when most of the sharpshooters are sent ashore to load ammunition and don't return before the ship sails. Idiots watch such things."

Marti mulls this over. A battle without sharpshooters. So what? In the old days they didn't even have sharpshooters. This Javert is a coward. He slides away.

Javert watches him go. He should've known better. The man's a fool.

His gaze travels west to the empty blue horizon. There, below the curvature of the earth, is Port-au-Prince and one particular whore about to bear his child. Once in his life, Javert has decided to take a responsibility. Besides, a white man can do well in Haiti, especially now with turmoil against France. Even a hunted Frenchman might do well if he sympathized with the Haitians, a protection against capture and hanging. A clever man may even prosper.

American upstarts enrich themselves by selling goods to both sides in this endless war, no reason he can't do the same. In time, the name Javert may mean something in the West Indies.

Far below, a drum roll. "Branle-bas-de-combat!" The "generale." The crew scrambles to battle stations. It's about to begin and Javert smiles. His last battle.

On the quarterdeck below, Vice Admiral Cortentin-Urbain Leissegues isn't quite the fool Javert and Sir John Duckworth believe, and unlike many French officers since the Revolution, is still in possession of his wealth. Many of the large timbers binding *Imperial* together were cut from mature elms growing on the Admiral's estate outside St. Cloud. Leissegues survived the French Revolution with his head and his lands, welcoming Bonaparte as the only man able to restore order. For that reason, more than any hatred of England, Leissegues fights for Napoleon.

Together with his aide, Pierre La Rue, Leissegues watches carefully as *Superb* and *Northumberland* maneuver into position one behind the other.

"What do you make of it?" La Rue inquires.

"Hmmm," Leissegues ponders. "Could be the obvious. Presenting us the smallest possible target. On the other hand, perhaps the Englishmen will attack port and starboard." He nods. "Clever, these English. Arrogant too, since Trafalgar."

"Every man aboard stands ready to sacrifice his life for the honor of France, our noble Emperor Napoleon Bonaparte, and for you, my Admiral."

Leissegues chuckles. "Let's hope they have as many reasons to live. Dead sailors win few battles."

Trapped between Charming Island and the British fleet, their position is hopeless. Given some warning he might've put on all his canvas and made for open sea, as it is, the enemy seized the advantage. He has only the power of *Imperial*, and even that is diluted. Many key officers and men were left ashore when the British surprised them at anchor. He was himself shamed by rejoining his squadron on a packet boat filled with bananas and mangos.

At best, the men left aboard are trash. He tries to remember what he'd heard another admiral say not long ago. "Ships so beautiful and strong manned by herdsmen and beggars," that was it. And quite true. The ships of his fleet were far superior to the British, but crewed by the dregs of humanity. Always it comes down to that. Man against man. Courage triumphant over sail and cannon. But men like these, what a pity.

"Pierre," calling the aide by his Christian name. "My regards to Captain Bigot. Ask him to please make a port turn and bring all portside guns to bear. We shall give these British a hearty welcome before they get close enough to shake our hands."

"Admiral. The distance is too great for accuracy."

"Accuracy be damned! Fire all three portside decks. All sixty guns. Even if just ten find their mark, we'll draw first blood."

Waiting for the order to be given, *Imperial's* gleaming canvas billows, white against a blue morning sky.

THE BATTLE

Across the pitted barrel of Number Seven, Reggy inhales the foul odor of Ian's sweat above the normal stench of animal excrement and hot tar permeating the vessel. He winks.

"That's the spirit," Ian whispers. "I'll be keeping an eye on you."

"You've become a good friend to me, Ian," Reggy answers. "The French are not my enemy but today I pray God we send them all to the bottom."

"Hush, now." Ian reaches for the tackle rope a second before the command to load is given. "It's on."

Colored flags go up, signaling the fleet to attack. Each ship is assigned a target for individual combat. *Imperial* is reserved for *Superb* and the frigate *Northumberland.*

A fresh wind at their backs, Duckworth and Keats devise a battle plan against *Imperial.* Making as much speed as possible before the wind, they plan to confront *Imperial* in single file, turning opposite directions at the last possible second and rake her down both sides, forcing her gunners to fire all guns at once. Both British vessels can then sail swiftly out of carronade range and repeat the maneuver until *Imperial* falters, unable to keep up the reloading pace, her rigging a shambles. Then they'll move in and broadside her at will with cannon and carronade until it's time to call away borders. The only danger in such tactics, Keats warns Duckworth, is similar to finding yourself in a game of draughts (checkers) where the opposing player tricks you into placing two of your draughtsmen on either side of him when it's his turn to jump. You always lose one.

"The French, luckily," Duckworth boasts, "are poor draughtsmen."

In the after cockpit, Surgeon James Heath and the ship's chaplain convert the junior officer's mess into an operating room. Pistol-handled crosscut saws protrude from a tin bucket under which a charcoal fire glows cherry red. The chaplain wrestles a large wooden tub alongside the mess table. This they'll fill with the amputated limbs.

The parson, just down from viewing *Imperial*, tells the doctor, "She's a horrid big monster, Jim. Go up for a look-see. I'll finish here."

The surgeon ignores him, handing across a corked bottle of seaman's anesthetic. "Last of the strong rum," he grunts. "I've a notion to drink it myself."

Without warning the chaplain stares heavenward and prays vehemently, "May Almighty God deliver that behemoth into our hands!"

"It's not God's work we're about this day, my friend. Slide that tourniquet here to me."

Across the narrowing gap of water, Admiral Leissegues on board *Imperial* watches carefully as *Superb* and *Northumberland* close the distance. *Imperial* has swung onto its port tack and the great warship lists beautifully to starboard bringing the portside batteries to maximum elevation.

"Fire now!" Leisseguses orders.

Through his long glass, Duckworth sees orange fireballs and smoke several seconds before he hears the thunderclap and receives the sixty rounds, soaring toward him at 1200 feet per second. Eight of the 24-pound balls strike *Superb*, the lead ship. Miraculously, no one is killed. Swarms of splinters explode like shrapnel drawing first blood from several dozen crewmen, including Duckworth, who is struck in the cheek. He dabs at it, coming away with red fingers. A piercing scream rises from below where a young midshipman staggers, a spike-like splinter protruding from his left eye. Even worse, a lucky 24-pound ball struck the bowsprit, stripping a great deal of rigging and luffing one of its four sails.

Superb carries almost three acres of canvas, and while she can maneuver quite well with less, it's a bad omen. The French have always been more successful at long-distance barrages, as many a British captain learned to his chagrin, with his rigging and sail crumpled at his feet. That won't happen this time, Duckworth promises. "Take in all but combat sail!" he shouts. "Signal *Northumberland* to do likewise."

Great activity aloft as the order is carried out. Their speed of nearly ten knots will be cut to perhaps six or a bit less. Better to allow the French to fire on them again than lose the canvas vital for close-in maneuvers later, he reasons.

"Return fire, Sir?" Keats asks.

"Not at present," the admiral replies.

"We're sure to be treated to more of this then," Keats persists. "My 32 and 24-pounders can respond now, I believe."

Duckworth places a hand on the captain's shoulder. "I understand your anxiety, Dick. Be patient. We've sustained no great injury. We'll give a much better account of ourselves presently, when we're in close and rake them down both sides."

Keats nods, unconvinced.

On the gun deck, Ian says softly, "What in bloody hell are they waiting for then, bloody Christmas?"

Dickey Kempenfelt provides the answer. "An easy target."

"So now you find your sense of humor," Ian says, smiling at Reggy.

"Most of their balls missed," Reggy observes.

"They'll do better next time," Ian predicts, gripping his amulet. "Are you really going to take the Captain's offer and go back to those miserable, mosquito-infested colonies?"

Reggy chuckles. "You'll miss me, you poor Irish bastard."

"Like bloody hell! Anyway, if you keep trading with the French, we'll soon have you back."

The French fire a second volley. It's thunder rolls once again across the water.

One of *Imperial's* 24-pound balls splinters the deck and strikes Ian's head, decapitating him and spraying brain matter, a gray foam across the faces of his two friends. Another ball enters just below and to the left, severing Dickey's leg and drenching the deck with blood and splinters of white bone. Reggy stands mute. He is unhurt.

Others around him aren't so lucky. Screams fill his ears and he can taste Ian.

Someone calls his name and he stares down at Dickey several feet away, lying on his back. His left leg is off several inches below the knee and the bone is splintered. It reminds him of a branch taken off in a storm, ripped instead of cut smooth. Dickey's knee is still intact and flexing repeatedly. His lower leg and foot would be kicking too, if they weren't lying there on the deck. It's Dickey, he realizes, who is repeating his name.

"I can't put it back on," Reggy explains to him. "It's all broken." This isn't entirely true because the calf, ankle, and foot are whole. The toes are dirty. The nails very long and yellow. You would think that Dickey, of all people, would take better care of his feet.

"Reggy. Good Lord, man. Get me to the surgeon."

"I'm sorry." There is an unreality to their voices and they seem to Reggy the voices of people speaking too loudly in an empty room. "Of course. Right away." Reggy hesitates, then rips a shirt sleeve from Ian's headless corpse and ties it snugly around Dickey's stump. "I'll have to carry you. Hold tight around my neck."

Reggy wants to cradle him in his arms but loses his balance, can't keep his feet under him. He slips and cracks Dickey's head on the deck. Where is the boy with the sand? They need more sand. "Can you crawl up on my back?" he asks.

Dickey's hands are like claws, a drowning man, clinging to his rescuer. Catlike, the Englishman crawls up Reggy's back, wrapping both arms around his neck. Reggy smells his sticky breath. But with his hands free to grab the bulkhead, the American gains his feet and struggles away toward the belowdecks ladder with his burden. The knee is still moving. He feels it thumping rhythmically against his buttocks as it kicks the imaginary leg.

Below, the junior officer's mess is a slaughterhouse. The roar finally of *Superb's* cannon clap the boards overhead, softening sounds of the bone saws and hatchets, the wet sounds of the big knives slicing flesh, and the cursing, crying, the vile oaths that escape the lips of the nearly dead. The sizzle, the sweet odor of cauterized veins and dripping skin as it cooks.

"This man has lost a portion of his lower leg," Reggy tells the butchers.

There is a system, he realizes. A kind of perverse order to things here. Two lines of wounded sailors are led staggering to the rear where two medical orderlies treat them or send them back up to the fight. The more seriously injured wait for the surgery table. "Two ahead of you," an orderly tells him.

Reggy nods. Where did all these men come from? How can so many be wounded already? This isn't his first fight, but he and Ian and Dickey, how can this happen to them? How did they so quickly become his people? His friends?

Beneath his bare feet the deck is wet with warm fluids and as the ship maneuvers and fires, reloads and fires again and again, the deck heaves and the fluids wash his toes. He struggles to keep his balance. He talks to Dickey and arches his back to ease the strain. The wait seems endless as the battle goes on and the slaughterhouse fills. Men scream, curse, sob like children.

To his right a large barrel is filling with limbs or pieces of limbs. Speedily, with ease and indifference, the produce of the men's maimed bodies is gathered. One of the hands still has a ring on it, and as he watches, an orderly, using the blood and slime on his own fingers for a lubricant, works the ring over the knuckle and pockets it. He shrugs when he spots Reggy staring.

After the table is squeegeed of blood, chunks of flesh and fluids, he finally lies Dickey down. He's been waiting a long time and notices now that his friend's eyes are closed. "Is he dead then?" he asks the surgeon.

"Not yet," he says, selecting one of the smaller saws from the heated pail. "All I can do is take off the splinters. Maybe he keeps the knee." He glances up quickly. "Or the whole mess goes bad in a couple days or a week and he dies. Get out now. There's no room here for gawkers."

"I'm his friend."

"Get topside, then. Kill the damned French. Kill them all."

The battle changes for him then. Men don't fight battles, he realizes, they just fight in them. They don't know who's winning or what is the strategy, and making his way back up on deck he doesn't care. Let the surgeon kill the French. Let him harvest his own bones for this pitiful sacrifice. Reginald

Wilson, American, from a small place called Maryland, is going home.

His back is sticky with Kempenfelt's blood and Ian's brain has hardened to the skin of his face. Reggy walks upright, unhurried to the rail, climbs over and dives into the cleansing sea.

Across the water and high above him, the Frenchman Javert clings to the mangled mizzen, the only stick left standing aboard *Imperial.* In less than two hours, the terror of the sea is reduced to a floating prison of the dead and dying. The officers who remain alive ordered the man-of-war run aground along the rugged Charming Island coast where they can remove the wounded to safety and abandon the ship. Javert works feverishly to set the remaining sail. He wishes to be gone.

Of all things, a grenade thrower survived in the tops with him. A patriotic fellow. When his grenades were gone he devoted himself to handling canvas, scampering out onto the yards as if he'd been at it since birth. His presence prevents Javert from jumping into the water and striking out for the furniture boat. The best option is to kill the man but he has to bide his time until all the sail is set and the ship headed for its final resting place. Too much attention now being paid the topmen.

Surprisingly the British fleet suffered few casualties. Even *Superb*, regardless of Reggy's gun crew, survived the battle in much finer shape than is usually the case, with six dead and 56 wounded. *Northumberland*, which joined in the attack on *Imperial*, at one point received a perfect broadside that killed 21 and wounded 80. Such losses were considered minor. Aboard *Imperial* things are different with half the crew either dead or wounded - at least 500 men, including Admiral Leissegues' aide-de-camp, Pierre La Rue.

Both British vessels stood out to sea once they recognized that Leissegues was headed for shallow water. He's only doing what they would've done in his place. All, of course, are gentlemen. They will in fact give the French two days to remove their wounded to safety, disembark the crew and their belongings before burning *Imperial* to the waterline. Meanwhile, Javert waits for an opportunity to rid himself of the grenade thrower.

Most of the longboats on deck were destroyed but three remain and they're being readied for launch. Only a matter of time before the officers start to concern themselves with their furniture and other belongings. Javert knows he has to act swiftly and take advantage of the confusion before *Imperial* strikes a reef and every boat is needed to abandon ship.

Despite a defeat that may yet cost them their lives, the grenade thrower curses the British as cowards. Javert has less love for the enemy than most but cowards they're not. The British gun crews worked like madmen reloading and firing two or three balls to every one fired by *Imperial.* What they lacked in firepower they'd made up for in manpower, but Javert listens as the man clinging to the yard beside him foresees the British Empire's collapse while the pride of the French fleet limps steadily toward imminent suicide on the rocks.

Javert's only weapon is a wooden fid, a tool he'd made himself and carries on his belt in a special leather case. The fid has been with him nearly seven years, during hundreds of splicing tasks. It brought him luck. Eight inches long, tapered, hand rubbed maple, it's an old friend. Twice he'd jammed it into a twist of rope and held himself safely aloft in foul weather. Its point would make a quick end to the grenade thrower but it might cost him the fid if he can't withdraw it quickly enough. This is no small matter. On the other hand, neither is staying aboard. Sooner or later the officers will hold muster to see who's left alive. Even if he's taken prisoner it's no escape. Prisoners are always traded, like cattle.

It's getting on toward noon, a beautiful sun-drenched day. Javert inhales the fresh air, blown clear now of smoke and gunpowder. He glances down at the confusion on deck far below and thrusts the fid into the grenade thrower's chest, aiming for his heart. It makes a mud-sucking kind of a noise and wedges firmly between two of the patriot's ribs. Javert fails to pull it back out before gravity tugs the imbecile down toward the deck.

He falls into the confusion of rigging and bounces only once. Several heads turn at the noise but no one observes the fall. Javert remains still. The men below go back to work. Javert shakes his head sadly. He'll miss the fid, but once again it saved his life. He grabs a long rope and prepares to climb down and over the side into the sea.

Reggy Wilson is a strong and natural swimmer. He finds the warm embrace of the Caribbean a welcome tonic to the filth and death he leaves behind. When he spots *Imperial's* elevated stern heading toward the coastline, he follows in its wake, hoping the French sailors will take pity on an American pressed by the British and return him to the harbor and the American vessels Captain Keats had promised him.

Two longboats are in tow some distance behind the French warship and Reggy finally decides to make for them instead of the ship. The more he considers his situation the more sense it makes not to rush into the same type of folly from which he'd only just escaped. The death and destruction aboard the French ship is likely to be much worse than that aboard *Superb* and the French officers and men might be hostile to anyone speaking English, even an American. In a bloody rage, they might strike him down before he has time to explain himself.

Water streams from his torso as he hoists himself over the stern-post of the furniture boat and flops face up onto the dry thwart. Safe at last, he allows himself a rare moment of ease, resting in the sunshine. It's a long journey home yet, but he's made a beginning. Weeks maybe, months depending on where the American merchantmen are headed, but one day before long he'll swing up the path to a white cottage snug behind a fine pair of druid oaks. He'll call to Mary and be home at last.

Hidden barely ten feet away, Javert edges a desk drawer open in search of a weapon. He's been through the wooden boxes and two barrels. Nothing. He taps his fingers softly along the inside until they touch something cool. A letter opener that brings a smile to his lips when he examines it. Gold plate, ivory handle, large emerald embedded above the hilt. An officer's souvenir gift from some lady he'd left behind, a memento of passion inscribed * *Je t'aime - Adrienne* * on its shank. It isn't a fid but it will do.

When Javert saw Reggy climb aboard the longboat he mistook him for an Englishman. Americans are a rare sight in the world and figure very little in the significant affairs of nations such as France or Great Britain. They're an upstart race and Francois Javert has never met an American, not that it would make any difference to him. Americans are thought to be exceedingly uncouth and miserable. He'd kill one just as happily as any Englishman.

The dagger-like letter opener has a nice balance and he grips it so the blade rests against his forearm. He plans to simply walk around the chests and other furniture, move toward the intruder reclining now at the stern, flash a welcoming smile, and slit his throat.

Reggy opens his eyes when he hears Javert clambering over a chair. "Hello," he says, sitting up. "Thought I was alone here."

The Frenchman smiles but doesn't speak.

"Are you French?"

The smile is frozen into the man's face.

"Speak English?"

Javert moves closer. He's carrying something in his right hand.

"Two can row faster and farther than one," Reggy tells him. A weapon flashes in the sunshine, bites the soft flesh of Reggy's neck. He chokes, tries to spit. His eyes widen and his larynx and both carotid arteries rip away.

Later Javert rinses the blade in the aquamarine waters and slips it into the old fid case. It fits nicely. Before the man bleeds out entirely, he eases the body over the stern and watches as it drifts, spinning slowly, toward the white sand bottom sixty feet below. A very neat job.

Shortly after noon, Javert has slipped the rope, cast adrift the furniture, and found the oars. It's a cumbersome boat to row alone, but he's spotted a beach a mile or so distant. He'll put in there, maybe even sell the thing, and be on his way before anyone's the wiser. He found more than a few pieces of gold coin and other treasures in the officer's cupboards, not to mention a very fine bottle of wine. Life is amazing and for the first time in memory he has an awareness of his own well-being, as if what he thinks and does might matter beyond the moment. Francois Javert is a free man.

Divers

CHAPTER TWO

Reggy Wilson's descendant, a boy of fifteen, closed the book and rested it on his lap. He'd read it many times before and recalled some parts from memory. Even boring parts, like all the "begats" of the family tree, but the fictionalized battle scene, researched and written in 1909 by his ancestor Douglas Wilson, fired his imagination. It remained a family mystery - Javert cutting Reggy's throat - but in 1961, Warren Wilson believed every word.

Hunched forward in the padded seat, head down, he clutched the wallet with the five hundred dollars cash inside, wondering if he dared unzip it and touch the money again. He liked the crisp bills, especially the 100s and 50s. The 20s were losing their grandeur.

The bus lurched over a set of railroad tracks. Not wise to flash your roll. He slipped the wallet inside the faded pocket of his jeans and burrowed back into the seat, turning his head toward the narrow window. He was young enough to feel cheated at not getting the window seat but old enough to take it in stride. The lady who did get it wore a creamy dress covered in tiny red flowers so small he'd stared awhile before seeing they were flowers. They might've been crabapples or cherries.

He thought the lady was a schoolteacher. She had the clenched jaw and pursed lips for it. Christmas vacation, so she was probably on her way to visit relatives in Minneapolis or St. Paul. He doubted she knew about Freddie-the-Frogman. He'd thought of asking her, but they'd been on the bus together almost half an hour and she had yet to speak. She might not even be a schoolteacher.

Warren stared out through frosted glass at the telephone poles slipping by in the snow, wires sagging like tired clothesline. He fought down a smile because he liked the bus. It was foreign and no one knew who he was. No one knew his mission to find *Imperial*, his own dead brother, a dead Wilson sailor, or what he was now about to do in order to accomplish these things.

"Traveling alone?" the schoolteacher inquired.

"Sure," Warren said. "I'm fifteen."

"Do you have family in Minneapolis?"

"Going to stay with my uncle. Tomorrow he's taking me to see Freddie-the-Frogman."

"Oh?"

"He's a scuba diver."

"You don't say?" Obviously amazed, her voice rose. "I didn't know they had skin divers in Minnesota."

Just the kind of comment you expect from a schoolteacher. "Land of ten thousand lakes," he said, not too smugly.

"Well, there's ice on the lakes now." A pert chuckle. She was one up on him. "I don't think Freddie will be doing much skin diving this time of year."

"That's where you're wrong," he said, grinning across at her. "He's going to dive tomorrow. And I will be too. In a swimming pool at the College of St. Thomas."

The schoolteacher looked out the window. "I doubt that," she said.

Her dismissal of his underwater dreams wasn't surprising. Tell them you were going to be a scuba diver or an astronaut you got about the same reaction. Not just from adults. His worst critics were his friends. Even his best friend Gilby called it "pie in the sky."

Basketball dominated everywhere as far as he could tell. You learned to dribble, run, jump, shoot, and you could do a lay-up, or you were nothing. Worse than nothing - sissy, weakling. People pitied your parents. You were never close friends with class presidents and cheerleaders and those who acted in plays or A-students. You couldn't be popular or be seen walking in the hall with anyone who was popular. You were junk.

This was 1961. The 1960s. Really modern times. High time, he thought, somebody came up with a sport without a ball in it. Once they invented ball games they just gave up. Freddie-the-Frogman was different, scuba had what no ball game could ever claim - high adventure. Warren loved baseball but it didn't promise what Mike Nelson or Freddie-the-Frogman aroused in him, a new way of life. He'd never met Freddie of course, but had great faith in him.

On the floor, locked between his legs, was his father's worn leather grip. The one he used when he hoboed across the country during the Great Depression. "Take it," Dad had said. "A traveling man has need of a good grip." Warren unlocked the brass clasps, slid the Wilson book inside and drew out a dog-eared blue folder. He opened it on his lap. In the right-hand pocket was a catalog of diving equipment and behind that a black and white, 8x10 glossy of Freddie-the-Frogman.

He held the photograph carefully by its edges so the schoolteacher could see it. "This is Freddie-the-Frogman," he announced.

She faked a smile and glared at Freddie. Couldn't she tell by the set to his square jaw and the steel in his silver eyes and the deep lines carved in his forehead that here was a he-man? A comic book character come to life. Not a man who played basketball or worried about a little lake ice.

"What's that thing around his neck?" she asked.

"Regulator." Recalling the catalog description, he said, "A double-hose, two-stage regulator."

"Looks like a fat rubber snake."

"It's a regulator."

She wrinkled her nose. "I wouldn't want one of those in my mouth."

Warren laid the photograph of Freddie aside and opened the diving equipment catalog to page six. "This is the regulator I'm going to buy tomorrow," he said, pointing it out. "The Royal Aquamaster."

"Do your parents know about this?"

"It's my money."

She looked again at the regulator pictured in the catalog. "Is that the price there?" she inquired. "Eighty-five dollars?"

He nodded.

"Young people today don't realize how long it takes to earn money like that," she concluded, turning back to the window and the snow-covered prairie.

He wanted to tell her of the cold days, humid days blistering with thick clouds of gnats, the Sunday mornings he wanted desperately to sleep in. How the satchel strap folded and furrowed as he walked, gnawing against the shoulder muscle. Times the delivery truck dumped his paper bundle in the rain. The deadbeats who ignored the door when he came to collect. She was right about one thing. People didn't realize how long it takes to earn that much money.

Since September 26, 1958, all he'd ever thought about was money. He'd gone that day to a local agricultural school and sat on the bleachers in the natatorium with the rest of his scout troop and watched the Viking Scuba Club give their thirty-minute underwater demonstration. Later, the scouts were allowed to leave the bleachers and mingle with the divers, touch some of the equipment. Gleaming tanks, hoses, galvanized pull rods, masks, fins, knives. Chrome-plated steel and the deep pressing scent of rubber, black and slick and wet. He sucked from a regulator and felt the snap at the back of his throat when its diaphragm opened and released a dry gust of compressed air. The divers were mostly young men and spoke a technical jargon he couldn't understand, like German, but he loved to listen. They were interested in him, sharing their secret underwater world. A place few had been or might ever go. No running back and forth, fish trapped in a tank or gymnasium, making or missing a basket, then back again and again.

That day he didn't remember the ride home. Not the scenery or what anyone talked about. It was as if a still voice spoke from somewhere deep inside, repeating over and over - *you can breathe underwater, you can breathe underwater*.

He was twelve that year, and got a paper route. Summers he mowed lawns, baled hay for Uncle Eb, sold cosmetics door to door after he bought a kit from an ad in the back of *Boy's Life* magazine. In three years he saved five hundred dollars.

But on the schoolteacher's face was the look. The look they all got when he said "scuba diver." He'd seen it through years of apologizing. It made him tired. People clucked like chickens or shook their heads or laughed outright. Some got angry at the very mention of scuba diving, like it was a sin. In eighth grade Dennis Dubbins told him he only wanted to dive because he was too chicken to play a real sport.

Why did it seem other people lived in a world different from his? When he saw the balding, pot-bellied fans hollering themselves red in the face, he knew they were reliving that one tense moment at the free-throw line when everyone held their breath and watched them. Now they were old, cheering to make it important for other kids because it was over for them.

He'd tried to explain this to Mom and Dad when he got home from the Scout trip that day but a short time later discovered their doubts when he came downstairs unexpectedly and overheard them talking in the kitchen.

"I'm just glad he's found an interest," Dad was saying.

"But scuba diving?" Mom's voice was scared. "It's so dangerous, Bill. And the water. Of all people, Warren should be afraid of water."

He could've lived his whole life without overhearing that, *of all people*. She didn't have to say it. Was he to blame for being alive? Did she think he'd forgotten that day? He was nine, Stephen eleven. Did she think he'd forget who taught him to ride a bike, pushing him hard long after Dad gave up and went in the house. They had a secret base in the willow swamp beyond the tracks. Stephen made furniture from branches lashed together with twine. They stabbed their fingers with Stephen's pocket knife and mixed their blood. Once they killed a blackbird and all its babies. No one knew.

So Dad answered her and said, "I know what you're getting at. Maybe it's like a psychological thing. Something he needs to do there. Under the water." He tried to sound cool for Mom's sake. "Anyway, don't worry. By the time he saves enough money to buy all the equipment he wants, he'll probably be onto something else."

"I hope so," Mom said.

During the next three years, Mom and Dad changed. Each came to share his dream in their own way. Dad, a mechanic at Larsen Chev, liked the equipment catalogs and the strange-looking mechanical devices that allowed men to breathe highly compressed air at underwater depths of over one hundred feet. Dad had great respect for any kind of machinery.

Mom loved to read, and when diving magazines, pamphlets, and books became an accepted portion of the coffee table library, she couldn't help herself, she read them and was infected with some of the same curiosity as her son. What was it like underwater? Three quarters of the earth yet unexplored. She'd no intention of going to look herself, but she began to understand Warren's fascination, and his courage. The world's first celebrity frogman, Jacques Cousteau, was yet then a young man. Warren's romantic childhood dreams warmed her heart. What happened to all that in people later on in life?

Now the day had come. It was Mom and Dad who'd driven him the twenty miles from their neat white house in Lake Darling to the bus depot in Alexandria. He was sitting here because Mom and Dad wanted their son to be a scuba diver.

The swaying bus rolled along steadily, clicking across seams in the concrete, rumbling over patches of ice and packed snow. It was warm inside and Warren closed his eyes. In his sleep he saw a boat. White. Gleaming as it sliced the sea. He saw the captain, who looked like Freddie-the-Frogman, but it wasn't. He was captain. He was on the high part of the boat. Smiling. Mom asked if he wanted cream in his strawberries. He saw a girl with dark skin and big teeth. He could smell cinnamon. He smacked his lips.

A sharp pain in his ribs. The schoolteacher's bony elbow.

"Young man! Young man!" Her voice sounded like it came through a tube. "We're in the Twin Cities. Your head is on my arm."

Warren sat up straight, blinking. The bus stopped at a traffic light on the side of a hill. Out the front window, over the heads of the other passengers, were the tall buildings of downtown Minneapolis, its skyline dominated by the Foshay Tower, a brown sugar building Dad said was the tallest man-made structure between Chicago and San Francisco - 32 floors, 447 feet. Funny airplanes didn't bump into it.

"First time in the big city?" the schoolteacher inquired.

"Heck no! Come here all the time. We got lots of relatives." This was partly true. Uncle David and Aunt Doris lived here, but visits were infrequent. Dad hated finding his way among the maze of unfamiliar streets and buildings. It made him angry, and that made Mom tense, so they usually visited uncle Eb on the farm instead. Warren preferred that too.

Minutes later the bus pulled into the depot, swinging through a door so low

Warren expected the paint to be scraped from the roof. Inside were other buses with names on their foreheads from all over America - Seattle, Chicago, St. Louis. Even one that said Miami.

Warren clutched his wallet and stood up.

"Sit down," the schoolteacher said. "Don't stand until the bus comes to a complete stop and the driver opens the door."

The bus stopped and the driver opened the door. Warren bolted down the aisle.

"Skin Diver!" he heard the schoolteacher say.

From the top step Warren saw Uncle David, a grinning giant with wide red suspenders to hold his belly up, standing with both hands in the air like he was flying down on a roller coaster. Uncle David was a gas. More then once Warren had seen him tickle people he didn't even know and saw now that the bystanders had already become his friends. Several called out Warren's name.

Warren waved, forcing his way down the steps through the crowd. "I made it Uncle David!"

"Here he is, my brother Bill's kid," David said, scrunching Warren's shoulders and showing him off to the bystanders. "Down here to get trained as a skin diver. Ever hear of such a thing?"

The bystanders shook their heads.

"Pleasure talking to you folks," Uncle David said with genuine warmth. "Lloyd Bridges here and me got to shake a leg for home. Auntie Doris is baking up a batch of kelp burgers for supper!"

He slapped Warren's back, swept him away through the door into the depot, laughing for no reason. The timbre of Uncle David's voice was penetrating, louder even than the voice calling the cities. It built his excitement and he glanced sideways at his uncle. How impossible to imagine this man as his father's brother. He talked loud, smoked Tiparillos, drank beer. But like Dad, you felt safe with him. He wasn't the kind of man who seemed to get beat down, like some Warren knew. Uncle David had pizzazz.

"What do you say we take a ride down Nicollet and have a look at this dive shop?" said Uncle David as they barged through the lobby. "Wasn't that the address you gave me on the phone? Nicollet Avenue?"

"Yes," Warren said, knowing it by heart. "1507 Nicollet Avenue North."

"Not too far out of our way. Like to take a look before I drop you off tomorrow. Okay?" They reached the street and Uncle David's tan-over-brown Plymouth station wagon. "But we won't go in. Save that for tomorrow. Agreed?"

"Sure."

For a fat guy, Uncle David possessed great dexterity. He handled the

Plymouth like a sports car, sweeping through downtown traffic, spinning the steering wheel knob recklessly with one hand and smoking his Tiparillo with the other. The steering wheel knob was clear plastic with the tiny figure of a naked woman inside. In back, the wagon was loaded to the windows with Uncle David's samples. Boxes of magnetic signs he wholesaled to hardware stores were the latest thing. Last year he'd been selling a miracle grease to revolutionize the wheel bearing industry.

"How's your old man?" Uncle David bellowed over the hammering rock and roll that poured from the Plymouth's dual speakers.

Warren shrugged. "Same, I guess."

"He should've come in business with me instead of staying back in Lake Darling where there's no jobs."

"He's got a job."

"Hump!" Uncle David's shoulders jumped. "Grease monkey."

Warren had heard this before. Obligated by family pride, he repeated Dad's argument best he could remember. "Dad wouldn't be happy in the city," Warren finished. "He needs the space. Breathing room he calls it."

"Breathing room? Lying on his backside underneath some guy's dripping Ford?" But Uncle David smiled, pleased by Warren's loyalty. This was an all right boy. He just might make a skin diver. Uncle David made rapid course corrections and the Plymouth entered an industrial area. Hot blue light from welding arcs sparked behind the frosted window panes of dirty brick buildings. They passed block after block of chain-link fence, piles of building materials stacked behind them, weighted in gray snow. Huge coils of wire, hose, and greased cable. Pyramids of pipe. Rusty iron. This was the kind of place you found a scuba diver. They were close to Freddie-the-Frogman.

"See a number on any of these buildings?" Uncle David asked. "This should be the twelve-hundred block, so it can't be far now." The cross streets had dips and Uncle David slowed the Plymouth to a crawl, saving his undercarriage. "We just crossed fifteenth," he said. "Keep your eyes peeled on the left. Odd numbers."

"There!" Warren said. "See the dive flag?"

Freddie-the-Frogman's dive shop was a house. Across the street, the station wagon coasted to a stop.

"Well?" asked Uncle David. "Whatdaya think?"

The house was old, out of place among the low sheds, warehouses, and machine shops. It reminded Warren of lonely farmhouses he'd seen driving across North Dakota. Someone had remodeled it with gray asphalt siding designed to look like brick and a steep concrete sidewalk led up to the door. A large display window had been added, the trim left unpainted. Dead center a neon diver with double tanks on his back hung from chains. Though it was mid-afternoon, the diver was lit. Mounted in the peak of the house, an immense plywood dive flag, red with white diagonal stripe. It was the most exciting place Warren had ever seen.

"Can't we go in Uncle David?"

"Getting late." To confirm this he consulted his watch, strapped to the underside of his wrist. "Aunt Doris told me to pick up dessert for supper. She'll want us to sit down and eat promptly at five." He looked up at the house, smiling sadly. "You won't care to leave once we get in there. Tomorrow's better don't you think?"

Uncle David was right, of course. Tomorrow would be better. It was just that he'd waited so long, and now to be right across the street with Freddie-the-Frogman just beyond the door and then drive away like they didn't have a care in the world. It was more than he could bear.

"Hard to wait," he told Uncle David. "Drive away quick."

Uncle David patted him. "You're a good boy, Warren."

The station wagon's transmission clunked and the car accelerated. Warren turned his head and watched the dive shop fade away among the sheet metal shops and bright forges of the tool makers.

* * *

Aunt Doris and the four Wilson girls - Darlene, Doreen, Denelda, and Daphne - lined up just inside the living room door when Warren and Uncle David arrived. Doris ordered everyone to kiss.

No one refused Aunt Doris anything. Not if they were smart. Warren bent forward, hands behind him, and accepted the indignity. When it came time to receive Daphne's kiss, she smelled so strongly of dill pickle he averted his face at the last instant. Her juicy mouth smacked his ear. He smiled. Aunt Doris said, "Welcome. Just enough time to wash your hands before supper." He complied quickly.

Things in this branch of the Wilson family were organized and structured: meals on time, children to bed at set hours according to their ages, and without argument. Everyone's role well-defined, except Warren's. He suddenly felt uncomfortable, afraid to venture further into the house. Strange being here without Mom and Dad.

Aunt Doris read his mind. "You'll fit in just fine over the next couple days," she said smiling. "We're all dying to hear about this skin diving business. Come sit down now. Let's eat. Then you can tell us all about it."

The tablecloth was immaculate white, the milk poured into a glass pitcher instead of left in the carton like they did it at home. Warren knew they were dressing things up a bit for him and this added to his discomfort. He was seated between Darlene and Doreen, the two older girls. They suppressed giggles, peeking at each other around his back.

Uncle David said grace in a loud voice and informed God that Warren would be eating with them awhile. Warren had been hoping to keep a low profile. Ever since he got his hands on the actual five hundred cash he'd been filled with dread. Worse - responsibility, like giving up things you wanted for things you should do to help others. Money as responsibility; an awful concept. Warren always thought of money as fun.

"Can't you pass the peas, Warren?" Darlene said, dragging the last syllable of his name out in a fakey Southern drawl.

"Pass the peas please," Doris corrected, enunciating each word.

Aunt Doris was a stickler for proper English, politeness, clean eating habits. Cursed as she was with an organized brain. On top of that she was good looking. Jackie Kennedy hairdo with a flip that made her light brown hair bounce whenever she moved. Wore makeup, pink lipstick and rouge. Her eyebrows had been removed, then drawn back in, an effect shocking to Warren, who was used to Mom's plain, scrubbed face and tangled head of dark curls so like his own.

"These mashed potatoes are great," he said, drowning them in brown gravy. "Sometimes you get lumps or they're too soupy. These are just right. Gravy's good too. Not runny."

"Thank you," she said, flashing a big smile, obviously pleased by such lavish praise. "Eat all you want. I have more in the kitchen."

"We drove by Freddie-the-Frogman's on the way home," Uncle David said. "Didn't go in. Just looked the place over."

"Are you getting anxious, Warren?" Aunt Doris asked.

He shrugged. "Naw."

"You've waited this long, you can wait until morning, right?" said Uncle David, grinning broadly.

Warren nodded.

"What will you do in the morning?" Aunt Doris asked. "When you get there, I mean."

Warren had hoped he'd get to finish supper before launching into a lengthy explanation of the technical training and equipment involved in skin and scuba diving. You could explain this stuff to a layman, or you could eat. You couldn't do both.

"It's sorta complicated," he said. "I've got all the information in my folder."

Uncle David and Aunt Doris exchanged looks. Uncle David said, "I think Warren will sit us all down after supper and show us his diving materials. Now he wants to eat."

This said, the remainder of the meal passed without mention of skin diving. When they finished, and the girls washed and wiped the dishes, Warren was led into the living room and placed on the large davenport between Uncle David and Aunt Doris. "Now," she began, "tell us everything."

Warren opened the blue folder and withdrew the photograph of Freddie-the-Frogman. "This is Freddie-the-Frogman." He allowed them time to study the photograph. "Taken when he was in the UDT."

"UDT?" Aunt Doris was lost already.

"Underwater Demolition Team, right?" Uncle David said, turning to Warren for confirmation.

"Yes," he said proudly. "The toughest guys in the Navy. Even tougher than the Marines. They were the frogmen during the war."

"Oh, I see," Aunt Doris said. "Like Mike Nelson on *Sea Hunt*?"

"Well, not exactly. Mike Nelson's a private eye. He solves crimes and stuff on TV, but a UDT man like Freddie-the-Frogman can swim fifteen miles and then attack." He paused. "He's the real thing. Tomorrow I'm going to be trained by a real UDT man and then I'll get a card with my name on it."

Hearing this, both adults glanced back to the photo.

"My," Aunt Doris said.

"I suppose it's kind of like having Alan Shepard teach you to fly," Uncle David offered.

Warren liked this analogy. As a hero, Alan Shepard fell in line just behind Freddie-the-Frogman.

"But you can't learn to fly in one day," Aunt Doris asserted. "Can you learn to skin dive?"

Both Warren and Uncle David gave her a sharp look.

"Sure," Warren said. "That's why you learn from a guy like Freddie. Besides, I'm not going to become a UDT man, just a civilian diver. An underwater explorer."

"How can you do that in one day?" She still wasn't convinced.

"First thing in the morning I'll pick out my equipment," he explained. "That's the most important part. The rest of the morning and afternoon I study written lessons - decompression sickness, nitrogen narcosis, air embolisms, stuff like that. Tomorrow night Freddie takes me to the swimming pool and I learn to operate the equipment, or gear, as we call it."

"And then you're a skin diver? Just like that?"

"It takes the whole day!" He wanted her to shake this time fetish. "I won't even be back for supper," he concluded, hoping a disrupted schedule would give her something fresh to chew on.

She slipped the equipment catalog from his folder, but instead of keeping it herself, she handed it to him. "Show me," she said.

He began with the regulator, the Royal Aquamaster. Then the 71.2 cubic foot cylinder - the tank. The backpack. The wet suit. Mask, fins, and snorkel. The olive green, military-simulated gear bag. Compass and depth gauge. Tank valve. Finally the various accessories, concluding with the seven-inch underwater knife and plastic sheath.

Each item was marked clearly in the catalog with a penciled circle around its price. On a slip of ruled paper clipped to the final page, was the total he'd worked out - $493.50. He allowed them to see this arithmetic as well.

"That's pretty much it," he said. Then added, "The knife has a sheath that straps to your leg."

Daphne crawled onto her mother's lap and whispered loudly, "I wanna watch Lassie."

"Me too," Denelda whined.

Darlene and Doreen were leaning over the back of the davenport breathing heavily on Warren's neck.

"There's a couple things I should do before tomorrow," he said, addressing them all. "Study this catalog some more and maybe take a walk to get limbered up. Haven't been swimming since last summer."

"Sounds fine to me." Uncle David struggled to his feet. "Go now before it gets too late. This is a safe neighborhood but the city's different from Lake Darling. Okay?"

"Sure," Warren said, in search of his jacket.

Outside, Warren zipped the jacket to his neck and pulled on his arctic mitts, the fur-backed ones he won for most new subscribers in a single month. He liked his aunt and uncle. They didn't slap you down because you did things a little different. There was a lot he couldn't tell them, or anybody. He couldn't explain the urgency. The terrible feeling that if he didn't hurry as fast as he could, he'd be left out. Men like John Wayne felt this way about war. Afraid it would end before they got to it. He mustn't let that happen. He turned right at the end of Uncle David's cleared sidewalk, shuffling along between snow banks higher than his waist.

And always, there was Stephen. Warren thought about him every day. Sometimes he prayed to him. Stephen was a lot like Jesus - invisible, but not dead. Warren never told Mom or Dad that he thought Stephen was like Jesus. They never talked about Stephen anymore, or what happened to him. It was as if they forgot they ever had another son. Pictures of him were removed. After the funeral his things were packed away, even his baseball cards, as if he'd just moved out.

Warren looked up at the unfamiliar houses around him. He'd been meandering along without looking. At the end of each block, street lights cast icy puddles of light on the snow.

He turned around and started back. The time had come. In the morning he'd begin his journey to find the brother he'd murdered. Stephen waited, somewhere deep underwater in the same lost grave as Reggy Wilson.

CHAPTER THREE

It happened in this way.

1955. Warren was nine. Stephen was eleven and a half. It was dark but they could see because of the snow on the ice and the starlight that was in the snow and the sky. Christmas was right around the corner but that night they played on the ice of the lake, forgetting the season, even the cold. Boredom drove them out of the fishhouse, away from their preoccupied father, and onto the frozen lake.

Lake Darling was average-sized. The town of Lake Darling was in a bay on the southwestern side where water stretched in both directions to form a female figure. Warren had never seen this, unless it was the flat-chested figure of a legless female. He suspected it wasn't the shape of a woman but some woman a lonely homesteader thought he saw across the water, like a mirage. "Darling!" he called, out of his head with loneliness. Lake Darling wasn't two miles from Square Lake - perfectly round.

Warren and Stephen were two peas in a pod, locals said. Always together. Look-alikes. Dark, lean boys on the move. They owned sophisticated toy weapons, Schwinn bikes, adult fishing tackle and did yard work for spending money. They went where they pleased and most people smiled at the sight of them. More than one widow called them to her porch for lemonade.

Out on the ice that night they had done the usual things - rolled in the snow, knocked on doors of other fishhouses and run away to hide, wrestled and made yellow snow in deep figure-eights under a twinkling, shimmering dome of sky. There wasn't one moment of apprehension or uneasiness. No warning. Nothing alerted them that their childhood would end that night and never return. They played and laughed under the heavens as if they didn't have a care in the world, just two peas in a pod. Perfect. Ordinary. Immortal.

The town of Lake Darling existed by virtue of the Soo Line Railroad. The rail line sliced the town to within sixty feet of the lakeshore and ran from St. Paul to Winnipeg, linking Lake Darling with a larger world of commerce and society. For its part, the town offered grains, livestock, block ice and a trickle of passengers. Freights came along the rail line at a rate of two dozen every day. Passenger trains were smaller and less popular then a decade earlier. Railroads were losing interest in passengers, preferring the greater profits of freight.

Dad told the boys that ice harvesting was passing into history too, and warned them to stay clear of the large area of open water formed by the ice crews sawing and hauling blocks to a conveyor belt that carried them to an ice house from where they were loaded onto waiting boxcars. The thick transparent blocks had a texture and three-dimensional depth that fascinated Warren. Giant cubes weighing 200 pounds. Hundreds of them. Why wasn't the lake empty?

Just then Stephen had said, "Look. They're still at it."

Warren, on his knees, pivoted away from a pile of snowballs he'd manufactured for the coming fight. The ice cutting area was awash with portable lighting and generating machinery rattled away the stillness of the night, keeping workers at their saws into the darkness. The lighting was pointed toward the ice and it seemed to him like stage lighting seen from a darkened theater.

"I thought they quit at dark," Stephen continued.

"Guess not. Anyway, it gets dark early and hasn't even been dark an hour. I'm hungry."

"All you think about is food."

Warren tossed a snowball into the air and caught it. "I could bust your head right now."

"In your dreams."

Warren hopped to his feet and fired. Stephen deflected the snowball with the palm of his left hand and laughed. "You're not exactly Mickey Mantle firing one from center field, are you?"

"You're dead." Warren fired again but it was low.

Stephen danced in a circle. "Come on there Mickey Boy, let's see your stuff. I'm over here."

Warren grabbed ice balls from his stash and fired them in rapid bursts. Only one found its mark but Stephen turned his back and it struck his heavy coat with little more than a dull thump. Warren was tired and sweaty. He flopped down cross-legged in the snow. "I could've had you," he said.

"In your dreams."

Stephen joined him in the snow and they sat side by side in silence until their breathing slowed and they grew restless again. Warren complained, "I'm hungry. Can't we sneak over and watch the ice cutters for awhile then get Dad to open the sandwiches? He's got cookies, too."

"He doesn't want us by the saws."

"So? Big deal. I want to see the lights. I've never seen the lights on before. It'll make the ice look neat. Two minutes."

Stephen turned and studied the ice cutters awhile. "Okay. But we stay to the right, away from the saws. If Dad catches us we're dead."

"I don't care. Just close enough so I can see the blocks."

The great brown blade spun like those in a sawmill. The boys stood back, covering their ears from the noise. With each cut the spinning saw descended into the ice pack and shavings filled the air high above the heads of the ice cutters. One of the men looked over and shook a finger at them, warning them back.

Stephen hollered, "Don't worry!" but the man couldn't hear him.

"Geez," Warren said. "It's loud."

Two men dragged a block out of the water and onto the pack. "Must be three feet deep, that ice," Stephen said. "Man, no wonder you can drive on it."

"Does the lake go down three feet then?" Warren wanted to know.

"Just freezes again."

"But if they take out three feet and then they come back after it freezes and take out three feet again, won't the lake be down?"

"What are you talking about?"

"I'm talking about the lake, Dummy."

Stephen punched him in the arm and threw him down. "Don't be calling me no dummy."

"Knucklehead!"

"That's Dad's word."

He jumped to his feet again. "So why isn't it empty?"

"How should I know?"

"You always think you're so smart."

"Smarter than you. Doesn't mean I know everything. Let's go back."

"I want to see the blocks over there I said."

"No," Stephen said. "We aren't going any closer to the saws."

"I don't mean where the saws are, I mean over there where they've got a stack."

Stephen followed Warren's finger to the area where the blocks were stacked waiting to be fed onto the conveyor. "Okay. We go, you see it, you don't climb it."

"Didn't say I was going to climb it."

"I know you."

"You're an old lady."

They didn't climb the ice mountain but they did sit on one of the loose blocks and Warren dangled his feet. The blocks were clear and crystal like.

Light came through them from the work area and lit them from inside so they glowed pale green, reminding him of the glass blocks alongside the door at the doctor's office where he went for polio shots, but bigger, grander. He jumped down and trotted around the other side to see if they were dark from there and if you could see stars through the top ones.

Warren didn't know they were stacked almost even with the open water and he was in the lake before he had time to yell for help or even get scared.

He bobbed to the surface. Surprised. He said Stephen's name but not in panic and not loud enough to be heard. Every kid stuck his bare hand in the ice fishing hole to see how long he could hold it there. Immersion was different. At first it wasn't even cold, and not very wet. His heavy coat, boots, jeans, gloves, cap, all protected him. The warmth of his body was in the cloth and it seemed to warm the water against his skin but it went everywhere and when it touched his face it stung like needle pricks. For some reason Warren thought his cap was pushing him under so he slung it up onto the ice.

He was a good swimmer for his age and his mother bragged he was like a fish in the water. He thought he could get out of this. Kick to the edge of the ice and grab hold with both hands. He'd climb out before Stephen missed him, then stand there all wet complaining that his brother didn't even want to take a dip with him. He couldn't get a grip. The ice was smooth where it made contact with the water. His gloves were wet too, and they slipped. He took them off and tossed them onto the ice. Tried again. Slipped again.

His bare hands soon began to throb. At first they were sore from the water but when he looked down they were a dull red and the fingers seemed swollen and when he touched his face or even the ice it was like the nerves were deadened, yet everything was painful. Clothes that a moment before kept him warm now became his enemy - saturated, heavy, freezing. Stabbing cold attacked his lips and made them swell. He felt them getting fat as if they'd been injected with something and when he looked down he thought he saw them sticking out like platypus lips.

The surface of the water was only inches below the ice. His eyes were almost level with it. Not so different from being in a swimming pool without a ladder. But the pool deck was ice and the water was cold.

It was creepy. Slow creepy. After the first cold shock a numbness embraced him. It didn't hurt - not then - just held him. How swiftly it entered his body, and how soon he knew it would never end. Cold possessed of a power to be colder still, and he hurt and tears sprang to his eyes. He'd known cold, and he knew it came on you and then stopped short. Not an end, but a place where it held steady. This cold only soaked deeper and deeper, eating through his skin into the meat, the bones, organs. It drank his warmth and numbed his brain.

He couldn't think straight. He had a headache.

And fright. Terror. Not like being scared of a thing, but knowing the truth that the fear is justified by the reality of certain death. He knew nothing could save him.

He cried in pain, far worse than anything ever imagined. A heartless thing that touched him deep inside - crotch, underarms - cooling him in a way that made his mind freeze. Then drew deeper, eating to the center, drinking the warmth that gave him life.

He balanced between pain and numbness, fear and acceptance, life and death.

He panicked.

Clawed the ice, kicked his feet. The leaden clothes drew him back whenever he raised himself even slightly above the water. He screamed for Stephen. Screamed his name again and again.

Stephen found him in seconds. "Give me your hand," he said.

Warren grasped Stephen's hand. Stephen braced his knees against the ice and pulled. Warren kicked and clutched at the ice with his free hand. He was lifted from the water but not high enough. Water sloshed onto the ice and smoothed it. Stephen tried again but his knees skidded almost off the ice and into the hole.

"Get Dad," Warren gasped.

"No. He's too far away. Try again."

Stephen used both hands and sat down flat on the ice digging his heels in. Warren raised several inches, then the weight of his clothes dragged him back. "I can't," he said.

"Take your clothes off," Stephen ordered.

"No."

"Do it!"

Warren cried.

"Do it. You're too heavy. I'll get you into the fishhouse. You won't freeze. Now do it!"

Warren tried but the clothes seemed stuck and he couldn't think straight. He couldn't pull his arm from the sleeve of his jacket, first one sleeve then the other he tried. Stephen grabbed him by the collar and helped. The jacket came off.

"Boots!" Stephen yelled.

Warren tried but they were laced tight. "I can't." He was swallowing water. He was going to die. A few inches from the safety of the ice and he was going to die. Stephen couldn't help him. Nobody could help him. It was an impossible thing. The water was stronger than anything. It wouldn't let go.

Nothing could move him those few inches. Not Stephen, not Dad. The force of the water was greater than human force. It pulled, drew him deeper, stealing his warmth. Then it would come into his mouth and run down inside and fill him with a cold so deep it went beyond pain, even fear. But he was afraid. He could hear himself screaming. Hysterical screams, high pitched, penetrating, uncontrollable.

Then, like a miracle, something pushed him up from behind. He turned. It was Stephen. He was in the water.

Warren was crying but Stephen said, "When I push your butt, kick your feet against my chest and shinny up on the ice."

At first it didn't work and Warren fell back again. Now they were both going down and he screamed and screamed, pounding his red fists at the water.

"Shut up!" Stephen said. "Kick against me like I told you. Now!"

Warren never forgot the anger of that night. His foremost memory should've been Stephen's bravery jumping into the frigid water to save him, or even the pain, terror, hysteria. But it was the anger he thought about, years later when he was past forty and his hair had grayed and memory should've faded. It was a hopeless anger at nothing. Not at himself for his carelessness or the ice or ice harvesting or frozen lakes. It was a frustrated anger at human frailty. The ultimate anger, he thought later, coming when he first discovered the body's betrayal, flesh that's nothing but a poorly warranteed obsolescent product of the here and now.

But that night anger saved him. The hard bone of his heel struck his brother's skull and he felt Stephen's bone against his bone and he pushed and kicked and pounded his feet against the skull, clawing with his fingers into the ice until one knee came free of the water and he slithered to safety like a fish from a net.

When he looked back he saw Stephen still there, face submerged just below the surface. Eyes open, his mouth forming some lost word or sentence. He stared as Stephen struggled to bring his mouth out of the water, to breathe. Stephen stared back at him but not in panic or in a painful way but just looking deep into Warren's eyes, holding on to them.

Warren did nothing. He didn't reach his hand out. Didn't grab his brother's hair or the sleeve of his jacket or even move an inch closer to the edge. He watched. Stephen drifted down. The darkness closed around him.

Warren sat very still, shivering.

* * *

Late winter dawn crept into the upstairs bedroom at 7:15, and found Warren sitting up in bed, waiting. A faint morning grayness, leaking between fat cracks of the blinds and outside a city stirring with an urgency and power unknown at home. Automobiles idling in neighboring driveways, warming up. Doors slamming. Crunching footsteps hurrying along the sidewalks. Shrill voices of children up early to play in new fallen snow.

Everything came down now to this moment, this day. The money, the work and waiting - all for this. Today he would breathe underwater and learn what only a handful of people on earth knew. Only those like Stephen, those who went below, knew what he would know. Not those who sat inside submarines or peeked down from inside glass bottom boats, not even the old fashioned hard hat divers locked inside their helmets and lead-soled shoes, only scuba divers who actually breathed in the water, feeling it against their skin, moving themselves through it, only they knew what it was. Divers, and the dead. Today he would begin searching for his brother.

Aunt Doris called, "Warren? Are you up?"

"I'm up Auntie Doris!"

"Come down then and get your breakfast."

He climbed out of bed, fully dressed since six o'clock, except for shoes. The greasy smell from the kitchen was delightful, maybe his all-time favorite, pork links. He ran down two steps at a time and heard the radio in the kitchen singing, "Salem tastes good like a cigarette should," and Uncle David saying, "Another inch and a half last night, would you believe? Breaking my back on that shovel."

"Do you good," his wife replied. "Might even shave off a few pounds."

"What'd you want, some guy with little toothpick legs and a sunken, denuded chest?" He chuckled. "Didn't hear any complaints last night."

"The way you talk!" Warren heard a slap. Uncle David laughed again. Aunt Doris saw him coming around the corner and shook a tight little fist at her husband. "Sit down and eat," she said as he came nearer and smiled at them.

"Good morning there, Mr. Skin Diver," Uncle David bellowed. "Side pork and eggs. We got scrambled, or any way you want 'em. Plenty of toast. Peanut butter? I bet you drink orange juice."

"Sure," Warren said, responding to the orange juice portion only. He'd suddenly lost his appetite. "I better not eat too much. Got butterflies in my stomach or something."

Aunt Doris drew out a chair for him. "Eat what you can," she said. "Not everyone wants to grow a belly like that."

Her insult gave Uncle David an excuse to let loose another bellow. "What time we gotta be there?" he asked Warren.

"Nine o'clock sharp."

"Plenty of time then. Plenty of time."

Uncle David was in no hurry. Breakfast dragged. All four girls awoke, fought, and brushed their teeth. The pulp in Warren's orange juice sank to the bottom. Uncle David asked for a third cup of coffee. "Seem kinda quiet this morning," he said. "Having second thoughts?"

Warren shook his head.

"He's just tired," Aunt Doris explained. "Look at his eyes. They're all puffy."

"Hate sleeping in a strange bed myself," said Uncle David. "Throws my bowels off."

"Be quiet and finish your coffee. Almost 8:30. Can't you see Warren's in a hurry?"

Heading downtown later, each signal light seemed stuck on red. Traffic crawled along, choked with lazy truckers and old ladies hedging their bets. Finally, the station wagon turned onto Nicollet. "Time to synchronize our watches," said Uncle David. "Got your money? What time do I pick you up? Where you going to eat lunch?"

"I've got the number. I'll call when I'm done." Uncle David's concern brought a smile. "Don't worry. Freddie-the-Frogman will take good care of me." He listened a moment to the dying words of *Candyman*, then added, "I *am* fifteen, you know."

"Shoot!" Uncle David said. "You can take care of yourself. I know that. You're a Wilson, like me and your old man. Those UDT guys ain't got nothing on us!"

Kind words. Better than he deserved. For all his bravado, Warren had yet to face the moment. Until now, scuba was talk. Once he got out of the car and walked into the dive shop, he'd be expected to follow through, really become a scuba diver. There were stories - shark attacks, mysterious underwater disappearances, a boy held to the bottom of the sea by a giant clam. There were killer whales, drownings, exotic diseases. In literature, scuba divers seemed foolhardy at best. In real life, insurance companies ranked them as daredevils and denied coverage.

The station wagon bounced against the curb and stopped. Warren looked up at Freddie-the-Frogman's dive shop. The sign read, OPEN. "Thanks for the ride Uncle David." He hopped out and stood a moment holding the door.

Uncle David leaned across the seat and looked up at him from the passenger side. "I make calls all over town, you know. Could stop by here again around lunch time real easy. I mean, just in case you need me or anything."

He tried to give Uncle David a confident smile. "Thanks. But I'll be fine. Call you tonight." He slammed the door and the station wagon pulled away. Warren watched until it reached the end of the block and sped around the corner, then turned to face the steps leading up to the place where Freddie-the-

Frogman waited.

Once in an eighth grade scrimmage, Warren was pulverized by Marv Pederson the human bulldozer. He badly skinned one elbow and the side of his face. He quit junior high football. Coach Ferris took him aside before he left and said it wasn't because he got hurt that he quit. "You can't stand to lose. That's your problem. That's why you're cutting out. If you don't try you can't lose. You're safe. Better watch out you don't end up running away all your life."

Too late for football. He wasn't big enough anyway, but if he tried hard maybe scuba would be the thing he could win. Show people he was something special - a frogman.

He stopped at the door. He didn't have to open it. He could give the five hundred to poor people in Africa. What if he was too dumb to be a scuba diver? Why should Freddie-the-Frogman even remember the letter he wrote? He probably got hundreds of letters from kids.

The outer door was homemade. A screen in place now, in winter. Warren tugged the latch, held the door open with his foot.

The inner door was solid, paint blistered, yellowed. The knob was ice in his hand and turned hard. Warren leaned his shoulder against it until it gave inward.

A Klaxon sounded, loud and impending like general quarters on a battleship. Warren froze in the doorway.

"Close that door!" A man's voice rose above the alarm.

The klaxon wailed. He couldn't move.

"What in hell's the matter with you, kid? Didn't you hear me? I said close the goddamn door!"

Trembling, Warren shoved the door closed. The Klaxon stopped.

"Don't tell me you're Warren Wilson?"

Warren nodded, staring. The man who spoke resembled Freddie-the-Frogman, but much older. His hair, what was left of it, stood straight on his head in a gristly crew cut. Flesh drooped under gray eyes set close together. The nose was large, puggish. The thin lips strangely familiar. Firm jaw. Skin sagging under the ears.

He came out from behind a service counter. He was short. Not much taller than Warren. A dingy T-shirt stretched tightly across his belly. Ironed to the front was a green felt scuba diver - over it the words Freddie-the-Frogman, and beneath, "Divers Do It Deeper." The man's frayed khaki shorts sagged to accommodate his belly. His legs however, were tan and muscular. Hips no wider than Warren's.

"Freddie-the-Frogman," the man said, thrusting his hand at Warren.

It was a lie. Some cruel trick. "You don't look much like your picture," he said, unabashed.

"Holy shit, kid! That was taken during World War II. You expect me to stay in my twenties all my life?"

"Guess not," Warren said, calculating the man's age then at about forty. Teetering on death's doorstep. The dive shop was stifling. Dry choking heat blew steadily from dusty registers set near the ceiling. Warren fought down a sneeze and removed neither cap or coat, not yet invited to stay.

"Bring your money?" Freddie asked.

Warren nodded.

"Come in then, we'll get you started."

Freddie headed back toward the counter and Warren shed his outer garments, surveying the showroom. It was dominated by pegboard sheets nailed to the walls. Metal hooks supported displays of dusty masks, regulators, fins, knives, and spearguns. Some of the pegboard was painted a drippy blue color, some left the original brown. Warren puzzled at the scarcity of merchandise on the hooks. A pegboard display nearest the counter had four speargun silhouettes painted on it in descending sizes, but all its pegs were empty except the smallest. Boxes were strewn about as if someone had just unpacked.

Freddie rounded the counter and made for a large cluttered desk at the back of the room. Warren halted at an orange sign that read: AUTHORIZED PERSONNEL ONLY.

"Well?" Freddie growled. "Are you coming?"

"Can I go back there?"

"Just invited you, didn't I? Sit here so we can talk." He brushed newspapers and sandwich wrappers from the chair parked alongside his desk. "Here," he said. "Sit here."

Warren, clutching his Freddie-the-Frogman folder, slid onto the chair. He wished Uncle David would come back for him. This was a terrible mistake. He shouldn't have come here.

"Over the years," Freddie began, "I've learned a thing or two about business. Number one is, get your financial affairs in order first. How much money you got?"

"Five hundred dollars."

"Just five hundred? No more than that?"

"I saved for three years."

Freddie dug at the clutter on his desk until he came up with a ruptured pack of Lucky Strikes. He gave Warren a toothy grin. "Don't worry. We'll get you outfitted for five hundred. You remember our deal don't you?"

"If I buy a complete set of gear, I get the class free."

"Right. You'll have to spend the whole five hundred."

"Okay." Suddenly, Warren relaxed. He wouldn't go home a failure after all. He'd have the equipment. With it, he could dive, Freddie-the-Frogman or no Freddie-the-Frogman. "I'll give you the money now." He placed the wallet on the edge of Freddie's desk and unzipped it. The sooner he got rid of it the better. He emptied the wallet.

Freddie grinned, counting out loud. "All there," he said.

Warren was relieved. Large transactions were unnerving.

"I expect you got some idea of what you want?"

Warren nodded.

"Let me see your catalog." Freddie wagged his fingers impatiently. "See if we got any of it in stock."

Warren handed the catalog to Freddie and waited, staring at the floor. Near the chair leg an army of ants fed on a cold French fry. He hadn't considered the possibility of things not being in stock. What if the Royal Aquamaster wasn't in stock? Grease from the French fry had soaked into the tile. Ants were licking it.

"Everything's here except the knife and mask you circled. I'll find you something better." He smoked for a moment. "You left a couple things out, like a weight belt and a hood. We're gonna have to make some adjustments to this list. Try to get everything you need and stick to your budget. Sure you don't have any more money?"

"I've got a bus ticket."

"Don't be dumb, kid. Who wants a bus ticket to some cow town?"

"Maybe you could sell it."

Freddie-the-Frogman laughed, looking a little like his photograph. His gray eyes narrowed and he stared at Warren. "One thing I got to know, Kid. How come you want to be a diver?"

Warren had answered this question a thousand times. Told some outlandish lies to keep people from laughing. Now Freddie-the-Frogman was asking. "Because I want to breathe underwater," he said, truthfully. "I want to explore the unknown. Be first to see new things." He felt like an idiot and wished he could change places with the ants, licking grease, but he couldn't stop himself. And he sure couldn't say anything about Stephen. "Besides, I'm no good at sports like basketball."

Freddie-the-Frogman didn't laugh. Nodding his head up and down, he made a humming noise. After awhile he said, "Don't worry about basketball, it's a spectator sport. A few play and many watch. You and I Kid, we ain't spectators." He ground his cigarette out in an ashtray made from an abalone shell. "Lots of you kids that come in here are pretty goofy - and you're skinnier than most of 'em - but if anybody can make divers out of you, it's me." He punched Warren in the arm. "Freddie-the-Frogman's gonna take good care of you!"

CHAPTER FOUR

"We've talked a lot about death," he said. "You're probably sick of it but kids your age think they'll live forever. Get that idea out of your head."

Warren, still sitting in the chair beside Freddie-the-Frogman's desk, swallowed hard. Freddie stood over him holding a giant placard that read: DECOMPRESSION SICKNESS KILLS.

"Take my word for it, kid. There's bold divers and there's old divers, but there ain't no old bold divers," Freddie said. "Obey the rules or you're dead."

Propped against the side of Freddie's desk were the death placards they'd already covered: AIR EMBOLISM KILLS, PANIC KILLS, NITROGEN NARCOSIS KILLS, and BAD AIR KILLS. They'd also discussed an enlarged photograph of a diver who'd been sliced open by a boat propeller. His back was especially gruesome, intestines exposed from the rear, bulging along the even slices dug by each propeller stroke. Warren hadn't imagined you could see a man's intestines through his back and the tissue cuts in the victim's flesh were fatty like that of a butchered hog. "Educational," Freddie said, he hadn't even minded the nine bucks it cost to have the photo blown up.

Now they came to Decompression Sickness, a diving disease almost everyone had heard about. "Of all the diving maladies," Freddie lectured, "decompression sickness - the bends - is the least understood." He paused to let this sink in. "We used to call the bends caisson disease, because many years ago tunnel and bridge construction crews got it when they worked in caissons."

"What's a caisson?"

"You don't know what a caisson is? Don't they teach nothin' in school these days?"

Warren shook his head. He must've missed this chapter in physics.

"Caissons are like watertight compartments where men work underwater or deep underground when they build a bridge or a pressurized mine, that kind of thing. Started way back in the 1800s, before the Civil War even. Understand?"

"I remember studying it now," Warren fibbed.

"Bends is just like everything else in diving - easy to prevent, tough to cure."

Freddie thumped the Decompression placard with his middle finger. "You get the bends and nine times out of ten you die. End up a cripple if you're lucky."

Warren stared at the placard. "How do you get it?"

"Going too deep. Staying too long. Coming up too fast."

"How can I keep track of all that?"

"With this." Freddie flipped the placard. On the back was a large chart titled: **U.S. Navy Standard Air Decompression Table.** Hundreds of numbers, times, and repetitive group letters set in columns. "Memorize it."

A hollowness grew in Warren's insides. It would take years. What if Freddie wouldn't give him his equipment until he learned it perfectly? "I can't remember all that."

"Not all of it." Freddie picked up a pencil and pointed to each depth limit beginning with forty feet going to two hundred. "You memorize only the no-decompression limits."

"What's that?"

"The depths and times you can stay without having to worry about the bends."

"Oh."

"Every depth has a limit. Learn 'em."

"What if I goof up?"

Freddie seemed prepared for this question. He grinned broadly, lighting his eyes with a mischievous sparkle. "Who can say, kid? Divers have lived by the Navy tables since the war." He let the grin fade. "Course they're just a bunch of numbers some guy made up. You could stick to 'em like gospel and still get the bends. Kind of diving we do hasn't been around long. You and I, we're pioneers kinda. We're making history. Not that anybody gives a shit."

Freddie-the-Frogman said that in diving, as in life, there is only one rule: don't get screwed. And even though Warren was just a lad, underwater he'd be taking on a man's responsibility. People who dove with him, his buddies, had to know they could depend on him. Not getting screwed, Freddie said, meant not doing anything unless you planned it ahead of time. Plan your dive. Dive your plan. That was the rule. Freddie taught him Boyle's Law, Dalton's Law, Charles' Law, Archimedes' Principle of Buoyancy, and the principle of accepting the world as a screwed-up place, and unless you took charge, anything can happen. All of it bad.

Freddie-the-Frogman fell silent. Finally he said, "That's Murphy's Law kid, and the law of the sea, too. It's always the damnedest little things get you killed. Remember that. Check everything. Every piece of gear. Then check it again to be sure."

"I will," Warren said, and he meant it.

At exactly noon, the telephone rang. Freddie picked it up but didn't speak into it. After listening awhile, gazing at the ceiling, Freddie said, "Just meet me there then. I'll pack two extra sets of gear." He hung up. "The wife," he told Warren. "Coming to the pool tonight to give us a hand. My daughter too. About your age."

Warren fought to maintain his composure. "You have a daughter?" He couldn't imagine this. "Does she dive?"

"Naturally. Started her in the San Diego tidal basin when she was four. Strapped an old 38 I stole from a scrap pile onto her." The memory pleased him. "I'll show you the pictures sometime. She looked awful cute with that 38 and my old Navy regulator stuck in her mouth. Had to carry her to the water. Couldn't walk with all that gear on." He grinned.

This image terrified Warren. What was she like today? A teenage version of Esther Williams? Built like her father? A girl who grew up tossing 38 cubic foot cylinders around wouldn't be likely to have mercy on a green kid from Lake Darling who had only just got his mile swim merit badge the year before. What if she laughed at him? His arms were skinny. He didn't have hardly any muscles and you could see his ribs. It hadn't occurred to Warren that girls could go diving. He'd never heard of it. He wondered if maybe it wasn't against the law. Freddie-the-Frogman was just the kind of guy who made his own laws, especially when it came to his family. "I never heard of women diving," he blurted out.

Freddie shrugged and seemed to agree. "I know it don't seem natural. Not to most men anyway. I only taught them because we lived way the hell down in Imperial Beach and I didn't have anybody to dive with out there." He shrugged again. "After I got out of the Navy they just kept doing it."

There was a long silence while Warren and Freddie stared at the floor.

"I never let 'em dive unless I'm there," Freddie said, demonstrating he hadn't taken complete leave of his senses.

Warren appreciated the shared confidence.

"Lunch time," Freddie said, slapping a hand against his leg. "Grab your Skin Diver's Bible. You can study for the final exam while we eat. You like chili?"

"Sure," he said.

"The Dew Drop Inn across the street's got the best chili in town," Freddie told him. "I'm buying."

"Thanks. I've never eaten at a Mexican place."

"Ain't Mexican," Freddie said, pushing him toward the door. "Owner's half Cuban. Did a tour at Gitmo and picked up a Cuban gal from down there. She does the cookin' so I guess it's Cuban chili." He grabbed his coat from a hook near the door. "Order two glasses of water."

Across the street, the Dew Drop Inn sat snug in a dirty snow bank. Like Freddie's dive shop, the building was elevated above street level and had to be approached by a set of concrete steps which the UDT man, still in his shorts, took two at a time. The cafe reminded Warren of a chicken coop and as they burst in from the cold, warm air engulfed them, laden with whiskey and fried onions. The men looking up from the lunch counter had flesh-colored rings around their eyes like raccoons. The remainder of their faces were black. Welders and cutting torch men, Freddie said, working in shops along the street. He'd taught several to dive so they could find work as underwater welders nearby in the Mississippi.

Freddie directed him to a booth near the window. The cushions were patched with duct tape, speckled with gravy, grease, and crumbs of bread. Freddie caught the sleeve of his thin jacket between his fingers and swept debris from the table onto the floor, then rolled his arm back and forth, polishing. Sliding in opposite, Warren gazed out the greasy window and said, "I suppose your daughter is tall."

"What?"

"Your daughter."

"What about her?"

"Is she tall? What's her name?"

"Ruth," Freddie said reluctantly. "I don't let her date. She's taller than you and probably out-weighs you by a good twenty pounds, all of which is muscle."

"Oh," said Warren.

"We didn't come over here to discuss women," Freddie growled. "I've only got one day to make a diver out of you, and not everything's in that book." He pointed to the Skin Diver's Bible. "You don't even know the most important rule of diving yet, do you?"

"I guess not." Warren shifted his brown eyes to the table. "What is it?"

Before answering, Freddie hollered at the man behind the lunch counter. "Bring us two chilis, Marcel!" Then he said, "Never hold your breath."

"That's the most important rule? Never hold your breath? In the book it says never dive alone."

"Diving ain't like sex, kid. You can have fun diving alone." He knocked on the book with his fist. "Books are just filled with stuff some guy wrote down. Doesn't make it right." He knocked on his own chest. "I'm telling you from twenty years' experience that the most important rule of diving is: Never hold your breath."

"Why not?"

"Because if you hold your breath on scuba your lungs will explode." He puffed up his cheeks and blew a blast of tobacco-soaked air across the table in Warren's direction. "You'll be dead."

Warren was beginning to understand why you didn't meet many scuba divers. "How come I never died before when I held my breath underwater?" he asked.

"Remember Boyle's Law?"

"I memorized it."

He scowled. "No good to memorize what you don't understand. Boyle's Law isn't just volume and pressure. It's about staying alive. About holding your breath." Two steaming bowls of chili arrived and Freddie crushed a handful of soda crackers into his bowl. "Your lungs are a balloon. Fill them with compressed air underwater, hold it, and go up - boom!"

"You're dead, right?"

"Right."

"Boom!" Warren said.

Freddie-the-Frogman nodded and went back to his chili.

They finished lunch and strolled across the street to the dive shop. Warren could contain himself no longer. "When do I pick out my gear?" he asked. This should've come first. Talking about death all day got boring.

"After you pass the exam," Freddie said. "No use picking out gear if you flunk the test."

"Like school? I can fail?"

"What do you think? You give me a measly five hundred bucks I'll let you pass?"

This was exactly what Warren thought, but as it turned out the test was a faded homemade mimeograph fraught with misspellings and unclear choices, and Warren had taken more tests than Freddie-the-Frogman had written. He psyched the answers and passed with eighty-six percent.

Freddie seemed pleased. He reached up the leg of his shorts to scratch himself. "I suppose you think this entitles you to some scuba gear?" An evil grin hinted he might not give it to him.

Owning his own dive gear wasn't like having a baseball mitt or a bicycle. It was like an astronaut walking into the hangar to see his capsule for the first time. To run his fingers gently over smooth, hard surfaces. This was serious. Scuba equipment was owned by people who weren't just cool, they were heroes. And Warren, who had killed his brother, wanted more than anything to be a hero.

"All right," Freddie said. "Let's start with the mask." He walked around the counter to the dusty pegboard mask display. "It needs to fit your face perfectly and have equalizer pockets."

Warren would have preferred to start with the regulator - the Royal Aquamaster - but joined Freddie at the mask display. "How about that one?" he inquired, pointing to a bright blue oval mask which seemed newer than the rest, not quite as dusty.

"Jeez, kid. Can't you see that's a skin diving mask?" Freddie snatched the mask from the display and showed Warren the inside. "Do you see any equalizer pockets? A nose pad? How you gonna equalize when you make your descent?"

Equalization was important, like not holding your breath or not getting the bends, and the principle of equalization was jostling around in Warren's brain somewhere with all the other "don'ts" and "nevers." You had to equalize air pressure inside your head with the increased water pressure outside, that much he knew.

Equalization was a concept foreign to humans, like most diving skills. Warren marveled at the idea of equalization, but would it really work underwater? How could there be so many things like that, that Warren had never heard about? He only had Freddie-the-Frogman's word for them. He trusted the old Freddie, the one in the photograph, the one he'd never met, but this one reminded him too much of Lucas Barnes, salesmen at Larsen Chev. "One of those slippery boys up front," Dad said. Never any doubt what he wanted - your wallet. Afterward, he laughed about how easy it was.

"Try this one," Freddie said, pushing an ugly black mask onto Warren's face. "How's it feel?"

It felt fine. The skirting was made of a thick, soft neoprene rubber that formed nicely to Warren's face. "I like the blue one better," he said.

"Forget it," Freddie commanded, slapping the blue one back on the hooks. "I've got a snorkel in back that'll work with this. Now, sit down and kick your shoes off so we can try on some fins."

Warren sat on a low stool staring at the ugly black mask in his hands. It had a purge valve nose piece that looked like a pig's snout. Did you have to be Jacques Cousteau or Mike Nelson before you earned the right to pick your own gear?

"Shoes?" Freddie repeated.

Warren pried them off without undoing the laces and grimaced at the stack of fins Freddie had assembled for him to try on. They weren't the kind he wanted. They were the kind of fins Warren had skipped over in the catalog. Open-heeled, adjustable fins. Ugly. Black like the mask.

"I want full-foot fins," Warren demanded.

"Those are skin diving fins," Freddie said.

"I want the blue full-foot fins to match the blue mask."

Freddie heaved a long dangerous sigh. "Listen to me, Warren." It was the first time he'd used his name. "Full-foot fins are worn barefooted. Do you want to go down below the thermocline, where the water is forty degrees, and swim around barefooted?"

"I want the blue fins."

"You can't wear wet suit boots with those fins. No room inside the foot pocket for your foot and a quarter inch wet suit boot. You'll freeze your damn toes off!"

"Then I want bigger ones." Warren knew he was just being stubborn. Freddie was probably right about the fins, but it was his money. He wanted the blue ones.

Freddie-the-Frogman looked as if he were about to explode, scalp gone pink under his thin hair. With effort, he held himself in check and left the room. When he returned, his face was a milder shade. "Here," he said, handing Warren an extremely large box. "These are double extra large, full-foot fins. Blue. They're too big for you but they're just what you want. And when you can't swim with them or stand up with a tank on your back or you kick them off at eighty feet and have to walk back to the surface, then you remember that I told you to get the black ones."

They never spoke of fins again.

They tried on wet suits, struggled with backpack harnesses, shot a speargun into an old cardboard box, selected a gold-colored tank, even laid knives across their forefingers to check balance. Warren could remember no happier time, but the main event was yet to come. The regulator.

Warren didn't have to ask for the Royal Aquamaster. Freddie set it before him and opened the lid on the box. "This is it, kid. Don't drop it. That's ninety bucks of chrome-plated brass, stainless steel, and high-grade neoprene."

"Eighty-five bucks," Warren corrected.

"Ninety. Your catalog's three years old. Price went up. Quit worrying about prices anyway. You got 500 bucks right? So it'll come out to 500 in the end see? Package price. No problem."

Warren relaxed. Freddie steadied the box and Warren carefully lifted the regulator out with both hands. Freddie spread a white towel on the counter and Warren placed the regulator on it, gently. Neither of them spoke. For this moment at least, they were in perfect harmony.

Just the hint of a smile creased the corner of Freddie's mouth as Warren reached out tentatively, allowing his fingers to contact the cool chrome, then the corrugated rubber hoses, circling, joined at the mouthpiece by two gleaming stainless steel clips. There was no doubt. This was the finest regulator ever built. It almost breathed for you. Each half-circle of hose, the inhalation and exhalation portions, had been hand-rubbed with lubricant, making the black neoprene appear wet and luxurious.

Warren forgot the fins. He had a regulator. His very own. Not a toy or a replica or a model. A working regulator. The same kind, exactly, that Freddie-the-Frogman used, a real UDT man.

"How's it feel, kid?" asked the frogman.

"Neat," said Warren.

* * *

That evening, Warren discovered the building that housed the campus swimming pool was constructed by the Romans. Giant grooved columns guarded the front door, supporting nothing but a tiny peaked roof purposeless as the columns themselves. An odd place for swimmers, Warren thought. Here people should study philosophy, or medicine, or spend years translating the Bible into obscure foreign languages.

Yellow light splashed the columns from inside hooded canisters deep in new snow, giving them a theatrical air. Snow-covered trees lent texture to surrounding lawns and leafless hedges along sidewalks plowed like country roads. He waited, watching for Freddie to come back around the side of the building. He'd gone in search of the janitor who was supposed to meet them and unlock the door but hadn't kept the appointment. It just showed, Freddie said, how really screwed up the world was.

It was almost six-thirty. They had the pool until nine. Freddie's wife and daughter hadn't arrived yet and Warren hoped Freddie would find the janitor and get back before they did. Once inside, the talking was over. He'd really do it, breathe underwater. What if he screwed up? Panicked? Sucked water? He knocked his feet together to warm his toes. Headlights rounded the corner. A car pulled to the curb and stopped.

Warren watched the passenger door swing open and a tall girl emerge. She was adorned head to mid-thigh in fur, face recessed inside an animal skin hood ringed by thick trimming so white he first thought it was artificial. Her legs were shapeless woolen stumps, feet hidden in snug boots with white trimming to match her hood. "Well?" she said, addressing him.

He stared.

She took several steps toward him. "Aren't you Warren Wilson?"

"Yes," he admitted.

"So, where's my dad? What are you doing standing out here in the cold?"

He didn't like being blamed for it. "Wasn't my idea," he said.

"Where's all the scuba gear?"

"In the trunk of Freddie-the-Frogman's car. Behind the building." He disliked defending himself.

The girl laughed. "What's this *Freddie-the-Frogman* crap?" She strolled to within inches of him and peered out from the fur. Black eyes shining. "That's a trade name. You don't call people by their trade names," she said.

The only trade names Warren could think of were like Ford or Coca Cola.

"Is that what you call him to his face?" she inquired. "Freddie-the-Frogman?"

"What should I call him, Mr. Frogman?" he asked crossly. "I don't even know his last name."

"Van Doren. Same as mine."

"You Ruth?"

"Ruth Van Doren. My mother's in the car, Marilyn Van Doren. My father, whom you seem to have misplaced somewhere, is Fredrick Van Doren." She uncovered her head, exposing a mountain of chestnut hair, ratted to a fine fuzz. "Now, if you don't mind holding the door for me, I've got a wet suit and a few things I'd like to unload."

"Door's locked. Your dad's trying to find the janitor so we can get a key."

She seemed skeptical of this, as if it might be some tale he invented. "I find that positively ludicrous," she said.

When they weren't giggling or discussing their periods, girls memorized words from the dictionary to prove everyone else stupid. Even so, Warren liked the way Ruth looked so far, her head anyway. She hadn't exposed anything else.

Freddie-the-Frogman-Van Doren came around the building, janitor plodding behind. They walked in brooding silence, as if covering up a fight they'd had. Freddie's face brightened noticeably when he saw Ruth standing next to Warren. "Hello, sweetheart," he called.

Such public gushing seemed almost feminine to Warren, maybe ludicrous, and he hadn't imagined Freddie even knew the word *sweetheart*. Now that Freddie had appeared, his wife joined them. She was the spitting image of Susan Hayward. In fact, for a moment Warren thought it was Susan Hayward. Her hair was dark chestnut like Ruth's with a mass of thick curls descending nearly to her shoulders and she had Ruth's lively black eyes, too. A small, turned-up nose and rich lips. The right side of her mouth was permanently hooked up, just barely, so it seemed like she was about to say something smart-aleck. But she didn't say anything at all. Not even hello.

"Quit staring," Freddie said in his ear. "Follow me around back and help unload the gear. You might as well learn now that hauling your own gear is the first rule of diving."

The gear consisted of five tanks, one for each of them and a spare, backpacks, weight belts, wet suits, and bags containing their regulators and other personal items. All of this, weighing hundreds of pounds, had been wedged into the trunk and backseat of Freddie's car, a green and yellow 1957 DeSoto.

"When you lift the tanks," Freddie instructed, "carry them vertically by the valve. Don't drop them!"

"What happens?"

"Kaboom! But you won't hear it, you'll be dead."

That afternoon Freddie had showed him a photograph of a scuba cylinder embedded in the back door of a 1960 Buick. This, he'd explained, was what happened when a tank valve snapped. Modern steel scuba cylinders contained 2,250 pounds per square inch (psi) of compressed air. They became rockets when dropped, or they exploded leaving a crater in the earth. According to Freddie, the tank pictured had been dropped in a railroad yard during unloading. It skyrocketed through several moving trains, the exterior and interior walls of a brick warehouse, finally coming to rest in the Buick several blocks away.

Inside the natatorium, humid air hung thick with chlorine. He struggled down a flight of worn metal steps to where Ruth and Mrs. Van Doren waited by the pool deck. Freddie's voice echoed from behind him. "Don't stand those tanks upright. Lay them on their sides so they don't fall."

Knowing the consequences, Warren gently lowered the tanks to the tile floor, then turned to face the pool. There were no swimming pools in Lake Darling, and though Warren had been in a few elsewhere, the flawless surface of the water fascinated him and he stood beside it transfixed. How was it possible for so much water to be so still? So motionless?

"Aren't you supposed to be helping my dad bring in the gear?" Ruth asked. She'd walked up behind, soundlessly. He noticed she had shed her Eskimo garb, but had not yet changed to a swimsuit.

"Checking out the pool," he said, on the defensive.

Ruth laughed. "Does it meet with your approval?"

Neither Freddie or his wife were nearby. Warren said, "You don't know much about business."

"I'm not in business."

"Your father is. Go around smarting off to his customers he'll go broke."

"Customers like you, I suppose," she said, crossing her arms. "You're just a kid."

"Big deal." He thought about mentioning the five hundred dollars, but even if she believed him, it wasn't proper to discuss such affairs. He turned away and trotted up the steps to the car.

"Shake a leg, kid," Freddie said. "Get this gear inside so I can close the door.

I'm freezing."

By the time they unloaded the equipment and Warren dashed into the boys locker room to change and had come back out again, Ruth and her mother were already standing at the edge of the pool assembling their gear.

Ruth in a swimsuit brought a lump to Warren's throat. She couldn't have been more than a year or so older, but she had a woman's figure. Even breasts. Shapely thighs and calves, thin ankles and long narrow feet. She didn't paint her toenails as some girls did. Warren glanced down at his own skinny sticks, white and almost hairless. One look at him and she'd double with laughter. He hurried to the pool's edge and dove headlong into the warm water before she had time to draw a bead on him.

"Get out of the water!" Freddie shouted. "Did I tell you to get in the water? You don't do anything until I tell you."

Warren swam to the edge. Slapping both palms flat on the tile lip above his head, he popped gingerly onto the pool deck without using the ladder. They'd see he was skinny, but limber and strong too.

"What are you, some kind of acrobat?" Freddie asked. "Get over here and pay attention. We're going to learn how to assemble the gear."

The humid air felt cold now and Warren wished he hadn't left his towel in the locker room. He shivered, trying to concentrate on Freddie's instructions.

"I'm going to tell you this once, and only once," Freddie growled. "Pick up that tank." He waited for Warren to obey. "Bring it here and stand it up." Warren obeyed. "Get a backpack." Warren left the tank and went for the backpack. "Damn it!" Freddie swore. "Didn't I just tell you a few minutes ago not to leave those tanks standing?"

"But you..."

"No buts!" Freddie cut in. "Learn the rules and stick to 'em, no matter what anybody tells you. I suppose if I told you to go jump off this building you'd do that too?"

Warren half expected it to be part of the course.

"Now," Freddie said. "Lay the tank down, then get the backpack." Warren obeyed, alert for new tricks.

"Okay. Shake the straps loose and slide the crisscross mounting bands - those metal ones - over the top of the cylinder and down about halfway," Freddie instructed.

Warren looked at the backpack in his hands. It was a confusion of straps, bands, and buckles. He shook the straps loose. A pair of metal bands were bolted to a painted metal plate. They were crisscrossed. He placed them over the top of the cylinder and slid them down halfway. Not so difficult. He looked up at Freddie and smiled.

"It's upside down," Freddie said.

Throughout the equipment assembly phase Warren came to realize that Freddie's main teaching method was trial, error, and humiliation. A system repeated again and again until each task was learned. In this way, Warren learned to assemble the backpack, mount it to the tank, attach it to his back. How to lock down the two shoulder straps, the waist strap, and the two crotch straps. Freddie made him do it over and over until it was routine. Then they did the regulator, the weight belt (mounting each lead weight separately), the mask straps and snorkel keeper, the wrist-mounted depth gauge, even the knife.

It all took time and once again, Warren felt deceived. He'd come to the swimming pool hoping to get underwater with his new equipment and was as far from breathing underwater now as he was three years ago. It wouldn't surprise him if Freddie-the-so-called-Frogman didn't even know how to scuba dive. Never been underwater in his life.

Twice Warren dropped the Royal Aquamaster onto the hard tile. The second time the chrome chipped. The bright gold paint job on his new 71.2 cubic foot cylinder was all but wrecked from picking it up and laying it back down a million times. Finally Freddie said, "Now we turn on the air. That's the final step before entering the water."

Warren reached for the tiny air wheel, a metal disk with two stubby legs that unscrewed counterclockwise, allowing air to flow from the tank into the valve where the regulator was fastened, and then through an orifice into the regulator first stage. "Not so fast," Freddie said. "Tell me again what the regulator does."

Warren sighed. "The two-stage regulator is a pressure reduction valve. High pressure air from the cylinder enters the first stage and is reduced from 2,250 psi to a breathable level of approximately 120 psi in the second stage. Because of this miracle of modern technology today's two-stage regulators can deliver air to a diver on demand at greater depths than ever before," he rattled.

"Jeez, kid. Do you have to memorize everything?"

It was the right answer. They got in the pool.

Warren was given Ruth as a "buddy" for the underwater training. She came with a warning. Freddie leaned over and whispered sternly into his ear, "Mind your manners and no playing grab-ass."

Warren flushed. Ruth either didn't hear her father's off-color remarks or had learned to ignore them, as she seemed able to ignore just about anything she felt like.

"Before we do anything too complicated," Freddie continued in strong voice, as if lecturing an entire class. "Let's see if you can really breathe underwater."

The moment had come. All of a sudden it seemed like he couldn't possibly get ready in time. Get the regulator positioned properly between his teeth. Inhale and exhale evenly through his mouth instead of his nose. Keep his mask from fogging up.

"Now," Freddie said.

Warren, standing in the pool's shallow end, sank to his knees and drew in his first underwater breath. There was a hissing sound. The first stage diaphragm inside the Royal Aquamaster opened, delivering air into the inhalation hose. It traversed a smaller diaphragm in the mouthpiece and rushed into Warren's lungs. He breathed. The air had a dry, rubbery-sweet taste. It wasn't the breathing, or the taste of it that took hold of him, but the sudden, complete detachment. It changed him forever. He made the physical transition to a new world. A liquid one. Like a dream made real, he breathed where no air existed, doing the impossible, like flying without an airplane. He knew now why he'd been born and why his brother had given his life for him. Or more accurately, why he'd taken it.

He turned and saw Ruth kneeling beside him. She took the regulator from her mouth and smiled broadly, her eyes strangely magnified inside a bright yellow mask. As he stared, she stuck out her tongue.

Freddie's vise-like hand bit into Warren's shoulder. His other hand formed various odd shapes and twists, as if trying to communicate. Finally he gave Warren thumbs up, a signal he'd seen in the movies when fighter pilots prepared for battle. They reached out from their cockpits, smiled bravely, and gave thumbs up to their loyal crew chiefs just before takeoff. Warren responded to Freddie's thumbs up by giving his own. Ruth rolled her eyes.

Freddie pulled Warren to the surface and spit out his mouthpiece. "Jeez, kid. What do you think this means?" Freddie gave thumbs up again.

Warren pulled the regulator from his mouth and let it bounce against his chest. "Don't know," he said. It seemed a safe answer.

"Up," Freddie said. "It means, go up."

"How am I supposed to know that?"

"Hold my thumb up, what'd you think? It means go down?"

He heard Ruth giggle. He turned and glared at her. She crossed her eyes.

This set the pattern for the remainder of the evening. He did things underwater. Freddie explained why he did them wrong. Ruth giggled.

Hours flew by. No amount of Freddie's harsh critiques or Ruth's cynical snips dampened his enthusiasm. A new power was awakening inside. When Freddie called him clumsy or knucklehead, he smiled. For once his mistakes didn't defeat him. He was becoming a scuba diver. He was learning what Freddie knew, what Navy Frogmen knew, what Jacques Cousteau knew, what only a few people on earth knew. No one could take that away.

When it came time - too quickly - for them to finish up and go home, Warren and Freddie were still in the deep end swimming lazy circles around the drain. Freddie pointed toward shallow water and gave the thumbs up. Warren nodded, then remembered the "okay" signal and made a circle of his thumb and forefinger. Freddie gestured for him to lead the way. Ruth had left the pool some time before, her lips blue. Now it was her father who signaled an end to the pool training, not Warren.

Warren had outlasted them both, and could have stayed underwater another two hours with ease.

Freddie-the-Frogman slipped from the complicated backpack harness smoothly, as a man might take off his coat, floated the tank on the surface of the water for a moment, then spinning it like a toy, flopped it onto the deck above his head.

He turned to Warren and said, "You done good, kid." Then he smiled, and looked exactly like his picture.

"Are you going to make me a scuba diver now?"

"Yes, I am," said Freddie-the-Frogman. "And I'll be proud to dive with you any day."

* * *

The new scuba equipment was laid out to dry on Auntie Doris' living room carpet. She'd insisted. Warren knelt on the floor with one of her best bath towels gently rubbing and rolling the epoxy-coated goldenrod tank. It gleamed like a chest of new sovereigns, except for the nicks.

Aunt Doris and Uncle David had listened to Warren's underwater success story. It didn't surprise them but Uncle David's reaction wasn't exactly what Warren expected. Uncle David was quiet. Not until morning when they slid to a stop opposite the entrance door to the bus depot did Warren learn the reason for his uncle's uncharacteristic reticence.

Banks of snow, dingy now from heavy traffic, crowded the sidewalk except near the door. Warren gazed above, marveled at the steam escaping from rooftop chimneys of the giant buildings, breathing like prehistoric beasts. His mind brimmed with hope and a long list of precautions in transporting his expensive equipment aboard the bus. He'd all but forgotten Uncle David.

"We're a half hour early," his uncle said. "I wanted to talk to you."

"About what?"

"Sort of a family thing," he said. "Not your brother's accident or anything like that. It's the story I gave you after the first time you told me about this diving stuff. Remember? Did you read it?"

"A bunch of times."

"Okay. Well, you know that's from way back when doggone Thomas Jefferson was President of the United States. A lot's changed since then, and now, well, you really are a scuba diver. You're young but I remember being your age and it's over so quick. You'll be grown up before you know it and I just didn't want you taking that thing too seriously, you know, basing any life decisions on it or anything. I mean it could all be wrong."

He had Warren's full attention. "Did that guy, Douglas Wilson, make it up?"

"No. It's accurate, far as I got into it, except maybe some of the family legend parts. Never sure about that. I just mean it's so long ago. Things get confused with young people sometimes and they might take a thing too seriously. Tempt them to go find the wreck or something."

"What's wrong with that?"

"Nothing's wrong, it's just not practical. Takes a small fortune for one thing, exact longitude and latitude, salvage rights from some foreign government, salvage equipment. All that expensive stuff. I started thinking about it when I realized how serious you were with this scuba thing, now you're the first certified scuba diver in our whole family. Hell. You're one of only a handful in the whole state! I just don't want your imagination kicked into high gear about something that's sort of a family conversation piece. Understand?"

Warren understood only too well that this was the major burden of adulthood - negativity. If it hadn't been done a thousand times you couldn't do it. "Uncle David," he began. "Why did you send me that story then?"

"Well, the story got first told to me by my grandmother, your great grandmother. She was an immigrant. Left her family in Norway, came here, married a Wilson. We were here before the Revolution but she had an immigrant's respect for American history. More than any Wilson I ever knew. We've been a sort of here-and-now crowd, I guess." Uncle David leaned back against the Plymouth's seat and fell silent.

Traffic rolled by and a bus pulled out from the narrow depot exit and turned away. Black exhaust from its straining diesel filled the air behind it and the heater fan drew the slick smell into the station wagon. "I don't mind if we're a here-and-now crowd," Warren finally said. "Douglas wasn't."

"No. Guess not. Sometimes I suppose, you got to look deeper. We weren't always auto mechanics and salesmen. Nothing wrong with that, having a regular job, it's just a thing got me wondering, you know, all those miles I drove. Why'd my grandmother tell me those stories?" He tapped the steering wheel. "She told me about Reginald Wilson maybe twenty, forty times, I don't know. I complained once that I'd heard it all before. She just smiled and told it again. Old bat was kinda loony, of course. She's been dead twenty years, and then some, but one day I got so curious about Reginald Wilson and the sea battle he fought way back in 1806, that I started doing research at the library. At first I just wondered, you know, was any of what Grandma said true? Well, it was true. I found the book, and there it was, even more than she knew. There were witnesses ashore who reported Javert's murder of Reggie." He glanced hard at Warren. "The Javert name appeared off and on in those islands over time. Maybe even today. But, you know, it still happened more then 150 years ago."

Warren smiled and patted Dad's leather grip. "Got it right here. You gave it to me. What did you want me to do with it?"

"Nothing really. If you'd known your great grandmother she would've told you this story herself, like she did me. On the farm they had a good sized pantry off the kitchen, and on the far wall of the pantry Grandma hung a family tree from Adam and Eve to Jesus. She told me it was there to remind her that we all had to know our place, even the Savior. I've got a feeling now that this story is intended more for you than anyone else, and maybe when you find your place in the world, well, it's going to be something more significant than the rest of us." He rested a large hand on Warren's neck and rubbed. "Get to your bus now. I'll help with the gear."

Warren moved to slide from the car. Uncle David's hand strengthened and held him. "Warren. I wouldn't have given you this story if you were a basketball player. Not all men play on teams or sit on their butts and watch others play. Just try and take it easy. Be careful, okay?"

* * *

The scuba tank was inside a heavy cardboard box but Warren stubbornly insisted it not be placed in the outside luggage compartment. The driver was polite and professional. "Sorry son, can't allow it. What if it got loose and started rolling around? Injured somebody? Nope. Thing's too heavy. Under here it'll be just fine."

Warren refused to be separated from the tank. "It's filled with air," he lied. "One bounce and it'll explode. Read the sign." The box carried a warning label: CAUTION! COMPRESSED AIR!

"Won't be any safer inside," the driver complained.

"I'll hold it between my legs all the way," Warren promised. "Please. I won't let go, not once."

The driver shrugged and nodded toward the door.

Once again Warren drew an aisle seat, this time across from a loose-jawed man with an enormous belly that filled his lap. "What you carrying there, sonny? Bomb?"

"Scuba cylinder."

"Explosive device. Ain't allowed on a public conveyance."

"Driver said it's okay as long as I hold it."

"Hold it my ass." The belly man stared. "You keep a tight grip on that thing. Hear me?"

"Yes sir," Warren said, turning to stare at the back of the seat in front of him. The rest of his equipment was in an olive green duffel bag with a coated lining and a thick drawstring. The bag was safely stowed in the luggage bin directly above his head.

They'd left the city far behind before he began to relax, to settle back. He glanced up at the sparkling landscape gorged in sunlight, void of warmth. The highway ran alongside a railroad track and ahead a train moved steadily toward them. Sleek diesel engines had replaced the steam locomotives of his early childhood and the great yellow headlight swinging side to side dazzled him even in full daylight, a magic of modern technology, like scuba equipment.

Aunt Doris had packed him a lunch. Meatloaf on homemade bread with raw onion and a sheet of crisp head lettuce. Back home they only had leaf lettuce from the garden, in season. She'd tossed in an apple too, some unshelled peanuts and three date cookies. The sack was packed inside his duffel only a few feet above him but completely out of reach unless he stood up and let go of the tank. He glanced at the belly man, tightened his skinny legs around the boxed tank and remained in his seat.

Uncle David's warning bothered him. He was a diver now and there was a card in his wallet bearing Freddie-the-Frogman's signature to prove it. There wasn't a doubt in his mind that one day he would dive that wreck and sift its sand for the bones of Reggie Wilson. He would tie the anchor rope of his boat to one of *Imperial's* cannon and a photograph of him in full scuba gear would appear in the newspapers.

But now there was something else too, and that day on the bus his mind wandered to what he'd seen, or imagined, in Ruth Van Doren's eyes. A come hither look he couldn't name until he'd learned a lot more about her, but had he known what was really in that story for him, how it would change his life forever and affect all that he did and all that he and Ruth would ever know of each other, he might've listened more closely to his uncle's warning.

CHAPTER FIVE

It was 1964 before Warren again stayed in Minneapolis with Uncle David, though he'd seen him at various family functions. Even then it wasn't Uncle David or his family he went to see, but Freddie-the-Frogman. And Freddie-the-Frogman's daughter.

Freddie often dove with his young students. He had few peers in diving and most of those saw him as a competitor. His old UDT buddies lived in far-flung places, like his closest friend Myron Bose, living in an obscure backwater, Charming Island. They drifted to warm ocean ports, setting themselves up as commercial divers, daredevils or beach bums. The world seemed to have little need of recreational scuba divers.

Freddie had another reason to dive frequently with his students. He needed the money. He met them at the shop where they'd shoot the bull awhile, and hopefully look around. Casually, he'd mention the new compasses or submersible pressure gauges, a revolutionary backpack - simpler, easier to use, no crotch strap.

Business went to hell by September and he worked driving school bus until spring. If not for his wife, the shop would have folded years before. Marilyn kept the same job she had before they married, Executive Secretary to the President of the College of St. Thomas. Her paycheck provided their only certain income - a situation he knew was not missed by Ruth. She demonstrated a fierce pride in her mother's ability to support the family.

Marilyn never spoke of it at home or at the office. She was a quiet, steady woman respected by her boss and revered by those bright enough to understand the administrative power she wielded behind the scenes. It was Marilyn who arranged for Freddie to use the swimming pool at the college free of charge. Freddie thanked God for her most of the time, and tried not to think of himself as a dependent the rest of the time.

Diving would catch on big one day and he'd be in on the ground floor. He had the know-how, the equipment, the air compressor. Most important, he had young people like Warren Wilson. His private navy. Someday they'd be instructors, shop owners, manufacturers' representatives, leaders in the scuba craze poised to overtake America. They'd remember Freddie-the-Frogman, the man who started them out. He'd be written about in magazine articles. His shop moved to downtown Minneapolis. Might get his own signature equipment line, like bowlers and golfers did. He felt it in his gut.

Freddie was a small boy when Lindbergh flew the Atlantic, but he remembered how the country went nuts over him for years afterward. A Minnesotan, Lindbergh was the hero of Freddie's generation. One day they'd go nuts like that over scuba divers. He just knew it. Oh, it wouldn't be ticker-tape parades and all that, but frogmen would have their day, too. Every dog has his day.

Striding toward the front door, Freddie checked his watch. Almost ten o'clock. Warren should've been here by now. It was Saturday. He peered out the door at the steady flow of traffic down Nicollet Avenue. Already the sun was hot. Unseasonably warm spring weather. Good for diving.

He stepped outside and looked both ways along the street. Warren was supposed to be driving his dad's pickup since his car wouldn't make it all the way to the Twin Cities. Just like a mechanic, Freddie thought, fix your kid's car last, take the paying customers first. He'd probably have done the same.

He came inside and heard the back door scrape stubbornly against its threshold. Fresh air and the faint scent of tangy perfume disturbed the dust and cigarette smoke. Marilyn and Ruth arriving to watch the store while he and Warren went diving at Pigeon Lake.

Ruth and Warren were dating now but Warren wasn't exactly an ardent suitor. Between drive-in movies and drive-in hamburgers he seemed to forget she was alive. Freddie was tired of hearing about it. Ruth was furious when he told her Warren called to line up a dive and hadn't mentioned her. Warren had, however, mentioned buying a second tank. Hopefully, Ruth would keep her mouth shut until he made the sale.

"Father," she addressed him. This formality had begun shortly after her first semester at college.

"Daughter," he said, noticing her eyes sweeping the room for Warren. "He's not here."

"Who?"

"That rippling mass of masculinity from Lake Darling - Warren Wilson."

"Daddy!"

"Fred," his wife warned. "Be nice. It's her first love."

"Oh, Mother! How can you say that? I couldn't care less about any high school boy. I'm almost nineteen. Before long I can drink whiskey."

"That's what you think," said her father.

They reached the desk and Marilyn kissed his cheek. Ruth, wearing extremely tight shorts, jumped onto the sales counter and crossed her long legs.

"I'm more interested in men with a universal sense of humanity," she explained, gazing at the ceiling. "Men who've lived, tasted the pain of our hopeless lives."

"Jeez!" Freddie groaned. "What do they teach at that dumb university?"

"Shhh," his wife said.

There was a discreet tinkling as the front door opened. (He'd replaced the old battleship klaxon after years of complaints from neighbors.) Warren stepped inside - tall, lean, duck-tailed - and smiled broadly. Everyone said hello except Ruth, who averted her eyes. Warren didn't seem to notice.

"Where'd you park the pickup?" Freddie asked.

"In back." Warren strolled up to the line of yellow cylinders displayed on dusty plywood steps.

"What'd you walk all the way around the building for?"

"Sign back there said employees only."

"Jeez, kid. You could've come in that way."

Warren shrugged. "No big deal."

"You must come to our house for supper after the dive," Marilyn said. "I just learned how to make lasagna."

"Sounds kind of Italian," he said, running his hand along the smooth surface of a 71.2 cubic foot cylinder. "What is it?"

"Jeez!" Ruth said. "You never heard of lasagna?"

"Nope," he said, oblivious to her sarcasm.

"Don't feel bad," Marilyn said. "It's something new. I'm quite sure Ruth's never eaten it either."

"Mother, really! We have lasagna nearly every week in the Commons."

"Ruth," Freddie growled. "Get your ass off the counter and see if my wet suit's dry. Put it in Warren's pickup." Another minute and she'd have the kid all tied in knots and he'd forget the tank deal. He joined Warren at the display. "Thinking second tank, eh?"

"Gotta drive a long way for an air fill," Warren said. "No compressors in Lake Darling."

"Two tanks make it easier," he agreed. "Might even be able to scare up a cross-over yoke and a set of double tank bands if you wanted some real bottom time."

"Hmmm," Warren said, inspecting the valve O-ring.

As far as Freddie could tell, nothing appealed to young divers more than extended bottom time. Their discussions included brags about depth, the years they'd been diving, and the longest time they'd spent underwater on a single dive. Though he'd been deepest, dove since forever and stayed under the longest, Freddie's greatest thrill - known only to him - was selling. His heart quickened before a sale. Sometimes it felt so good he sold things for less than he paid for them.

"Dove Superior yet?" he asked.

Warren appeared wounded by this inquiry. Lake Superior was the dive in Minnesota, maybe the Northern Hemisphere. Freddie knew this was a sore point.

"You'll need two tanks up there," he said.

Warren asked, "How much?"

"Tank, three-quarter inch reserve valve - $75." He added it on a scrap of paper. "$15.95 for the solid bar yoke. Twin harness, another $13.95." Prices had inflated. "$104.90." He sighed to let Warren know the price wasn't his fault.

Warren continued to stare at the tank.

"Tell you what," Freddie said. "Make it an even $95 for the works."

Warren nodded, smiling.

Freddie threw in a free air fill.

Ruth and Warren dated three times over the winter. He hadn't kissed her. Far as she was concerned, hell could freeze over before she'd make the first move. When he left that morning to go diving with her dad she decided never to speak to him again, but less than a week later, a warm, pink evening in late May, he called. "How's your dad?" He didn't bother to say hello.

"He's fine."

"Home from work yet?"

"Yes," she said. The guy was a dope. "Would you like to talk to him?"

"I guess not."

She listened to the long distance humming, the overlay of distant voices echoing on the line. She waited for him to speak again. The pause lengthened.

"Maybe you'd like to talk to my mother?" she asked. "Or my Aunt Sally?"

Finally he said, "No. I called to talk to you."

He didn't say anything more.

Warren Wilson was the biggest dope in Minnesota. Maybe in the world. She was the only freshman at the U dating a high school boy. Several of her friends knew about it too. Of course Warren never once gave a thought to her problems or imagined what it must be like for a nineteen-year-old woman to be hopelessly in love with a boy. In fact, he seldom called at all. Their dates were more like palling around.

"What did you call to talk to me about?" she said finally.

"Graduation."

"Yes?"

"It's a week from next Friday. Mom's having sort of a party like, afterwards. At our house. She says you can come."

"I love it when you talk to me like that." She breathed heavily into the mouthpiece.

"Huh?"

"Never mind. What should I wear? Is it formal or casual?"

"My relatives will be there."

"What are you wearing?"

"Mom bought me a new suit."

"Pretty formal then," she said. "For Lake Darling."

"I guess."

Seconds ticked away. Long distance noises dominated the line again. Had he hung up? Tossed the phone down and gone off to do something more important?

She sighed. "Was there anything else?"

"I don't have any classes the day before. Do you want to go diving?"

It was her turn to pause. Was he asking her to come and spend the day with him and then stay the night? Spend a night in his house? Sleep under the same roof? More likely he hadn't thought it out. Didn't realize Minneapolis was a long drive from Lake Darling. How foolishly inconsiderate.

"Do you want me to spend the night in Lake Darling?"

"People do it all the time," he said, laughing.

"What about your parents?"

"What about them?"

"Do they want me around?"

"They like you."

"They've never met me."

"I told 'em all about you."

"Jeez," she said, sounding just like Freddie-the-Frogman.

"I found an old ferry boat in Oscar Lake."

"How deep?" He didn't need this enticement to get her to spend two days with him, but she took it as a compliment. He was trying to win her over.

"Only about twenty-five feet," he said. "It's wooden. Has an inboard engine. Steam, I think. I haven't told anyone."

This must be costing him a fortune, or his parents, which was worse. "We better hang up," she said. "I want you to have enough money left to buy me a hamburger or something. What time should I be there?"

"I'll come and get you if you want."

"Don't be silly. It's five hours round trip. I'll drive my own car. What time?"

"Early."

"Okay."

"Bye."

She listened a moment to the noises still linking her to Lake Darling. Then the dial tone interrupted, shutting her out.

The next ten days were bleak and slow-moving. It rained off and on and the thermometer seldom got out of the 50s. She was afraid Warren would call the whole thing off, like a ball game. Canceled due to weather. Wednesday night, the night before she left, was the worst. She was convinced he'd call any second.

"Will you please sit down?" her father begged, tossing aside a recent issue of *National Geographic*. "You're making a path in the carpet."

"I just know he's going to call," she said, perching finally on the edge of the coffee table. "He'll mumble something about it's no use to dive in this kind of weather."

Freddie-the-Frogman leaned forward and examined his daughter closely. "Jeez," he said. "You got it bad."

"Daddy!"

"Robbing the cradle to boot!"

She refused to answer when he got like this.

"You've only dated the kid a few times," Freddie said. "How'd you get so flipped over him?"

"I'm not flipped." She slid from the coffee table and strolled to a plant stand near the window, picking at the leaves. "I just think he's cute, that's all."

"Boys aren't cute," he said flatly.

"You wouldn't know," she said in a rich, husky voice. "That curly, mussed up hair. Always needs a haircut. Sleepy eyes. Little smile wrinkles at the corners of his mouth. The fluid way he moves, like a cat."

"Sick!" Freddie burst out. "Sounds like James Dean or one of those creeps."

"Better," she said, like a father could understand. It wasn't really his looks at all. Warren was nothing like any boy she'd dated, or any man for that matter, except maybe her father, though she didn't like to think about that. He didn't seem affected by what others thought of him. That took guts. It also took patience and self-reliance, making him independent as hell and hard to deal with.

Life with Warren would be an adventure. He'd never sell insurance or teach high school or live in the same house very long. Of this she was certain. At the same time it frightened her. Already she'd been a bridesmaid twice. Cheryl, her third best friend from high school, got a dental student. She quit college to work and help him pay his way. And Mary Beth, shy, unassuming. Gone now to California with a real estate man she met in a hotel bar. He'd promised to buy her a house in Beverly Hills. All good matches, people said. While they were caring for their husbands and finding homes and maybe even becoming mothers, what was she doing? Waiting for Warren to get out of high school.

"You like Warren, don't you Daddy?" she said suddenly.

"Course I do." He smiled. "Trained him myself, didn't I?"

"I guess I have flipped over him," she said, choking a little on the words. "I just worry he hasn't flipped over me."

Freddie-the-Frogman stood up, facing his daughter squarely. "Come here," he said. She nestled in his outstretched arms. "I'll kick his scrawny butt if he doesn't flip over you."

"Oh, thanks!"

"Don't worry about tomorrow. He won't call it off."

"How do you know?" She leaned back to see him.

"Because whatever else he is, even cute, that boy's stubborn." She frowned at him. "I mean that as a compliment," he said. "Even if it snows, he won't cancel."

He retreated, crossed his arms and gave her the old lecturing stare. Father to daughter. Pay attention. "Understand this, girl. If you get mixed up with him you'll end up like your mother." He glanced around to make sure she hadn't snuck in. "He's really the first generation of scuba divers. The first to learn as kids. No telling where it'll lead. Are you ready for that? I don't think the rest of the world is."

Seemed the kind of question only a parent asked. Ready? Of course she was ready.

Next morning on the drive north, speakers cracking whenever Elvis hit a low note, she sang "Love Me Tender" with so much feeling it brought tears. The D.J. was already calling it an oldie. This made her feel old, too.

Ruth liked to drive fast. The sun had returned, bringing with it the promise of summer. All four windows on the 1956 Chev were rolled down. She hung one arm out, steering casually. The car's swaying course along the uneven highway kept time to the music. Disconnected from earthly cares she ballooned along, drifting over hills dotted with Holsteins, across nameless streams, following the raised embankment of the Soo Line.

A meadowlark called to her from a fence post along the road as the Chevy blew over Roger's hill at 70 MPH and began its descent to the valley containing Lake Darling the town and Lake Darling the lake. Sunlight shimmered blue and silver on the water, but the town, a lush canopy of trees cloaking white homes and two-story stores, had turned its back on the lake to face the railroad. She pulled to the side and stopped. It wasn't possible to take it all in at seventy. She didn't want to miss this first view of Warren's home.

The engine and radio died. Ruth got out and stood by the car. No traffic. Sun-warmed pavement radiated upward, warming her. Another meadowlark warbled in the dry grass rustling along a nearby fence line. Above, unending sky. Bursts of popcorn clouds gathering to the west where the land flattened and sky leveled to match it.

Somewhere below, in one of the white houses peeking through the leaves, Warren waited. If she went down to him now she knew she'd never leave him. It was a strange thing to know. But she knew it nonetheless.

Ruth straightened the blue seat cover and slid behind the wheel. The engine drowned out even the radio as she pumped the gas, spitting sooty liquid from the dual exhaust. She gunned the engine and sped away toward Lake Darling and Warren.

They were lying back in the tall grass with their knees up. Warren observed that his legs were longer from hip to knee than Ruth's. Hers more substantial though, better formed.

Quite some time had passed since Warren bravely reached over and took her hand. She hadn't seemed surprised or offended and toyed with his fingers in a particularly pleasing way. Not that she was the first girl he'd held hands with. Who could forget that night in the backseat of Wayne Turner's Dodge? The night he and Evelyn Lundquist got drunk on Hamm's. But he couldn't get serious or sustain seriousness with a girl. Girls were foreign, peculiar of habit and language. Hearing his scuba ideas they often said, "Don't be silly." Ruth seemed more his type, so here he was, holding hands with a college chick. He'd have to tell Gilby, his best friend, about it.

Ruth rolled onto her side and leaned so close her hair brushed his face. She did it on purpose. "I bet I know what you're thinking," she said, dark, thick curls glistening from their first dive.

"I doubt it," he chuckled, rolling to meet her.

"You're comparing me to all the other girls you've dated." She said this softly without the slightest edge of hostility.

Warren felt his face redden.

"You don't have to say anything," she said. "I understand. Cute guys get plenty of dates." She plucked a long blade of grass and traced his jaw line with it until he brushed her away. "What I'm wondering," she said, "is what about now? Is there a girl now?"

It occurred to Warren how really little she knew of him, and how easy it would be to lie. He might have lied to Evelyn Lundquist, but not Ruth. He wanted her to know the truth about him, even the unsavory parts, because her hair was thick and because he was beginning to think they belonged together. Not just boyfriend-girlfriend. Something deeper, more personal. Time she knew the truth. "I've never had a real girlfriend," he said. "Just girls I've gone out with. Mostly, they like guys who can shoot baskets or run with a football. I was never good at any of that."

For a moment he thought maybe she didn't believe him, suspected he was shooting her a line. But she nodded slowly and smiled. "No crowd in the bleachers," she said. "No rah-rah or cheerleaders in red panties out here I guess."

He shrugged.

"I'm here," she said, black eyes suddenly large, searching. He allowed her to push him back as she lowered herself gently onto his chest, pressing her mouth against his. Her lips were soft and dry, full of strength. They kissed again and again.

"Jeez," she said later. "I like the way you kiss."

He kissed her again. "Practice," he said, tossing his head. Ruth's laughter shook them both. Warren turned serious and said, "I'm really crazy about you."

She answered, "Me too."

Warren guessed this must be love. Mosquitoes fed joyfully on his naked limbs and he made no move to slap them. He wouldn't disturb Ruth's head, resting on his chest. He imagined Ruth couldn't live without him. She'd go home and tell this to Freddie-the-Frogman. They'd get married and move to Charming Island and run a dive shop while they searched for *Imperial*. He picked up his watch from the towel. They had enough time and enough air for another dive.

"Do you think we could kiss underwater?" he asked her.

"You mean is it physically possible?" She sat up and looked toward the water. "Or is this an invitation?"

"Both."

She began gathering her equipment. "Let's find out," she said.

All at once it didn't seem right that she should be struggling with heavy scuba gear. "I'll help you," he said, picking up her tank and holding it with the backpack facing away so she could slip into it easily.

"Put that down!" she ordered.

"Why?" The sharp tone alarmed him.

"Because I've been doing this since you were in diapers, and I don't need any help."

He only meant to be polite. "Yes, Ma'am!" he said, dropping the tank with a thud.

For a moment they stood a few feet apart, staring at each other. Warren had no idea what to do next. He was surprised not only by her anger, but by the suddenness of his own.

Ruth, too, seemed bewildered, as if she hadn't meant to be so harsh but still thought she was right. "It's rare to find two people who love each other exactly the same," her mother had once said, explaining her twenty-five years with Freddie. "In any real lengthy marriage, or even a friendship, one partner loves more than the other," Mom said. "In our case, I'm the one who gives in. I'm the one with the greater love." Maybe, Ruth thought, it's going to be that way with me.

"I was only trying to help you," Warren said, staring down at her bare feet.

Her anger evaporated. "You're a gentleman," she said, dropping the mask and snorkel, moving closer. "My gentle man."

Their embrace was tentative at first, then wholehearted. Warren felt the weight of fear lifted from him and quickly forgot his anger. How could any man fight with a woman this beautiful?

"Let's leave our wet suits here," he said. "Then we can dive without weights. If we get cold we'll come up."

Ruth agreed, suspecting his motives ran deeper than just to simplify their equipment load. She couldn't decide if she wanted these suspicions confirmed or not.

The spring-fed waters of Oscar Lake, cooled by a long winter, engulfed them, pressing against their skin in a way not experienced by swimmers. The cold being more intense at depth. The wetness more encompassing and sensual. The separation from an air environment complete, detaching.

Since receiving instruction from Freddie-the-Frogman, Warren had made dozens of dives. That first summer, between May and October, he'd entered one hundred and eighteen dives in his logbook. His right eardrum exploded the next summer, due to something called a "reverse block," caused by diving with a head cold. The third summer he'd taught Gilby to dive and helped him pick out a set of used gear. He hadn't dove with Ruth since they'd been in the pool together three years before.

Underwater, he quickly relinquished his grip on the topside world. The transition was total. He often wished it were irreversible, this metamorphic passage from air to liquid. Euphoria washed over him, providing today the same exhilaration as the first time he'd breathed underwater. It never became routine.

Beside him, Ruth slid through the water with such economy of motion he could only marvel at her efficiency. Her body swept downward into the deeper blue of the lake in perfect balance. She had long ago mastered the greatest skill of diving - neutral buoyancy. Exciting to watch. Women like this weren't growing on trees.

He reached around and centered the tank on his back. Ruth's bubbles burst against his mask as he drifted slightly above and behind her. They'd descended no more than fifteen feet and already the water felt perceptibly colder without their wet suits. His plan to kiss Ruth underwater in her natural state - no rubber coating - might've been reckless. What kind of kiss could you manage with the shakes?

Ruth located the ferryboat unassisted and glided across its bow. Arching her body, she swam back around, pivoted in mid-water and settled onto the wooden bow dodger. Very slowly, her legs sank beneath her and she sat upright, hair floating free in a dark halo above her head. A striking sight.

Ruth reached out and drew him close, lifted the mask from her face, freed the strap from her hair, and ran it up her arm. Eyes open, widened, blinking to see him in the blur, she withdrew her mouthpiece and parted her lips. He did the same. They kissed.

This was not as daring a maneuver as it appeared, but it took concentration. Forced to hold their breath throughout the kiss, Warren thought of Freddie-the-Frogman's First Rule of Diving. It took the edge off the romance.

He drew back from her, blinking. She replaced her mask and cleared it using less than a full breath. Though the mask and mouthpiece hid her mouth, he could tell she was smiling from the way her eyes squinted.

A moment later she took his hand and they swam side by side toward the stern of the ferryboat.

Of all Warren's underwater discoveries - outboard motors, fishing tackle, anchors, rusted bed springs, old bottles - the ferryboat excited him most. Only Gilby, now Ruth, had been taken to see it. This was no sunken galleon, no *Imperial*, but Warren relished the discovery as if it were. The accomplishment was the same. Maybe Ruth could understand that. Finding the boat gave him what his friends got from finding the end zone. The sad difference, of course, was no one saw him score.

Until now.

On their first dive much of their air was consumed relocating the boat. Now they were back for a closer look. He guided Ruth over the end of the stern, straight down standing on their heads until in synchronized flight they somersaulted under the hull. He dug a hole, exposing the brass propeller and Ruth ran her finger gently along the edge of the blade as if it were made of glass. What might have been junk in some waterfront scrap heap, seemed a precious underwater discovery. Ruth was clearly impressed. Her fascination made Warren feel as if he were discovering the boat all over again.

From the propeller, he took her to the inboard engine, fanning silt away with his hand to show her how the propeller shaft was braced and shimmed in the bilges. He pointed out the fuel tank, the flywheel, the cylinder heads - and she seemed fascinated by it. Suspended upside down, she poked her face-plate directly at the sights he brought to her attention, often positioning her mask within inches of an item and studying it with the concentration of someone looking at a rare sight under a microscope.

Even the smallest discoveries seemed to intrigue and delight her. Prying, lifting, prodding the silt and debris, she edged along the ribbed insides of the ferryboat's exposed bilges. The gray, faded world of an old photograph. Water absorbs light and washes out warm colors. Ruth's bright yellow fins appeared anemic and artificial as they moved lazily above her head, holding her body in place.

Carefully, she lifted a gray-brown piece of bark, then suddenly jerked her hand back, making an "Eeeek..." noise from inside her regulator. Warren laughed as a four-inch crayfish marched out from under the bark holding both its pinchers above its head, snapping them menacingly at Ruth.

He gave the crayfish his right index finger and the angry crustacean gladly accepted, pinching the skin until it puckered. Warren lifted the crayfish up from the bottom and held it out for Ruth to examine. Parrying a small twig, she teased the crayfish, working up the nerve to allow the critter to latch onto her finger as well. It soon tired of this game, released its pressure on Warren's finger, fanned its tail and swam away backwards at high speed. A moment later it was lost among the leaves and sticks on the ferryboat's skeleton.

At almost the same instant, Warren's Royal Aquamaster delivered its last breath. He had exhausted his air supply.

Reaching around with his left hand, Warren groped for the small eye of the reserve pull rod which extended along the side of his tank. It was always just a little higher than he remembered. Once he found it, he inserted his thumb and jerked downward. This movement tripped the reserve lever on his valve and sent a welcome surge of air through his regulator and into his lungs.

No matter how many times Warren performed this vital, yet routine maneuver, it always gave him a moment of apprehension. Always a chance the lever wouldn't work or had already been bumped into the "down" position during the dive. A special danger when he dove alone. Warren thought many times there had to be a better way to monitor your air supply then to wait until you ran out - then try and save yourself. Ruth watched him switch to reserve, then held the OK signal until he returned it. A moment later they began their slow ascent to the surface.

On shore, Warren stared as Ruth patted herself dry with his towel. "That's the best dive I ever had in my life," he said, staring openly at her lips.

"Shut up!" she said, punching him.

"Maybe we should try it again, up here?" He closed in on her. "And a few other things."

She held her ground and smiled in that knowing way girls have of smiling and said, "You get all you want, the day I'm Mrs. Warren Wilson. And not one day sooner."

This response both pained and pleased him.

He couldn't keep his eyes off her as she broke down her equipment. The practiced hands, delicate against the steel and brass, moved swiftly, professionally. She cleaned each piece as it was disassembled. The yoke screw spun off the regulator - she used a single hose affair thought by most men to be feminine - blew into the orifice to clean it, replaced the dust cap, stored it in a special small bag. Bending over, she examined the tank valve carefully, eyeballing the O-ring seal for cracks or sand, then covered it with a homemade dust protector that looked like a large rubber band - a Freddie-the-Frogman original no doubt.

Ruth strolled past him toward the water, carrying her regulator.

"Are you going to stop staring at me?" she said.

"Sorry."

"If I'd known underwater kissing was going to send you into outer space I'd of kept my mask on and mouthpiece in," he heard her say as she trudged into the water. "I didn't mean to tease you or anything," she said.

"That's not it," he said. "We kissed before."

"What then?"

He kept his eyes on her hands swishing the regulator back and forth in the water, cleaning it. "I don't know," he said. "I'm afraid you won't understand, like when I tried to help you with your gear. I'm not good at explaining."

"Warren!"

"Okay." He took several steps toward the water's edge and halted on the sandy bank, legs apart. "I don't think women should dive. But I like the way you do it."

Her reaction was quieter than before. Her face showed no signs of anger. "You like the way I do it?" she repeated.

"I mean it's a man's thing, but you do it like a woman. I don't know. Does that make sense?"

"You mean like a woman trying to throw a baseball?" Her voice cautiously optimistic.

"No," he said. "I mean you do it well. You just take a man's thing and make it girlish. I can't explain it."

"Is this a compliment or an insult?" she demanded.

"Neither one."

"So you don't think I can dive as good as you?"

This response alarmed him. "Better," he said. "That's the whole point. I see you move through the water and it's like I'm watching a dance or something. I can't move like that. I feel clumsy beside you. At the same time I want to be close to you and be ready to help you and take care of you. I feel funny because you don't need my help."

She draped the regulator around her neck and walked out from the water. She slid both her hands along his naked sides and up his back, drawing him to her. "I really am stuck on you," she said.

"You're not mad?"

"Because you want to protect me?" She smiled. "No. I'm not mad. I'll tell you something I just figured out." She reached up and kissed him before going on. "I've been diving almost as long as I've been walking. Today was the first time I felt really comfortable underwater. I mean really safe, secure. It was because you were there. I just knew nothing could hurt me if you were there. Even my dad, nobody, makes me feel as safe as you do."

Warren lost himself in her black eyes. "I'm stuck on you, too," he whispered. It was the first time he'd ever said words like that to a girl.

The idea that Ruth could feel safe with him made Warren giddy. He felt like having a cigarette. He'd been smoking lately, keeping it secret from his parents as they both believed smoking to be bad for your teeth. Several girls he knew also smoked, and though he disapproved, it was daring. He offered Ruth a cigarette.

"I don't smoke," she said, brushing twigs from the blanket she'd spread on the ground. "But maybe today I will."

Once he'd lit a cigarette and placed it between her lips - a particularly intimate gesture, he thought - he lit his own and knelt on the edge of the blanket.

Ruth had arranged the blanket to flatten the tall grass edging a large cottonwood. She leaned back against the tree and motioned for Warren to lie his head on her lap. This seemed even more intimate than lighting her cigarette. Men often rested their heads on women's laps in the movies. But it was usually in the South, along a river, under a giant tree with spreading branches hung with Spanish moss, and a woman wearing a wide skirt. But Oscar Lake, a cottonwood, and Ruth in a swimsuit would do fine.

Her thigh felt cool against the back of his neck. "Are you cold?" he asked.

"Not anymore." She ran a hand through his damp hair. "Your head feels good there. Cozy."

From beneath, her face looked longer, almost like his mother's. There were things about Ruth that reminded him of Mom, though he'd never admit such a thing to Ruth. How could any woman understand that? "I'm glad you said that about feeling safe with me," he said.

"I meant it." Her other hand gently massaged his chest.

"In a way, it's sort of crazy," he said. "Thinking that you could ever feel scared underwater. Not scared. I mean, feel anything but perfectly secure even all by yourself."

She stared out across the lake for awhile before answering. "People weren't meant to go underwater," she said. "We didn't come equipped with gills anymore than pilots came equipped with wings. It's foreign to us. Yet I think some of us, like you and I, and Dad, were meant to be divers. So we feel safe with each other."

He followed her gaze across the water. The thought of Freddie-the-Frogman having to feel safe with someone made him chuckle.

"What's so funny?" she asked.

"Your dad holding someone's hand underwater." He laughed aloud. "If he ever ran into a shark, it'd be the shark who'd get eaten."

"You think a lot of my dad, don't you?"

"Don't you?"

"Yes. But he's human too," she said.

"Well, I didn't think he was Martian."

She pinched the tight skin of his belly. "I'm going to tell you a story," she said, as if she really were his mother.

"About what?"

"Malta. The Mediterranean. Freddie-the-Frogman. And sharks."

"Is it true?"

"Shut up and listen," she said, grinding her cigarette in the grass. "During World War II, Dad was stationed for awhile with the British Royal Navy on Malta learning their underwater demolition techniques, or something. Anyway, the water was warm there and very clear. On his days off he'd check out a set of gear and go spear fishing. (To this day we eat fish four times a week.) One day he'd been diving a sixty-foot reef several miles from shore. Enjoyed the little swim out and back. Along with his speargun - a three rubber job with lead-filled bone handle he'd made himself - he carried a stringer for the fish.

"On the swim home this particular day the stringer was full. It being only mid-afternoon, there was no hurry so he swam lazily, letting the sun warm his back, the temperate water slide along his body. He cruised on the surface, the stringer of dying fish resting on his back. From time to time one of the livelier fish flopped against him or pricked his skin with a sharp fin. Satisfied and content, he slipped into a trance, swimming along in the Mediterranean Sea.

"Later, unexpectedly, he felt a bump, as if someone had pushed him, gently. Not hurt, he was confused. After all, there was nothing but water for miles around. He couldn't have run into anything. Glancing around, he saw a shark swimming away with something dangling from its mouth, dripping blood.

"The realization of what had just happened came slowly. The bump had been the shark going for the flopping fish on his back. But what else had the shark taken? A piece of his back? The right arm which held the fish?

"Scared, he craned his neck to see. Blood trailed behind him in the water. His mask restricted line of sight so he couldn't see the source of the blood, though it was obvious. How long before the beast came back to finish the job? Should he move the arm to see how much of it remained? No. Movement would undoubtedly bring excruciating pain.

"Miraculously, to this point, there'd been no pain. He thanked God for sparing him that at least. No doubt he was in shock anyway. Before long he'd simply pass out and drown. He preferred this ending to the return of the shark. He swam on.

"The water became like glue, resisting him at every stroke. The sun menacingly hot now, searing his back. The speargun in his left hand weighed him down. The distance to shore seemed a million miles. Where were the boats? What became of the fishermen always on the bay? If someone found him, they might get a tourniquet on his arm and stop the bleeding. Save his life, though he'd be a cripple. Half a man.

"On he went, head swinging side to side relentlessly searching for the shark. He couldn't see directly behind, of course, where it had attacked the first time. How far had he come? Perhaps the shark lost sight of him? Lost the scent of blood trailing from his stump? Or maybe not.

"At that moment he didn't really care. All during the war laying explosives, disarming underwater mines, surviving long night swims onto treacherous beaches, he'd been afraid. Now that he faced death, saw the certainty of it, he found peace. And with peace came the key to survival. You had no fear of trying the impossible. He decided to toss the speargun, detach the knife from his calf and use one of its straps to tourniquet his stump, stemming the flow of blood and denying the shark a trail to follow. Then swim until he died.

"Using his left hand, he reached around carefully and took a firm grip on his right arm just below the shoulder. This, he knew, would be the worst of it - seeing the damage.

"He'd been holding the right arm up, over his shoulder, to carry the heavy stringer you see. Closing his eyes, he brought it down, but when he opened them, he saw two arms with matching hands, attached and whole, one holding a broken stringer. He wiggled the fingers of his right hand to make sure they were real, then suddenly terrified again he reached for his back. The hand returned bloody, but only from abrasions caused by the shark's barnacled hide brushing against his skin.

"The shark merely snipped the fish from his stringer and swam away with them. Grinning, no doubt."

Her voice died away like notes of a pleasing tune. He wished the story hadn't ended so soon.

"I bet Freddie-the-Frogman has told you that story a hundred times," he said.

She laughed. "Quit calling him Freddie-the-Frogman. And it was at least a thousand."

"I like it."

"He says we compete with some ocean animals and eat the rest. I don't know. Sometimes I think I'm more at home there than he is." She swallowed. "The shark taught him that once you face what you're most afraid of, you really start living." Her voice trailed off and Warren thought he knew why she looked so comfortable underwater.

"Don't you think he's right?"

"Sure," she said, smirking. "It just tickles me every time I think of him swimming along with this perfectly good arm stuck up over his shoulder holding an imaginary stringer of fish while he thinks it's in some shark's mouth. What a geek."

"What could he have done different?"

"Looked."

Warren thought about this a moment. Yes. Ruth would have looked right away. All her actions, her speech, her emotions too, were direct - straight ahead. He liked that about her. There were already enough sneaky people in the world. He was glad he hadn't fallen for one of them.

Ruth's skin had gathered a blush from the sun, setting her face aglow and bleaching the fine hairs on her arm, resting across his chest.

"I don't want this day to end," he said.

"It won't," she said, puckering her lips.

But Warren didn't follow Ruth to college after graduation. He enlisted in the U.S. Navy and shipped out to Vietnam. They wrote letters, of course, saw each other briefly during a leave or two. Then at the end, he attended college on the GI Bill - he a freshman and she a senior and leader in the anti-war movement. It was a difficult time and their cohesiveness underwater was replaced by adversity in almost everything else.

Ruth had been attracted to another member of the anti-war crowd - Bobby Slovnik. The pigs and hired killers like Warren offended Bobby and he planned to build a power base in the Minnesota DFL (Democratic Farmer Labor) Party and try his luck at politics. He promised her he would be Governor of Minnesota one day and then the pigs would answer to him. She kept her relationship with Bobby secret from Warren but they had argued about the war and on his return home, when he joined the vets club on campus and openly defied her and everything she'd come to believe, their differences finally came to a head.

They picked a back table in the student union and tried to keep things civil.

"I'm glad we're getting this out in the open," Warren said. "I don't hardly dare talk to you anymore."

"That's because you've been brainwashed by the military-industrial complex," she answered. "You need to think for yourself."

"Really? The 'military-industrial complex' is a slogan. How is that thinking for yourself? You're more brainwashed than you say I am."

"You should talk to a few people like Bobby Slovnik instead of that bunch of hired killers you hang with!"

Warren still wore his hair shorter and ran a hand across the top of his head and sighed. "You know, Ruth. I must be a hired killer too then, by your definition. Name-calling isn't thinking for yourself. And you know what else? I'm damn tired of hearing about Bobby Slovnik. He's a skinny, pasty-faced punk. Somebody should kick his dumb ass."

"You, I suppose?"

There was venom in her voice and a challenge that he'd fail against Bobby if he tried to fight him. Something clicked then in Warren's head. "You're sleeping with him, aren't you?"

Ruth looked away and her unwashed hair obscured most of her face. She said nothing.

"It was a question," he continued. "Why don't you answer it?"

She remained silent.

"Okay," he said. "I guess I've got my answer. I knew it a long time ago when the letters hardly came anymore, and when they did, all you wrote about was your hippie politics. The one you wrote about how I should go AWOL was the best. I tore it in about a thousand pieces and threw it into the South China Sea."

"Oh please! I'm sure you were an angel all this time, right? No sailor's liberty in Hong Kong with some Chinese slut? Right. Don't you dare question me!"

Warren lit a cigarette. His hands were shaking. "Sluts? Sure. That's all we hired killers can get. Not like we had any hippie chicks in Hong Kong to fuck the fleet. We had to pay for it. And all this time you're back here giving it for free. Guess I really missed out."

Ruth swung hard and hit him squarely in the temple. He saw stars and she was gone.

But in the weeks, months and even years that followed the blow was nothing compared to the damage to his soul. He might have survived the rejection of his affections, since he had been anything but celibate himself, but the disregard she demonstrated for him as a human being, a man, boy really, who did his duty and buried his friends, that was unforgivable. Like the death of Stephen, it ate at him and soured his opinion of the world. Where did he live that such things happened? How could she go from loving to hating him?

He saw her for the last time six years later. He had dropped out of the University of Minnesota, which had a lousy marine biology course track, and gone west to Stanford in California. He'd completed his master's but had tired of the academic life, though he'd taken some fine trips to Baja, Hawaii and the Aleutians. The *Imperial* story had stuck with him and Stanford had sharpened his research skills. He discovered that islands, like nations, sometimes traded names and the spellings and pronunciations depended on the occupants and languages spoken at various times in history. Or who drew the maps. Charming Island was still the most logical resting place for the wreck but Hispaniola gave him a starting place, and he had found a job there, in Santo Domingo.

Warren's GI Bill was exhausted and so were his other financial resources, including a part-time teaching assignment at Stanford. He owned nothing but an eleven-year-old Ford so it was a good time to follow the family legend. He sold the Ford and flew to Minnesota to see his parents before heading south.

He walked up the jetway and spotted her in the departure lounge, slumped in a plastic seat, reading a paperback. She'd lost much of the hippie look and washed her hair. Even given in to some light makeup. He thought maybe she was thinner in a more athletic way.

She was intent on her reading and he started to walk away toward baggage claim but changed course almost without thinking and stood beside her. "Hi," he said.

Her mouth opened at the sound of his voice and she raised her head. "It's you."

"It's me."

"What are you doing here?"

"Just got off a plane." He tried to smile. "I'm from here, you know."

"I heard you were in California."

"Finished up there," he said. "Going to visit my folks before I take off again."

"Oh."

He drew a deep breath. She was embarrassed and that made him feel foolish. She'd moved on obviously and wanted no reminders of the past. "Ever been to the Dominican Republic?" he asked.

"Trujillo and all that other right-wing shit?"

"I guess. I'm not a politician."

"That's for sure."

"Thought I'd go see some of the Caribbean, then look for the *Imperial*. Remember?"

Then she smiled. "You never grew up did you Warren?"

"If you mean by that I didn't give up dreams I had when I was young, well, then you're right. I didn't grow up. I don't plan to get old and miss the adventures of living my dreams either."

She shook her head. "I married Bobby, did you know that?"

"I heard."

"Did you also hear he was elected to the Minneapolis City Council? The youngest person ever to win? That's what I call living a dream. Not a pipe dream like sunken ships. The kind of a dream that makes history."

"Minneapolis is a bunch of dumb Swedes and they'd elect anybody long as they got the old DFL stamp of approval. And as cities go, Minneapolis isn't exactly the big time. Come on! If you ask me you're the one who hasn't grown up."

Her faced reddened but she held her tongue.

"Well," he said. "Guess it's a good thing you married Bobby Slovnik. Before long you'll be the First Lady of Minnesota or Pork Queen."

He hadn't really meant the last part, and when she burst into laughter he watched a moment to be sure it wasn't feigned.

"Oh, Warren," she sighed. "You really are a smooth talker. Let's not fight. Can't we just agree to disagree?"

"Sure," he said. "We can do that. Anyway, you're the best kisser in Minnesota."

"Thanks. But how about Hong Kong?"

"Don't start that again."

They both smiled and for a moment it seemed there was no angst between them. But there was nothing to say really, so they chatted randomly and parted. Warren felt an oddly familiar hollowness in his stomach as he walked through the crowd and then he was glad they'd met. Glad they'd reestablished their animosity. Walking away from each other was the best thing that could happen to them. That's what he told himself. That's what brokenhearted people always tell themselves, like when they kill their brothers or begin to deny their parents or lose their old girlfriends.

CHAPTER SIX

Two weeks later when Warren Wilson landed at Aeropuerto Las Americas in Santo Domingo he began the most absurd years of his life.

Months before, sipping a fine Pinot at a bayside bistro he frequented on the California coast, it had all seemed so simple and well-planned. The story of the Wilsons and Charming Island was imprinted in his head, but he had no intention of going there straight away. First he had attended scuba instructor school to learn as much as possible, and get certified as an international instructor, then spent time crewing on a dive boat leaving from Santa Barbara until he was proficient at boat handling and able to find underwater sites using shore marks and electronics.

During his naval service he'd learned much about ships and boats at sea. Now he applied it to diving. Within the required time Warren Wilson was a licensed captain, scuba instructor and equipment repair professional. He brought those talents to Santo Domingo because he knew little about the Caribbean. The Dominican Republic was the second largest island, with a sizeable population and big cities. Plenty of job opportunities and centrally located so he could explore the other islands, learning as much as possible about them before he struck out for Charming Island and the search for *Imperial*.

Ruth hadn't even asked why he was going to the DR instead of Charming Island. She didn't care, of course. Had lost interest in where he went or why. He wished that didn't bother him as much as it did.

But his plans were well-made. He had contacted the only diving operation he could find in Santo Domingo - Sol Survivor. Since "sol" was sun in Spanish he didn't understand, beyond the obvious catch phrase, why anyone would name a diving operation Sun Survivor. He soon learned that the name was the least of his worries. But the owner - Salmagundi "Sal" Jarvis - had promised him thirty-five thousand dollars per year, a furnished apartment, and use of the company vehicles. Cars were prohibitively expensive there, he'd said. In addition, they would meet him at the airport since it was miles from the city.

Thirty-five thousand was more money then Warren Wilson had ever made or hoped to make. His parents, now both working, didn't make that much together. You could buy anything you wanted for that amount of money. In a few years he'd accumulate enough to buy his own boat and sail for Charming Island, probably with money in the bank and a sweet little Spanish gal on his arm. Ruth Slovnik could kiss his ass.

No one met him at the airport except arrogant customs inspectors who tore his dive bag apart, questioning him at length in Spanish about what was in it. Diving equipment, he said. Diving equipment. No one knew what that meant. He should have studied a little Spanish before deciding to live in a Spanish-speaking country. Repeating "scuba" over and over did nothing for the inspectors either, who seemed to think the equipment was subversive until he donned his mask and snorkel, then acted out swimming and looking around underwater. They finally got it, and laughed at him just as people had done most of his life. What a relief.

Outside, once he realized he was alone, he found a cab driver who claimed to speak English.

"How much to Santo Domingo?" he asked.

"Que?" the cabbie said.

Warren made the international sign for money by rubbing his thumb and first two fingers together. "How much?"

"Aw," the man said. "Fifty dollar."

"Are you kidding me? I'm not paying fifty dollars. Ten dollars."

The man laughed, shaking his head side to side. "Jus' for you. Twenty-five dollar."

Warren pointed to the trunk. "Open! Open!"

He loaded his own equipment and they sped out between honking taxis, buses, private vehicles and the raised voices of two hundred shouting speakers of Spanish. The place smelled like sweat, rotten mangos and sewage. For goodness' sake, what had he done?

The coastal drive into Santo Domingo would have been the loveliest stretch of Caribbean highway in the West Indies if the inhabitants hadn't tossed every banana peeling, plastic bottle, old tire and sack of garbage they owned along the road, in addition to scrawling all manner of graffiti on anything that held still long enough - road signs, palm trees, buildings, large rocks. A thirty-five kilometer long garbage dump.

Halfway there the driver wanted an address. Where were they going? Warren had no idea.

Finally they stopped at a small café. The driver knew a woman there who spoke English. The woman's name was Rita. She had large brown eyes, shoulder-length black hair and a shy smile.

"You are from New York?" she asked Warren.

"California," he said, figuring she'd never heard of Minnesota.

"Ah," she said. "Hollywood."

Warren nodded. "I'm trying to find this address." He thrust the Sol Survivor brochure into her hands.

She studied the brochure. "Buceo submarino," she nodded. "The scuba diving?"

"Yes," he said, relieved.

"This is the address in a neighborhood. A house. Maybe not such a good part of the city, you know?"

"Like poor?"

She had an aggrieved look now, as though she didn't want to say more. "Like drugs and prostitutes. Robberies. Violence sometimes. No good for a foreigner. Someone who does not know the city." She shrugged. "Maybe you go tomorrow? Early in the morning."

Warren was tired, short on cash and in no mood to check into a hotel and begin the search all over again tomorrow. "I'll be fine," he told her. "You've been very kind. Thank you."

She would accept no tip, said goodbye, finishing with "Buena Suerte, Señor."

Back in the taxi the driver was getting cold feet. "Tomorrow is better," he said.

"Let's go," Warren told him. "Before it gets any later."

Afterward, when the sun began to dip and the neighborhoods no longer contained paved streets or noteworthy lighting, Warren was having second thoughts. There were open fires everywhere and groups of people standing about, staring as the taxi passed. He smelled raw sewage and wedged among the small concrete houses he noticed mean shacks with tin roofs and crooked pole walls. Many of the people they passed were drinking rum from small bottles and others made catcall noises or called out to them. The driver sat straight in his seat and kept his eyes on the road.

At last they came to the Sol Survivor address - an oasis of overpowering light and the rattle of a generator in need of maintenance. The driver all but bolted from the taxi and unloaded Warren's bags and diving equipment, dropping them in the dust. A second later he had his hand out for the fare and without so much as a good luck he roared away, the springs of the taxi groaning in protest. Warren was alone before he had time to find the entrance of the concrete building looming above him. All he could see were spotlights. He heard the barking of dogs.

Warren found the door and knocked.

He had an ominous feeling about the whole thing now, but he was there and no other choices existed. He waited, sweating, and knocked again, louder.

When the door opened he saw Sal for the first time. A tall, broad-shouldered man in his 50s, nothing like the thirty-year-old in his brochure photograph. His sandy hair now streaked with gray and knotted in a ponytail at the nape of his neck. The skin of his face resembled the leather skin of a scuffed football with a mouthful of yellowed laces. But the smile seemed genuine and welcoming. "Warren Wilson, am I correct?"

Warren nodded.

Sal pivoted and screamed into the house. "Come on girls! Wilson's here!"

Warren heard the slapping of bare feet on tile and two women appeared, dressed like twins in sagging tank tops and bikini bottoms. They were grinning at him but holding onto Sal. They had Sal's baked and dried skin. He guessed them to be in their 40s, but both were slim with nice figures and he hesitantly smiled in return.

Sal drew the one closest almost into his armpit and said, "This is my wife, Ava." He released her and the other woman snuggled against him and kissed his cheek. "And this is Eva, my girlfriend." Sal noticed Warren's confusion. "I named them myself," he explained.

"Sally baby," Eva said. "You never told us Wilson was so cute." She slipped out of his arms and embraced Warren, grinding against him. "We gonna have so much fun," she breathed into his ear. "Ava and I gonna take such good care of you."

The darkness surrounded them. The dogs were barking. People were laughing, swearing, singing in Spanish. He heard the tinkling of breaking glass. A nearly naked woman was gnawing his ear. So Warren wondered, what could possibly go wrong? He was trembling. Eva might have guessed it was because of her.

"Pick up his stuff," Sal told the girls. "Let's get him settled in, have a couple drinks, smoke a joint or two and talk about the future. Eva. Let's go. You girls shake your pretty asses."

Sal took hold of Warren around the neck and dragged him inside. He was too weak to resist, or run.

So that was the beginning. Over the next few weeks Warren learned there was no dive shop, just the house. There was no new scuba gear inventory, at least not in the Dominican Republic. Sal explained to Warren, "I got me $150,000 in brand new U.S. Divers equipment on the docks in Miami. All we gotta do is get it here and we are in business, man. Big time. Look around. Second largest island in the Caribbean and we own it. Own it! All ours. Like an unmined mountain of gold."

The gold was rather deep underground. Sal had no compressor either so when the tanks came there would be no air to fill them. There were no students clamoring for scuba lessons or lining up to purchase the equipment rusting on the Miami docks. Santo Domingo had never hosted a cruise ship and local politics scared even the locals. There were a bucketful of good reasons why nobody had discovered the place as the new dive Mecca.

"We just got the one problem," Sal explained. "Getting that gear from Miami to here. Ava and Eva will bring in the trade. Both of 'em are promotional geniuses. Eva went to college. Smart as a whip. We'll make a hell of a team."

"Have you sent for the equipment?" Warren had asked one morning while they enjoyed their coffee in the shade of the littered courtyard patio.

"We gotta go fetch it," Sal said. "That's where you come in. You got the boat expertise. The skills we need."

Warren thought there must still be a way out for him. He'd seen no boat and mentioned this to Sal. "I haven't seen a boat."

"I'm working on it." Sal grinned. "Negotiating. These damn wogs take a month to do a day's business. We're just about there. All I gotta do is mortgage the house. Stupid banks. I'll get it done."

"You got some equity then?"

"Well no, not really. It isn't my house. I got a lease and they don't need to know that. Paperwork's kinda messed up so who knows who owns what." He grinned. "Don't you worry, we'll get what we need to start this baby up. We're going to make some real money down here. Tons of it."

"You don't own the boat. Can't you just ship the equipment down?" Warren asked.

Sal heaved a sigh. "You got to understand the tropics, man. It ain't like the States. They got massive like duties. I mean that $150,000 would turn into $250,000. Maybe more before we were done. And it would sit in some customs shed where these buggers would pilfer it until there wasn't anything left worth keeping, see? We got to fetch it ourselves."

Warren stared at Sal's leather face a long time before asking, "Does this mean you want me to travel to Miami in a stolen boat to 'fetch' thousands of dollars' worth of scuba equipment and smuggle it into the country without paying the customs duty? Is that what you mean?"

"Wilson, come on now, really. Everybody gets paid in the end. This is the way it's done, man. You're young. You worry. How about a little smoke with your coffee? Chill you out."

Warren had refused repeated attempts made by all three for him to join in the daily marijuana smoking that was a systematic part of their lives. He had managed to go through two tours in Vietnam without it and he wasn't inclined to become a pothead now. They were disappointed. His stubbornness had finally turned Eva against him and she no longer tried to entice him. This might have bothered him but he always imagined her with Sal, maybe Ava for all he knew, and as she became more familiar he lost interest in even her sexuality. He thought of her now as pathetic.

But that morning he decided to go home. His spending money was almost gone and his safety stash was just enough for airline tickets and a taxi.

The next day he realized they had robbed him even of that small amount. He kept the greenbacks rolled up in his underwear and shoved at the back of his shabby dresser drawer. Every dollar was gone. They were understanding when he lost his temper. Sal explained the maid had quit that very morning. No wonder, they said. She'd stolen his money and fled.

The maid's name was Tonya and she was the only person in the household he liked and trusted. She stole nothing. Of this, he was certain. They must have realized he was ready to scram and concocted a scheme to keep him. Why, he couldn't imagine until two months later, when he was completely broke and they were tallying his living expenses against him. Now he was nearly $800 in debt, and the amount grew with every meal and every night he slept under their roof. But the boat deal was done. Sal had the key and Warren prayed it wasn't stolen.

Sal took him to see it and explained what was about to happen.

Warren would sail the boat to Miami with forged customs papers, load the scuba equipment and transport it back to a small bay near a coastal fishing village where small boats would unload it so it could be transported to the Capital.

"I don't want to talk so plain to you," Sal had said. "But here's the deal. Maybe you get tempted to jump ship in the States or make some other plans. So I figure two, three weeks to cross. And that's liberal. After the third week you need to call me from the dock and tell me the deal is done and you're coming back here. If I don't get a call, I make a call to U.S. Customs and report a theft of a boat and an attempt by my employee Warren Wilson to steal my scuba gear. Now they're gonna contact the Coast Guard, and maybe after a couple months it all gets sorted out and you skate. Or maybe not." Sal smiled and patted Warren's knee. "On the other hand, you bring the gear back, I give you a chunk of the tourist action and pretty soon you don't owe us nothin' and there's a nice bit of cash in your pocket so you can go where you please. Come on man, it ain't such a bad deal. You might have a nice time here for awhile. Anyway, Eva's going along and though she ain't too fond of you just now, who knows? You might be able to sweeten her up." Sal chuckled. "You got no idea what you're missing. For real."

All of this rested in Warren's guts like a landmine, just waiting for him to take one wrong step. He had been thinking seriously of ditching Sal's boat somewhere in the Keys, hitching up to the Gold Coast, find a diving job long enough to save money and get back home to Minnesota. But Sal had been thinking too, and now he was stuck with Eva. He didn't like her so maybe she'd have an accident along the way. It was a big ocean. But of course, he was not going to do that.

While this was going through his head, Sal said, "You leave in the morning."

"How? The boat's at the dock and nothing is ready."

"Is now. Ava and Eva spent the day putting enough food and fuel aboard for you to make it all the way without stopping."

"What if something breaks down?" Warren asked. The boat was far from new.

"Eva has her credit card and you're handy enough to jury rig something to get into port someplace." He grinned. "I have a lot of faith in you Warren. That's why I hired you."

Warren shook his head. "You hired me because you needed a sucker."

"Whatever. Just get it done."

Salmagundi Jarvis named his boat in the same way he named his women. He called it *Free Love*. He had painted a red heart between the two words and it dripped blood. Nevertheless Warren loved it the moment he saw it. Originally a sport fishing yacht built up north, it was heavily beamed with elm. *Free Love* took the sea and cast it aside. The new fiberglass boats seemed like toys by comparison, bobbing and bucking high in the water, while *Free Love* challenged the sea, split it away from its bows in a thunder of gushing white spray.

Warren had done whatever he could manage to improve the boat. He repaired the raw water pump, fidgeted with the electronics, especially the LORAN and ship to shore radio. He had the bilge pump singing and the brass work polished. Sal had noticed the effort and praised him. But Warren knew he cared nothing for boats and *Free Love* was like everything in Sal's life, existing only to serve him.

Santo Domingo was a crease on the horizon when Warren first spoke to Eva. The morning had been cool and she wore shorts and a windbreaker over her bikini. He thought she looked almost normal.

"This will be a long trip," he informed her.

"No shit," she said.

"Listen. I was hoping maybe we could be civil at least. You know, leave everything back on shore and just stand our watches and have like a pleasant voyage."

They were on the flying bridge - he in the captain's chair and Eva standing alongside him where she could see the compass clearly. Did she really think checking his heading was necessary? He wasn't about to sail in circles.

She ran her left hand along his back, rubbing in gentle strokes. "We can have a very pleasant voyage if you let go a little. Quit being so uptight."

Warren was tempted to take her up on the offer. He might win her over and find a way out of his mess. "I'm not uptight," he said. "I just have trouble with people forcing me into things. That's what's been happening to me since I got here. Do you like to be forced?"

"Sometimes," she said. "I like a strong hand."

"Don't you think about anything besides sex?"

"Better then never thinking about it," she said, dropping her hand. "Unless you like boys."

Warren stared at her and knew nothing would work. She was Sal in female form. "No. I don't like boys. Think what you want. Just remember, the nights are long and dark and we have hundreds of miles of empty ocean to cross. You want to piss me off go ahead. But I have my limits like anybody. Come across the line too far and things might not go so well for you."

"That a threat?"

"Exactly. There's a lot of work ahead and you're going to do your share. It will be easier for both of us if we work together, but if you really want to make it miserable, well, there is not one thing on this boat I can't do alone. But if you're left alone you're going to die long before anybody finds you."

"Bullshit," she said, but he saw the doubt in her eyes. The sea frightened her, and so did being left alone.

Warren doubted that Sal or Eva had any notion of the time it would take to make a trip of over 700 nautical miles. If everything went perfectly then Warren guessed three or four days, granted a true course and speed. At 15 knots it might happen. In reality, he'd guessed five or six days. The Gulf Stream favored them but everything else wouldn't. His repairs on the boat were still incomplete and that worried him, though he reasoned the vessel was seaworthy and capable of making good headway, even in rough seas. But there was only one engine and he didn't have time or parts to restore it to prime condition. And would Eva stand her watches so he could sleep? Could she keep to the course, even at night or in rough water?

During that first day and night he taught her what he could, and while she remained hostile and suspicious, she cooperated enough to give him hope. She caught on to steering the boat and watching the sea for other traffic. He made her understand the compass but the LORAN was outside her intellectual range and he gave up. She did want to talk on the radio and he decided it did no harm.

That first night he awoke hourly to check the heading and make sure she was awake, alert and in charge of the vessel. She didn't appreciate him watching her. "At least bring a cup of coffee up here if you're going to bug me," she told him on one of his trips to the flying bridge.

An hour before dawn he fell asleep. When he awoke sunlight was streaming into the galley from the east. She had done her first full night watch. It tested her, and he hoped it also gave her confidence.

He splashed water on his face, put on a fresh pot of coffee and went topside.

She was at the wheel and swung to face him when he climbed the ladder. "This was some kind of test wasn't it?" she asked.

"Training," he answered.

"Did I pass, teacher?"

"What do you think?"

"I'm not as dumb as you think I am."

Warren sat down on the life jacket locker and sighed. "Eva, why don't you just lose the attitude. You're older then I am and act like a teenager in heat or something. Shouldn't you grow up pretty soon? Quit competing with me. Let's just do this and get it done without all the drama. Okay?"

Whenever she spoke to him her face twisted into a wrinkled knot. Now it relaxed and she shrugged before standing and giving him his seat. "I'll go get some coffee," she told him.

"It's on the stove," he said. "I wouldn't mind a cup either. Do you know how to cook?"

She smiled for the first time. "Yeah. I'm a real little Susie Homemaker."

Half an hour later she returned with his coffee and a fat omelet stuffed with green pepper, cheese, onions and jalapeño. He was hungry and ate without looking up until he'd finished. "You are a Susie Homemaker."

She shrugged. "I like to cook."

That day marked the beginning of their getting along. Tensions subsided, and while they weren't necessarily friendly, they worked together, standing their four-hour watches and managing the difficulties of life at sea without the hostility they felt in the beginning. Warren loved being at sea and now he thought of it as almost an enjoyable trip. There was scuba gear aboard and he planned a stop at Great Inagua Island in the Southern Bahamas where he'd always wanted to dive. Eva was a diver, after all, and might enjoy it too. Not to mention a fresh lobster should they be so lucky.

The next day the storm came.

Free Love had no radar or weather radio. So when they looked behind them to the southeast they had no place to go. No safe harbor they could reach in time. The wind, rain, and heavy seas would soon overtake them in an open ocean far from land. Warren had survived many storms at sea, even typhoons in the Pacific, yet he worried, because he'd never done it in a 55-foot boat and this old vessel was about to be tested beyond anything it may have ever endured before. Eva faced a violent test he thought might destroy her at the very time he needed her desperately. The fierceness overtaking them was a rare experience for most people and she seemed to him least prepared for it. The intensity of the ocean's savagery is remarkable at first, then overwhelming in its disregard for anything but its own menace and the peril it builds in the hearts of those who face it.

They were together on the flying bridge when they first spotted the blackness rising high into the heavens sucking at the sea and charging the air. The wind was calm before the monster, as it drew everything toward itself like some great pulling force alive with its own wicked cravings. They named the really big storms, the hurricanes, but this wasn't a hurricane so it would wreck and kill without being known or remembered. They too might perish and remain anonymous. Sal was unlikely to report them missing and radio calls were useless since they survived, or not, by luck and their own skill.

"Eva," Warren said. "We're in for a spot of rough weather."

"No shit."

Her brown, blond-streaked hair, hung limp to her shoulders. "Put your hair in a ponytail," he said.

"We're about to die and you want me to look like your high school sweetheart?"

"No," he said, smiling. "You're going to be very busy in a few minutes and that lovely hair of yours is going to be whipped into your eyes like steel spaghetti."

"Fine," she said, walking toward the ladder. "I'll go down and see if there's a rubber band lying around so my hair's nice and neat when the storm of the century clobbers us to death. Maybe I should put on my heels."

"Barefoot, I think," he said, still grinning at her. "There's some coils of rope in the bow locker. Bring a couple of those up with you too."

She paused halfway down the ladder. "I was hoping you'd want to tie me up sooner or later."

"We're going to make lifelines. Now get going. We don't have a lot of time."

Like most dive boats, *Free Love's* stern had been cut out above the main deck to accommodate divers, giving them free access to the swim step when it was deployed port to starboard across the stern at the water's surface. But unlike most dive boats *Free Love* had not suffered the usual removal of the full stern, but accessed the swim step through a removable gate. The gate was in place now and the swim step swung up and chained. If the gate held, they were as solid as any sport fishing yacht in rough weather.

He hoped it would be enough as long as the pumps remained on line and nothing came apart. And the old diesel engine didn't stall or get flooded. And if nobody was flung overboard and the two life rafts remained secure on deck, and the wind wasn't so strong it blew them into the trough of some giant breaker and they turned turtle. And if nobody panicked and when they lost visibility no big container vessel piloted by some Panamanian drunkard didn't come roaring out of the rain and split them in half. And then there was the little matter of Captain Warren, who had never piloted this boat in heavy weather. Captains usually know their craft and what it is capable of. He knew nothing.

Eva had returned to the flying bridge on quiet bare feet. He glanced up and she was staring at him. "Scared?" she asked.

He nodded. "Yep."

"How scared?"

He smiled. "Not as scared as I've been a couple times before, but ask me again in half an hour."

She continued to stare. Finally she said, "Sure you don't just want to go downstairs, crawl in the sack and smoke a couple joints?"

"No."

"Good," she said, still staring. "I figure my life depends on you. And I don't even like you. I'm not even sexy to you."

"Eva, for crying out loud! This is not the time."

"I think it is. We're probably going to die."

"We all die, Eva. Just a matter of timing, so the way it works is you be ready all the time. I lost my brother to a hole in the ice when we were little kids. You're dead when you're dead. Old. Young. It comes when it comes."

"Today?"

"Maybe. Or maybe we rig the lifelines, get our life jackets on and when this baby gets close we swing the bow around take her head on. Can't hurt to try."

Eva moved close. "Could you stand up maybe? Give a girl a hug? Is that too much to ask?"

He took her in his arms and she was trembling.

And then they ran before the wind. Warren had the throttle full open and kept it there even as the old diesel barked in protest. The sea was relatively calm before the storm and they covered their wake in black smoke and still he knew it wasn't enough. The monster raised itself higher and higher, leaning forward like a sprinter at the blocks. His orders were obeyed and Eva managed to double tie the two forward life rafts, rig the lifelines, secure the scuba tanks and equipment, lock the galley door, close up the salon and get their life jackets.

"One last thing," he told her. "When this bastard is on us I'm going to switch helms. Steer from the pilothouse down below instead of the flying bridge, and you need to be there with me. Understand?"

She nodded.

He spared her a grin. "And if you start puking don't worry about it. Just heave up on the deck."

"I'm too damn scared to puke," she said, returning his grin.

"Me too, but don't let it get you down. I've done this before, in the Pacific. This is just a pond compared to that. We'll be okay. Though I'd rather be afloat in a steel destroyer two football fields long with an experienced crew and well maintained engines."

"Are you trying to cheer me up?"

Warren glanced over his shoulder. The time had come to turn the boat into the wind, what there was of it. A calm preceded the storm and now it rose so high above them it seemed they were trapped in a deep mountain gorge. The air tasted like something you sucked from your snorkel. "Okay," he said. "Let's go."

"Downstairs?"

"Below, sailor. We say below."

She dropped down the ladder like a fireman on a pole and her voice drifted back, "Sailor my ass."

Once inside the enclosed pilothouse Eva latched the door. Warren took the helm and spun it right to make a starboard turn. As the bow came around the monster roared, the wind began to shriek, the seas increased and rain like hail beat the windows.

"The windows are going to break," Eva said. Her eyes were wide with fear and her head and hands were shaking.

"No they won't. I have a job for you. See that light? That one? It's for the bilge pumps and if the bilges get flooded we're going to sink, so watch it. Be sure the pumps are running. There are two electric ones. I fixed them both but if something goes wrong we have a hand pump that I rigged for backup. It's down below and you're the only person available to man it. Hard work but it will keep us afloat. Okay?"

The idea she would have to leave him and the safety of the pilothouse dawned slowly on Eva's face and the trembling gave way to anger. Her jaw set below eyes flinty, sparking with malice. "I'm going down there alone?"

"Do you see anybody else around?"

"I won't."

"Eva. You will do it or you will die."

For a time there was only the pounding of the rain and howling of wind. Then Eva said in a quiet voice, "I hate you, you son-of-a-bitch."

He shrugged. "The truce is over then. Too bad. But we are going to make every effort to survive this storm and you are half the crew. You will obey me immediately. If we survive you'll have the rest of your life to hate me, so do what you're told and we'll deal with the rest of it later."

"It's your fault we're out here. I don't want to die. Which light is it?"

"That one," he pointed.

They had rigged a lifeline suspended by stanchions from the overhead so they could walk side to side, hand over hand. Eva hung from it with both hands but her eyes were on the bilge pump light.

Free Love climbed the first of the giant seas and their bodies took on the weight of it as the force drove them nearly to their knees. Then without warning they crested and the bow fell into the trough leaving them to all but float above the deck with their stomachs jamming upward in a retch of surprise, fear and sourness.

They raced down the backside and Warren saw the height of the seas were beyond freakish. At the bottom he thought the old boat would simply drive itself below the surface and keep going. "Aw shit," he cried softly.

Just before they reached bottom he heard Eva say, "I'm sorry."

He was too frightened to accept the apology and *Free Love's* bow plowed into the water and sank far enough below the surface to allow tons of green water to strike the pilothouse, smashing windows and scattering shards of glass across their faces and bodies and the deck where they stood barefooted. Sea water washed around their calves, flowing in angry swirls across the deck, out the passageway and in a foaming waterfall into the galley and birthing areas below. Thousands of gallons of it.

The old boat reared her head and shuddered. The rudder had gone slack when they dove into the trough but now it bit the water again and Warren could steer. But he was in shock and did nothing but hold it steady as it climbed the next high ridge of water. He thought the boat was already sluggish and when it fell again into the next trough it would be finished.

Warren realized the throttle was wide open. Had he driven the boat deep into the trough himself? He reached over and pulled back to about half power. If they survived the next cresting he vowed to throttle back even more and ease her down the backside of the fresh wave. They couldn't afford to take on that much water again. What if the pumps failed?

Eva said, "The pump light went out."

He glanced away from the towering wave and saw her face was ashen and void of expression, but her voice had been strong. "You remember the manual pump, right?"

"Sure."

"Can you go down and work it?"

She took a step closer to him and he noticed her feet were bleeding. "I will obey your orders. I can do the pumping or I can untie the lifeboats. Just tell me."

He grinned and shook his head at her. "When it's time to untie the boats we'll do it together. We aren't quite finished here yet."

"We're going to die," she said.

"Maybe. But not quite yet is what I'm saying. This old boat is still fighting to stay afloat and we're going to give her every chance."

"Do you believe in God?"

Warren didn't think it was the time for a philosophical discussion. *Free Love* was reaching the crest. "We've had a falling out since my brother drowned. Now's not the time. Pump the water overboard."

She turned and started below, but added, "If you're right I'll make you tell me later."

He had no way of knowing if she could work the pump, or if it would matter. A few gallons more or less in a trillion-gallon sea.

The old boat crested the next wave and the rain beat in through the broken windows and he saw the next one and the one after that and how their tops were torn in a blizzard of spume beneath acres of spray flying horizontal to the sea, driven by the howling wind. It was likely Eva was right about dying.

The bow dropped and they surfed the backside. Warren throttled back and watched as the bow once again pointed toward the trough and the bottom of the sea. "One more, old girl," Warren said. "One more."

He sensed no slack in the steering this time and when the bow burrowed into the water it felt as final as the first time but the green water came across only as far as the fo'c's'le where the lifeboats were lashed and then washed over the sides in a gushing sound like water spewing from a rain gutter.

"Eva!" he screamed over his shoulder. "Pump! Pump! She's doing better. We're going to make it."

He had no way of knowing if she heard or was even there. They began to climb the next wave and he increased the throttle. At the crest he cut the engine back again and thought maybe the third wave smaller, more compact, and then they headed down toward it.

Once again the boat took the sea and rose above it. The bow hatch had held and the scuppers flowed in compressed rivers but he was certain no more water was entering the boat, weighing it down further. Below Eva must be pumping.

He thought how hundreds of gallons of bilge water was sloshing fore and aft by the pitch and how the electric pumps would be shorted out by now. How long could she keep it up? He thought of turning with the wind and riding the waves but if water came across the stern no amount of pumping could get it over the side. No. He would keep his head into the blow. And damned if this wasn't one sweet old vessel. If it sinks, it's a privilege to go down in her. A real fighter.

They maintained their heading for another two hours or more and his legs wobbled and he shivered with cold and fatigue. The muscles in his upper back, arms, and neck twinged. He relieved the tension by shifting his weight from side to side and using only one hand to steer as the height of the waves diminished.

In all this time he had heard nothing from Eva. He couldn't hear the pump or see water going overboard. If she was hurt he was helpless. The autopilot was a piece of crap and broken anyway. He could tie the wheel and run below but if *Free Love* yawed and went abeam into a trough they were finished. If she wasn't dead now, she would be.

Another hour slipped by and it was getting dark. The rain hadn't let up but the seas were far less dangerous. The generator had flooded and they would spend a night without power. Not even running lights. Eva would be there below, alone in the dark.

Warren removed his belt and tied off the helm. It would be good for a short while he hoped and he staggered from the pilothouse and climbed below.

At first he saw nothing in the heavy gray dusk below, but heard the sucking of the pump as it slowly cycled the water from the bilge and out into the sea. And then he saw her and heard the keening that came from her slack mouth. Both hands on the handle she worked it unaware of him or her surroundings. Her skin was as gray and colorless as the air.

"Eva," he spoke softly. "You can stop now."

She went on pumping and he noticed how her back remained straight and the pumping motion occupied her entire body in the manner of a bowing wooden bird. He feared to touch her.

"Eva," he said in a stronger voice. "Stop it. Please. You need to make coffee and get us something to eat."

He moved forward then and wrapped his arms around her, tightening the grip until she could no longer work the handle. Her breath came out her mouth in a dry rasp. Her eyes misted and she collapsed against him.

"Walk with me," he said. "Easy. Come to the galley and rest awhile. Then both of us need water, food, coffee."

"Rum," she answered. "I want rum."

He unlocked a cupboard and took down an unbroken tumbler, pouring a stiff drink from the bottle of rum wedged in the door shelf. He held it as she drank. The tears were an unnoticed stream now. She pushed the glass away. "Take some," she said. "Who's driving the boat?"

"My belt," he said, and drank.

"Well, that's okay then." Her cheeks flush with rum, she tried to smile but the tears seemed endless. "I can't be alone down here in the dark," she told him. "You have to take me up with you. I thought I was going to die at the bottom, and then later I thought I was going to die from the pumping. It hurt me."

Warren felt tears come to his own eyes, and reached up to brush hers away. "You saved us. Come up with me then. I'll bring the bottle and we'll have a few drinks before dinner. We can have soggy sandwiches. You can hold the wheel and I'll even make them so you don't have to come back down again."

"I can come down if you're with me."

Without thinking he drew her into his arms and kissed her lips. She neither resisted or cooperated. "I'm sorry," he said.

"I don't need a pity kiss."

"It wasn't that," he said, releasing her. "I just wanted… I don't know, to comfort you, I guess. Let's go topside and check on things. Get you set at the wheel and I'll make us something to eat. Come on. I've got the bottle."

She followed him to the pilothouse where he removed the belt from the wheel before they climbed to the flying bridge. She sat in the captain's chair and took the helm. He dropped onto the life jacket locker, drank from the bottle and passed it across. "Tastes good," he said.

Eva drank sparingly and handed it back. "Why would you want to comfort me?"

"Maybe I'm not quite the jerk, or sucker, you and Sal and Ava think I am."

She said nothing for some time. "You aren't a jerk," she said, keeping her eyes on the darkness ahead. "You're harsh. Even when you kissed me your mouth was tight. It's your brother isn't it?"

The wind was still raw and the darkness complete, without running lights or starlight or anything to give focus to the eye except the phosphorescent wash alongside the vessel. As suddenly as he wanted to kiss her before, he wanted to tell her about Stephen now.

It took more than an hour and the rest of the bottle. By the time he finished they were both a little tight.

Finally she said, "You blame your parents don't you?"

"My dad for not being there out on the ice to save him. We were just kids. And my mom for putting him in the ground and removing his things and seeming to forget about him. To me he became more than before. A real spiritual presence. They told me his death wasn't my fault. All very kind and final. We just put it away and never talked about it again. I hated them for that, too. Maybe I still do, but I don't mean to."

"Go down and make the sandwiches," Eva said in a firm, steady voice. "It's going to be a long night."

"Aye, aye Captain," Warren said. He tossed the empty bottle over the side and climbed down the ladder. Expressionless, Eva watched from above.

The sea was still rough but she felt it more then saw anything in the blackness of it. Her mind traveled instead to Warren, then to herself. She wasn't accustomed to men who refused to sleep with her. It hadn't happened in years, and while she was offended at first, now she drew a kind of strength from it. As she worked the pump in the dark and dared not give it up, she found a different kind of thing inside her that she could only describe as faith or maybe dignity. There was no Sal with her at the pump, or anyone like him, to encourage her, keep her struggling beyond the point where it seemed pointless. Her own lonely spirit rose to the task - the physical pain, the mental clarity. She credited Warren for opening the door to this, but he too was absent when new confidence grew within her.

Awhile later when Warren returned with a paper plate loaded with sandwiches, she kept her seat at the helm and said to him, "My name isn't Eva."

They chewed and swallowed awhile before she continued. "My name is Sharon Carlson and I'm from Indiana. Terre Haute. You know that place?"

"Heard of it. Never been there."

"Yeah. I couldn't wait to get out."

"Why are you telling me this?"

"Because I want you to know me."

Warren reached out his hand and she shook it. "Pleased to meet you, Sharon. Do you want me to call you that now?"

She shrugged. "I don't care. Right now I feel more alive on this stupid old boat then I have since I was a little kid without a care in the world."

"You did a good job down there. Didn't panic."

They ate in silence for a few more minutes and then Warren flipped the empty paper plate into the sea.

They were silent a long time and then Warren said, "You aren't going back, are you? That's why you told me your name."

She nodded agreement. "I'm done with them, and you are too."

"I am?"

The new Sharon smiled exactly like the old Eva. "You're really a bitter kind of a person," she said. "Frowning at everything. You seem to expect the worst, but don't do much to prevent it. Maybe you like self flagellation. Oh, don't get all mad. I'm about to save your ass."

Warren was angry and snapped at her. "What are you talking about?"

"Do you really think Sal would send you off alone with me if he didn't have a plan? I'm here to learn about the boat, then once the new scuba gear is loaded, take it back. Meanwhile, about the time I clear harbor, a guy he knows in customs busts you for stealing it. While you're sorting all that out, if you can, I'm long gone. Since you own neither the boat or the gear, what can you do about any of it? You're screwed, get it?"

"You crazy?"

"Sal figured after awhile they'd let you go and no harm done. He likes to think of himself as harmless." She released her hair from the ponytail. "I had a lot to question down there in the dark and my mind needed something to do while I pumped."

"So you decided to confess?"

"No." She shook her head. "I decided to help you because you're just too dumb to help yourself."

"What's that mean?"

Sharon grinned the Eva grin again. "Means I have a plan. Sal's going to pay us back for using me as his whore and you as his scuba patsy."

"I was right before," Warren said. "You are crazy."

"Listen first. Who is in possession of the boat and will soon be in possession of the new scuba gear?" She waited for his answer, and when it didn't come she said, "We are. We have the boat and soon the gear. I'm supposed to call Sal when everything is loaded, let him know, then get you off the boat to handle paperwork or whatever bullshit I come up with, then sail away. Adios. Sayonara, baby. But we are going to change this plan. Just load the gear and disappear. How do you like that?"

"Steal it?"

"Does Sal owe you money? Does he owe me even more? Listen Mr. Happy, sometimes nobody takes care of you but you. I'll make the call to Sal for you so he doesn't put the customs after us. We sail this thing south and you drop me in Cancun, I take enough gear for myself and you take the rest and do what you intended. Start a dive business somewhere. Just has to be a boat charter instead of a shop. So what? You'll make more money anyway."

"I don't have any money."

"No kidding? Who watched him take your money? I know that, but I've been saving for years - just in case - and I've got five grand down below and I'll give you two of it. And I don't want you to pay me back."

"All seems crazy."

"It is. Wanna do it?"

Three days later Warren sailed out of Biscayne Bay in a stolen boat with a new name - *Esteban* (Stephen). He was at the helm and Eva Sharon perched on the life jacket locker, grinning.

Two and one half days later he dropped her on the Yucatan Peninsula of Mexico without incident and they said goodbye.

They stood close together, leaning against a customs shed on the pier to escape the blazing sunshine. "I doubt I'll see you again," she said. "But if I'm ever at sea in a storm I wouldn't want to do it with anybody but you as my captain." She reached up and stroked his ear. "Someday my friend, you will know you aren't the cynic you think you are. It's integrity, I think. You have it. It's part of you and that helped me find some inside myself. But man, sometimes you just got to be cool and quit holding all that past stuff in your heart, torturing yourself. I got to go."

He reached out and drew her in. "Not until I thank you. I've always had a plan for my life but when it went to hell I didn't know what to do, and who should hand me two thousand dollars and a boat? Some girl from Terre Haute. How does that even happen?"

"It's only money and a pile of old boards," she said. "Kiss me. I'm going to kiss you back this time, just to teach you something about what you missed."

She was right. He'd missed something extraordinary.

Seekers

CHAPTER SEVEN

Nearly two hundred years had passed since that day Javert killed Reggie Wilson. And twenty-seven years since Warren Wilson learned scuba from Freddie-the-Frogman, and twenty-four since he loved Ruth.

Charming Island waited almost unchanged, its green back hunched to the east, coconut-coated arms open to the west, and golden hands folded across a lap of jade sea. An emerald Buddha squatting in a tub of warm water, thought the fat man. Not unlike himself. The comparison dislodged a chuckle.

His pupils, damp onyx, darted back and forth between rolls of flesh, watching the busy little harbor below. The canopied veranda of the Pink Sands Hotel was the best vantage point in Edward Town. The old Victorian house, a rousing bordello a century ago, rested dead center at the crossroads of downtown, upholding the past and one too many coats of fresh paint. Rarely an afternoon passed when the fat man did not take his ease there in the shade fanned by an ocean breeze, and no one in Edward Town found it mysterious that a fat man enriched himself by sitting and talking on a hotel porch. More than a few owed him money. Some owed things more precious. And always, the fat man smiled.

He worked the trickle of tourists too. Those who happened by and paused awhile in the shade or ordered a rum punch. North Americans mostly, some from Europe, a few Australians. The man sitting opposite him at the table, mopping sweat from his face and repeatedly photographing the harbor with an undersized Japanese camera, was clearly American. From Texas.

"Last year we was in Anteegwa. You been there? Anteegwa?"

"Antigua, you mean?"

"That's it. Just northa Gwadaloopa."

"Guadeloupe," the fat man corrected in flawless French. He had French ancestry, among others. Tourists found his heavy French accent colorful, though he could have spoken to them in clear, almost generic English had he wished.

"Wife's always after me to come down here on accounta her fish tank. Nets tropicals. Cheaper'n buying 'em, she says. I reckon that's where she's got off to. Finding out where to hire a dive boat. She can net a hunnerd a day."

The fat man's eyelids peeled back in the manner of reptiles. "What is your name, sir?" he asked in his amiable accent.

"White, Robert E.," the Texan said, flashing a set of perfect teeth. "Bobby to my buds."

"Well, Monsieur White. I think you'll have quite the surprise for your wife when she returns to find you sitting here in the shade having accomplished more - much more - than she did by running about town." The fat man smiled.

"Oh? How's that?"

"As it happens, you are currently speaking with the man who arranges dive charters on Charming Island. At the most reasonable rates."

The tourist shook his head happily. "Shoot!" he said. "She'll just shit."

When you heard about things they did, you thought Americans must be the most ingenious people who ever lived, but meet them one at a time and there wasn't anyone quite as pedestrian. The fat man smiled at his fresh catch. "Perhaps a drink while we wait for your charming wife to return?" he suggested.

"Now you're talkin' my language. Say, what's your name anyhow?"

"Javert. Jacques Leon Du Gard Javert."

"Ah," the Texan said. "Like Jack Cousteau."

"Exactly." Monsieur Javert signaled the waiter, who, knowing the routine, arrived moments later and flourished two large rum punches. Both would go on the tourist's bill, together with an eighteen percent service charge, five percent of which belonged to the fat man.

"Say. Speaking of Charming. What kinda name is that anyway? For an island, I mean?"

"It's a man's name," the fat man said, sounding every bit the local historian. "Sir Edward Charming of Her Majesty's Royal Navy stumbled onto this island and the cays surrounding it in 1687. Menaced by several large pirate ships and dangerously low on provisions, Sir Edward supposedly ducked into the harbor you see below you and sent a party ashore in search of fresh water. They returned with coconuts, breadfruit, plantain, sand crabs, and a turtle. He was heard to comment that this was indeed a charming place to hide from his pursuers, and because his officers found the play on words so amusing, the island was ever after referred to as Charming Island. Or so the legend goes. The French inhabitants prefer a different version." The fat man shrugged - a rippling motion. "Myself. I think the British story is better scripted."

Monsieur White stared back at him in a most vacant way, having already lost interest. "Place is kind of a dump," White said, folding a sweat-soaked handkerchief into squares. "Far as I can see, there isn't even a Burger King."

Javert took no insult from this remark. Only shrugged. His fat, watchful face remained a mask. "We are what you may call a backwater," he said. "The terrain is rugged and mountainous, but the soil is rich and produces delectable fruits and other produce. Enough to export. The people are mixed as people are on most Caribbean islands. A British government and English the official language, but most Charming Islanders also speak fluent French and Spanish. In times past, the French ruled here and so did Spain. My own family came from Haiti and brought their French along. You North Americans speak your own language and have little patience for another, but here people switch languages sometimes within the same sentence. The only thing they all agree on is religion. They are Pentecostals to the heart. Leave a stack of one hundred dollar bills on your hotel room dresser and nobody will touch it. That's faith, my friend."

"We're not staying at this hotel," the tourist continued, glancing around in obvious distaste at the Pink Sands. "We're at the Royal Colonial around the bay there." (As if Javert, a resident, had to be shown where it was.) "More modern. Got a package deal from Three Forks Travel in Dallas. They know their stuff. Eight nights, seven days, all meals, and a complimentary rum cocktail on arrival. Garden room, though. Can't see the ocean. I told the wife, I said, who gives a shit? Nothing but a big lake, when you think about it. Did we come down here to sit and look at the ocean or get under it?"

Javert listened patiently, sipping his drink through a straw. It was always the same. The deal I got. Better than anyone else's. What simpletons, these Americans. Nauseating. Yet, he was one who realized their importance. While the island's short-sighted populace dozed in the sunshine, Javert saw opportunity hanging heavy on the limb. Tourism was the future. Islanders must be weaned from their agricultural tradition, which gave nothing but sustenance. Cash in, embrace the Bobby Whites waiting by the thousands to be exploited. After all, how did anyone make money but by exploitation? You exploited people and natural resources. A direct route to wealth. Charming Island possessed an abundance of natural resources - sun, sand, clear waters. Sell that and reap the reward in hard currency. Was it so difficult to understand? Wasn't it being done on every island in the Caribbean? Why were these people so complacent?

He knew the answer, of course. Religion. The British rulers, their families and a gaggle of British merchants, were Anglican, Church of England. The French had been mostly Catholic and attended the one Catholic church in the town. There were a few Baptists as well, but most of the island people were Pentecostal. White people attended either the Catholic or Anglican churches and black people attended at least two dozen Pentecostal meeting houses spread across the island. And they took it seriously. Unlike the other faiths, which mostly consisted of a worship hour on Sundays, Pentecostals tended to gather often for prayer, Bible studies, food, fellowship and work projects. They lived their faith and when there was a choice between it and a social or political issue, they held to their beliefs. This was Javert's biggest problem. He wanted to entice more tourists, and they did not. And the black Pentecostal population held the power. Except for the Governor and his staff, the British Consulate people and a small business community, all important positions of power were held by islanders. And this was the foundation for a society split by color, religion and politics.

Javert spent half his time plotting to change this dynamic, but had failed. "Hotel space is limited," he admitted to the Texan. "But the weather, Monsieur? You must agree, it is lovely, no?"

Leaning both elbows on the table, the lanky tourist seemed to consider this awhile, then he said, "I don't suppose you'd know if the Jazz did any good this week?"

"Pardon?"

"Utah Jazz? NBA?" Frustrated, he asked, "Comprendo basketball?"

The conversation's new twist caught the fat man by surprise. "I am afraid I do not follow North American sporting contests. We are more interested here in soccer."

"I've heard that. Basketball's my sport."

"You are a participant?" The fat man stared at the tourist's sloping shoulders and stooped form.

"Played in high school," Bobby replied. "Utah's my team. Might've gone all the way last season, but the Bulls - that's Chicago - pretty much dominated all year."

Monsieur Javert had no idea what the man was talking about, but nodded agreeably.

A freshening breeze sent napkins scurrying across the table, carrying a variety of ripe odors from the harbor - diesel fuel, garbage, rotting vegetation washed by the tide, sewage discharged from the small packet boats tied at the wharf.

"Perhaps Monsieur, it is time we conduct our business?" coaxed the fat man.

"Huh? Oh. The dive trip. Yeah." The Texan thought a moment. "How much?"

The fat man withdrew a worn yellow rate card from the breast pocket of his oversized, off-white blazer. "It is all here." He handed the card across the table.

The American studied the rates thoroughly. After some haggling, a price was agreed upon. Less than the listed price, fifty dollars more than Javert was willing to settle for.

Another drink was ordered to seal the bargain when Javert observed *Esteban* struggling to dock. "And there, Monsieur, is your boat."

The tourist spun around and squinted into the late afternoon sun. "That scow coming in? Estabone, whatever?" He wagged his salon-styled head from side to side in disbelief.

"*Esteban* means Stephen in Spanish," Javert instructed. "The Captain acquired his boat on one of the Spanish islands further north, I believe. Granted, most boats are christened female."

Mr. White failed to notice the fat man's eyes focused not on *Esteban*, but farther out in the harbor on a smaller craft slipping along the far shore, keeping well away from the main dock. The corners of Javert's sagging mouth lifted ever so slightly, as the smaller boat disappeared to the north and was lost in the forest of masts growing from Sailfish Marina. Once again, his money had been well-spent. This boat carried the communist insurgent he'd requested from Cuba. Wesley Bens, a competent and dangerous man hired to carry out Javert's plans against the powers of politicians and Pentecostals. His patience was at an end and now it was time for action.

Javert was aware of the risk Bens posed. Cuban communists were not easy to control, but for Javert the wiser choice. The Cubans were still bristling and red-faced since their 1983 trouncing by Ronald Reagan in Granada, an almost laughable defeat of the great Cuban military modeled after the powerful Russian Army. Now they were anxious for revenge and that gave Javert a chance to borrow some military muscle without spending too much of his money or being suspected as the instigator. He had been careful in his clandestine negotiations with the Cubans and succeeded in persuading them that Charming Island was ripe for the picking where Granada had been too closely aligned with the U.S. and U.K.

They fell silent awhile, watching *Esteban* backing down against a cross current holding it from its berth. The diesel engine rattled in response to the strain of additional RPMs and dense clouds of black smoke drifted across the water, adding to the noise and confusion of the harbor. A dangerously thin boy, naked but for ragged shorts, leapt to the wharf dragging a dirty length of line that he deftly looped over a bollard to secure the boat. Cat-like he sprang back aboard, with matchless speed and agility scaled the front of the pilothouse and swung inside through an open window.

"Just like a monkey," the Texan observed. "Cute though, when they're little."

"This one's a bastard," Javert said, confidentially. "Mother's a local tramp.

They share quarters with the Captain. None of them eat very well, I'm afraid." A pleasing thought.

A figure emerged from the pilothouse and stepped gingerly onto the wharf. Bare feet shoved in salt-stained deck shoes, one with silver tape wrapped around the toe. Khaki trousers streaked with fingers of grease where he'd wiped his hands. A crew-neck shirt, navy blue, faded, a full size too small, hanging just above his belt. He said something to the boy and started up the wharf.

The Captain's shoulders and upper body moved mechanically like the bare-chested stevedores on the dock. They were black men. He was tanned brown. His facial features, coming into focus now as he drew near, held an expression Javert thought heroic - a tragic, tolerant, puzzled look. He didn't like to admit it, even in secret, but there it was. You couldn't look at those intelligent, brooding eyes, with their deep creases growing back across the temples to the hairline, eyes that changed color to match sea or sand, without noticing their ageless quality. Below, the nose and lips were thin, almost unnecessary. Javert despised his own envy for this American at the same time he thrilled at the power he held over him. It made him shiver in the heat.

He wore no hat over his long, slick hair, much of which had gone gray, tied carelessly back in a knot at the nape of his neck. His weathered skin, mapping years spent squinting over tropical waters and reflected sunlight, stretched tightly across the bones of his face, beginning to sag slightly beneath his chin. The fat man thought it a handsome face, though too angular, scarred on the upper lip, salted with three days' growth of beard. Far from pretty.

"What's his name?" White asked.

"Will."

"That's all? Just Will?"

"Captain Will."

"Doesn't look like much." The tourist leaned across the table. "He a doper?"

The fat man chuckled, waving to the waiter. More drinks were ordered, along with a basket of garlic bread and fresh oysters. His commission grew.

"First of all Monsieur, I must confess I do not know the whole story. Captain Will came here fifteen or sixteen years ago, slightly younger of course, more enthusiastic perhaps, but very much like you see him today. A man with few friends, shadowy past, no ties, little ambition. What happened to him before he arrived on this island, I cannot tell you. Some say he escaped from the authorities in his own country. Others say his heart was broken in some torrid love affair. Who knows? I for one, am not curious."

"He's American?" The Texan was shocked.

"Ah, yes!" the fat man confided. "He is from your USA."

"What state?"

"That I do not know. He speaks as someone from the northern regions, unlike yourself with that delightful hillbilly accent we find so colorful."

"It's not hillbilly." Mr. White was offended.

"A thousand pardons," soothed the fat man. "I meant no disrespect."

"There's more big cities in Texas than any other state in the Union," White informed him. "A lotta people forget that."

"I am dreadfully sorry," said Javert in his most obsequious tone. "Let it suffice to say that our Captain is certainly not from the great state of Texas."

"Hardly!" Bobby White narrowed his eyes and a new firmness grew around his flaccid mouth. "Where's he going?"

"The Tortuga. The bar across the street. There he will take his afternoon rum." Javert lowered his voice to a confidential rasp. "Many of us here do not associate with the Cuban, Carlos Orizondo, who owns the Tortuga."

"Oh? I thought the ones who left were on our side. Anti-communist, I mean."

"There is much doubt as to Señor Orizondo's loyalties," said the fat man. "A man without a country. Not to be trusted." Javert fell silent. There was more to say but this was not the time or the audience. His hatred for Orizondo was already too widely known.

Orizondo's friendship with Captain Will was also well known. The Cuban and his cronies opposed Javert's plan for the island, but Captain Will paid his commission and drew, through his dive boat, a steady, thin stream of tourists. Charming Island was no Antigua or Guadeloupe. The mountainous terrain forbid an airport. Cruise ships were forced to anchor outside the harbor and bring their passengers in by small boat, an inconvenience most refused to accept. Javert and his friends were unable to convince the British governor to dynamite a hole in the barrier reef, dredge the harbor deeper and allow ships to land their passengers at the pier. Only shallow-drafted pleasure craft and small inter-island packet boats crossed the reef and tied up inside.

All his life Javert had been frustrated by shortsighted fools like Governor Sir Henry Leach. In the shantytowns of a half-dozen Caribbean ports, Javert discovered that only power yields success, and a full belly. What a shame those like Leach, who had power bestowed upon them, were too stupid to exploit it. How lucky in another sense, because it made them vulnerable. Nothing crossed Javert's path unnoticed, no opportunity regardless how small or insignificant, was overlooked. Everything made him money. And money made him fat.

Javert carried his weight as some men do wealth. He made the most of it. Let it stick out, protrude in billowing rolls so flagrant people either stared or turned away. But everyone noticed. And of all Javert's fears, the worst was anonymity. He'd had enough of it.

Judy Ann White chose that moment to materialize in the dusty street below, lugging a large straw basket filled with colorful souvenirs she'd bought from the natives, who imported them from Taiwan.

"I half expected this," she said. "Sittin' in the shade boozin' while I'm out taking care of business. I got a coating of dirt on my feet an inch thick."

The whining, strident voice didn't fit the lovely vision the fat man saw standing before him. Judy Ann was tall, willowy. In her thirties. Frosted hair, long and tangled by the wind, reminded him of ripe peaches. He imagined himself gripping her head between his meaty fingers, sweeping the long body against his. He had an appetite for women.

Bobby bolted from his chair, bounding down the wooden steps to greet his wife with an overpowering smile and clearly unwelcome hug. "Here," he said, jerking at her bag. "Let me take that."

"Keep your drunken hands off!" She yanked it clear and struggled up the steps.

"Allow me, Madame," said the fat man, rising to his feet with surprising agility, whisking the shopping bag from her grasp. "Please." He withdrew a chair for her. "Won't you join us?"

Judy Ann stared at him a moment, decided to trust him, then sat down. "I'm thirsty," she said.

Javert summoned the waiter and issued a string of commands - rum punches, more garlic bread, oysters, a damp towel for the lady. "Quickly! Quickly!"

"Well, Bobby E.?" Judy Ann inquired. "Aren't you going to introduce me?"

"Oh, sure," he said, relieved by the opportunity to deflect her annoyance. He sat down. "This is Mr. Jack Javeer."

"Javert," the fat man corrected gently. "At your service, Madame."

"And what services do you perform, Mr. Javert?"

"For a lovely lady such as yourself," the fat man opened his arms as if to embrace her, "you have but to ask and I will perform."

Judy Ann nodded her appreciation of this imposing promise. She was coy, this one.

"Jack here is gonna fix us up with a dive boat, native lunch from the sea, the whole nine yards," Bobby brayed.

"Oh?"

"A real pirate captain," he plowed on. "Captain Will somebody. Boat right there." He pointed.

"I have a standing agreement with the Captain, Madame," explained Javert. "His bookings go through me."

"*Esteban*?" she inquired. Receiving nods she said, "I booked it with the Captain's wife an hour ago."

Javert's pink jowls trembled as he shook his head. "Captain Will has no wife, Madame."

"Oh?" she said, momentarily confused. "Woman in her late 30s?"

"Black. Poorly dressed?" Javert prompted.

"Yes."

"Rosa Lionelli, the illegitimate issue of an Italian sailor and a Haitian cane cutter's daughter," Javert related in a gossipy tone. "We import Haitians, you understand, to cut our sugarcane. The Italians, I'm afraid, are everywhere. She has a bastard child herself, Armando. They live with Captain Will in his shack near the mountain. The boy works on the boat. The woman - to be delicate - performs other services."

"Oh," she shrugged. "I haven't met Captain Will."

"He's white. American," Bobby explained. "Shacked up with a Nigger."

Javert, though white-skinned, had an array of black ancestry he regularly denied. An idea struck him. "I am sure Madame Judy Ann, that you made a much more accommodating bargain with Rosa than I could have arranged," he said, smiling broadly. "Therefore, I will withdraw my offer of one hundred seventy-five dollars, U.S."

Judy Ann's face clouded. "How much?"

"One seventy-five, Madame."

"And how much is that in Charming dollars?" she inquired.

"One hundred and forty CI."

"I can never get used to that," Bobby complained. "Their money's worth more than ours. Their dollar bill is white for crying out loud, and has a conch on it where Washington's head oughta be."

"Well," Judy laughed. "I guess we better stick with Mr. Javert's offer. The best I could get was two hundred."

"Ah," Javert nodded. "This will present a problem for us both. Rosa will inform the Captain of the higher price, making it most difficult for me to settle with him for a lower one." Javert stared at the table. "But leave this to me. Perhaps I can arrange a compromise."

"Guess you wasn't so smart after all," Bobby told his wife. "How much you spend on all the junk you got there?" He sneered at the shopping bag.

Avoiding an argument, Javert suggested, "Another round of drinks?"

"Settle this boat thing first," stated Bobby. "Let's go over to the Tortuga and straighten everything out."

"If you wish," said the fat man, shrugging. "However, you can expect to pay the full price on that account. Captain Will is not a sociable fellow. He drinks alone. Always. If we interrupt him now, he will simply quote us the full price of two hundred and fifty CI."

"Then we'll just hire another boat."

"I am sorry Monsieur. There is no other boat."

The conversation had stirred memories of Javert's own beginnings here. His parents had escaped the poverty of Haiti when he was very young and he remembered little of it. His father was a French expat without a dime and his mother descended from black Haitian, Irish and French ancestry. Shortly after their arrival on Charming Island, the senior Javert succumbed to drink, fell from a pier and drowned. His mother was left to support the two of them by spreading her legs until she disappeared seven years later. Javert, in his early teens, hated both his parents and felt no remorse at their departures. He was relieved, in fact, and made a better living than either of them, and mostly by using his wits and daring. He was a thief who never got caught, a con man who was never uncovered and a gigolo when it served him. Before he was twenty he owned land, a share in two hotels and an old dredging machine that he refurbished and used to clear silt from various island docks and piers. He was an accomplished smuggler who avoided the drug craze and kept to more acceptable contraband such as liquor, cigars and delicacies of the palette. By so doing his apprehension was never a police priority, even though enough people knew of his darker activities. But Javert had learned the art of bribery too, and more then a few customs officials were willing to turn a blind eye on Javert's cargoes if the price was right. He was a social fellow who mixed well with the elite of the island, even though some of the British residents found him repulsive. Javert prospered while many others failed and his bank account grew with his girth. He achieved respectability in the end, and that was more valuable to him than all the money he had stashed away.

CHAPTER EIGHT

Tuesday afternoons at the Tortuga were slow. They'd always been that way and Carlos Orizondo had no explanation for it. Late afternoon sun worked on the tin roof, ticking. He flipped the ceiling fan switch to medium. Carlos was hard-working and shrewd, like many Cubans who fled Castro, and the run-down Tortuga Bar and Grill was indeed a thriving family business.

The building had no windows or walls, built in a rectangle with mildewed concrete posts and waist-high barrier connecting them. The posts supported rafters and a metal roof. The absence of walls gave the bar an unfinished look. Exposed wiring connected ceiling fans that dangled from cross beams and wobbled dangerously, threatening to spin loose and decapitate the patrons. Homemade leather chairs and brilliant cascades of bougainvillea along the building saved it from being a dive. An ancient mango shaded the packed mud of the yard, banging fruit on the tin roof when the wind blew.

Small groups of island girls skipped and danced their way home along the dusty street dressed in pale green and white school uniforms. They carried books and flashy folders with garish titles and photographs of bright monsters. Behind them, Captain Will made his way inside, shuffling to his usual table facing the harbor without so much as a glance around the room.

Carlos was simpático to Captain Will, admired North Americans for their audacity, mourned their self-destructiveness. In the Caribbean, everything depends on the American cow, its love of being milked - fingering its teats, filling their buckets. He read the *Miami Herald* - a day late - and its scab-picking editorials fed his deep frustration with the Yankees these days. He was determined not to repeat their mistakes, or Cuba's, here on Charming Island.

Captain Will had flopped into one of the straight-backed chairs. A man who never looked comfortable sitting. He fidgeted and it made Carlos smile. There'd been a shyness about him when they first met, though it had long ago given way to a more combative camaraderie. He trusted the American, who was dependable in spite of his beach bum reputation. Maybe when the trouble started he'd be a man in whom they could hope.

Carlos tucked a bottle into his armpit, took glass in hand and strode toward

Will's seaside table. The Captain was a stickler for a clean glass, though rarely clean himself.

"Your rum, Señor," the Cuban said, placing the bottle, which had a yellow mesh around it, in the center of the table. "The glass." This also he placed before the American, addressing him formally as though they were strangers.

"Gracias." His eyes remained locked on the harbor. "That dredge of Javert's is getting on my nerves, hammering all day."

"And all night." Carlos looked around, staring openly at Javert sitting on the veranda across the street. He spat on the floor. "Fat pig!"

"How's he get a government contract anyway?"

"Llaves." Keys.

"Dredging pier channels so far. Hasn't talked them into blowing the barrier reef yet."

"Matter of time." The Cuban wished to discuss more pleasant matters. "Any luck today?" When Captain Will had no charters he searched for a sunken warship.

"Just smoke from the cannon."

Carlos laughed. "Where there is smoke there is fire, no?"

"Only applies to politics and women," said the Captain.

This was an old topic the Cuban knew never failed to widen the Captain's eyes. Stories of gold and galleons circulated constantly, the kind of thing you either laughed or marveled at, depending on how you viewed life. The Captain searched for the French man-o-war *Imperial*, sunk by British naval units in 1806. While not a treasure ship, it carried gold to pay its crew and purchase supplies. But *Imperial* slipped beneath the waves and disappeared. "You will find it," Carlos assured him with real conviction. Only a fool, after all, lived without hope.

"Of course," replied the Captain, still watching the dredge. The Javerts haven't changed, he thought, since that day in 1806, when Reggie Wilson felt the steel wielded by another Javert. He'd thought of it often. Javert himself had confirmed his ancestry dating back to a French seaman. Few things remained in Warren's possession from the old days, but Uncle David's account of *Imperial* was one of them. "Anyway, gets me up in the morning. In the end, persistence defeats everything, I suppose, even stupidity."

"If I had a lovely brown-skinned woman like Rosa rubbing against me in the morning," Carlos told him, grinning, "I would not need to search for treasure, or get out of bed."

"Your wife know you talk like this?"

"She encourages talk." He laughed. "Has a butterfly knife for the rest."

"Don't you have any other customers?"

"No," Carlos said, sadly. "None."

"Then go bother the cook."

"I am the cook. You know that, Señor Will."

"Well, buzz off anyway. Enough Cuban prattle. I got mail to read. Private."

"Si, Señor!" The Cuban bowed, worshipfully. "First, I tell you of the meeting tonight. Eight o'clock. The old refinery."

"Told you before. Your political intrigues are your own. Not interested. Don't give a damn which bunch of vipers governs this rock, just so they leave me alone."

"You don't care that the fat man and his amigos plot to overthrow the government? You let this happen? No. You help us."

"Don't bet on it. Javert has me by the ass and you know it."

"Señor Will. We can help each other."

"I said, don't bet on it. Go on now. Leave me alone."

Carlos sighed and walked away. Americanos. Carlos saw his two-story house in Habana "liberated," his father butchered, a sister raped and beaten, his defeated mother a dullard living and breathing in a Miami barrio until she died there brokenhearted. For what? Politics. A refugee life on Charming Island earned him another family, another house. These he kept, or they killed him.

Behind his back, Captain Will poured the amber liquid slowly along the inside edge of the glass. He used no ice or mix. The Dominican years had taught him how to drink rum like a Dominican.

The first sharp taste filled his mouth and numbed the back of his throat. He closed his eyes and thought of nothing. Then came back to the letter.

All day he'd been avoiding it. Last night Rosa had been pleased to hand him something from home. No letters came for her. He was casual about it. "Just my mother," he'd said.

She wrote less frequently now, since Dad died. What was there to say? Time slipped away. She'd just written at Christmas. What could've happened in Lake Darling since then? What ever happened in Lake Darling?

The letter was folded once and stuffed deep inside his back pocket. He retrieved it. The envelope was sweat-soaked, his address an unrecognizable smear.

He picked at the seal, breaking it off in pieces.

Finally, he removed the contents.

Dear Warren,

It's hard for me to write this to you. I don't know any way bad news can be broken to a person, except to come right out with it. When you read this I will be dead. I'm sorry. Breast cancer. I've had it nearly three years. Suppose

I should've told you before, but we don't see each other anymore. You don't come home and it wasn't the kind of thing to say in a letter, until now.

I'm writing this at the table in the breakfast nook where you used to sit and eat my chocolate chip cookies after school. Once I made two batches for some doings at church and you came home and ate them all. Remember? I didn't have the heart to get mad at you. I've been remembering a lot lately, of course, but in the end there's no mystery to life, I suppose, greater than we make of it. The Bible says we're like flowers in a field, the wind passes over it, and we're gone, and our place knows us no more.

I don't want to make you sad, that's why I kept my cancer from you so long. I'm writing now while I still feel pretty good. Anna Kaye will mail this for me after I'm gone. She's been a constant strength all this time. A true neighbor and friend. If not for her, I wouldn't have been able to deal with dying in any kind of dignified way - I mean, if dying can be thought of as dignified. I decided not to have anyone notify you about the funeral, burial, and such. This will have to be your notification. This way it'll all be over long before you know about it. Unless I die in the winter. Then they stick me inside the cemetery shed with the lawnmowers, rakes and things, until spring. Maybe you don't remember, but I'm afraid of the cold.

Whatever happened to us, I wonder? It started when Stephen went under the ice. Though there were many happy years after that. When you moved away the years slipped by and we waited for you to invite us for a visit or come home yourself, but you never did. When Dad died and you still didn't come, well, after that I guess I gave up. Last Christmas you answered my letter with a card and wrote at the bottom: "I'm still alive. That's life in the tropics." It made me cry. You're right, you see, you are still alive, and in the end that's all we have - time. I don't mean to lecture you from the grave, but what have you done about it?

I should cross that out, I suppose. I won't, though. You need to think it over. I'm not suggesting I'm any better. My life didn't amount to much. I was born in a small town less than seventy miles from the one I'm dying in. I've never lived in a city or traveled to a foreign country, and I've only been on an airplane twice, for funerals. Never held a job, like women now. I raised you, Stephen for twelve years, and took care of your father. I miss him every single day. He wasn't a duty or drudgery, like some people think. You kids weren't either. It was what I wanted and what made me who I am. The idea that I could've been more fulfilled by some career, and that somehow make me more a woman, is just foolishness.

But we're all gone now, Warren. Stephen, your dad and me. There's no one left who loved you when you were young, wedged your head in the crook of their arm and watched you drink milk from a bottle, or had tears in their eyes when you struck out. No one who knew you from the beginning. It's going to come to you now, that loneliness. Life has no sappy Hollywood ending. My spirit won't hang around to comfort you, even my body rots in a gruesome way, and this place, Lake Darling, will know it no more. I hope you'll think of me once in awhile.

Otherwise, I've left you a small insurance policy. It's all I could afford, I just had the Social Security at the end. (My funeral was prepaid.) I'm buried between your father and Stephen where I belong. If you ever get back here to Lake Darling you'll find us there, but don't make a special trip. I sold the house to pay my medical bills so you'll have to find a motel. But if you didn't come when we were alive, I don't suppose you'll come now.

I should say one more thing - I love you. After Stephen drowned you became my only son. It's hard to explain but I just wanted to give you everything I had left over from him. I couldn't of course, or I would've smothered you. Besides loving you, I pity you. I mean that in a compassionate way. You had your heart set on such lofty, adventurous things and I knew from your silence all these years how short of it you fell. But what maybe you don't know is that we all did that, fell short I mean. It's unavoidable, and I wonder if that's what you've done, tried to avoid the unavoidable.

Maybe you can make something out of these words of mine after awhile. I'll pray for that. I hope you still pray sometimes. And I can give you some news. Your old girlfriend Ruth Van Doren is alone now. Her husband died in a small plane crash last year. I read it in the paper. He was in the State Legislature. I didn't vote for him though. He was a Democrat. She went back to teaching. I only mention it because they - her and her father - are coming to Charming Island.

This was a funny letter to write. I'm glad to be done with it, except that for the first time in years I feel like I'm talking to you again, like when you used to come in after a dive and I'd be fixing dinner and you'd talk on and on about fish and old tires and boat motors you found underwater. Find yourself now, Warren. Don't think we held anything against you for staying away. You can't face those you love when your heart is heavy. When you're lost.

Your Dad loved you. I love you. Goodbye, Son.

Mom

Captain Will ripped the letter into two equal halves, placed one on top of the other, making a coaster for his drink. Her voice rang inside his head as if she'd spoken the words aloud and the past rushed back upon him. He should cry for her but he couldn't. She'd taken this one last opportunity to nag. To have the last word. What was it about his life that offended them all so?

He ignored his glass and took a long pull from the bottle, impatient for the numbing liquor. Sometimes she'd clipped newspaper engagement photographs, Chamber of Commerce awards, gossip columns concerning people he knew. These were mailed to remind him of all the time he'd wasted waiting for his life to begin.

"Carlos!" he shouted at the kitchen. "Hey! Cubano!"

No answer.

Since Santo Domingo he'd been keeping a low profile. Damn near invisible. He drank from the bottle.

"Carlos!"

The little Cuban made himself scarce if he wanted to. He refilled the glass, drank from the bottle. What happened to all that piss and vinegar everybody started off with?

"Carlos! Damn it!"

This time he drank from the glass. His lips were numb. He sucked at his cheeks and bit the end of his tongue to check it.

"You are calling to me?" Carlos inquired, almost on top of him.

"Huh?"

"I hear you. 'Carlos! Carlos! Dom it!'" the Cuban mimicked. "I hear you."

"Oh, shut up," Warren said. "I can't remember now why I called you. Go back and skin a chicken or something."

"You no skin a chicken. You pluck it."

"Pluck it, then."

"I have a glass." Carlos held it up and smiled broadly.

"I drink alone," Warren growled, but before the Cuban could walk away he said, "Go ahead. Sit down."

Carlos saw the Captain had downed half the bottle already. On the table was a letter torn in two pieces. He pretended not to notice and filled his glass.

"Salud, Señor," Carlos said, raising his glass.

The Cuban didn't know the source of his old friend's pain, but he'd long ago recognized the anger. Anger born of shame, failure. Captain Will had no exclusive rights to that. Carlos fought the gnawing stomach, sudden explosions of temper, sleeplessness. It began at night in a boat, crossing the Florida Straits toward freedom, leaving behind in Cuba all that he'd ever loved. A thousand nights since in sweat-soaked beds, running to the same place Captain Will hid now, a bottle. Today, so many years later, it was still not far away. Though he'd licked the bottle, more or less. He tipped his glass and drank the Captain's health again, offering a silent prayer for them both.

An hour later Carlos had gone back to work - four inspectors from the dockside customs shed came in for happy hour - but Captain Will remained at his table drinking steadily.

He'd changed his name, his appearance, certainly his address. Today Warren Wilson lost those trappings, the layers of camouflage. All his efforts since Santo Domingo unraveled by one letter. The rum he drank seemed like water and the usual conversation with the Cuban felt strained and scripted. It was his mother, of course, who was in error. Who knew nothing of the death of Warren Wilson, her son, and the birth of Captain Will, a man whose eyes had been opened in Santo Domingo, where he had been so easily deceived and humiliated, saved only by a woman from Indiana. He questioned his mother's love. What could she possibly gain from writing him now? She was dead. She might've had the decency to do it quietly.

The past is an emotional trap. A trick to divert attention from the truth. Pain makes life more potent, adding texture to form something passionate or purposeful so we don't make fools of ourselves chasing faith or God. They all chase God in the end, but if there was a God, Stephen would still be alive.

So he'd torn the letter.

He stared at it. It was limp beneath his glass. Her voice was still in his head. He'd never seen her old, not really old. He belched. She was almost a fairytale character. Nothing in childhood proved true in life, and remained where it belonged, behind. He'd really done more than suppress it. He'd disavowed it. Hell, he could even laugh at it. He drank. Other times his mind ran slide shows, home movies, and the voices in his head started again. A scar that itched now and then, that's all. Be careful not to scratch, it went away. His parents, even Stephen, were biologicals that really had nothing to do with him except in the way a turtle might hollow out the sand and lay some eggs, forget them and return to the sea.

He stared at the two halves again. He removed the glass and picked them up and shoved them back inside his pocket.

A moment later a Pink Sands' waiter arrived with a note and pointed to Javert sitting on the veranda. The note read: *Time we had a visit.*

"Go tell him....never mind. Thank you," he told the man politely. Yes, this would do fine. That bastard Javert. He wanted to talk to that son-of-a-bitch anyway.

The Pink Sands was no longer the largest hotel on the island. It couldn't even claim to be the oldest, but remained a potent symbol of colonial power, however faded, because on its veranda islanders conducted their business over lunches or evening cocktails. On the rare occasion the Governor was seen in public, he dined at the Sands. Warren wished they'd bulldoze the place and build a Radisson, then fill it with scuba tourists.

His oily deck shoes made a squishy noise as he ascended the immaculate white steps to the veranda, leaving behind greasy footprints. He disliked being summoned, and would normally have ignored Javert, but he was drunk and bilious from the letter, and anyway, it was time he gave the fat man a piece of his mind about the dredge.

Already the sun had gone. Followed by a brief twilight and then the night, thick and heavy with reggae and cooking smells drifting up from the charcoal fires of shantytown. Plantains in peanut oil, Warren thought, staple of the Caribbean.

Javert was no longer on the veranda, where a sizable crowd of Charming Island's elite had gathered, filling every table. Warren felt the tension, and catching a phrase here and there, knew the topic of conversation was politics. Not the usual gossip but serious talk full of fear and frustration. The vote on independence drew ever closer.

Perhaps Javert had moved to the bar, or even his suite upstairs. Warren wound his way through the tables, accepting a nod of recognition now and then, even a "hello" from the passport control officer, Leroy Paquette. He'd taught Paquette to dive last year, along with several others at these tables. It earned him a certain amount of respect, if that was the word. Call it civility or nervous affability. You taught someone to dive and it took time, patience, effort from you and the student. Even if a student fails, gets a certification and never uses it, the instructor is never forgotten. You can't hold someone's life in your hands and not impress them just a little. Not that teaching diving today was anything like when he'd gone to Minneapolis and met Freddie-the-Frogman. Divers today didn't have the fire in their bellies he had then. They didn't have the love of a good regulator or the desire to feel a steel tank resting against their spines. Not that he blamed them really, just felt sorry. They played at diving. It had become chic. Something to brag about when the girl on the next barstool notices your dive watch. "Sure baby, I'm a diver." But rarely a way of life, as it was for him.

He'd assumed the reggae was the jukebox, but as he rounded the corner and stepped through the double doors, he realized it was live. He didn't recognize the singer, a light-skinned, shirtless Rastafarian in tight copper-colored trousers. Behind him, his band sweating like cane cutters, bent to their work. Javert was nowhere in sight.

To hell with him. Warren turned right and exited into the quiet of the dim lobby.

"Captain Will." Javert's voice.

The lobby of the Pink Sands survived from Victorian days when anything with fringes seemed decorative and a room could never have too many potted plants. The fat man sat in a sturdy chair near a round table of dark mahogany.

"I was just about to leave." Talking to Javert without growling took effort.

"So I observed." Javert's voice smooth as grease.

"What do you want?"

"A moment." He gestured to the other chair opposite. "Please."

"I'm on the way home for supper."

"Your little Negress will wait. What I have to say is important to you, and extremely urgent." He shifted in his seat and again gestured to the chair. "Please."

Warren sat and lit a cigarette. He smoked sometimes when he'd had a few.

"That's better," Javert continued. "Please don't be rude when I'm about to offer you financial independence."

"Seems like there's a lot of independence talk going around today," Warren said, flicking his match onto the polished floor.

"Oh?"

"Veranda's packed. Bar's overflowing with too much good fellowship, like people huddled together before a hurricane."

"Undoubtedly a storm is coming."

Warren's eyes had adjusted to the dark and he made out Javert's face clearly. Calm, almost serene. "That what you want to talk to me about?"

"In a manner of speaking, yes. Like all of us, you must decide the issue of independence."

"No, I don't. Not my island."

"You've lived here nearly as long as I have and I consider it my island."

"You consider too many things yours."

Javert looked thoughtful. His serene face clouded. "Why is it you and I can never have a polite business conversation? Why do you insist on this belligerence?"

"I don't like you, Javert. I see only two possibilities for our relationship - it can stay the same, or get worse." He blew a cloud of smoke. "Interviews like this make it worse. Do you have a charter for me or what?"

"I do, but there's more." Javert reached for a dainty stemmed glass of clear liqueur on the table. It looked ridiculous dangling from the thumb and forefinger of his fat hand. "Political change is coming. Soon. What you think about it is unimportant, but the side you are on when it's over will mean everything." The serene look had returned. "We are already partners of a sort, since I hold *Esteban's* mortgage. Why not extend our partnership in ways that profit us both as these changes - opportunities - come upon us?"

"I dream only of ending our relationship." A day seldom went by when Will didn't kick himself in the ass for borrowing from Javert to start his scuba business and fund vital boat repairs.

"How sad." Just the hint of a smile. "The borrower's natural resentment for the banker who helped him get a loan. Biting the hand that feeds you, I believe is the expression."

"Debt free, I call it." Warren was beginning to suspect Javert's motives and they frightened him. He'd avoided politics to such an extent as to not even laugh at a political joke or answer a political question. He left the flying bridge of his own boat when the conversation turned political. "Politics is the plague of the Caribbean," he'd once told Rosa. And he was right.

"I fear, Captain Will, that you are attempting to run between the rain drops," Javert said quietly. "What I am about to offer you is an umbrella."

A hollowness grew in his stomach. "And what will it cost me?"

"Very little. A few days of your time. The use of your boat."

"Doing what?"

"Importing."

"Smuggling, you mean."

The fat man chuckled.

"Drugs or guns?"

"Guns," Javert said without hesitation. His truthfulness disarming. More dangerous than a lie.

"You shouldn't be so candid, Javert," Warren said. "I might talk."

"I'll give you the mortgage to your boat and five thousand, CI. Our commission agreement remains the same. Agreed?"

Warren marveled at the scene. It seemed the West Indies grew larceny like a greenhouse. People discussing subjects such as smuggling with the aplomb of questioning the weather. Perhaps he should be more insulted then tempted, but it was the other way around. Five thousand dollars and *Esteban's* mortgage would solve every problem in Warren's life. He could even buy a used pickup.

"Why not use your own boat?" he asked, hedging.

"Obvious reasons."

Warren's head buzzed as the rum wore off. Why was he even considering this? "No." He shook his head. "A mortgaged boat is better than no boat. They impound smuggler's boats. Or blow them up. No thanks."

Javert didn't appear disappointed by the rejection, as if expecting it all along. With a suddenness that caused Warren's head to jerk, the fat man snapped his fingers sharply. "Can I interest you in a Tia Maria? Something stronger?"

"Rum," Warren said. His mouth felt pasty and parched.

They sat in silence until the waiter had come and gone and come again.

"You are not a man who is easily persuaded," Javert said. "Commendable."

Warren waited for the other shoe to drop, sipping the fresh drink.

"Don't give me your decision in this matter now, before you've had the benefit of further study and reflection. As I've said, the political storm will come. Those with protection from the rain will remain dry. The others, well..." His voice trailed off into the darkness.

It seemed wise to keep quiet. Wait the fat man out.

At last Javert resumed, "I have a charter for you tomorrow. An obnoxious Texan and 'the missus.'" He laughed with considerable gusto, but it got mislaid somehow in the cavernous lobby.

"What time?"

"Eight o'clock."

"How much?"

"One hundred, CI. Less my commission, of course."

"Not enough."

Javert only shrugged, unconcerned. "It is up to you, of course."

Warren knew Javert was pocketing more than his usual share. Punishment for not taking the smuggling deal? A warning? It didn't matter. *Esteban* was sucking fumes. A hundred might buy a quarter tank. "I'll take it," he said. "No smuggling." He tossed back the remainder of his rum. Without another word he rose to leave. "Why *Esteban*? Why me? There's a dozen captains on this island who'd jump at the chance to make that kind of money."

"Yes." Javert's black eyes caught light from the bar. "There are many, but you alone come and go without fear of customs. Only *Esteban* cannot be searched. Total immunity."

Warren nodded. Of course.

"I've often wondered," Javert continued, "how you attained such exalted status. They say the Governor himself signed the order. True?"

"Yes."

"Why?"

"Promotes tourism," Warren lied, hiding his surprise. Javert always knew too much.

"How convenient for you."

"Tell the Texan and his wife to be on the dock promptly at eight." Warren felt unsteady on his feet. Javert had discovered his exemption. How would he use the knowledge?

Javert sat in the darkness, pleased with himself. He was, after all, a student of human nature. He'd handled the captain well, unnerving him just enough. Difficult to speak of violent things like weapons without evoking the passion for which they were designed. He'd managed it well. He wasn't a man of violence. Many thought so, but it was not true. No. Jacques Leon Javert was not a man of violence. The weapons were defensive only. Not a drop of blood would be shed because of them. In fact, they would have the exact opposite effect. They would save lives. And Captain Will would deliver them. Of that he was certain.

Warren's eyes swept the harbor and focused on the gaily-lighted dredge. "Don't you ever turn that thing off? Give the crew a rest?"

"Oh, the dredge. Let's not argue that again. With independence comes progress. The harbor will be opened and bring prosperity." The fat man sipped his liqueur. "A reef more or less. Have you no compassion for the poor?"

"Javert the humanitarian." Warren snorted. "So eager to make waiters and chambermaids of them. Your idea of independence."

"Tourism has saved the Caribbean."

"Bullshit. It destroyed it." Warren ground his cigarette into a nearby plant and steadied himself. "Worse. I'm part of the problem. In bed with you people, all you people who robbed them of their pride, even if it was only the pride of catching fish or growing yucca. You're bastards, all of you."

Javert's tiny eyes settled on Warren's face. "Your colonial ideals are passé. Run along now. There are arms there, in your tin-roofed house, to comfort you, no?"

"Fatso," he said and lurched for the door. Maybe he was tighter than usual. He'd saved that torn letter, too. There was a big dull spot in the middle of his brain, a gray fuzzy place, that had never been there before. A place you didn't bring your mother.

CHAPTER NINE

Wheezing deep within, *Esteban* caught her breath. The sadly maintained diesel coughed, choked, and coughed again - a heavy, phlegm-laden sound. Sour smoke belched from the stern and the engine noise grew to a steady rattle. Warren felt a reassuring shudder under his bare feet.

Morning sunlight streamed through the pilothouse windows, and alongside him Rosa and Armando stood grim-faced and silent, no doubt pondering the recent lack of cash flow. Both took the boat very seriously. Rosa held her head up, tight dusty curls absorbing the light, chin raised parallel with the deck. The full mouth set in a straight line, an expression so unnatural Warren fought to keep a straight face.

He brought *Esteban's* bow around evenly, flicking the wheel between his fingers. The refueling pier slid away behind. Because *Esteban* was originally constructed as a sport fishing yacht, it lacked the utilitarian character of most dive boats. Much of the stern had been cut away and an aluminum swim step bolted on near the waterline. This step, which extended the entire width of the vessel, could be raised and lowered on two metal chains. Running fore and aft along the fantail were plywood seats and tank racks made of PVC. Other than these modifications, *Esteban* looked like someone's old pleasure boat. The main salon enclosed most of the forward and middle deck space. Three steps above was the pilothouse, and atop that the fly bridge with duplicate steering, electronics, and throttle controls.

"Armando," he said. "Have you forgotten the drift line?"

"No señor."

"Then get it out. Wedge the float ball under a seat when you're done, I don't want it bouncing around." Warren kept his eyes on the bow, swinging toward the open sea. "That idiot Geraldo spilled at least a gallon of fuel on deck. Clean it up before all the paint's eaten away."

"What paint?" said Armando's mother. She talked bad about *Esteban* sometimes, from jealousy.

Armando went aft.

"Don't be a smart-ass," Warren told Rosa, steering toward the rusty buoy marking the narrow channel through the barrier reef.

Rosa allowed herself a sideways glance, envious of how his palms caressed the wheel. A superstitious sailor, she spoke little once land slipped astern, working tirelessly, ignoring her surroundings until the dock was again in sight. Like many islanders she hated the sea. It surrounded and hemmed them in, and beneath its mirror death awaited.

"So?" she inquired. "You saw El Gordo?"

"I told you."

"You were drunk."

"I was not."

"You had the red eyes." She leaned close and ran a long nail across his forearm, scratching. In a more soothing tone she said, "You only want to sleep when you drink rum."

This was doing his headache no good. "Get off it," he growled. "I got a charter, didn't I?"

"Those two?" She jerked her head toward the Whites, sitting out of sight on the fantail. "Have they paid?"

"What do you think I bought the fuel with?"

"How much?"

"Enough."

"Humph! The woman offered me more. I handle the business, we make money." But it was no use. "Where do we go?" she asked, more out of a need to quell his irritation than curiosity.

"Sting Ray Flats."

She swung her black eyes to bear on him. "Almost six miles! An hour, at least. And how much fuel? Take them somewhere close."

"The Flats," he snapped. Then more softly. "Woman wants to net fish. Take her to some reef and she'll load up. Nothing on the Flats but sand and rays. They'll be so busy butting heads with old Darth Vader she won't have time to think about netting."

"You care more about fish than people, I think."

He didn't deny it. But the only thing Rosa appreciated from the sea was a hot fillet or cold cash. Lately, they'd been short of both.

"We're almost to the channel buoy," he said. "Go back and tell the Whites to sit down and put their weights on the deck. Check to see if Myron's got his O2 bottle strapped to a bulkhead." The channel was often rough even in calm weather. Freak waves bounced off the shallow bottom sometimes and appeared out of nowhere. Not more than a month ago a fishing boat capsized on a perfect day much like this.

"I don't like this Myron!" she said vehemently, rhyming the end of his name with "moon."

"Just because he pinched your butt a couple times."

"Once, and I hit him. Like this." She shook her fist. "No. I don't like him because he rides free. Never pays. Eats more sandwiches than the tourists who pay. How come we run a business like this, huh? You tell me."

"Because."

"I know because. Because of this Frogman!"

"Freddie-the-Frogman," he said, running low on patience. "They've been friends since World War II." He'd explained this a dozen times. Freddie got him started and any friend of Freddie's was a friend of his.

"I want to see this Frogman," she said. "I give him Myroon back!"

Myron Bose was indeed costly. The old diver had barely enough money to eat. Unknown to Rosa, he slept in *Esteban's* V-birth cabin whenever his Navy pension check got delayed or he spent it on things other than rent, like rum. He ate whatever was left aboard, thanking Warren in the only way his pride allowed; he treated him like an equal.

"Are you going?" he asked, glaring at her.

She started down the steps to the main cabin. "Frogman. Old man. And now what we got back there? Cowboy?"

A few minutes later Armando relieved him at the helm. "I can take it through the channel?" he begged.

"If you're careful."

"Si, Señor."

"Knock off the Señor crap."

"Si, Papa," said the boy, grinning.

"I'm not your Papa."

This was true, of course. Armando had no Papa. None he knew about, anyway. When he got old enough to ask his mother she'd shrugged as if not having a father were the most minor of inconveniences and he should concern himself with more important matters. He'd lived with Captain Will all his life, been disciplined by him, rewarded by him, even hugged a time or two, but never claimed by him. The man didn't claim Rosa either, but he'd learned not to talk to her about it. "He is a good man," was all she said. "There is love between us and we are safe with him." That was enough for her perhaps, but not for Armando. One day, Captain Will would become his father. On that day no one would dare call him hijo-de-puta.

"Don't worry about the compass in here," Captain Will was saying. "As the buoy passes to port read the current from it. Is the tide incoming or outgoing? Understand?" The boy nodded. "Look beyond the reef now, out where the waves build. They appear as ground swells, smooth and wide, but sometimes they crest suddenly in the channel. When that happens, be ready to pull the throttle back and put her nose square into the wave. If you don't, she'll be furrowed under like a stick." His eyes never left the water. "The sea has no respect for anybody."

The tide was incoming. Armando applied even pressure to the throttle. Captain Will nodded his approval and they stood silently side by side until *Esteban* cleared the channel.

The dangerous part of their journey complete, Warren relaxed and left Armando alone at the wheel. Dropping onto the main deck and approaching the others near the stern, he heard Myron ask, "You folks from the Midwest?"

"Texas," Bobby answered proudly.

Myron lit a cigarette and sucked smoke deep into his remaining lung. "Never been to Texas," he said. "Used to live in Hawaii. Got bent there twice. Once in '56 when we dove Molokini Crater - two hundred and fifty feet. Then again in '61 when I took one of Cousteau's people on a little two hundred foot swim. Threw up inside his regulator. Nearly fucking choked. Ever hear a Frenchman puke underwater?"

The Whites shook their heads.

"Kinda froggy, slurpy sounding. Makes you wanna gag." He bent forward and simulated gagging. "All I could think of later, when they laid me out in the recompression chamber, was that Frenchman puking and gagging. Took the hit to save him. Carry oxygen with me all the time now." He pointed to a tank on wheels, secured to the bulkhead with a multicolored elastic cord.

"How often do you get the bends?" Bobby inquired.

"Not once since I turned seventy," he bragged.

"Shoot," Bobby said.

Myron gazed off into space, mentally shifting gears. "September '68 I drilled my left testicle with a speargun."

"Oh!" cried Judy Ann. "Gross!"

Warren had heard this story several times, seen the remains one night when Myron got drunk. "I was at sixty feet doin' the splits over a crevice. Giant lobster wedged in just out of reach. I had this short little single-rubber gun." He held up the imaginary speargun pointed at his crotch. "Shouldn't of shot between my legs." He shook his head at the memory. "Big mistake. Course, I got the lobster. Twelve pounder."

"You expect us to believe that?" Bobby asked.

"Don't much care if you do."

Addressing all three of them in a commanding voice, Warren said, "We're leaving harbor now. Better see to your gear. Get things hooked up."

"When do we get there?" asked Judy Ann.

"Hour, more or less."

"This boat's too slow," she complained.

Warren returned to the pilothouse and found Rosa.

"They are okay?" she asked. She knew they took a toll on him. That his shoulders would be knots by evening and she'd spend the better part of an hour kneading and calming him down.

"No worse than usual, I guess." Warren fought to keep the tiredness from his voice.

"You should eat something," she said, by way of scolding him for drinking too much last night. "The boy has some bread here. Not fresh, but not hard."

"Later."

"There was a noise," she said, pointing. "Back there."

"I didn't hear anything."

"When I first went back. Under the deck."

Esteban, a wooden vessel built Norfolk, Virginia, in 1969, carried her age and abuse with greater difficulty each year. Her hull, fouled with barnacles, needed a good scraping and painting. The diesel's raw water pump was clogged with rust. Worst of all, the electric bilge pump had a short somewhere. Had to watch it on every trip. One minute it was running fine and the next it stopped.

Returning to the fantail, Warren lifted the hatch cover and dropped below the main deck into the dark, stifling engine compartment. He crawled forward on all fours, bilge water sloshing against his legs and soaking his trousers. The compartment smelled of oil, sludge, and decay. The pump, however, was working.

"What are you doin' down there?" came a voice from above.

Warren ignored the question.

"Engine sounds okay to me!" Bobby White shouted above the racket. "You ought to paint this tub. Costs enough to go out on it."

"Don't bother the captain," Bobby's wife cautioned.

White glared at his wife. "Slipshod outfit," he said. "Little Nigger kid's driving the boat while the so-called captain's down there lapping up another bottle of rum."

"Careful, Señor." Rosa came up behind him, placing her lips very close to his ear. Her voice hoarse with anger. "You are a guest on this boat. My son's name is Armando. You will not refer to him as a Nigger again or I will put you ashore myself."

Warren's head came up through the deck. "What's going on here?" he said, hearing only the last few words. Rosa's face dark.

"Bobby and your maid are having a little discussion," Judy Ann said with feigned interest.

"She's not my maid." Warren sounded worn out. "She's part of the crew. I think you both better go and sit down. Rosa, see if the boy needs anything."

Rosa's eyes never left Bobby White's reddening face until she turned and walked stiffly up the pilothouse steps.

"If you don't watch your mouth," Warren heard Myron say to Bobby, "you could end up with a missing testicle yourself."

Warren climbed out of the bilge and replaced the hatch cover. He was glad the boy had been in the pilothouse, unable to hear. Why hadn't he said something? It wasn't Myron's place to speak for him.

He reached the pilothouse, avoiding Rosa's eyes.

A moment later he felt her hands sliding up and down his back. She leaned close to him and whispered, "You are my man. Don't trouble yourself about these touristas." She brought her arms around, encircling his waist. "You will find a nice lobster when they are done. Tonight I will cook for you. Then we make love."

"Rosa. The boy."

Rosa laughed. A deep, gentle sound that always reminded Warren of home. There was a lot of his mother in Rosa.

She slapped his rump. "The boy knows more than you think," she said. "Anyway, soon time for him to learn. If he is going to be a man he must first learn about women."

"That's the dumbest thing I ever heard," Warren said.

Armando kept his eyes straight ahead, grinning at the azure sea.

"Watch your heading," Warren ordered.

The boy nodded, shifting his gaze to the hooded compass. He'd been allowed to stay at the helm through the channel. Captain Will may have enough confidence in him now to allow him to navigate all the way to Sting Ray Flats.

"What are you looking so smug about?" Warren asked.

Armando tried not to smile. He didn't know what smug meant.

"There are some pastries in the galley," Rosa informed them. "A day old, but I will serve them to our passengers and make fresh coffee."

"No," Warren said. "Make coffee but leave the rolls on the table in the salon. Serving gives these people the wrong idea."

"It's my work."

A kind of formless guilt seemed to have settled over Warren. He should've turned the boat around and taken the Whites back in. Given them a refund. Why hadn't he? "Today it's *our* job," he said to Rosa, and followed her down to the galley. Together they began setting out rolls and snacks on the salon table.

On the fantail, Myron wondered why the Whites hadn't bothered to attach their regulators or BCDs. "How long have you folks been diving?" he asked, struggling with his tank harness.

The Whites looked at each other. "This is our first time," Bobby whispered. "Keep still about it."

"You didn't tell Captain Will you're beginners?"

"Don't be dumb."

"You people are the dumb ones," Myron said. "Don't you think he's going to find out soon as he talks to you about it? Tell him. Chances are he'll get mad as hell either way, but if you confess he might let you snorkel at least."

"He ain't got nothin' to say about it," Bobby said. "We paid our money."

"It's his boat."

"Shut up, both of you," ordered Judy Ann. "I'll tell him."

She slipped off the short terrycloth robe she'd been wearing over her swimsuit, stood up and stretched. The one-piece suit plunged in front, had virtually no back and not much of a bottom. Myron drew a sharp breath, openly admiring Mrs. White's smooth buttocks. Bobby was pleased too, as if she were something he'd created.

Judy Ann scanned the fantail portion of the boat for Warren. "Where'd he go?"

"Up front," said her husband.

On the bow, Warren pounded his fist against a stubborn anchor clamp. Rosa had kicked him out of the galley for being clumsy and having dirty hands. Without warning, Judy Ann rubbed against his back and said, "Oh, pardon me. It's kind of bumpy up here."

"Then go sit down," Warren answered.

"Can I ask you something?"

"What?"

"You won't be mad at me?" She laughed. "I'm such a dope."

Warren kept his back to her.

"You'll think it's silly," she continued. "Happens all the time I'm sure, but we were just wondering, do you have to be, like, certified divers to dive here? Or can we just sort of learn on the job?"

"Are you telling me you don't know how to dive?" Warren sighed. It happened time and again. Scuba certification is required. Everyone knows it, like everyone knows you need a pilot's license to fly an airplane, but people like the Whites try to bluff through. Warren was tired of pointing out the dangers, tired of their sour looks and excuses.

"We did it in a swimming pool once," Judy Ann said. "In college. Bobby and

I met in college, you know."

Warren turned and looked at Mrs. White. Lord, the woman was nearly naked. "Don't worry about it," he said. "I'll give you a resort course, so you can make a couple shallow dives." Luckily the water over the Flats was no more than ten or fifteen feet deep inside the reef. Outside, it dropped thousands.

"Cool," she said. "I'll tell Bobby E."

"You can also tell him it's an extra fifty bucks per head for instruction."

"Oh!" she said. "He won't like that."

"I don't work for free. Teaching someone to dive is a lot of work." Especially someone like Bobby White. There wasn't enough money in the whole world. Suddenly, he thought of the letter. Time, his mother wrote. Time. This was how he spent it. Warren Wilson, underwater explorer. World traveler. Adventure seeker. Loser.

"Men are so stupid," Judy Ann told Bobby and Myron when she returned. "Captain Will was quite pleasant. Says he'll teach us to dive good enough for today."

"You're lucky," Myron said.

"We have to pay some extra," she said, adding hurriedly, "and I think that's only fair."

"You do?" Bobby looked up from studying his pinkish-white feet. "We've paid him enough," he said, but didn't seem interested in debate. "Say Myron, what's the story on this place we're going? Sting Ray Flats?"

"Huh?" Myron couldn't keep his eyes off Judy Ann. "I don't get you?"

"Funny name."

"Real name's Ragged Man Cove. Only been called Sting Ray Flats since Will brought the rays in."

"Brought 'em in?"

"Yeah. So you can feed 'em."

"So who can feed 'em?"

"Us." Myron was still feasting on Judy Ann's buttocks. "Nothing to it. Just don't stick your hand in too far."

"What?" Noting the subject of Myron's gaze. "Like my wife's ass?"

Myron blinked, reluctantly turned his head. "It's a corker," he said, grinning, unembarrassed.

Judy Ann, standing a short distance away, made no move to don her beach robe. Myron decided he wasn't the first to notice her buttocks. White had his hands full with that one.

"Not everyone gets to come here," Myron said to clear the air. "Took Will and me years to bring the rays in. There's not another spot like this on earth that I know of, except Sting Ray City in the Caymans. You'll be able to hand feed ten, maybe fifteen rays."

"Is this another dive story like your testicle?" White asked.

Myron began untying his swimsuit string.

"Never mind!" Judy Ann injected. "We believe you. Sounds dangerous, that's all."

"Well, it is," Myron said, relaxing, his integrity no longer in question. "These aren't some kind of zoo animals. What we got around here mostly is Southern stingrays. Not too big. Fifty to seventy pounds, wing spread of about four feet and maybe six feet long with the tail. Some smaller, some bigger."

"Aren't they poisonous?" Judy Ann asked, swinging around to sit opposite him on the plywood seat.

"Yep."

"Then why would the captain be fool enough to take us there?" White asked.

"I told you," Myron said. "He's got 'em trained to come in and hand-feed. Long as you don't provoke them, no problem."

Both Whites looked at him as if he were insane.

"Listen," he said. "Stingray's got one defensive weapon, a venomous dart-like spine gadget growing partway down his tail. Really pissed off ray can whip that baby right over his head and drive it through the planking of a boat. Or someone's head. You take a hit in the stomach, forget it, but most likely he won't use it. More people get hurt stepping on old ones washed up on the beach than ever get struck with one from a ray. Captain Will shows you how to keep the rays calm anyway. We never had anyone hurt in over ten years."

"What kind of venom's in the spine?" Judy Ann asked, unable to shake the image of a giant ray driving its spine deep into her pale flesh.

"Got me," Myron shrugged. "Like a snake, I guess. Heard of a Mexican kid one time dragging in a fish net. Ray was caught in it and drilled the kid in the stomach. Died in less than two hours. Does something to the muscle around the heart too. Shuts it down."

"Always fatal?"

"Naw. Saw this tourist in Hawaii thirty feet down on the sand. Ray put a spine in his leg. Hour later the poor bastard lost all control of his bodily functions, if you know what I mean." He looked at Judy Ann and smiled. "Next day I spotted the same guy drinking beer at one of the joints in Lahaina."

"That supposed to be comforting?"

Myron shrugged.

"This is a screwball outfit," Bobby White said.

"Have you fed the rays?" Judy Ann asked Myron.

"Hundreds of times. Capitan Will and me is pretty much partners."

"So you don't limit yourself to gazing at women's behinds," White offered. "Seems to me you're a little old for either one."

"Older the stag, stiffer the horn," Myron explained.

Hanging over the water, Warren walked the gunwale aft around the pilothouse to the stern, landing on deck with a catlike thump. "Would you like to snorkel or dive first?" he asked the Whites.

Ragged Man Cove took its name from the legend of a mysterious shipwrecked sailor who appeared many years ago and stood high on nearby limestone cliffs and warned certain people - those who could see him - of impending storms. The hard, porous cliffs reminded Warren of blackened Swiss cheese, and were undercut by the sea and tufted in sea grape and green vines, hanging like Pentecostal stoles above the water. There was no beach. Even the Whites fell silent as Armando throttled back the engine and *Esteban* glided onto the quiet water of the Flats.

"I've never seen water that color," Judy Ann said. "It's like looking into a jade swimming pool. Flawless, like..."

"Water," Bobby finished for her.

"You're so trite, Bobby E. There's not one teensy bit of romance in you."

Bobby wanted to dive and Judy Ann wanted to snorkel. The discussion was brief. They decided to do what Judy Ann wanted as the snorkeling would get them used to the water before trying scuba, and Warren agreed. It also postponed the encounter with the stingrays, but no one said that.

Myron, already suited up, opened *Esteban's* stern gate, paused a moment on the swim-step, then catapulted himself into the water with a somersault.

"Crazy old bastard," Bobby said.

After the Whites too had gone, Warren stood watching a moment. They swam toward a shallow, wave-beaten reef he'd recommended. Few suitable specimens there for the fish tank in the Whites' den. Judy Ann's rump stuck up almost as high as her snorkel. He couldn't decide whether she intended it to be admired or had just lost track of it.

"So," Rosa said behind him. "You admire the white woman's hinder?"

"Hinder?" Warren laughed. "Where'd you get hold of a word like hinder?"

"You make fun of my English?"

"Neither your English nor your hinder," he said, patting the latter.

More than a mile away, the 32-foot sport fisherman *L'Etrangere* cut her engines and drifted to a stop. Todd Slitter leaned back in the captain's chair, switching the key off with his naked toes at the same time he brought up a pair of high-powered binoculars and adjusted the focus. Known on the docks as Slither, Todd was extremely short and had to stretch his neck to see over the helm.

"Now I got him," he said, resting a pair of grimy elbows on the instrument console.

His companion, towering over him as he gripped an aluminum brace on the boat's Bimini top, didn't answer, only squinted in the direction of Sting Ray Flats. Too far away for him to see much with the naked eye.

Slither disliked the new man. Not the usual drifter Javert hired. This was, as the Americans said, "a serious dude." His accent clearly British. Physique overdeveloped by zealous exercise. Hard eyes. Colorless, thin lips. Focused and disciplined, even handsome in the way Slither thought a four-inch dagger was handsome.

"Get closer," the man ordered.

"Cool it, Comrade," he said in his best American slang. "You don't give me orders." He tossed the binoculars on a cushioned seat beside him. "I work for the fat man."

"Comrade?" The man smiled but there was no joy in it.

"You're the new one Javert shipped in, aren't you?"

"Shipped in?"

"Mercenary? Revolutionary? Whatever we're calling them this week." Slither's black eyes widened. "Maybe an off-shore political consultant?" Tickled at his own cleverness, he mouthed it again.

The man's face remained unmoved. He studied Slither as if he were a fly caught in his fist, then in a gentle, unhurried way, he picked the smaller man up by the front of his neck and the back of his pants, carried him to the rail and asked pleasantly, "Do you swim?"

Slither, to his own astonishment, croaked, "Yes. Quite well."

He struck the water face first, barely having time to close his eyes and draw a deep breath. He wasn't scared. Not really. He came up and cursed the man in Spanish, then called him a queer and a son-of-a-bitch in English.

He heard the engines start.

Slither was less than five feet from the boat.

"You're not going to leave me here?" he cried above the exhaust noise.

"I told you to move the boat closer," the man said, shoving both throttles forward. "Now I do it for you."

L'Etrangere surged ahead, spinning Slither in a circle and leaving him in its wake.

Again, Slither swore.

Like many Caribbean islands, Charming Island grew from violent upheavals in the earth's crust, leaving volcanic mountains ringed with shallow, underwater plateaus. These steep plateaus led to surrounding waters that dropped to incredible depths, even very near shore. Slither knew the rich blue color of the sea went on and on, three thousand fathoms down. Eighteen thousand feet of water beneath his pumping white legs.

Last year Captain Will caught and gaffed a shark nearly half the length of his boat. Slither had been one of the people standing on the dock that day when the Captain made port dragging the giant hammerhead alongside. He'd helped string the creature up by its tail and then gone home for his camera. He wondered how a beast like that looked in the water, swimming in circles around you. Or maybe you never saw it. Maybe it just blasted from the depths and ripped meat from your bones.

Captain Will told him once that sharks were overrated as killers. They were, he said, no more dangerous than any wild animal, like a bear in the woods. He knew he wasn't supposed to like Will. Javert and his crowd belittled him, but Slither found him fascinating. He knew the ocean and its underwater mysteries, diving there often, unafraid. Few people have enough sense to know how important this is. Slither even spoke against Javert's plan of persuading Captain Will to move the weapons over from Guadeloupe. No one listened. But his immediate problem was to survive the next few minutes. A problem the Englishman would soon share if he was lucky. He felt the small of his back for his dagger. It was there.

Uncertain of his ancestry, Slither spoke three languages fluently: Spanish when he swore, French when he made love, and English to figure things out. Solutions seemed more logical in English. Like now: Swim or tread water? If a shark comes, just as well to be eaten on the way back to the boat as hanging here like a useless jellyfish.

The Englishman had moved *L'Etrangere* about a quarter mile away, not an impossible swim. He might reach the boat with enough energy left to open the Englishman's stomach and uncoil his blue guts.

Spreading his short, muscular legs wide in the water, he thrust them together and began his swim with a powerful stroke. Arm muscles tightened as he dug handfuls of water and pushed them behind. The sea was reasonably calm and the tide with him. He swam steadily toward the boat, a white speck against the dark cliffs riding up and down like a fisherman's bobber.

On board *L'Etrangere*, the Englishman had his back to the open sea and the binoculars trained on Sting Ray Flats.

* * *

Isn't it odd, Warren thought, how sometimes the greatest achievements come so easily, like feeding the rays. He took no credit for it. The stingrays themselves initiated contact. More accurately, one ray. Elmo. (Named after an uncle.)

A decade ago he sat on the sand in twenty feet of water for the better part of an hour watching Elmo sleep, though he wasn't Elmo yet then. The shallow water made it possible for him to stay a very long time. When Elmo awoke he wasn't frightened by the sight of a man kneeling there. Instead, seemed curious and flapped his rippling wings and rose from the bottom, streaming sand like snow from the roof of a speeding car. Warren held very still. Elmo circled and then without warning came straight on, gliding swiftly at Warren's head. He put a hand up to fend him off but the ray was not deterred by this and angled his body so the hand brushed along his white underside, receiving a stroke. The skin was dry, smooth, and cool. The touch sent shivers of haunting recognition along Warren's back and the ray sensed something too, because he banked and returned for another caress. And so it began.

Over the years Warren established strict criteria for bringing tourists to feed the rays. His instructions were obeyed without question or the encounter was terminated. There were now between fifteen and twenty rays coming regularly onto the flats to feed. They relished the iced baitfish Warren brought, demonstrating the same trust and lack of fear first displayed by Elmo.

Like most great discoveries, feeding the rays was simple. Slide a baitfish between the forefinger and middle finger, hold the hand aloft, the ray closes its large mouth around the hand and sucks the fish up into its teeth. A ray's mouth is positioned underneath, teeth recessed up inside. No one lost a finger or suffered a sting from a tail spine. The only danger seemed to be the ray's unfamiliarity with human anatomy. Rays often opened their mouths and attempted to swallow someone's head. One of the reasons for the tight knot in Warren's ponytail.

"Do they have names?" Judy Ann asked. All three of them sat in a row along the swim step, their feet dangling in the warm jade water. Warren in the middle.

"Yes," he said, pleased she'd asked. With names they became individuals, harder to kill. "There's one called Darth Vader. He's coal black on top. Whiter than the others underneath. The only one I've seen with that coloring."

"Is he more dangerous than the others?"

"They're all wild animals." A little fear is a healthy thing.

Warren's fear of teaching the Whites to dive never materialized. They were quick learners. Even Bobby E. In itself proof that anyone can scuba.

There hadn't however, been a ray in sight when they finished the lessons. They'd come to the flats too early, he explained, but that was only partially true. While the rays did prefer to feed later in the afternoon, they also gathered almost anytime they heard his boat, and he knew they could distinguish his engine noise from any other.

"I'm going in for another look," he told the Whites. "I'll swim out and lie on the bottom awhile. Once you see they've come and started feeding, ease into the water and join me. Don't forget the bait. Keep it in the plastic containers until it's time to feed, then take out just one baitfish at a time. Hold it up like I showed you."

Water closed over his head and he sank. A swift transition, gas to liquid, clamor to serenity. Years ago, Ruth Van Doren said diving was returning to the womb, rediscovering the liquid quiet and security lost when we're born. He'd made fun of her. He accepted the sea's embrace in nothing more than a faded swimsuit, galvanized steel tank and four-pound weight belt. The old UDT knife Freddie-the-Frogman had once given him, strapped to his calf. No wet suit or buoyancy control device or dive computer, now common among well-equipped divers.

Warren inhaled. Dry air hissed. He drew in enough to fill his lungs and bring his body off the bottom. The slightest motion of his fins and he glided ahead, leaving *Esteban's* dark hull behind, a shadow against the sun. He noticed again that the reef fish seemed skittish, but he saw nothing out of the ordinary. No large predators about. Without thinking, he reached down and patted the knife.

On the sand, a few kicks further along, he spotted a large conch. It was old. Grass like slippery green feathers grew on its weathered shell. The claws of the hermit crab that carried it kicked up sand as in a desert. What compulsive journey, he wondered, drove the crab on, dragging its armor? A doorstop in the Whites' bathroom if it came within Bobby's grasp.

Lately too, there'd been a disease among the black sea urchins. He'd found piles of dead ones rolling like tumbleweeds along the sand. Warren closed his fist on a handful of the sand. Pink. Flaming scarlet. Golden amber. Shades of pearl and blue. Unique as snowflakes. Grains that were really bits of coral, ancient fish, conchs and crabs, polished green glass, spines of dead urchins, maybe the bleached bones of Reggie Wilson. Remnants of history. Someday, God willing, his bones too. Opening his hand, it slipped through his fingers.

The first stingray, a large brown, came along as if by happenstance, gliding near the bottom in casual arcs until it reached the spot where Warren waited. Warren raised his hand, as he'd done that very first time with Elmo, in what looked now like a greeting. The brown came in, pushing with his nose and brushing his body against it. With his other hand Warren held the baitfish. The ray's cool, rubbery lips slid over the hand nearly to the wrist and vacuumed the fish up into the grinding teeth.

Sound travels many times faster in water than air. Warren heard the Whites before he saw them, swimming in lurches along the bottom clanging their gear. Attracted to the noise, more rays arrived. With stingrays suddenly surrounding them, the Whites seemed unable to function, ducking their heads, crouching and flinching. Streams of eeks escaping Judy Ann's regulator.

Hoping they would calm down and follow his example, Warren rested on his knees, allowing rays to swoop and pivot around him like rubber eagles. He counted eleven. Not a bad showing. Darth Vader was with them but no sign of Elmo. This disturbed him further. Elmo was often the first to arrive and played long after the bait was gone and the other rays retreated to the depths. Elmo, slowed by age and flecked with pale scars, might be injured or ill. The unlucky recipient of a fisherman's spear? Something more ominous?

Rippling sunlight, magnified by the water, danced on the sand and the backs of the circling rays. A rare marriage of man, beast, and paradise. The Whites set aside their fear and gave in to fascination, fumbling with the plastic containers, shoving the baitfish into the ray's mouths. For once in their lives, Warren thought, they're totally occupied with something besides themselves. Who can place a hand inside the grinding mouth of a wild animal, caress its cool hide, see the look of acceptance and trust in its black eyes and go away unmoved? It's a peek back to the beginning of time. Why did the stingray, one of the most ancient of creatures, choose this place to come and mingle? He only knew how really impossible it was, and how likely sooner or later, somebody would screw it all up.

He studied Bobby White's movements. Stripped of pretense and Texas bravado, he swung his torso from one diving ray to the next, excited hands feeding, stroking, pointing. Warren heard him shrieking with muffled delight inside his regulator - "Guk! Guk!" Judy Ann, fewer than fifteen feet away, ignored him. She'd adopted Darth Vader, pushing the others aside to stuff fish into his mouth. The black ray responded by coming in low over the sand, running his white underside along the full length of her kneeling body. She trembled with anticipation, then fear, then fulfillment. No matter what happened on the rest of their vacation, these were the moments the Whites would remember. This was the story they'd repeat again and again. A long-term memory. He had shown them something.

An hour slipped by without notice.

Back on board *Esteban* with their air supply finally exhausted, it was Bobby White, pink belly pressed against the gunwale, who summed it up best: "I felt like they wanted to be our friends." His bushy eyebrows glistened with drying salt. "Do people know about this?"

"For sure!" Judy Ann said. "Shouldn't this be in, like, National Geographic or something?"

"I've been trying to keep it quiet," Warren said.

The Whites exchanged a look.

From the salon doorway, Myron belched loudly and addressed them. "How'd you like the rays?" He had been alone, diving the caves and undercuts near shore instead. Unknown even to Warren, he'd managed to coax several green moray eels into accepting food by hand, a surprise he planned for Warren when there weren't any tourists around.

"You people don't know what you've got here," Bobby White enlightened. "This thing's a gold mine."

Judy Ann nodded. Years of tending the aquarium gave her unique insight.

"Too many people know about it already," Warren complained.

"You're looking at this from the wrong perspective," Bobby said indulgently. "I'm in security back in Texas. Security systems. We tell our customers one thing: the best-kept secret is the one everybody knows."

"Is it?"

Bobby had seen looks like the one on Warren's face a thousand times before. In selling security systems your main job was education, not sales. "Let me ask you, ever seen a house with one of those eyeball crime watch stickers on the front door?"

"Yep." It was Myron who answered.

"People have those stickers for one reason, to tell crooks that everything inside is listed with the PD. All the serial numbers are recorded. It ain't worth the trouble trying to fence. Get it? The best-kept secret is the one everybody knows."

"What's that got to do with stingrays?"

"Instead of trying to keep everyone from finding out, you should be advertising. Tell the world. Then nobody'd dare bother your rays, see? They'd be a national treasure." He smiled triumphantly. "And you'd be one rich dude."

"The rays couldn't survive all that," Warren said. "Hundreds, maybe thousands of people coming here."

"That's a risk you've got to take."

"No," Warren said. "It's not."

"We got our own way of doing things," Myron added. "To me it's like standing in a field at the end of a runway, see, and planes fly just over my head so I can pet their bellies."

"You're nuts," Bobby said, then shrugged indifferently. "Maybe y'all should take a trip back to the States now and again for a recharge."

"Bobby E. gives seminars on self-motivation in the security industry," Judy Ann told them. "He's thinking about doing a video."

"Probably be a big seller in Texas," Myron said.

"Rosa's making lunch," Warren said to change the subject. "Armando's snorkeling for fresh conch. There's lemonade in the cooler. Maybe you'd like to snorkel around until it's ready."

"So you're not interested in hearing my ideas for this place?" Bobby tried one last time.

"No," Warren assured him. "Let's leave things like they are. I ask everyone who comes here to keep quiet about it. Less talk the better."

"Sure," Bobby said, straight-faced.

CHAPTER TEN

The last hundred yards Slither did the breaststroke. Slipping silently onto the teakwood swim step he drew the knife from its sheath at the small of his back. It would be like that time in Port-au-Prince. Then, it was a big man too, and he died like a sow.

Slither brought his head up level with the stern gunwale, holding his breath, praying the Englishman had eyes only for the flats and had forgotten he'd left him to drown. Slither peered inside the boat.

A moving wall of flesh blurred his vision. An alarming thud. His head smashing against the stern, blinding pain. He heard the Englishman's high-pitched laugh. Trying to think what had happened, he sat stunned, staring at the man's bare chest. Only then did he think of the knife and bring his hand up. It crushed against the gunwale under the Englishman's heel. There was a popping noise. Bones breaking. The knife clattered onto the swim step, found a crack, and disappeared beneath the water.

"I have no wish to do you further damage," said the Englishman. "Remain quiet."

Slither lost his courage. "Fine," he muttered, dangling his broken hand in the water to cool it.

"Too bad about your hand," the Englishman said pleasantly. "I'm not fond of knives."

Slither stared at the man's wide, ruddy face. "Who are you, anyway?"

"Wesley Bens. Big Ben, if you like," he said. "Some find that amusing."

Slither feigned a smile. So far, there was nothing amusing about Big Ben. "What are you doing here?" Slither asked. "The fat man has plenty of Big Bens already. What's he need you for?"

"Good thinking," Big Ben said, glad to see Slither exhibiting such mental agility. "I'm a scuba diver."

"Ah!" Now he understood. "So we're taking the stories of Captain Will's treasure more seriously these days."

"You do not?"

"Let's say I'm skeptical."

"Why?"

"Years ago, when I first came to this island from Port-au-Prince, I heard the story of the *Imperial*," Slither said. "The lost French warship loaded with cannon and gold. Fairy tales."

"Mr. Javert doesn't share your skepticism," the Englishman replied. "He wants this wreck examined and anything of value removed. Then we destroy it so your Captain Will cannot make it some kind of protected diving site and persuade this weak government to abandon ideas of blowing a hole in the reef to bring in cruise ships. I also have other talents he admires. Those I acquired in Havana."

"Do you mind if I get inside the boat?" Slither thought his sarcasm brave under the circumstances. His hand throbbed and he wanted to elevate it. He was beyond caring what the Englishman thought.

"By all means," said Big Ben. "We're both employed by the same firm. Come into the salon and let me take a look. I have first-aid training."

Before Slither could protest, the big man hoisted him over the stern as easily as he'd thrown him overboard before, but gently, almost kindly.

Inside the salon, Big Ben examined the broken hand. "The pinky," he said, bending over the small Formica table on which Slither's hand rested uneasily. "I think the ring finger, also. This may be painful."

Swiveling in his seat, the Englishman put his back to Slither and pinned the broken hand to the table. Clearly, from the way the pinky drooped at the knuckle, the finger was badly broken. Without warning, Big Ben pinched the knuckle and pulled. It popped.

Slither screamed.

Just as the scream reached its height, the man gripped the next finger. It seemed to come apart and snap back together like a plastic toy. The pain was beyond the range of Slither's vocal cords. He settled for a low moan.

"Shhh," cautioned Big Ben, in a motherly tone.

Slither nodded, sweating. What possessed him to placidly give this man his hand? Undoubtedly their history of comradeship.

The Englishman taped the two fingers together with sticky, black electrical tape. "This should hold it." He seemed pleased with his work. "Bones knit rather quickly, don't they?"

Slither drew his first full breath in some time and closed his eyes. "I need to rest awhile," he said, falling back on the vinyl cushion.

"Of course," said his companion, genuine concern in his voice. "I'll fix you a spot of tea."

"Just what I need." He squinted at him from under the table.

The Englishman drew fresh water and placed it on the small galley stove to heat. Slither marveled at the large man's deft movements around the small galley, slipping cups from the cupboard, searching for sugar, opening the silverware drawer, humming while he worked. Slither's hand throbbed, forcing his eyes shut again.

He passed out for awhile, came to staring at the Englishman's broad back. He'd given the fat man years of loyal service. How like him now to put this Castro-trained goon in charge. How typical to end up flat on his back while the man who hurt him hummed a Bob Marley tune and made tea. Slither closed his eyes again. There was a new day coming and he'd be ready.

"Our friends have finally left the flats," the Englishman observed. "Would there be any crackers about, do you think?"

"Chips," Slither answered, sitting up.

"Chips?"

"Bag under the sink."

Big Ben came up with a large bag of American made potato chips and held them to the light as one might hold the tail of a dead rat. "Onion and dill pickle?" he said.

"Fat man's hooked on 'em. Has them flown in from the States."

"Oh, my!"

"You get used to them," Slither remarked. "Aren't you afraid Captain Will spotted us so close in like this?" He'd been wanting to ask this question since the Englishman first told him to move the boat, but things had gotten out of hand.

"I wanted him to see us."

"Why?"

"I wanted him to know what it's like to be stalked."

"That makes no sense," Slither said, swinging his feet to the floor.

"Fear, my little friend. We are making the Captain afraid of what he doesn't know or understand. Frightened men make mistakes."

"Ha!" Slither slapped his good hand against the table. "You don't know Captain Will. He won't be frightened. He's more likely to come over here and run a spear through your muscular torso."

"I believe the tea is ready," the Englishman replied. "You overestimate the Captain's powers, and his courage." He served the steaming cups. Onion and dill pickle chips lay in neat rows around the saucers.

"You're wrong," he said flatly, hardly caring if he took a hit for it or not. "No man who faces a shark half the size of this boat and kills it is lacking courage. Be careful you aren't next to be gaffed."

"I've no fear of Americans," said the Englishman, but Slither saw the muscles tighten along his jawline.

It was Slither's turn to smile. "You are a communist then?" he asked.

No answer.

"Of course you are a communist," he went on. "Hasn't anyone told you? Communism is over. Ha! The cowardly Americans beat them at their own game and now have them eating McDonald's hamburgers like everyone else."

"Not in Cuba."

"So you are a communist?"

"Don't I look like a communist?"

Slither said nothing. Whatever scruples or politics the man had, he was no slave to ideology. Money might motivate him, but he was a brute, a monster, and whatever drove him, it wasn't devotion to some failed system in Cuba, last starving bastion of communism in the Western Hemisphere. Even the Russians had embraced détente. Slither shivered. He knew how to watch his back, and success didn't always go to the strong. This Englishman, for all his power and self-confidence, was vulnerable. But right now he feared him.

"I've nothing against communists," Slither said. "No doubt you're worth whatever the fat man's paying. How often can he find a man who's both a communist and a scuba diver - a man who can bring up treasure and rid the island of the Brits? And is one himself. Appeals to Javert's sense of irony, I'm sure."

"Your sarcasm bores me," the man said. "Keep still and drink your tea."

But he couldn't keep still. His future was tied to Javert, and the success of Javert's ambitions. Pain gave him courage to speak. "A referendum on independence is coming soon. You help in this?"

"I will help throw off the yoke of British colonialism," affirmed the man from Britain.

"And replace it with Castro?"

"Socialist revolutions return power to the people."

It was all Slither could do to keep from laughing. Grown men no longer believed such nonsense. "We're going to finance the revolution with Captain Will's treasure?"

"Don't be daft," said the Englishman, sipping his tea - the teacup nearly lost inside his massive hand.

"Then why spy on Captain Will?"

"What did Javert tell you? You've been watching the Captain yourself for months, have you not?"

"Yes," Slither said. "I do what I'm told. Fat man never seemed too worried if I saw anything or not. Many times Captain Will took his boat out and I was not told to follow. Javert does business with the Captain. Maybe he thought he was being cheated. I don't know."

"Then continue to do what you are told."

"The fat man knows he can depend on me," Slither said, "but his preoccupation with politics is dangerous. Captain Will never mixes in politics, so why spy on him? Why try and frighten him?"

The Englishman considered these questions but the answer was slow in coming. "Perhaps," he said at last, "we will have need of another boat one day."

"There are a hundred boats better than Captain Will's on this island," Slither asserted.

The Englishman placed his cup and saucer on the galley table. "Enough questions," he said.

Slither saw something in his eyes that reminded him of the shark Captain Will gaffed that day - a kind of pitiless stare that even in death had made him shiver.

"Raise the anchor," Bens ordered.

"With a broken hand?"

"Use the other while you have it."

Elmo was late arriving on the flats. He'd dallied too long with the young female after *Esteban's* unique sound waves washed against his sensitive skin. The boat had gone. Four younger rays patrolled the stretches of sand, swimming aimlessly. A hundred yards farther on Darth Vader, his appetite inflamed by the hand feeding, flopped against the seabed grinding a conch beneath him.

The falling sun, its brilliance reflected away at the surface, angled into the water, scattering soft green light along the sand. Elmo had gone without food since early morning. Though quite capable of feeding himself, he'd grown dependent on *Esteban's* easy pickings. No stubborn shells to crush or crabs to open. No tireless hunting.

The boat had gone. The mysterious sputtering and knocking noises no longer audible. No sign of the man with the ponytail. Everything was quiet. Surge worked the small purple sea fans and swept the blueheads to and fro outside their coral doorways. A spotfin butterfly fish, distinctive black stripe slicing its eye top to bottom, darted along, fanlike yellow tail and fins in sharp contrast with its pearl-white body. A short distance behind, a trumpetfish positioned itself to appear as part of the meager growth of soft coral sustained on the shallow bottom. Things on the flats were returning to normal.

Elmo glided to a stop and settled onto the sand. With a movement that set his entire body rippling, he fanned the sand into a tight cloud that rose above him. An instant later he ceased all movement and the sand fell back over his body, covering him completely. Only his breathing spiracles remained exposed. They drew water in, extracted the oxygen and passed it out the gills underneath his body. Elmo was invisible.

On the flats and inside the cove there is always eating and killing. Day creatures. Night creatures. Monotonous noises of parrotfish gnawing the hard corals with oversized incisors. Squeaking lobsters wrestling in the sand. Sometimes whales, miles away, bellow like cattle. Only the sound of men can nourish terror.

L'Etrangere slid onto the flats, a long dark shadow eclipsing the white sand - Wesley Bens at the helm. The twin engines purred in harmony and gradually stopped.

"Tend the anchor," Bens commanded.

Slither kicked at the rigging, cursed and held his sore hand tight against his chest. You give some asshole a pair of throttles and the next thing you know he's Captain Queeg. "It's stuck."

"Bend over and work it."

Slither worked it. The chain rattled and the anchor crashed into the sea. "What are we doing here? Feeding the rays?" Everyone on the island knew Captain Will's so-called secret.

The Englishman smiled and disappeared down the ladder from the flying bridge only to emerge a moment later gripping two M-16s. "American," he said, raising them above his head. "Here." He tossed over one of the weapons.

"What am I supposed to do with this?" Slither asked, genuinely confused. "Everybody's gone." He half imagined the maniac was going to pace off a few feet and suggest they have a shoot-out.

"You're familiar with this weapon?"

Guns were unpredictable and noisy. Slither preferred knives. "I'd much rather have my SRK."

"Watch closely," the Englishman ordered, snatching one of several ammunition clips stuck in the waistband of his shorts. "Insert the clip so." He jammed it home. "Fire only short bursts. Don't jerk the trigger. Fire from the shoulder, not the hip."

Slither leaned his weapon against the lifeline. "Nothing to shoot at."

Bens flipped him a clip. "The rays," he said.

Catching the clip one-handed, Slither couldn't hide his amazement. "Why? Doesn't make sense."

"We're going to reduce the Captain's assets." Bens shrugged as if he knew of better ways. "Javert wants use of the Captain and his boat. This will persuade him not to change his mind."

"No!" Slither shook his head vigorously. "It will enrage him."

"Load your weapon. I've several coolers of fish. We'll bait them in close and shoot them at the surface. I don't know how easily they die."

Eyes alight with pleasure and anticipation, Bens upended a cooler of what smelled like rotten bait into the crystal sea. Slither looked on in disbelief.

"Pick up your weapon," Bens ordered.

"You can see it's impossible for me to fire with only one hand, even if I wanted to."

"Pick it up."

"No."

"I can make you."

"As you wish. I can't hold a machine gun and I won't kill the rays." Slither dropped butt first to the deck and grasped his wounded hand firmly, ready for the consequences.

"You have more courage than I thought, little man." The Englishman laughed. "Help me with the bait at least," he continued good-naturedly.

At first the rays seemed oblivious to the feeding. Maybe they take bait only by hand, Slither thought. This amused him.

The Englishman cursed. "Where are they?"

"Captain Will has them trained. They come only for him." The rays might escape slaughter.

Bens beat the butt of his M-16 against the deck, hoping the sound might attract them. He paused, peering into the water, then pounded again. "I'll get my gear and go after them one at a time if I have to," he threatened.

"Look what's happening to your bait," Slither teased.

Dozens of sergeant majors, porkfish, grunts, and a host of others thrashed the water, devouring the bait. There wasn't a stingray among them.

An instant later two dark shadows glided across the sand. The reef fish disappeared. "There!" The Englishman pointed, forgetting for a second his M-16.

When the two rays drew almost abreast of the boat Bens fired a quick burst at each. The water foamed white momentarily hiding the rays swimming beneath. But they either didn't hear the gunfire or chose to ignore it. Both rays, unharmed, swam beneath the boat and circled back again. "It's not even ten feet deep," Bens complained, glaring at the machine gun. "Lousy piece of shit."

Slither could no longer suppress his glee. "You Cuban guerrillas are bad dudes!" This phrase, partially taken from a movie and spoken in his heavy Caribbean accent, opened the floodgates and his shoulders shook with laughter.

Once again the Englishman's disarming calm surprised him. "These small caliber American bullets travel poorly through water. There's another way," Bens observed dryly.

Rummaging belowdecks, Bens came up with a handful of large hooks and a ten-foot length of PVC. Using bits of wire he attached the hooks to the top side of the pipe at evenly spaced intervals. He baited the hooks and lowered the PVC on lead-weighted ropes several inches below the surface. "There," he said finally. "They will be nearly out of the water when they take the bait."

Despite his repugnance of the plan, Slither edged closer to see if the rays could be fooled into taking the risk. Would they actually come to the surface and feed?

He didn't have long to wait. The two circling rays took an immediate interest in the baited PVC, swimming first beneath it then alongside, end to end. Bens held his fire, though the rays were now less than two feet below the surface. First one, then the other rose and took the bait. Bens waited. A third arrived. When all three were feeding, he climbed onto the gunwale and sprayed them with steady fire. This time the water frothed white, then red.

Two died instantly. The third spun like a tattered kite to the bottom, trailing blood.

Uncharacteristically, Bens shook his weapon above his head and yelled. Slither's eyes remained glued to the water, where a large shadow nearly the width of the boat had suddenly appeared and rose slowly, purposefully from the sand.

Elmo's ascent was slow and steady. He positioned his body carefully, achieving just the right trajectory to deliver the poisonous projectile in his tail. The dark enemy was large, silhouetted clearly against the light. No chance of a miss.

An instant later Elmo struck, driving the spine deep into the boat's hull. It punched the gleaming fiberglass and the boat lurched. Bens, thrown off balance, corrected in time to save himself but not his M-16. It pitched into the sea and was lost.

Slither's first thought was *Jaws*. He'd read the book, seen the movie, read the book again. Never dreamed any ocean creature could attack a boat anywhere but Hollywood. Attack a man in the water, certainly. But not a boat. This ray was trying to kill them. He attacked the boat not for something done to him, but because of something done to other animals. That showed planning and cunning - a range of other concepts he didn't associate with animals.

"Let's get out of here," he told Bens.

"Give me the other M-16."

"Are you crazy? It attacked the boat. We might be sinking right now!"

"The weapon!"

As happens sometimes with large stingrays, Elmo's tail was equipped with two poisonous spines instead of just one. He circled wide off the boat's port beam and prepared for a second attack.

Bens climbed onto the gunwale again with the M-16.

Elmo came as before, an angled attack allowing his speed to build gradually until he reached the target. Guided by fierce instinct, this highly intelligent animal clearly identified his enemy, the boat, and would persist in his attack until it died. Elmo aimed the second spine for a portion of hull less than six inches from the first. A concentration of poison to disable such a large, formidable enemy.

Bens wrapped one arm around a stanchion to secure himself, aiming the M-16 at Elmo's rising form. Forcing himself to wait, he let the ray come almost near enough to touch. Its size was staggering, a wing span nearly equal to *L'Etranere's* entire 12-foot width, like photos he'd seen of the American stealth bomber. In the clear water Bens could see Elmo's black eyes set on either side of his tapered head. They were unblinking and determined. The beast showed no fear, coming straight for the boat, straight down the barrel of the M-16.

Machine gun fire shattered the air, tearing at the water. Thunk! The boat rocked.

"Bullets won't stop it!" Slither shrieked.

Blood boiled up close to the boat on both sides. "I got him," Bens said softly.

Time seemed suspended.

Thunk!

Again the boat rocked.

"How many spines do these fucking things have?" Slither asked.

"No," Bens answered. "It's another one. See? A black one."

Darth Vader, like Elmo, had two tail spines. He'd delivered the first quite accurately into the boat's hull near the keel. He circled now for a new attack. But Bens was ready. He fired earlier this time, his bullets catching the ray squarely behind the head, sawing into his slick flesh, mushrooming, chopping him to pieces. In the mindless throes of death, Darth Vader's tail came out of the water one last time and thrashed at its enemy. It was only luck that the long, sharp spine nailed Wesley Bens' foot to the gunwale. Darth Vader's inert body drifted lazily to the bottom, seeping blood.

Even Slither had to admit that Bens demonstrated great courage. With both hands, he grasped the tail spine and tried to pull it out. Unfortunately, the spine had entered through the top of his foot and exited the bottom, nailing it quite securely to the gunwale.

"A pliers," Bens gasped.

Slither obeyed, more out of curiosity then fear of anything Bens was capable of at present. It would've been simple to slip a knife between the big man's ribs and have done with it. He hoped he wouldn't later regret his decision to get the pliers instead.

CHAPTER ELEVEN

The butchery at Stingray Flats remained secret for less than a day, and when it came to light it was Warren who took the blame. Lester Ebanks, a fisherman, and his son Edward discovered the slaughtered rays an hour after Javert's men had vanished. Sharks and hundreds of smaller reef fish were feeding on the remains. This frenzy in the water convinced the Ebanks something significant had taken place. They told the story in a harbor café and it came to the attention of Carmen Asenjo, an onion picker who lived in a shack not far from the flats. She'd heard strange noises that afternoon she said, like fireworks. "Ah!" Carmen said, "Gunshots." Who could've done such a thing?

So the rumor was born that Warren, who everyone knew swam with the rays, had become angry when they refused to perform for the tourists and shot them. An evil act against nature and the sea. It explained the bad luck many fishermen were having.

Esteban blew smoke as Warren sailed back to the Flats at full speed. The rumors couldn't be true.

Once there, he saw nothing at first. The sea cleaned its own mess and left little evidence of slaughter. He donned scuba and swam below.

The water felt foreign to him. A cherished place; now altered, unfamiliar.

On the sand, not far from each other, he discovered two tails, one still attached to a partially devoured carcass. A short distance away, an M-16 rifle. The carcass was unidentifiable but its tail was missing both defense spines. The other tail still had one spine in place - a third. Two sand sharks remained, swimming lazy circles just at the edge of his visibility. Satiated, no doubt. He picked up the M-16, the tail with one spine, and swam to the surface.

He tossed the tail and rifle aboard and pushed himself up onto the swim step, unbuckled his tank and slid it along the deck, then flung his fins after it. The tail was Vader's. It contained an extra, small spine. He'd never seen another ray so equipped. Now it lay alongside the machine gun, and was of similar color and size. Two weapons, he thought - one manufactured, one natural. Both deadly. He stood, raised the swim step and fastened it across the stern, then slumped onto the plywood bench. The animals, he knew, must've been defending themselves against the human attackers.

A tightness grew inside his chest. Who sent this kind of message? Not Javert, or superstitious fishermen. The senselessness frightened Warren a little, concealing the path for his anger. He stared at his feet and said, "I'll kill the bastards myself when I find them." And he knew just how he'd do it.

By the time Warren arrived to investigate, rumors that he'd been responsible were so exaggerated he should've laughed them off. Instead, they'd deepened his depression. He was responsible, as if he'd fired the shots. He'd tinkered with nature. Created neutral ground on the flats where man and beast came together, and inevitably, man exploited the animal's trust. Even sharks often flee when they encounter men in the water.

Later that day, he tried to explain this to Rosa. "Might as well take Javert's deal," he said. "At least we won't have to grub for money. Screw this subsistence living. I'm tired of it. Yesterday was bad, today is worse."

"It has not occurred to you perhaps Javert killed the rays?" Rosa spoke firmly.

They stood together on the sparsely furnished veranda of their tin-roofed cottage at the base of Dunnmore Mountain. The house, reached by a narrow gravel drive, was cloaked in lush vegetation and well hidden from the main road.

Rosa leaned on the wooden railing, lit a thin, dark cigar and studied him. Blue smoke curled into the windless air as the heavens opened and a sudden downpour beat the bushes with its fury. Raindrops pounded the tin roof and washed red gullies in the rich volcanic soil of the yard. She was sure she knew her man. "You are not guilty of this thing. Javert tricked you."

"So what?" Warren said more loudly, staring purposefully across the yard at a stand of plantains gushing water from their giant split leaves. "Maybe it's time I start letting him trick me. It pays."

"Evil always pays," she said flatly.

"Please, Rosa. Don't moralize."

"So you will become a smuggler now?" Her voice distant and musical, like part of the rain. "Armando will have criminal for a father?"

"I'm not his father."

"In his mind you are."

"The boat will be mine again and we'll have five thousand cash."

She turned and leaned lightly against the railing, her back to the rain. She wore a faded red blouse and simple straight skirt of crepe-like material that hugged her hips. The skirt was a creamy beige. Her feet were bare. "Tell me what we will do with this money."

He shrugged. He hadn't thought that far into it, and just wanted her to agree for once.

"Buy your truck?" she asked. "Clothes for me?" She twirled in a circle. "Parade down High Candle Street in designer blue jeans? You rent an office in one of the new hotels, buy a cellular telephone. Little cappuccino cups and saucers so I can serve Javert and his friends when they come to talk business with you. Que fino!"

"Shut up," he said. "I know the downside as well as you. I got to do something. Play it smart for once. You can't handle that, find another man. Shouldn't be fooling around with white boys anyway."

"Talk sense, hombre."

"If life made sense somebody would've figured it out long ago. "

"Somebody did," she said angrily. Rosa's strict Pentecostal beliefs surfaced only periodically, but always with volcanic result.

"I won't argue religion with you," he said. Warren thought the Brits pretty fair rulers, lousy missionaries. One steepled Anglican church on the island faithfully attended by a handful of white people, but dozens of clapboard Pentecostal meeting houses with peeling paint, jammed each Sunday with gyrating, hymn-singing islanders. Even the demise of Jimmy Swaggart, who'd walked in the shadow of God, didn't shake their faith. An irony of the Caribbean: British government, American religion, African music, and not a single murder since 1937.

"Why argue? Better we make love, no?" She rested her hand lightly on his arm. "Too much death."

"Huh?"

"Your mother."

"Oh."

Rosa's African heritage was strong in her - broad-shouldered, tall, large hands and feet - and a pride he never opposed. At the same time the gentleness with which she caressed him was more feminine than any woman he'd known. The timbre of her voice was powerful. "I love you," she said. "I have not questioned you. This thing with your mother is not a thing I like." She rubbed her body against him. "Tell me why you hate her."

"Don't be stupid. I don't hate her."

"She dies. You find out in a letter. You show more emotion when you pay *Esteban's* fuel bill. Am I blind? Stupid?"

They were close and her breath touched his cheek. "I'm sorry. It's something I don't talk about.

"Another woman you don't talk about. Lose a fight you don't talk about it. Your mother? The woman who gave you life?" She drew him still closer. "Your mother is your mother."

He thought of orange peel whenever he inhaled her scent. "It won't make sense to you."

"I am stupid?"

"No." He slid from her arms and backed against the porch rail. "Long before I came here I had some trouble in Santo Domingo. I told you. My life went to hell, that's all. One day I woke up and knew I was another person. Changed my name to Will when I came here. This Warren my mother loved is dead. Dried up." He turned away. "Nobody lives in the past, Rosa."

"Not you, huh? You have some trouble, you forget your mama?"

"I told you you wouldn't understand."

"Esplain it."

"I can't! I just needed the separation. That was then, this is now. I was that, now I'm this."

"Coño!" she swore. "You are politician or a man?"

"Rosa!"

"When will there be this money from Javert?"

"When the job's done. I move the cargo from —"

"No." She moved close again and covered his mouth with a long slender hand. "Tell me nothing."

He nodded.

She looked deep into his eyes. "You love your mother?"

"Yes," he said. "I've explained before. Got my brother killed when we were just kids. Instead of making something of myself, I made a mess of the life he saved for me. You don't go home after that."

She slipped into his arms. "Home *is* where you go," she said. "You are home now."

"You're my woman again?"

Her lips opened and he felt her hunger. Outwardly placid, Rosa's passion was always surprising, deep-rooted in love, proven by strength. He never questioned it or the shame it brought her. Life with Warren ran against the strict teachings of her faith. "I know this is hard on you," Warren had said years ago. "Should we marry?"

"Do what seems right to you," she'd answered.

"In my heart, we're already joined."

His answer was a disappointment. An easy answer, like the one he now gave Javert. They never spoke of marriage again. Of Javert they would speak.

Now she leaned away slightly, unbuttoning her blouse. He heard her light skirt flutter to the floor and felt her fingers move to his belt. He made love to her there on the floor, rain drumming the tin.

No one ever spoke to Warren about his color blindness. Indeed, many in

Edward Town never spoke to Warren at all. But there were looks. Snickers. The whiter or blacker the person, the more likely they were to disapprove.

But it was Rosa's color Warren loved most.

She was black in the warm way night seas are black. Luxurious, deep. She filled him with longing and lusty desire never aroused by any woman of his own color.

Rosa knew this and used it to her advantage - especially when they fought or disagreed about disciplining the boy. She thought him far too easy on Armando. "He could be working," she'd scold. "Let him sell fish in the market or run the fat man's errands if you are going to let him skip school. He is a truant, and you take him on the boat whenever he wants."

Warren had chuckled. "He is truant, not a truant. Anyway, he's in school some of the time."

"So, he will be able to add *some* numbers?"

Conceived when Rosa was nineteen, Armando seemed to Warren more like her younger brother, though he'd never mentioned this. Armando's father and the circumstances of her affair with him remained a mystery and sparked speculation among the locals because Armando's skin was a full shade lighter than Rosa's. Nearly every white male on Charming Island had been suspect at one time or other.

Years passed and Rosa said nothing, even to Warren. The less charitable islanders decided she was a whore who knew a good thing when she saw it in Warren - a convenient meal ticket for her and the boy. Oddly, Rosa did nothing to correct this impression. Sometimes, Warren thought, she purposely reinforced it.

The identity of her lover remained secret. Warren knew only that the man still lived in Edward Town. (This he learned one night when she had too much rum.) A man of some stature. A white man.

Now Warren attempted to push himself up from her, but she had both arms locked securely behind his back.

"Let me go," he protested. "The boy will come up the path any minute."

"I like to feel your weight on me," she whispered. "Stay for awhile."

"Rosa."

She kissed him, wrapping her long legs behind his knees to trap him. The rain had stopped, leaving behind a sound of dripping.

There was a dampness to her skin that smelled now of femininity and sweat, the oil she used on her legs. Warren had first seen Rosa washing dishes at the Pink Sands Hotel, a tall, big-boned woman with a protruding belly. Pregnant with Armando. Even when she wasn't pregnant, he thought her a tall, big-boned woman with a protruding belly. Not fat, but embodying a kind of female ripeness Warren found irresistible. He became her lover just before she gave birth to Armando. He felt safe with her.

"Rain stopped," she said, spreading her legs to free him. "Go."

He traced the broad line of her nose with his finger until her arms came up and hugged him again. "I wish I could cry for my mother."

"Men cry late," she said. "It is one good thing about them. But not a thing women understand." She smiled. "You are not tired of me?"

He shook his head. "I better go down and help Myron get the boat ready for tomorrow." He stood and glanced around for his clothes. "He'll want to know all about the rays."

"Fine," she said. "Go to your old drunkard, now that you have satisfied yourself." She was smiling.

"Yes," he admitted. "I'm very satisfied." She extended her hand and he pulled her erect. There was no shyness between them as she stood naked helping him button his shirt.

"It's the taste of rum he loves. I know he drinks too much."

"You drink too much."

He slapped her behind. "Get dressed."

Rosa was self-conscious about her "tall" legs. She wore flat sandals and lengthy skirts when she went out. At home she was barefoot. Warren couldn't remember seeing her in shorts or slacks. Sundays there was the dark blue dress for church, the only dark piece of clothing she owned. Everything else was multi-colored, red, or cool white. She had little use for underwear.

She noticed his admiring eyes. "You are the only man who can look at me," she said, as if that proved something.

"Doubt that," he said. "I think we *should* get a truck. Been years since I've driven anything but a boat. I'd like to go fast."

"Men are stupid." Rosa glanced at the ceiling. "Forget Javert. This gordo. If you find the barco *Imperial*, can you not buy a truck and pay him so he doesn't own *Esteban*?"

"Maybe," he answered.

"Go to your drunkard then." She fastened her skirt around her bare waist. "And tomorrow look again. Search the sea. You know the sea. If you know it is there, you will find it. Empeñarse en hacer algo. Understand me?"

"Si, mi amor. Persistence. As if I haven't already had it. How many years have I looked?"

"It is not a thing, mi querida, that you have for awhile," she said more seriously. "It is a thing you have that dies with you or you die because of it."

He retrieved her half-smoked cigar from the railing and relit it with a wooden match from his shirt pocket. He drew the smoke into his mouth, exhaled and handed it to her. Then he smiled.

"What is this, some kind of wisdom of the Dark Continent?"

She inhaled smoke and blew it from her wide nose. "No teasing today," she said. "Javert has killed the rays to ruin you. He is without patience and moves in shadows. Javert schemes for independence from Britain and the British do nothing." She shook wrinkles from her blouse. "If there is trouble they will find it convenient to grant independence and they will leave. Then Javert can own us. He and his friends will have power to rob us. When the money is gone he can open the reef, build the tall hotels and restaurants. Then you and I will serve the tourists and all those here will serve them."

Warren shrugged. "So what am I doing now?"

"You teach." She held the cigar between her teeth and buttoned her blouse. "Why does Armando say you are his papa? Because he loves you? Not only this. Because the boys, his friends, respect you. A few of the older ones you have taught to dive, and there will be more. Some will serve the tourists, yes. But some will dive to fish, others clean the bottom of the small ships that come across the reef, and those who leave the island will have a useful thing to take with them. You offer them something more than to be pool boys. If you find the barco can you not teach the tourists about it? Is this not a warship of Napoleon? Does it have nothing to say? The British who rule this place, why are they not pleased when you find the evidence of their colonial victories? Teach them to protect this history, and the water."

"All this if I find one little hunk of coral with some corroded cannons sticking from it?"

"I will tell you the truth," she said, smoking the last of the small cigar and tossing it into the yard. "The young ones go to New York or Miami. A few to Europe. Chasing a white world - television, cars, stereo music and fast food. What have you made them want, you Americans? Freedom? To do what? Spend money? Live rich until nothing is left? Glotón! A foolish freedom. Embaucar a alguien para que haga algo."

"Rosa. I'm not sure you know what you're talking about. You've never been to the States."

She had not intended to go this far and he was getting defensive. "So, maybe I am your lover. Yes? I help on the boat. Care for my *illegitimate* son. This is enough for me. It is too much for you that I have an idea, huh?"

"Of course not." He'd waited too long before going up the path. "Your opinion is more important to me than anyone's."

"Except your own."

* * *

For a drunkard, Myron seemed level-headed and in good voice. His favorite new tune came from Lacy J. Dalton, "16th Avenue". Myron had a decent voice and sounded almost like the woman who'd taken it to the top of the charts, less a certain amount of belching. Under a darkening sky his voice carried out across the harbor. Myron was forbidden to drink onboard. Warren rowed toward him, and listening to the song his anger evaporated. Let the poor bastard sing, he thought, he's got little enough to sing about.

The dinghy he'd borrowed bumped the port side and the singing stopped.

"Who's there?" Myron called.

"Just me."

"Will? Shit. I'm drinking onboard. I'm sorry, Will."

Warren climbed over the gunwale. Myron was up on the flying bridge. "Got any of that stuff left?"

"Sure do. Come on up."

Myron scooted from the captain's chair to the side cushion as Warren's head cleared the upper deck. Warren took his seat, swinging it to rest both feet on the cushion next to Myron. "Got some news for you," he told the old man. "We're going to have company tomorrow."

"Yeah?"

"Freddie-the-Frogman."

"Freddie?" Myron passed the bottle and shook his head. "Not here?"

"Morning ferry is my guess, judging from a letter I got from my dead mother and a few calls I made to the airlines in Guadeloop. Got his daughter Ruth with him."

"Freddie?"

"The man himself."

"I'm sorry about drinking on the boat, Will. You know? It's old man melancholy or something but I can't take it ashore sometimes and I need to be here on the water where all the people noise and shore noise is distant. You've been fine to me, Will, I don't mean to go against you."

"Forget it. Aren't you glad about Freddie?"

Myron didn't answer for so long a time Warren thought maybe he'd nodded off in the dark. Then the old man said, "No. I don't want him."

Warren sat up and stared at the old diver's silhouette, etched dark and hard against the water.

"Myron. You haven't talked about anything but you and your UDT buddies in all the years I've known you. What's going on?"

The old man sighed and shook his head. "I lied."

"About what?"

"I lied to him first. Told him I owned this boat and you worked for me. Then I lied to you because one time when I was drunk I called him and invited him and his girl to come down here on vacation and they could stay at my house, which is your house because you know I don't have any house, and then I lied to you some more when I didn't tell you I've known all along he's coming because I didn't want to have to tell you all the lies I told, and so just now again I was lying when I seemed like I was surprised because I'm supposed to pick him up at the ferry dock tomorrow. I got confused with all the lying going on."

Warren suppressed his laughter. "Where were you planning for me to live?"

"Thought maybe some of Rosa's church folks would take you in for a week or so. Them Pentecostals are pretty thick. Can I still have that bottle back?"

Warren handed it across to him. "It's your bottle, Myron."

"Well, not really. Found it in a sock drawer in your cabin."

The mirth broke loose in Warren's chest and his laughter echoed back from the ketch moored nearby. "You're a prize, Myron," he told him.

"You ain't pissed?"

"I'm pissed. Just can't hold onto it. What does bother me is that you didn't just come and talk to me. Hell, I'm not that much an asshole, am I?"

"No sir! Not a bit of it, Will. But the money and everything. Javert, that prick, and people like them mealy-mouthed Whites and I just couldn't get up nerve to make your life more a mess. Even Rosa, who's always the sweetest thing, gave me a tough look and didn't say much lately and I've been thinking maybe you'd be better off if I just drifted someplace else and got out of your hair, that's all."

Warren gazed out across the water, eyeing the ketch's anchor light winking as darkness deepened and the boat rode gently on the harbor swell. "We'll handle Freddie however you want, Myron, but just telling him the truth is going to make it easier, since you can't remember all the lies you told. He isn't going to kill you over all that small stuff. You own a boat, you don't own a boat. Who cares? I don't think he owns a dive shop anymore either. You're both old enough to be beyond all that."

Myron was confused. More than a little drunk. "So it doesn't matter, you think?"

"It matters to some people, Myron. Not people like you and Freddie. When I was a kid I thought he was a hero. Maybe he still is."

"Okay." Myron thought Captain Will usually had a thing straight. "I'll tell him the truth right away."

Warren grinned in the dark. "Don't just blurt it out. Give it to him a bit at a time." He slipped from the chair and stretched his back. "Come on. Let's get the gear ready for tomorrow."

"Okay, but damn it Will. I'm sorry." He sniffled, felt tears running, as they did more often these days. "Sweet Jesus, Will. Some crazy bastards killed our rays."

"I know, Myron. I know."

Rosa climbed the hill. It seemed to her that every path, road and sidewalk on Charming Island led uphill. But it was a warm night after the rain. Will gone to load the boat for tomorrow and Armando spending the night with his best friend Jaime, freed Rosa to make her rendezvous.

The church was hidden from view in the trees halfway up the mountain. There were many Pentecostal churches on Charming Island. As far as Rosa knew, not one had a white member. She felt the tension of the climb in her thighs and calves. A youthful aching.

Rosa's parish was one of the smallest and poorest. No electricity. She watched for the lamp light she knew would soon flicker behind the trees where Towanda Johnson and Antonia Gutierrez waited to greet her. They met often like this, in the dark, an appointment of righteous love and overpowering sadness, and the only thing that kept Rosa from despair.

No honest person denies their own spirit, and Rosa refused to cover her sin with self-justification or delusion. Rosa saw no humor in fornication, any more than she saw humor in the horrors of abortion or genocide. She was Christian to the core and living with sin - loving a man not her husband - ate at her insides with steel teeth.

"Sister Rosa," Antonia said.

Rosa halted in the path and stared, sighting Antonia up ahead. She nodded and walked the rest of the way to the small porch, wooden steps leading to where Towanda, known as To-John, waited.

An oil lamp and two candles lit the porch, church façade, flickering in the branches that enclosed them. "Good evening," Rosa said formally. "Thank you for coming."

To-John was a heavy woman who walked down the sides of her sandals and never appeared in public without a string of plastic pearls around her neck and cotton dress ending mid-calf. Her cinnamon face was round, soft and expressive. She hid nothing, and Rosa knew she could hide nothing from her. "Come, Rosa. Antonia," To-John said. "I have special news tonight."

"A surprise?" Antonia asked.

Rosa knew Antonia was the meek who would inherit the earth. The meek who resisted lions and beasts of a new age. Small, dainty and soft-spoken Antonia. Rosa knew too, how different she was from that quiet, secure faith that made passivity a powerful weapon. "This has been a day of surprises,"

Rosa said.

"Margarita Ramos came round after supper and told me Pastor has a son. Sheila is doing well and this baby was delivered in hospital." She shook her head. "At some cost."

"The complications did not arise?" Antonia asked.

"No," said To-John. "Thank you, Jesus."

Rosa smiled at the thought of new birth. She wanted more babies. "I'm happy. Pastor and Sheila are good people who are patient with me. How I thank them for that."

To-John's soft face hardened. "Did your man kill the rays in the sea?"

"No," Rosa answered. "He harms nothing in the sea. Looks. Photographs sometimes. Takes only what we all take to eat. If he loves anything, it is the sea and all that's in it."

"Humph! If he loved you he would marry you. He is like many men. Users of women." She plunked herself down on a wooden bench. "Users."

"To-John," Rosa addressed her. "I love you, but he is my man. He is my sin and my choice."

"A choice you make for your son."

"Partly, yes. I want a life for him, but for myself too. It isn't Armando I embrace in the night. I love that man and I won't leave him."

"So here we are again," said To-John.

"I'm sorry," Rosa said. "You understand my dilemma. Forgive me."

They sat quietly for some time, listening to sounds of laughter and music from the town and the pounding of Javert's dredge in the harbor far below.

"Rosa," To-John said. "Sometimes I wonder. God knows we are all fornicators, in bed or in our minds. Sin isn't why we're here tonight. Not church either. We come because we love you. I see what's in your heart. We all see it. Antonia and I see you mourning. We understand a dilemma of love for a man and love for God. But who do you love more? Who do you obey?"

Rosa moved to the top step and sat with bowed head and answered softly. "I pray for a way to please God and keep my little family." Rosa lifted her head to face the two women. "Maybe it is too much to want. It makes me a hypocrite. Maybe a whore too."

To-John was quiet. She'd wanted to tell Rosa to make the choice - God or man. Force a decision on her that would break the deadlock. Now she said nothing.

Antonia had followed Rosa to the steps and taken a seat just below her. She extended a hand and Rosa gripped it. "I see Captain Will almost every day," Antonia said. "He is one of the few who sees me. When I come out from the scullery and my apron is dirty and my dress soaked with sweat, he has never seen the dishwasher, but me, a person. He's not a smiley man, nor a rude one either. He will speak my name and greet me kindly, though we have never spoken at length." Antonia reached for Rosa's other hand before she went on. "There is good in him. Does he hate God, do you think?"

Rosa had thought about that more than anything else. "No," she said. "He's angry. Yesterday he received a letter from his mother. She died and he's angry with her. He's been angry with God since the day his brother died saving his life. Injustice. Misfortune. Life is a source of anger for him and I can't break it. I throw my love against it and a thousand times I've thought to leave him when he throws it back in my face. What can I do?"

"Kick his ass," To-John suggested.

They all laughed, but To-John continued. "Faith is a problem. People live fine without it. We can't. It's in our blood. God's law is not a burden to us like it is to many."

"Will wants his own way," Rosa said. "And I have gone the way of Swaggart. But for love."

Her friends nodded and neither spoke.

"Do we have the polish?" Rosa asked.

"I have it," To-John said.

"We won't finish tonight," Antonia warned.

The three friends stood, and as they moved toward the door Rosa held it for them. "Can we sing a hymn or two while we rub the pews?" she asked.

"If you'd come back to church Sundays," To-John said. She held the lamp higher as she passed through the weathered door. Inside, they raised their voices in song.

Rosa joined in the hymn and bent her back to the work. She asked God no special favor, no exceptions for her. But here at least, those who sang His praises would do it in pews polished by her hands.

CHAPTER TWELVE

Next morning the Leeward Island Ferry docked thirty minutes late at the public pier in Edward Town Harbor on its twice-weekly journey from Guadeloupe. Freddie-the-Frogman and his daughter Ruth Van Doren-Slovnik filed down the brow and onto the dirty concrete pier. Each staggered under a heavy scuba equipment bag, towing wheeled luggage.

Gerald Jeffers spotted them immediately. Gerald was a visa clerk at Government House, bribed by Javert to take the afternoon watch on the dock. He nodded to Philip Drew, a customs official standing near the shed where new arrivals were processed. Drew in turn signaled inside to Leroy Paquette, a passport control officer.

Paquette smiled knowingly. He was prepared to ask them some difficult questions, to which he knew they lacked answers. They'd be back on the ferry and gone within the hour. He planned to spend the money in Javert's envelope on his girlfriend Marisa - some dinner, drinks, a modest piece of amber he'd seen in a duty free shop, and get laid. All on Javert's dime. Life was good, and not his concern why the Fat Man disliked these newcomers. He didn't know Javert had never met them.

Javert, as always, was scheming. He had good reason to be rid of them. For years Javert had offered bribes to Myron Bose. He hoped to use him against Captain Will, but Myron refused. No matter how drunk he was, how broke, he rejected Javert's offers, and often with resentment. He had listened with interest to Myron's drunken stories of World War II and Freddie-the-Frogman. If even half of them were true, Freddie's arrival promised Javert more trouble. Myron would talk with his UDT comrade and Javert would gain another enemy on his home ground.

The Van Dorens walked boldly through the wide customs shed doorway, unassisted by the usual hordes of baggage handlers eager for tips. They approached Paquette's glassed-in cubicle. He looked down, studying an array of papers on the counter before him. He neither acknowledged their presence nor looked up from his reading, hoping it would soon become painfully obvious he was ignoring them.

It did.

"Excuse me," Freddie said, "We're waiting here."

Paquette was a handsome man of thirty-one. Neatly trimmed black moustache and dark curly hair. Unmarried, he delighted female tourists with his suave manner and swarthy good looks. He marked those he found interesting, memorizing the names of their hotels. Later, he'd arrange a chance meeting at the Tortuga, or other local hangout, and eventually sleep with some of them. A constant flow of fresh meat from the States made stamping passports for a living a little more palatable.

When Freddie spoke, Paquette looked up briefly and sneered, then went back to scanning his papers. An old man for crying out loud, on the short side of five-foot nine and the far side of sixty.

Freddie was surprised and turned to Ruth. "Think he understands English?"

"Must," she answered. "It's the official language. He looked right at you."

"Am I supposed to say anything special?" he asked. Several barefooted men squatted just outside the door smoking. They feigned disinterest but remained there to see what happened.

Ruth observed another line forming to her right with the official behind that cubicle stamping passports, smiling at the guests, and passing them along quickly. She nudged Freddie and indicated they should change lines.

As they gathered their bags from the dirty floor, Paquette spoke in accented but clear English. "You will remain in this line," he ordered.

"Well!" Ruth said, letting the bags drop. "Don't you want to see our passports then?"

"Yes," he said. "Now. Quickly. Both of them." Suddenly impatient, he stuck his hand out from under the glass window, beckoning with great annoyance.

To her left Ruth noticed yet another cubicle opening, more people filing through with barely a glance given their passports by the grinning customs official.

"You are both North American?" Paquette asked, holding the United States of America passports in his hand.

"Yes," Freddie answered. "What's it look like?"

This brought a mirthless smile to Paquette's lips.

"Traveling together?" he asked sarcastically.

"Yes," Ruth said. "That's obvious. And we're in a hurry."

"North Americans are always in a hurry," Paquette observed dryly, thumbing slowly through each of the passports, determined to read every line and double check every number. He repeatedly consulted a large book, mounted facing him on a metal stand inside his cubicle. He flipped the pages with painful slowness, licking his index finger tediously and comparing whatever was written there to each of the passports.

Ruth watched the wall clock tick off twenty-two minutes. Still Paquette studied the passports. A band of four middle-aged musicians, playing merengue for the tourists, finally coasted to a discordant finish and lit cigarettes. Three of them squatted against the shed's outer wall. The fourth guarded the instruments and watched Ruth with interest.

Lines of incoming ferry passengers now dwindled to fewer than half a dozen. Baggage handlers stood idle, visiting with customs officials who'd finished inspecting suitcases spread out on the long, low tables. Tourists were being loaded into buses or taxis and whisked away.

"This is stupid!" Ruth said at last. She leaned over, pressing her nose almost to the glass. "Who's in charge here?"

"I am," Paquette said.

"Of the whole island?" Ruth shot back.

"I am the passport control officer."

"Big deal!" Ruth shouted. "You're an incompetent boob as far as I'm concerned. I want to see your boss or the American Counsel or the police or somebody who isn't going to sit around with my passport up his ass!" Ruth sounded very much like Freddie-the-Frogman's daughter.

"Watch your crude lesbian mouth!" Paquette warned.

"My what?"

"I will not repeat," he said, smugly turning his attention back to the big book.

Ruth turned to the remaining tourists. "Did you hear that? Lesbian mouth! He said lesbian mouth." She stepped more toward the center of the shed. "Did you hear this man?" she shouted. "This man called me a lesbian!"

Those who did not understand English only shrugged and smiled. The others grinned openly, some shaking their heads. Freddie, who had been bending over one of his bags, came up with a marlinspike tool perfect for glass breaking. "Don't call my daughter a lesbian," he said in an even tone. "Not today, anyway. I'm tired." A second later Paquette's cubicle tinkled and shards of glass showered the passport officer as Freddie reached inside and dragged him out by the shirt. Without comment, he beat Paquette unconscious in far less time than it took three customs officials to drag Freddie away.

"I don't understand," Ruth said reasonably. "Why are they treating us like this?"

Leroy Paquette had failed. Freddie-the-Frogman and his daughter were arrested, handcuffed, and transported to jail in the rear of a small, dented Toyota pickup. Javert had wanted them placed back on the ferry to Guadeloupe.

He wouldn't know that Javert's fear of them was probably unfounded, exaggerated by dozens of stories, spun by Myron Bose on occasion of his having a few too many at the Pink Sands bar or anywhere else he found an audience. Javert had all too often been among the listeners.

Colour Sergeant Gladstone Cumberbatch carried a riding crop. He'd never mounted a horse. Mostly he stuck the crop in his armpit, marched that way, stood at attention or parade rest. The Colour Sergeant, a six and one half foot tall policeman, had a low tolerance for nonsense. His black eyes kept Freddie-the-Frogman nailed to a straight-backed chair at the High Candle Street Station House.

The Colour Sergeant's baritone filled the station office, and he had yet to raise his voice. "Not in all my years has any man come onto our soil and attacked a passport official of this government. Not since the pirate era." He held Freddie's bent passport like it was scrap paper. "Do you fancy yourself some kind of pirate?"

Freddie waited to see if this was a rhetorical question. Finally he said, "No."

Ruth, seated at his immediate left, said, "This is your problem, not ours. It's you people who started this."

"*You people?*" inquired the Sergeant. "As in *you* Negroes? *You* natives? *You* who are appointed to serve us?"

"I didn't mean that."

He tossed Freddie's passport onto his immaculate desk and fanned Ruth's from his giant hand, reading, "Van Doren-Slovnik? Ruth Van Doren-Slovnik? What's your relationship to this man?"

"My father."

"Uh-huh. Another divorcée. I'll get to you later. Now be still, girl." Heavily starched white uniform shirt catching the light, he turned back to Freddie. "You are the father? This is the example you set for your children? You are a violent man and you have injured someone. I've been informed that Passport Officer Paquette has lost part of a tooth. I happen to know that he's quite proud of his teeth, in particular. And very nice teeth they are too. We have good dentistry here."

"Listen," Freddie said. "I'll buy him a new tooth. I'll apologize. I *am* sorry, actually. I lost my temper because he called my daughter a lesbian. I just lost my temper. Don't you have any children? You'd defend them, wouldn't you?"

The Colour Sergeant snatched up Freddie's passport again. "It says here you were born in 1924. Is that correct?"

"Yes."

"You're an old man. Why are you fighting? Do you have some sort of senility affliction?"

"I just lost my temper, that's all. I'm fine. I swim every day and I take vitamins and eat meat. Just lost my temper."

"You're an old man. Why are you coming to this country?"

"Vacation. I know some people here."

"On Charming Island?" Cumberbatch studied him as he would any liar. "You know people here?"

"Myron Bose."

"Ah-ha! Who works for Captain Will? Yes?"

"Something like that, I guess." Freddie was confused. "I know Captain Will too. Warren Wilson."

"Who? Wilson?"

"Another name he uses."

"Another name he uses?" The Sergeant was puzzled by these people. Looked like tourists, but picked fights. Said they'd never been here before, now it turned out they knew two people who'd been here many years, and knew one of them by another name. "I know Captain Will very well. I will send one of the boys to fetch him."

A full hour later, late morning sun cooking the tin roof of the Station House, Warren came through the door, followed closely by Myron. "Morning, Mr. Cumberbatch." He nodded at Myron. "He was supposed to get them at the dock. Overslept." Warren glared at Myron, then turned to Freddie and Ruth. Freddie had aged and was nearly bald, his shoulders rounded, knots on his knees, arthritic hands. But Ruth was still beautiful. Signs of wear, but nothing like he might've expected in a woman her age. It made him slightly light-headed. "May I speak to you privately, Mr. Cumberbatch?"

They went into the Sergeant's private office and closed the door.

"The old man is my teacher," Warren began. "The guy who taught me to dive. His daughter, well, she was an old love when I was young."

"They have done violence."

"Leroy?"

"Yes."

"If I talk to him, and maybe a few dollars would pass his way, do you think it might be cleared in that way?"

"Are these people staying with you?"

"No. Myron's getting them fixed at the Sands. I haven't seen them in many years and only just learned they were coming. Not to see me. Myron and Freddie were in the Navy together. Old sailors, you know."

"Yes, I know." Cumberbatch tossed the riding crop onto his desk. "The man called you Wilson. Are you Wilson?"

Sergeant Cumberbatch was nobody's fool. He'd spot a lie. "Yes," he confessed easily. "People called me Will for many years. Nickname that stuck I guess. Thought you knew."

"Maybe I'd heard it somewhere," the Sergeant said. He smiled broadly then and placed a heavy hand on Warren's shoulder. "We've known each other many years. You will be responsible for this Van Doren? And the Van Doren-Slovnik?"

"Slovnik?"

"The woman," Cumberbatch explained.

"Oh. Her married name. Husband's dead. Plane crash."

"Has the pursed lips of a divorcée."

"Nope. Dead husband."

"It's the same. The divorced have alimony, the widows, insurance. Too many strangers. I long for the old days. Bananas, sugarcane, copra, rum, some fruits going out maybe. Life was simple. Now...." The Sergeant sighed, walking Warren toward the door. "No more violence. You tell them. And talk to Leroy."

"I will."

When they came back into the room, Warren noticed Ruth staring at him with what he could only describe as shocked sadness, like when you've found your dog struck and bleeding along the highway and can't quite make up your mind if you hope he lives or dies. He glanced at Freddie, then back at her. "You're looking good," he said.

She nodded.

"Warren?" Freddie was still unsure.

Warren extended his hand and Freddie stood to take it. "Long time ago now."

"A lifetime," Freddie said. "Still diving I guess."

"Every day. How about you?"

"Summers."

"Let's get you out of here and into the hotel."

They both nodded and Myron said, "Got 'em a suite on the second floor so they don't have too many stairs but they still get a harbor view and it ain't far from the bar."

They'd been walking in the street, forever. Ruth trailing behind, grumpy. "Where is this hotel?"

Warren halted and pointed ahead. "There."

"The pink thing?" Freddie asked.

"Yeah."

"No modern hotels?"

"Sure. Consult your travel agent there."

"Dumb ass," Freddie told Myron.

Myron shrugged and they walked the rest of the way in silence.

After they checked in, Warren explained he had a charter, if the Whites weren't scared off by what happened with the rays. As he started across the lobby, Ruth caught up to him. "Warren. I want to talk to you."

"I gotta go now."

"I don't mean now. I mean later. Alone."

It seemed impossible after all these years, but Warren still felt shy around her. Unsure of himself. "I'm with someone now."

"Sure," Ruth said. "Of course. You would be. Dinner, is all. Bring her along."

"She's not going to want a walk with us down memory lane. Let's start with drinks in the bar, say five o'clock? See how it goes from there."

"Here?"

"No." He pointed at the Tortuga. "There. Across the street. Nothing fancy but we can talk. Be alone." He added that without thinking, and wasn't sure what he meant by it.

"Okay," she said. "See you then."

Later he persuaded Bobby White to advance him some fuel cash, half of which he put in the tank. The rest he pocketed for drinks with Ruth. He didn't want to look broke. She obviously saw him as some sort of beach bum.

The Whites were subdued by what happened to the rays. He thought Judy really did care for them at some level. Bobby bemoaned the lost revenue opportunities and asked how long it would take to train more rays. Warren told him he wasn't going to try. The ray circus was finished, forever.

They dove Dead Man's Wall off Dunnmore Head. A spectacular dive he usually reserved for the end of a charter, but he wanted something to get their minds off the rays and keep them paying the rest of the week. Might even wean them from Javert. He'd done it before, usually with promises of a whole other kind of diving experience if the Fat Man wasn't in the picture. Take the boat out farther, dive spots tourists didn't see, if he had extra cash and wasn't paying Javert's commission. Javert caught on to this, of course, but there wasn't much he could do about it.

Late that afternoon he washed down the boat and took a freshwater shower on board. He hadn't done that in months. He found clean clothes, a pair of sandals with all the straps intact, and decided the ponytail gave him a rakish air when it was clean, free of salt water. Thick hair, streaked with gray but alive still with highlights and curl. It wasn't primping, he convinced himself, but just making a better impression. Ruth had seen him at his worst - poorly dressed, shocked at seeing her. He'd said little and now it was time to step back a pace from the beach bum image. He was a local businessman after all. Owned the only dive boat on the whole island. No small thing.

Stiff northerly breezes cooled the night. Ruth leaned over the balcony, absorbing a babble of voices from the veranda two stories below, faint odors of cigarettes and candle wax, the dim lights along the street and tender rhythms from the Tortuga Bar on the other side. She'd learned Tortuga meant turtle. The music she couldn't identify so she hummed a little of "Teenager in Love" and it made her laugh.

The darkness was heavy. She closed her eyes. A foreign place but homey. Warren? A loud cricket noise pierced the night, drowning the music for several seconds. Warren wasn't anything to her. Old friend. Acquaintance. Where'd he get that little ponytail?

She opened her eyes. This was the last balcony on which Ruth expected to find herself standing, and Warren the last dinner date. Her marriage to Robert V. Slovnik was about as perfect as marriage got. His death changed everything in her life.

She'd married him right out of college. His father immigrated from Bulgaria to the Iron Range and Bob, raised on unionism and socialism, came to Minneapolis to major in Political Science and begin his career as a politician. His liberalism was rock solid and so opposite Ruth's upbringing that she was immediately attracted to him. His view of government as benefactor, even sovereign over the lives of common people, was foreign to what she'd learned at the knee of Freddie-the-Frogman and tempted her in the way too much money tempts young celebrities. Her father's creed of self-sufficiency seemed outdated against the social justice agenda Bob sketched as the political ideal. And to some extent she supposed, her attraction to Bob was rebellion against parental authority.

Senator Bob Slovnik's plane crash devastated the Minnesota Democratic-Farmer-Labor Party and gave Ruth Van Doren-Slovnik a widowhood status not unlike that of a queen. The true believers loved Bob Slovnik in such a worshipful way his televised funeral turned into a liberal political rally in such obscenely poor taste she found herself crying not for Bob but for the shameful rantings she was forced to endure in his name. Then and there she knew it was time for change. For the first time since she'd met Bob, she began to think he'd been wrong about everything. How could it be?

She'd told herself she wasn't looking for a man. She'd simplified and wasn't unhappy with the single life, though she regretted their decision not to take time for children. "I'm not looking for a man," she told the night wind. But isn't a woman always looking for a man?

Warren arrived at the Tortuga by boat, but not his own. He persuaded Stanley Burke and his boy Cullen to run him over. Evenings they fished the bay near the anchored *Esteban* and had done it before. The Burkes noticed tonight that Captain Will wore good quality sandals, and kept them raised from the oily water sloshing the deck. Stanley winked at the boy and he giggled. The Captain was an odd duck.

Unobserved, Ruth watched Warren climb the ladder to the pier, wave a goodbye to the Burkes and turn toward the Tortuga. In the moment it took for this to happen, Ruth became anxious to check her makeup again, find her wrap and hurry down to the bar across the street. She had no second thoughts.

Outside the Tortuga, Warren split his ponytail with both hands and tugged, tightening the hair at the base of his skull. He waited a moment longer before stepping out from under a mango tree and striding into the bar. In the evening Carlos brought his wife and daughters in. There were candles on the tables, cloth napkins and white tablecloths. Not classy but less shabby. Service also improved and Carlos' daughters were easy to look at.

Carlos met him at the city side entrance. "You are here for dinner?" he asked, eyes widening.

"Anything wrong with that? You serve dinner don't you?"

"Si Señor."

"So shut up and find me a table by the water."

"Si Señor! A table for one."

"Two."

"Ah, Rosa is coming."

"No. An old friend from the States. Old girlfriend in fact, and that's all I want to hear about it. Just try and be a host for once without asking any damn Cuban questions. And we'll be drinking wine if you have such a thing."

"Of course we have wine, Señor Will."

"I'd prefer you call me Captain Will. I am a businessman in this community. People forget that. Boats cost a lot of money. More than restaurants, I can tell you. I'm tired of everybody thinking I'm some kind of beach bum or hippie or something."

"Si Señor. I will be very respectful so this *friend* from America can see what an important man you are here in Edward Town. Don't worry."

"That isn't what I meant."

"No Señor. Some nice red wine perhaps? Two glasses. I will polish them myself."

"Goodbye."

"At your service, Señor."

Warren nodded. He should've planned things better. Taken Ruth somewhere else. Some tourist spot where hardly anyone knew him. There were a few.

A moment later Ruth paused at the entrance and Carlos pointed the way. She'd inherited her mother's classic beauty. Middle age had stolen her youth but replaced it with strength. He liked the way she walked up straight, projecting confidence when she must be feeling as nervous as he was.

"Not much of a view," he said as she approached, "but we're on the water."

"I think it's lovely." She smiled. "I'm glad I came. The smell of the harbor. Lights. Suppose you're used to it by now."

"Suppose I am, a little." He watched her, not the lights. "But some views you never get tired of looking at."

"My goodness," she said, flushing under his gaze. "You've learned to be charming."

"Must be the island."

She wrinkled her nose in a way he'd forgotten.

Carlos appeared with the wine. Two clean glasses. "So wonderful to have you dining with us again Captain Will." He uncorked the bottle and poured a taste. "At your service, Señor. It is acceptable?"

"Great. Pour."

"Si Señor." He smiled at Ruth. "Welcome to Charming Island," he said.

Warren glared at him and he left smiling.

"Service here isn't the best," he told Ruth.

"I think it's great." She tasted her wine. "Hmm. Good."

They both seemed to run out of conversation then and Warren was actually wishing Carlos would return. Finally he said, "I'm not expecting anything out of tonight. No leftovers from the past. Old embers we have to relight or anything."

"Do I look that nervous?"

"I think you're smashing. Best looking forty-year-old dame I've ever seen in my life."

She smiled. "Forty three, but don't spread it around." It seemed to Ruth, Warren was making a conscious effort to be charming. Something he'd never seemed capable of before.

He'd noted her bare legs under a white, lacy skirt so fine he could see through the lower half. Billowing above the wide waistband was a skillfully batiked blouse of pale blue and green with large leather buttons. The top buttons were undone and the blouse pulled down to expose her broad shoulders. She wore a beige shawl draped carelessly alongside her breasts. He smelled no perfume, just the heavy fragrance of flowers and spicy sauces going by to the tables.

"You're staring," she said.

"Sorry. I forgot what you looked like. Well, I don't mean forgot. I mean, I knew you right away and everything." He laughed too loudly. "What I meant was I forgot the details. The little mole on your neck, that smirky way your mouth lifts at the corners, frank eyes. Sorry. You shouldn't have said I was charming. I just wanted to say you were beautiful."

"You're doing fine," she said.

"Lot of years. Well, I suppose you'd like to know something about the island. It's sort of a backwater, which is what I like about it. Named after a British guy, Edward Charming. Let's see..."

"Can you go back to the part about my eyes?"

Instead, he said, "I came alone."

"Rosa had other plans?"

"No."

"I see."

"I want to tell you about before," he said. "That time when I told you about Stephen."

"You don't owe me any explanations."

"I want to tell you," he said. "I was immature. A kid. Things were going on in my head. It took a long time to sort it out. Maybe it's not done yet, but what I felt for you was genuine. Not childish. I just wanted you to know that."

Suddenly she wanted to cry for both of them. "I was young too. What can it matter now?" She placed her hand lightly over his. "Let's dance."

He hated dancing but pulled out her chair and slipped the shawl from her shoulders, his hand brushing her skin. She pretended not to notice.

There was a small band with loud drums. Had it always been here? At first Ruth held his hand, then dropped it and draped both arms around his neck. Her body, stretched lightly against his, was softer than Rosa's, slipping back and forth inside his hips.

They danced like that until the music stopped. Nobody said anything. Then he took her back to the table but they didn't sit down, walking instead to the waist-high edging nearer the harbor. She leaned against him. "I should never have come here," she said.

Warren pulled her from the edge and turned her slowly in his arms. She wasn't crying but her eyes were wet.

His eyes went to her lips. He bent forward, placing his mouth tenderly over hers. Their touching was delicate, her softness retreating before him. Slowly she lowered her eyelids and tilted back her head. Lips parted, she drew a quick breath, suddenly astonished.

It was a kiss every bit as stirring as the first one she'd given him when they were young and had plenty of time.

"I didn't want this to happen," he said.

"No?" She turned away.

"Well. I did and I didn't."

Her eyes had focused somewhere below, on some distant point of light.

"Which one is *Esteban*?" she asked.

Before coming ashore he'd set anchor lights, something he rarely did. The old boat was easy to spot and in the darkness appeared large, almost mysterious and grand. Not as showy as the ketch anchored nearby. "That one," he said, pointing. "Next to the one with all the lights."

"I see it." She turned to face him. "*Esteban* is Stephen in Spanish, isn't it?"

"Yes."

"Your brother?"

"You'll think I'm crazy," he said. "But sometimes I feel like I'm living for both of us. Trying to give him a chance, sort of, at everything he missed because of me." He watched the way the harbor lights shone in the strands of her hair. "Maybe I am crazy."

She shook her head. "Still blaming yourself."

"I won't run from it," he said.

"You were a kid."

"Yeah," he said, "but he's still dead."

"Well," she said, "there's a lot to be said for the way you kiss. Must be the romantic Caribbean living. You've really made it. Got the success the rest of us dream of."

"Me?" Warren laughed. "You've got a warped sense of success. First, this whole island is about to blow up in our faces. Politics. I just decided to help this fat jerk smuggle a load of illegal weapons into the country. I'll probably lose my boat. Your father's best friend, poor old Myron, is mixed up in it too because of me. I don't have enough money to buy socks or decent clothes for a little kid who wants me for a father." His wind gave out. He took a breath and said, "If the guy who owns this joint didn't owe me a favor, we couldn't even afford to eat here."

Ruth pulled him close and rested her head on his shoulder. When she opened her eyes a moment later, she said, "Don't look now, but half the people in this restaurant are watching us."

"Marvelous," he said, and led her back to the table.

She saw the worry lines in his forehead. "Can we begin with the present?" she asked.

"Huh?"

"The owner here really owes you a favor?"

"Yeah."

"Good, because I didn't bring any money."

They laughed easily together.

"Now, about the rest. The island's going to blow up? Sounds like a long story."

He nodded. "Let's order first. I'm in the mood for some raw oysters."

"No doubt." She smiled.

It took a plate of oysters, a Caesar salad, a surprisingly good piece of lamb, and mountains of pasta before he got it all out. She listened quietly, stopping him just enough to get her facts straight. When he told the part about the rays, and Elmo, she cried. But when he told her about Javert, she was angry.

She went to the bathroom and by the time she returned he'd already decanted another bottle of wine. "I'm back," she announced, sliding into her chair before he could move. "Can I talk to you about my husband?"

He laughed. "Of course."

She took him through it all then, and somehow, saying it aloud, was an epitaph of sorts for her previous life. Creating a watershed moment. As she spoke, simply and without great emotion, it moved her in a way Bob's rally funeral, interment, and private memorial service had not come close to doing. Maybe, she thought, it was the audience. Or the time that had passed. Whatever it was, it unstrapped the constraints of her heart and granted a level of freedom she'd not known in many years. Whether he deserved it or not, Warren got credit for it.

He had listened attentively and half the wine was gone before she wound down. "What a bore I am," she said. He didn't answer at first and his eyes remained down. "I said I'm a boring old cow and I'm going back to the hotel before you fall asleep."

"Ruth." He'd been holding back something. Talking around it, feeling his way.

She noticed his lips were slightly parted, waiting for the words to come. She wanted to reach out for his hand but remained still instead.

"All this is wrong," he said. "Isn't it? I mean, we blew it." He poured wine into their glasses. "I'm not saying anything is wrong with what you just told me. Your life. I just mean we missed a life too, didn't we?"

"Don't say any more," she told him. "I'm not going to like it."

"My mother died," he said suddenly. "Hadn't seen her in years. Like my dad. You. Everything back there in Lake Darling. Stephen. Mementos, old photos in a bottom drawer, never discarded, never used. I wasn't honest. Didn't turn history into experience like I should've. Buried it instead. But you lived an honest life, best you knew how. The right way. So my mother died forgiving me."

Ruth wasn't sure she understood all that he said, but she knew pain. "No one outlives their past, Warren. It's the one sure thing. We carry it to the end. After that, I guess, our history either saves or destroys us."

He smiled. "Well then," he said, "I'm screwed."

"Hold my hand instead."

He complied. "You're still kind of bossy."

"I missed you. Right now, I'm glad we're becoming acquainted again. Can we start there?"

"Sure," he said, patting her hand then leaning away. "Anyway, I saved the best for last."

"Best what?"

"Best part of the story of my life. Sunken treasure."

"Warren."

"I'm not kidding. When I came to Minneapolis and your dad taught me to dive, I carried along that old family story one of our ancestors wrote about a Wilson who was shanghaied by the Brits and fought in a battle just off this coast. One of the biggest ships in the world, *Imperial*, was sunk and never recovered. Thought I told you. Anyway, it's here and I've been looking for it."

Ruth laughed louder than she'd intended and glanced accusingly at her glass. "You haven't changed," she said. "Sunken treasure! But I suppose you did tell me once, and I forgot."

Warren accepted her laughter. "Just because everyone talks about sunken treasure doesn't mean there isn't any."

"Silly boy."

He smiled at her. "It's the silly boys who don't go and look."

"Tell me the story again," she said. "I need some coffee though, and some water."

One of the Orizondo girls brought the order and Warren talked for an hour, relating every detail of his uncle's tale, adding some of his own. Ruth sipped her strong coffee and listened, some of it coming back to her across the years. The darkness surrounding the glowing lights of the Tortuga was almost complete.

Here, Ruth thought, I can believe in ancient sea battles and sunken treasure. Was it Warren's voice, or the dance or the kiss or the smell of the sea she'd almost forgotten? When Warren finished and she recognized the hope lingering ever so reluctantly at the corner of his eyes, she said, "I'm sorry, Warren. It's more than a tale isn't it? It's history. Yours."

Warren was relieved. "Do you want to come for a look yourself tomorrow?"

"Just you and I?"

Warren stared at the table. "No. I have a charter. Two people. Rosa and Armando will be there to crew for me. Myron. Your dad too, I guess."

Ruth smiled. It was, after all, just their first day on the island. "That's fine. Freddie will love it. Some adventure now in his old age, no matter how far-fetched."

It was Warren's turn to smile. "Not as far-fetched as you might imagine. I've been narrowing the search for years, and in a methodical way. Can't say we'll find it tomorrow, but one day soon I think. Process of elimination. This island has a finite amount of coastline and *Imperial* rests here. That's a fact everyone agrees with. So, it's just a matter of time."

Ruth nodded. "But there's really no treasure? I mean, it's a warship, right?"

"Yes, of course. But every ship in those times traveled for months or years without seeing their home port, and carried gold to pay for supplies, pay the crew, deal with emergencies. Many officers were rich gentlemen who never sailed without considerable funds to purchase the amenities, pay their servants and the like. There won't be treasure in the sunken chest sense, but there will be no small amount of gold. Even one coin of that era has value."

"Like how much?"

"Couple thousand - maybe."

"I had no idea."

"Several years ago a small group of underfunded salvagers came to the island with a chart, purchased a permit from the government, and removed crates of tumblers - hand-blown drinking glasses - from a well-known Dutch wreck that I'd dived on myself. I used one of those tumblers for a toothbrush holder until it slipped off the sink and broke. The salvagers off-loaded thousands of them. They were 360 years old. Packed them up and shipped them to Europe. Sold them there for $6,000 apiece. Not gold. Not sunken treasure in the Hollywood sense. But not too shabby either."

"So," she said. "It's worth looking."

He smiled at her again. "Yes, for the money, it's worth it. I'm not really after the money though. I want to find it to find it, and to open it to the public. I want to take divers down for a glimpse at a real piece of world history. I'll take what gold I find and the rest can remain there. I'll tell the divers that. What kind of dive will it be then? And if they find a piece, let them pay the tax and keep it. The only alternative is salvagers sucking it up from the bottom with dredges, then grinding it to extract the gold. Gone forever, and much of it winding up in some politician's pocket."

"You're destined to die poor, I think," she said. "And maybe die early if someone desperate knows about it. Just like the rays you told me about. I wonder, can we save anything in this world?"

"Think I'm naïve?" He sipped his cold coffee. "We save it the same way we saved the Yellowstone or Old Ironsides or anything else of historic value. Islands like Cayman, Bonaire and others, have declared their waters national parks. Underwater parks. We can do the same here. It's got the greed motivator. Even some of my detractors among the local gentry might sign on for a profit, or an imagined one. If I find *Imperial* I will have a card to play with the government. The Brits are very green, you know, and this has the appeal of tourist money and political purity. The Governor will look like a saint at a time when Britain could very well lose this island."

Ruth knew instantly that she had underestimated him. The beach bum image was more image than substance and she regretted most of what she'd just said. "You've thought this out. I'm sorry. I'm new here and it shows. Will you still take me along tomorrow?"

"Of course. We haven't been underwater together for a long time."

"Don't you dive with Rosa?"

"She snorkels but I have yet to get her on scuba."

The idea of Rosa chilled the warmth they'd enjoyed.

"Time for me to turn in then," Ruth said, slipping from her chair. "Thank you for a wonderful evening, and sharing so much with me. I look forward to tomorrow. Really."

Warren watched her walk away and said quietly to himself, "Good night."

The hour was late. Other patrons were strolling away from the Tortuga. None observed the tall shadow as it separated from the corner of the Clyde Import, Ltd., warehouse and slipped inside the cracked trolley door. Wesley Bens had found his quarry and waited patiently until they could be alone.

CHAPTER THIRTEEN

Wesley Bens loved to jump rope. From where he'd hidden himself in the shadows of Clyde Import, Ltd., he spied Captain Will's date strolling back to the hotel. He jumped an imaginary rope to keep busy - wrists twisting, arms swinging, feet dancing in a rhythmic motion of his slick, beefy body. He glowed with excitement and the rope came alive, spinning invisibly round and round. The deep ache in his foot kept him sharp. Pain often quenched his thirsty bloodlust.

The stingray spine had holed his foot, leaving a boiling scab to remind him Javert was a fool and Captain Will an unwitting accomplice. He needed enemies - lots of them. Suspicion, fear, hatred - ingredients of unrest. Castro's Cuba, like its Russian sow bear, stumbled along the path of socialist hopelessness and lethargy. Few cared or excelled in Cuba anymore, except Wesley Bens. Teams sent by the Partido Comunista de Cuba (PCC) to Guatemala and elsewhere were weak. Bens knew it was too late for communism. Sent alone to Charming Island, thanks to his British heritage, his mission here was hopeless, too. Here again they would auger in the pathogens of corruption, fear and unrest, an evil strain disproven across the globe. But Wesley Bens had his own plans.

He had to play it cool with Javert, until the time was right. The Fat Man had contacts in Cuba and persuaded them to help him seize power in Charming Island. If it hadn't been for their humiliating defeat by Reagan in Granada a few years before, Bens doubted Javert could have persuaded them to move against a backwater like CI. But Bens saw his chance to jump ship now and swim to safety on another island he believed much easier to control.

His plan was simple - deceive them all - take them all, kill them all, steal from them the power they sought and rule in their stead. He had the brains, the ruthlessness, and now the perfect opportunity. Already he had moved against the only real threat to his plans - the American Captain Will. He alone stood up to Javert and he perceived in him a stubbornness and independence that might pose a threat. He smiled to himself. Already he had moved against his stingray asset, eliminating it and causing suspicion to blossom between the

American and Javert. In a few minutes he would surprise the captain again. Plant fear in his mind. Keep him off balance. Create sleeplessness and doubt.

Captain Will exited the Tortuga and took a lonely route toward his house at the foot of the mountain. Bens had guessed his course. A well-worn path leading behind the hotel, uphill away from the harbor before turning left to wind through a poor neighborhood and away from the lights of the town. Bens concentrated on walking without limping. This increased his pain.

The Captain was in no hurry. Twice he stopped to stargaze. Once to light a cigarette. Bens felt the pain spread along his foot, encompassing heel and lower ankle, but had no real difficulty pacing the American.

Americans were his hobby. The 20th Century would be their last, he thought. He wasn't fooled about the Caribbean. Everything here depended on America, and America had turned the corner, losing the moral high ground, doubting itself, blustering and threatening instead of leading. Hadn't Britain done the same thing? Most European nations, once great colonial powers, now weak, banding together to save themselves. Their true individuality passing into history. A nation unto himself, Wesley Bens wasn't following that road.

The pain in Bens foot radiated along his calf toward his knee. He'd had enough climbing for tonight.

"I say there! Up ahead. Aren't you Captain of the *Esteban*?"

Warren paused and turned toward a large man limping from the dark. "Yes?"

Bens continued to gain ground until he reached the level spot where Warren waited. "Just a word, if you please."

Warren waited in silence.

Bens smiled. "Do you know me?"

"No."

"You've had some trouble with your stingrays I believe."

Warren shifted his weight and studied the man, sensing danger. He was without a weapon and the man was large and seemed physically very fit.

"Did you hear what I said?"

"I heard. They weren't my stingrays."

"You exploited them."

"You with the government?"

Bens laughed aloud then. "No. Not at all. I'm the man who killed your rays."

Warren's fists clenched and despite his growing fear he moved a step closer to Wesley Bens. "Who are you? Some goon Javert sent out?"

Bens closed the remaining distance between them and leaned down. "My name is Wesley Bens. Isn't it funny how so many people believe you killed the rays? People so often believe one thing, when in fact, something else entirely has occurred." He reached out and gently patted Warren's cheek. "Don't draw back. I like Americans. It's been told to me that you avoid politics and mind your own affairs. I applaud that. You have a woman, a boy, a boat, and apparently a mistress. A great deal to lose. For now, do as I do, obey the Fat Man. Later on, things will change quickly and I may need you."

"You may need me?"

The large Englishman smiled. "Javert told me an interesting story about you. Said you claim to have some colonial ancestor who was pressed into service in the Royal Navy and was gutted by a French sailor named Javert, not far from here. Is that true?"

"Who knows?" Warren said. "That's the story."

"Well, you wouldn't want history to repeat itself, now would you?"

"This isn't 1806. It's my ground and I know my enemies. I don't give them an opportunity to sneak up and stab me in the back."

"I just came up behind you."

"Yeah, you did." Warren smiled. "It won't happen again. Now run back on down the hill to the fat man and tell him I've already decided to fetch his guns. I'll be taking the mortgage in advance and half the money. Tell him that."

Wesley Bens reached for the smaller man and drew him close. "*You* tell him." His voice barely a whisper. "Think you're someone who can make demands? You're nothing. A middle-aged drunken loser. Next time I speak to you things will be different."

Bens lifted Warren and thrust him back hard onto his heels. Warren kept his balance but felt the overwhelming strength Bens exerted. It shocked him. He knew without a doubt the outcome of any hand-to-hand contest. Bens would kill him without breaking a sweat. This realization wasn't as frightening as it was humiliating and Warren moved closer. "Keep your hands off me."

For a moment Bens stood silent and Warren thought they were coming to blows, then Bens shrugged. "There's plenty of time. Later on you and I will visit again. That meeting you will remember forever."

"Yeah? I'm scared to death."

Bens smiled patiently. "You should be." He turned and made his way slowly downhill, soon lost in the darkness.

Warren stayed a long time on the path, listening and watching, mind racing through lists of options, most of which didn't seem pleasant. To fight a man that powerful took more than skill, maybe something large caliber. All he owned was an old rifle not fired in years. Good thing he was about to go into the weapons business. The irony of the thought made him smile. Oh, well. They hadn't beat him yet.

But that night he lay in bed listening to Rosa's rhythmic breathing and reviewing his options. They were few, disappointing, and mostly dangerous. Spurn Javert and expect more visits from Bens, more danger at sea. Fetch the weapons and climb into bed with the crocodile. Gather his forces and fight? There was Rosa, an unemployed dishwasher. Her son Armando, nine. Myron Bose, a horny old man. And his former scuba instructor, Freddie-the-Frogman, another old duffer who couldn't get into the country without being arrested. And Ruth. She had much to offer, but nothing to stem the power of men like Bens.

He turned onto his right side, staring at the window. Night breezes lifted the light curtains. He smelled forest and decay. Rat them out to the police? Sergeant Cumberbatch was an honest man, but the Sergeant, like the rest of his small force, carried no gun. Probably never shot one. Was more likely to scold a miscreant than take hold of him. Warren had seen him round up any number of drunkards ready to fight. Cumberbatch handled them like squalling three-year-olds, held firmly and lovingly against him as they were marched blubbering away to sleep it off, finding a hot home-cooked breakfast awaiting them in the morning. What could he possibly do against a brute like Bens?

While no painless choice presented itself, Warren did grasp that this was his problem. He had borrowed money from Javert. He had gone behind the pile of ice blocks that night with reckless disregard for what his father and Stephen had told him. He had fallen into the water and it had cost his brother's life. Now who should pay for this mistake? Rosa? Armando? Old friends? He'd run out of brothers. His mother's words came back to him. *There's no one left who loved you when you were young. No one who knew you from the beginning*. In the clarity of the moment, he heard her voice as clearly as if she stood alongside his bed as she'd done a thousand times when he was a child. And for the first time, felt the weight of her passing. He was alone. No wife, child, or friend replaces the love of a parent. How many times had Rosa promised him that only the love of God was like it. But God was his adversary too, a father who never came to the rescue.

Warren drifted into restless sleep as he'd done many times before, alcohol on his breath and limbs heavy with a fatal aching. Sleep left him unrested, and new days dawned in red-bright hope, only to vanish in harsh light, revealing a world beyond his understanding and out of his control.

In the morning he rose early, leaving Rosa and Armando asleep, and made his way down to the town where he knew Javert, also an early riser, would be enjoying a solitary breakfast on the Pink Sands veranda.

Javert was surprised to see him. "Good morning, Captain."

Warren took the chair opposite to spoil his view of the harbor. "You killed the rays, you Bastard."

"Nothing of the kind!" Javert said.

"Don't bother lying. I've already talked to your boy Bens. He threatened me and my family. He's a big boy. Even scares me a little." Warren smiled. "In war, Javert, I was forced to take lives. Most at some distance, others very personal. I didn't like it much, but one does become accustomed to such things. What you need to know is that I know how, and have the means. Should one hair on Rosa or Armando's head be disturbed, I'm going to kill you. Not Bens or your other boy Slither. You, Javert. We won't talk it out first, no fair fighting, just - bang, you're dead." Warren smiled again, lowering his voice even more. "And I'll tell you something else. Bens is more dangerous to you than to me. Big men, fat or muscular, are just big targets." He stood up. "I'll go to Guadeloupe on Saturday and pick up your weapons. Find the mortgage for *Esteban* and get some cash. Half now, half when I return."

Javert made no move to stop him or speak to him as he turned and trotted down the steps toward the harbor. He hoped Javert didn't know it was a bluff, but maybe even if he suspected, he'd never be sure. At the very least, call Bens off until the guns were delivered. Rosa and Armando would be safe until after he returned.

Only light activity on the town dock. Most fishermen long gone, having left before sunrise, but several still readied their boats and Warren hailed first one then another. Both ignored him. No open hostility, just found him invisible. A dozen times he'd towed them in from miles out to sea when their poorly maintained outboards failed. Today they didn't know him.

He stared into the deep water below and spoke no more to them. Kicked his deck shoes off, pulled his shirt over his head and tied them inside. Jumping clear, he swam toward *Esteban* several hundred yards out in the bay.

The water was warm and cloudy from Javert's dredge. The Whites wanted to leave at eight when he called them earlier. He promised adventure searching for a genuine shipwreck and Bobby parted with two hundred for extra fuel and supplies. Warren's research suggested a rough coastline site miles from harbor and he'd been concentrating his search there for nearly six months. It was an unlikely place with a murderous surge, high limestone cliffs and rough water, but might explain why the wreck escaped discovery for two centuries. The *Imperial* was documented, after all, and he wasn't the first to go looking.

The wind was calm. Water subdued and inviting. He tossed his clothes up, placed both hands on the swim step, popped from the water and sat down. The swim had cleared his head. He planned to top off the potable water tanks, add a hundred gallons of fuel, then put in at the dock. Rosa and Armando should arrive to load food, beverages and ice. Besides the Whites, he'd also invited Ruth last night. Freddie and Myron too. Eight mouths to feed, two paying customers, Rosa yet to be told. He smiled to himself. He may soon have a longer swim than the one he'd just made. Rosa watched every penny like it was her own.

Warren hadn't planned to mention Bens to Rosa or Ruth, but warn Freddie and Myron instead. They were linked to him, maybe seen as allies. Bullies are usually cowards, but he sensed in Bens a brutality that endured pain and withstood impatience until threats turned to action. Wesley Bens was a dangerous man. Maybe more dangerous than any he'd ever faced. He posed a serious threat and it wasn't fair to leave the two old men in the dark, though he doubted either of them could do more than bluster and swagger. Their time had long passed.

Rosa and Armando were waiting when he docked. Armando handled the lines, then helped his mother load supplies aboard. "I can steer the boat?" Armando asked.

"We'll see." Warren's predictable response.

Rosa wore faded pink capris and a white blouse that accented her dark skin and high breasts. Her face a mask of indifference.

Warren trailed her into the salon, carrying ice and dumping it into the large cooler. He glanced up and smiled at her. "Going to be a fine day," he predicted.

"The woman is coming?"

"What woman?"

"Your lover."

"Damn it, Rosa! She's not my lover."

"Your old lover. Very old," she laughed. "Old like my mother."

"If you knew who your mother was." He regretted it instantly. Saw the hurt on her face. "I'm sorry. I didn't mean that."

"I've heard it before. But not from you." She turned her back to him and walked away, up the three steps to the pilothouse where Armando was busy preparing for sea.

Warren worried about Bens, but Ruth boarding a boat with Rosa aboard might be worse. Grinning, he thought, Ruth and Rosa. Not exactly R&R.

The Whites were first to arrive. Judy Ann was naked, or nearly so, wearing thick-soled high-heeled sandals and transparent beach jacket over her scant bikini. Bobby lugged several straw bags and a large wheeled cooler.

"I've already got cold drinks in the boat cooler," Warren told him.

"I ain't drinking my beer out of some bait cooler," Bobby replied, straining to lift it aboard. "Take these damn bags, Judy Ann!"

Warren spotted Ruth, Freddie, and Myron as soon as they stepped onto the dock. Each carried a large dive bag, nothing else. He waved. Ruth waved back, and as she approached he felt a lump in his throat. Where Judy Ann was tawdry, Ruth wore a simple black bathing suit of conservative design, accenting her hips and long legs. Warren's vision of kissing her underwater in Minnesota flashed into his head and he blushed.

All three stopped on the dock. Freddie and Myron saluted. "Request permission to come aboard, Captain."

Ruth shrugged. Warren said, "Permission granted, if you two geriatrics can get over the gunwale."

At that moment, Myron spotted Judy Ann and all but leapt into the boat, dumping his bag on deck and dashing to her side. She sat cross-legged on one of the tank benches digging in a straw bag. "Remember me?" he asked her.

"Don't be stupid," she said.

"Them is real titties, ain't they?"

Judy Ann sighed and looked around for Bobby, who was struggling to stow his cooler. "Bobby. Bobby. Myron's bugging me."

"Tell him to shut up."

"Did you hear that?" she asked Myron.

"Don't suppose I can touch one sometime." He tried a charming, yellow-toothed smile on her. "I mean, they're so damn pretty and what's it cost you?"

Judy Ann stared at him in a strange new way and for a moment Myron thought she'd give in. "You're the dirtiest old man I've ever met." She covered herself with the transparent beach wrap. "Has it been a long time? Years I bet. Suppose I'm tempting you, showing you what you've never had or ever will."

Myron growled and stood up. "You don't know what I had or what I'm gonna have." He turned away, then paused. "I had better than you many times."

Warren gripped the back of Myron's neck and whispered, "Damn it! These are customers. Now shut up, or get your gear on the dock."

Myron nodded stiffly, but Warren saw his shoulders slump. He'd never decided if Myron was a letch, or just overpowered by his misplaced ribald sense of humor. Usually he ignored it. Not today.

He shouted at Armando, "Start the engine," and hopped onto the dock. The diesel rattled. He smelled its acid smoke as he slipped the stern line from the dockside bollard, then trotted forward to the bow line. Armando was grinning at him from the pilothouse window. "Do you think you can get us underway without crashing into the dock?" he asked the boy. Almost before he could jump back aboard Armando engaged the engine and *Esteban's* reversed propeller spun in response. Minutes later they were headed for open ocean.

On the fantail, Warren addressed them as if they were newcomers. "We're clearing harbor. Gets rough in the reef cut sometimes so stow your gear and sit down until we make blue water. Okay?"

They nodded.

Bobby White said, "Same-o, same-o."

Seagulls squawked in their wake, trailed by a lone pelican skimming the frothy surface. No matter how many times he went to sea, Warren felt his spirits lift. Then thought of his dread going out after the rays. Thankfully, not today. They were alone on a sea of gentle swells and sleepy breezes.

Esteban plowed through the heavier swells of the cut and was free of the harbor, Armando at the helm. The bottom dropped out beyond the reef and Armando felt the same astonishment he experienced each time he stared into deep water so blue it seemed freshly distilled from heaven. While his mother's Pentecostal faith often confused him, the sea did not, and if God left any undeniable evidence of His creation, it wasn't mountains or the heavens themselves, it was the sea. No wonder many islanders feared it.

The boy's concentration deepened as he sensed Captain Will enter the pilothouse. A warming presence that also made him watchful.

"Watch your heading," Warren said.

Armando grinned. "I want to drive all the way," he said.

"You don't know the marks."

"I know them," the boy said. "The three palms. The two near the cliff and the one far behind we bring to the center and then a little south. Back farther to sea then until it is half size. That's the marks. I can do it."

Warren stepped around and leaned on the console so he could see the boy's face. "So you're confident?"

"I've watched you."

"And you remember the rocks that extend underwater from the headland just before the place we've been searching?"

"Yes."

The boy was eager, and clever about the sea. Awed by it but seldom afraid.

"Okay," Warren said. "Stay alert. Where's your mother?"

"On the flying bridge."

"What's she doing there?"

Armando's grin widened. "Hiding, I think."

Warren slipped away and scaled the aluminum ladder to *Esteban's* flying bridge. "Crew Only" was painted in red on the upper portion of the bulkhead behind the ladder. Two cushioned seats that doubled as life jacket lockers enclosed the space port and starboard. Rosa was lying on the starboard seat one arm across her face. She was crying. Warren's first thought was of the many times they'd slept up here on balmy nights.

He stood beside her only a moment before she too sensed him and rolled onto her side to face the sea.

"You're crying," he said.

"Yes. I'm crying."

"Well. Stop."

A moment passed before she spoke, "Won't do for people to see your nigger crying, I suppose."

"Rosa."

"No," she said. "Don't talk. My tears are drying up. Leave me alone so I can clean my face and serve your guests."

Warren held his tongue. Rosa was stubborn and he'd learned not to push her, back her into a corner. She was on edge with Ruth aboard and he'd recognized the fear in her eyes this morning when she first came aboard. He didn't want to lose her and at the same time discovered a hole in his heart suddenly plugged by Ruth's presence. Freddie brought something too. A measure of stability only home can tender and no amount of years forsake. And the letter, of course, nagging his conscience like the endless pounding of Javert's dredge.

He glanced ahead before climbing down. Their heading was true, and dropping onto the main deck he saw a straight wake astern. Armando was becoming a fine sailor at the age of nine.

"Excuse me Captain," Judy Ann said at his elbow. "Can I ask you something?"

"You don't have to call me captain. Just Will." He paused, forced to take note of her large breasts, swaying against his forearm. "Or Warren, my full name."

"Oh. Okay. I just wanted to know how deep it was, where we're going. How long can we stay down?"

"Do you have a wet suit?" he asked.

She shook her head. "Just a Second Skin, you know, lycra body suit. Why? Is it cold?"

"No, but there's a lot of surge and some fire coral. The surge pushes you around and it's just nice if your body is covered. Protected."

She looked down at herself and shrugged. "I'll put it on. I don't want fire coral. I know about it. But you didn't say how deep?"

"Shallow," he said. "Thirty, thirty-five feet down to about fifty. We've been searching an area about a half mile long and one hundred yards wide."

"Oh," she shrugged again. "I'm not sure I know what that means. How deep are we going to go?"

Warren forced a smile he feared must look strained. "I'll tell you when we get there."

Underwater searches in a vast sea are often futile, justified by suckers who reason that after all, somebody has to win. Warren thought of the chart he'd been using all these years. Little more than "X marks the spot." Symbol on a piece of paper of questionable authenticity. Even worse, very little would remain of the actual *Imperial*. Metal, of course. Much of that corroded and overgrown with corals. What he usually looked for, or tried to visualize underwater, was the outline of a ship. A reef shaped as a ship. Only in Hollywood do wooden ships remain ships after centuries underwater. The ocean begins destroying wooden vessels almost immediately. Currents and surges rock it, storms batter it. Worms come to eat the wood and corals feed on it. In a short while, nothing remains. Warren searched for ballast stone, cannons, anchors, and the gold, of course. Little else is to be found, except maybe the bones of sailors, now mixed with the shifting sands of a restless sea. Not a bad end, he'd always thought. He hoped for none better.

Warren found Armando still standing at the helm, straight-backed and steady. He smiled. "Watch your heading," he said.

"The wake is straight?" Armando inquired without taking his eyes from the sea.

"Not bad at all."

"How far now?"

Warren allowed his hand to rest on the boy's shoulder. "Try and imagine more than you see," he said. "Picture as much of the coastline as you can, but only as it fits in the water. In the sea. All the world is in the sea. Land people forget this. Their lives are on land and the sea is just something they look out on. But here it surrounds us. Boats are like airplanes, not wheeled vehicles. We drift and maneuver on a liquid that can act upon us much like floating in air. Understand?"

The boy nodded.

"Make the boat an extension of your body," he told him. "Feel it move as you move - walking, running, turning. How you put your back to the wind, or face it dead on. Don't forget it's running out from under you, pulling you down and pushing you up." He grinned at the boy again. "It's a ride."

Armando said. "But I am driving. I'm in charge."

"Most of the time," Warren agreed.

Armando glanced up at him. "That's the little headland," he said, pointing across the starboard bow.

"Yes, it is. You've done good. Now swing her out to port ten or fifteen degrees and come back in on your marks. When you get close, shout for me to stand by the anchor and when the marks are perfect, back the engine until the boat is dead in the water. I'll let go and when the anchor line is slack you back down again until it sets. Understand?"

"I understand."

"It's tricky."

"I'm tricky," the boy said.

Twenty minutes later *Esteban* swung at anchor. The pride Armando felt in that accomplishment was swelled by the little Captain Will had made of it. Almost as if he'd come to expect such accomplishments from his son.

Warren had occupied himself with boat chores, speaking to his passengers only in passing, but now there was time. He unhooked the chains and allowed the swim step to drop, rattling and slapping the water. He turned to the five divers. They sat in a tight row along the starboard bench with their tanks, BCDs and regulators ready in the cut-out PVC pipes behind them. Warren had mounted the PVC into the seating. Each pipe held a tank securely and was further secured by a length of elastic rope knotted into the top of each pipe in such a way it could be wrapped around the tank valve in each diver's pipe.

When Bobby White first saw this system he said, "Looks like a plumber's nightmare. What is that, sewer pipe?"

It was ugly, even Warren agreed, but worked in the simple way all great ideas work. After using a system that allowed each diver some personal space and a way to don their tanks effortlessly, even Bobby White soon came to love it. And he sat there now in line with the others, almost smiling.

Warren was standing a bit splay-legged before them to keep his balance as *Esteban* rocked at anchor. He was looking at Freddie-the-Frogman. "It's tough," he said, "to give a dive briefing to the guy who taught you how to dive. Except for the Whites, everyone of you has been diving longer than me."

"We never dove here before," Freddie said. "You're the resident expert. We're just here to learn."

It was a relief to hear him say it, but Warren nodded. "Thanks. This is a pretty shallow and easy dive, especially in these seas. We fight a surge here off those cliffs." He pointed. "Even today I expect you'll be moving back and forth at a good clip every few seconds. Maybe swaying like three, four feet side to side. Long as you don't line your head up with something solid, you get used to it pretty quick."

"How do you want us buddied up?" Freddie asked.

"Myron's the only one besides me who's ever dove here, so why not you, Ruth and him together?" He turned to the Whites. "Since you're new divers stay around the boat, don't venture too far. I'll have a drift line out 150 feet. Depending on the current it should be seaward. Look for the orange ball on the surface. If you're in trouble swim to it and pull yourself back on the line attached."

"How we gonna find anything lollygaggin' around underneath a damn boat?" Bobby wanted to know.

"I'll be there too. This water is rougher than it looks. When the ocean is suddenly stopped by something like those cliffs, its energy bounces back. It's going to push you. It's your first dive here. Take it easy. We'll come back again. Wreck's been here nearly 200 years. I've been looking more than a decade. No hurry."

Turning to Judy Ann, Bobby said, "There's a lotta *no hurry* around here."

Warren got Myron and the Van Doren's onto the swim step first. Ruth had barely glanced at him since coming aboard and they'd found no moment to even exchange a private hello. He had caught her studying Rosa whenever she got the chance to do it unobserved, and he wasn't pleased with the forlorn expression it lit in her eyes.

Myron, Freddie, and Ruth took giant strides into the water together and were underwater within seconds. Warren lectured the Whites about the surge again and sent them on their way, promising to follow once he had the drift line out.

When all divers were in the water, Rosa came back to him and said, "You are diving with her."

"No," he replied. "I'm diving alone. Have to watch them and the Whites, plus run my patterns. I'll let them play at looking."

Rosa nodded. "You will be diving with her."

Warren turned his back to her, coiled the 150 feet of orange line in his right hand and swung it and the ball away from the stern. It spooled in the light breeze and slapped into the sea, ball drifting rapidly away. Then he snapped the brass clip to a D-ring on the stern and donned his gear.

When he looked for Rosa, she was gone.

Warren dropped into the water, relieved to be free, and sank to the bottom. A sinking most people experience only in the first stage of drowning, but for Warren, a familiar weightless transition from air to liquid, care to carefree. Different rules, different physics. His clarity underwater married him to a world others found frightening. Their fears had prevented diving from becoming a major sport, as Freddie-the-Frogman had once so ardently hoped. But today it seemed to Warren that he and Freddie were completing a journey begun long ago when adventure was still fresh in them, and the waters surrounding them, clear and warm.

CHAPTER FOURTEEN

No two dives are ever the same in the sea's endless panorama, and unlike a subdued and populated land, it remains wild. Warren recalled how, after *Imperial's* defeat, the British fleet stood off for two days until the surviving French sailors and their goods were safely ashore, and only then burned the ship to the waterline. Their reasoning was simple - sailors fear the sea most, though it's their livelihood. Warren accepted life on those terms, joined to an untamed environment, working, as he could, in harmony with it. The Whites, on the other hand, struggled against a light surge. Aliens.

Warren had searched alone for *Imperial* all these years, except for taking Myron off and on. He knew it had become a private matter, and sharing it with people like the Whites was tantamount to offering them his virgin daughter to ravage, not that he had any daughters he knew about. Why, then, did their presence somehow complete the adventure? Several handfuls of Judy Ann's fine hair had loosened from her mask strap, waving above her head like a blonde sea fan. Neither of the Whites moved with the surge well enough to keep themselves stationary. Warren swam toward the couple. Ruth, Freddie and Myron had disappeared.

With so many people present, Warren decided the most ruinous outcome of the day might be if they actually found the wreck. Luckily the odds were stacked high against it. He'd searched many years, and in places much more promising than this, but dark thoughts crept in when he imagined how bad things could get - Bobby White discovering *Imperial.*

Warren often doubted *Imperial.* Battered by 200 years of hurricanes, currents and endless surge, odds were that nothing remained. Her cannons buried deep, anything else scattered along the bottom or carried away into the depths. The bones of Reggie Wilson mixed with the sands. Anyway, it was the hunt he loved. And today more people made that hunt more real.

Once he got the Whites' attention, he signaled for them to relax and let the surge swing them side to side. He demonstrated this using his own body, achieving neutral buoyancy and showing how without flailing arms or legs, he allowed the surge to sway him gently. He even tried to smile at them around his regulator mouthpiece. Bobby cocked his head, but Judy Ann mimicked him and before long was suspended in the surge, nodding her approval.

Their depth was shallow, less than thirty-five feet, and the towering black cliffs of sharpened limestone barely a football field's distance away. The ocean swept across the breath of the Caribbean from the Colombian Basin across the Beata Ridge, its swells and wind-driven waves mounting to great heights before crashing and thundering into the cliffs of Charming Island. Warren marveled that the surge was as civilized as it was that morning.

Even the mildest of storms or nor'easters obliterated the coastline with mountainous seas and spray that rose high into the air. At times the salt from these seas blistered onion crops a half mile inland and growers covered their trucks to keep them from the corroding sea water. At such times the surge grew deadly and the sea swept the bottom clean of all but the most stubborn hard corals. The soft corals too were stunted. Sea fans displayed tattered edges, vase sponges their rips and holes, and pale anemones hid themselves in rock crevices and ridges.

They picked their way along this battered seascape walking on their hands, heads down, like picnickers in a wheelbarrow race. Warren had tried to sell the Whites two pair of light gloves to protect their hands. This entrepreneurship set Bobby growling about nickel-and-diming him to death when he'd already paid through the nose to ride on the crummy boat. All the extras should be free, he said, and bought bright yellow work gloves from a hardware store instead. Judy Ann lost hers whenever she moved, and finally tucked the clumsy things under her weight belt.

So the search began in haphazard fashion and without the stringent grid system Warren had long employed to cover each foot of bottom only once. He was delighted to be free of that today and just enjoying a dive. The Whites wouldn't know the difference. He imagined Bobby telling his buds back home how he searched for sunken treasure.

Sunshine warmed the sand and shallow waters, sparkling with lazy energy and yellow light. He led the Whites out to sea, away from the search area toward deeper water. He'd check *Esteban's* anchor and give them a peek at the deep blue, he thought. Once in awhile a large grouper wandered there, or barracuda, something for them to talk about later. A little danger, even imagined, spiced things up for the telling of it back home.

The bottom gave way to rippled sand, mirroring the water's surface. Their descent was gradual and when they reached the anchor Warren saw it was held fast with plenty of chain resting on the bottom. Judy Ann lost her fear entirely and treated the anchor as a treasure itself, kneeling beside it and petting the shank.

Descending from the anchor, the water assimilated the blue color that has fascinated poets and song writers for centuries, that indescribable deep blue, never successfully photographed or brought to life by anything but the eye. They swam abreast across a small field of turtle grass and out onto the trackless white sand. The shark appeared at the far reaches of their vision and only Warren saw it cruising there. A silhouette. He couldn't identify it. Most likely a sand shark, he guessed. Or even a nurse. No danger either way, except from the panic it might generate in Bobby and Judy Ann. Since shark sightings were rare he hadn't covered the possibility with them, nor the action they should take. More correctly, the actions they should not take.

He swam slightly ahead of them, turned and settled to the sand on his knees, motioning them to do likewise. He made the sign of a swimming dorsal fin, followed quickly by the universal OK sign. Judy Ann's eyes grew large inside her mask. With both hands, palms outward, he indicated the importance of remaining calm. Only then did he turn and once again locate the shark swimming in the distant gloom and point it out to them. Judy Ann slid close to him. Bobby jerked his thumb toward the surface. Warren shook his head and repeated the calm down signal.

Bobby bolted upward, his fins leaving a cloud of sand and silt behind. Warren grabbed Judy Ann's upper arm and calmed her. She nodded and remained by his side, trembling. If Bobby had enough sense to inhale and exhale normally on the ascent he'd likely survive, though Warren marked their depth at just under fifty feet. Deep enough for serious injury.

The shark had bolted too, frightened by Bobby's sudden ascent. He pointed that out to Judy Ann and it relaxed her.

He spotted Bobby on the surface treading water, pumping his legs. If he'd embolized, that wouldn't last, as the compressed air in his blood streamed upward to kill his brain function. Slowly, he led Judy Ann to the surface. If Bobby held his breath during ascent, he had about five minutes to live. If not, he could still exhibit a number of serious air expansion symptoms. Warren swore to himself. A panic reaction to sharks is foolish, but predictable. He should've anticipated, and warned them.

Their heads broke the surface behind Bobby, several yards away. Warren was alert now and cautious about confronting a panicked diver. He spit his mouthpiece and grabbed Judy Ann's BCD with both hands, pulling her close. "Stay put," he ordered in a firm, quiet voice. "I have to calm him down. Understand?"

She nodded. "Doesn't seem like he knows we're here."

"Panic. Sees me, he's going to lose it and try to climb on my head or something, so stay back. Be calm."

Warren swam a wide circle around Bobby White and approached him face on, stopping more than a yard in front of him. “Inflate your BC!” Warren commanded. “Relax!”

Bobby pounded his fins against the water, thrusting himself at Warren. Panic on the surface is usually more dangerous to the rescuer than panic underwater, which is most dangerous to the panicker. Warren repeated his command. “Inflate your BC! Do it now!”

Bobby’s eyes were glazed. His mouthpiece was gone and he sucked at the air with quick labored breaths that came in loud gasps, drawing in more salt water than fresh air, pushing Bobby even further from reason. “Damn it, Bobby! Calm down. Calm down,” Warren continued, though he saw now how hopeless it was. He’d never get through to him in this condition.

All along Warren was backing away from Bobby’s pumping legs. The Texan seemed almost superhuman, with enough strength and stamina to last the day. Ideally there would be help from another diver, but Judy Ann was frightened and keeping well away from her husband. Warren wished for an oar, even an article of clothing to make contact, so Bobby couldn’t get a grip on him, but there was nothing and Warren knew before long Bobby would be lost. He’d exhaust himself and drink salt water.

He knew the risk when he finally stopped retreating and let Bobby come to him. The man was howling now, like some poor beast in a trap. His irises were flat, pupils black with horror. He thought he was dying. Warren faced him and remained still.

A moment later Bobby’s arms crashed from the water and closed like jaws around Warren’s neck, while the tireless legs pumped and pumped their hard punches along the front of Warren’s own legs and groin. Bobby climbed onto Warren’s head and pressed his face underwater. Warren had forgotten to replace his mouthpiece after shouting his commands, but drew a short breath just in time to save himself from drowning.

Warren usually dived without any type of buoyancy device but had donned one today because of the surge, and it saved him. He’d inflated it before allowing Bobby to approach and now it supported them both, though just barely. Bobby continued to struggle and kept Warren’s face in the water. The first priority before he could take charge was to recover his mouthpiece and get an air supply, then do what needed to be done, and do it quickly.

He knew the regulator mouthpiece, the second stage, was dangling somewhere along the right side of his body, though it might easily be tangled among both divers’ sets of equipment. It might be pressed in between them, twisted in a tangle of nylon webbing, D-rings, buckles and rip-stop nylon that made up the BCs. The best way to find it was to begin at the source, where the first stage valve was attached to the tank valve, then follow the hose to the second stage mouthpiece. He tried to reach over his right shoulder but the crush of Bobby's death grip made it impossible. Warren knew the regulator was there and without it he would die. Drown with his mouth and nose only inches below the surface. But it was there, because it had to be there. Two thousand pounds per square inch of air pressure said it was there. But he couldn't reach it again on his second try and he was fast becoming disoriented himself for lack of oxygen. He needed air. He needed to breathe now.

His left hand was free to deflate the BC. If he did that he would sink and Bobby would loosen his grasp because the last thing a drowning victim wants is to go down. That meant Warren had one chance to find and recover the regulator. He would have to do it quickly and get it right the first time or risk losing his own life, and Bobby's for sure. And those pumping legs might easily smash his face as he descended.

The inflator hose needed to be held above his head to drain the air. Bobby saw it, screamed like a madman and tore at Warren's mask with both hands, grasping the snorkel and ripping the strap from its stainless steel buckle. The mask fell away toward the bottom and Warren had now lost both breathing and sight.

But the air squeezed from the BC bladder and Warren sank. At first Bobby held tighter and Warren felt the knotted muscles of his forearms smashing his ears and the pumping legs came to the level of his chest pounding his rib cage, threatening to force Warren to lose control of his lungs. The stored air would gush out and he'd suck water instead. At some level of Bobby's semi-consciousness he must've understood the greater horror of following Warren underwater and he kicked Warren repeatedly in the head, first with his knees, then his feet.

Warren groped for the regulator hose when he was free and found it almost immediately, followed it to the mouthpiece and slammed it into this mouth. He exhaled forcefully and blew the water clear, then inhaled a joyfully sweet breath of air. It arrested his freefall slightly and cleared his head enough to tap a small amount back into his BC to maintain himself just below Bobby's flailing fins.

Salt water stung his eyes and the bubbles created by Bobby's struggle made it difficult to know which side of Bobby he was looking at. He must come up behind him.

Now the difficult part, Warren thought. He must subdue Bobby physically before he hyperventilated and passed out. Though Warren had done this before on several occasions it was never without serious risk and a bit of luck. And this was the first time nearly blind, without a mask to see everything clearly.

He moved to position his body just behind and below the struggling swimmer. He hoped Judy Ann wouldn't get any ideas in his absence. He glanced over to where he'd left her and he thought she was still maintaining her position. He flipped her the OK sign but couldn't tell if she saw it. He checked Bobby again then moved up quickly behind him, grabbing his thighs and climbing to his weight belt, reached around he flipped the quick-release buckle, unthreaded it and pulled the weights away from his body and dropped them. Without hesitation he continued his climb up Bobby's back until he locked his right arm over Bobby's shoulder and around his chest. With the other hand he found the Texan's inflator and mashed the inflate button until the glorious sound of low pressure tank air hissed into the bladder. It rolled Bobby onto his back, pillowed his head and forced him to float face up.

Warren held him by the tank valve, stripped his mask and placed his mouth against Bobby's left ear. "Listen to me, you dumb son-of-a-bitch! If you don't quit kicking and struggling I'm going to deflate that BC and let you sink. Do you hear me?"

"Bobby! Relax for crying out loud!" Judy Ann shouted from a safe distance. "You're going to herniate yourself."

They spent more than a quarter hour like that, floating and waiting. Bobby struggling from time to time, then resting from exhaustion, panting. Warren repeating again and again. "Slow your breathing rate. Slow your breathing rate. Relax. Relax." Judy Ann picked up the litany but Bobby didn't respond to either of them.

"He's lost it," Judy Ann told Warren. "Like he's in some other world. Should we call 911?"

"There's no 911 here," Warren said. "We're all he's got, so let's just get him calm, so he can breath normally. Most likely has a splitting headache by now. When he's calm I want to check him for lung injuries. Make sure he's only suffering from panic, not something worse."

"Seems to me like there isn't anything worse."

"Well, not in the water, I guess."

"He just lost it."

Warren asked, "See my mask and Bobby's weight belt down there anywhere?"

She bent over and popped her head up almost immediately. "Yeah, I see them. Can I go down and get them?"

"Sure. Take it easy though."

Judy Ann swam close to him. "Do you want to know something?"

"What?"

"You're my kinda guy. Bobby'll never thank you for this but I know what you did." She pushed her mask up and kissed his lips. "Thanks."

He watched her descend and thought, despite himself, that she really meant it.

Warren first decided to take them back to the boat, which wasn't far, but it finally occurred to him that it was better for Bobby if he recovered and continued the dive, making his panic a smaller part of things, easier to recant later. Even a jackass hates to feel like one, Warren reasoned.

He explained this to Judy Ann and she agreed almost immediately. They floated near Bobby's feet and for another fifteen or twenty minutes said very little. Then Judy Ann pulled her mask and snorkel down around her neck and said, "That's what you told us to do. Put it around the neck so it wouldn't get lost."

Warren smiled for the first time that day. "Just one of those little things."

She smiled back. "Okay if I go up by his head? He won't go crazy again now. I want to talk to him."

"Sure."

He could hear her soft voice clearly. "Bobby. It's me. You got to snap out of it boy. You almost died. Scared yourself to death. Scared me too."

"I'm sorry," he answered. "I don't know what to do now. I'm scared."

"I know."

"Can I talk to the instructor?"

Judy Ann motioned for Warren to come up the other side of Bobby's prostrate body, and when he looked into the Texan's eyes he saw that reason had returned with remorse. "How you doing?"

"I screwed up."

"Everybody screws up."

"I really screwed up."

"Pain anywhere?"

"My legs hurt."

"No doubt. You ran a two-minute mile. I mean like pain in the chest, any trouble breathing, that kind of thing."

"Don't think so. I'm just sore."

They were silent awhile.

Finally Warren asked, "Ready to go back down?"

Bobby rolled to look at him. "Am I okay?"

"You shouldn't be, shooting to the surface like that. If you'd held your breath we'd be turning you over to Ebank Brothers Mortuary now. When you're in the ocean, expect to see things that live there, like sharks, eels, barracuda, whatever. This ain't the damned zoo. Just don't panic. Don't bother them and they won't bother you. Most of the time anyway. Get it?"

Bobby surprised Warren with a grin. "Yeah," he said. "Let's get back down there."

Their descent was uneventful and Warren's careful scan of the bottom revealed nothing that could be *Imperial* or any part of her. Once again, he thought, the only remaining monument to his ancestor's struggle and death hid itself from him.

Bobby White returned Warren's OK signal and they moved off three abreast toward an isolated coral reef, a colorful island in a rippling white sand sea. Common reef fish flicked and zigzagged above their lonely island - brilliant porkfish, yellow striped grunts, parrotfish and the ubiquitous blueheads. At this depth the sea fans and other soft corals seemed less bruised and beaten by the seas, with several large tube sponges growing long as Warren's arm. Peeking inside, he found a tiny spider shrimp that he pointed out to Judy Ann. She eeked in her regulator, then cooed. Bobby kneeled nearby, scanning their periphery.

Even the tiniest reef is a microcosm of all the great barrier reefs of the world. Large reefs are a smorgasbord for the eye but there's too much of it, but here, just enough to teach them something about the whole. Warren remembered how years ago he'd loved to lie on the sand in shallow waters and wile away an hour watching a tiny and industrious spectacle of underwater life such as this. Unlike one of Judy Ann's aquariums, with faded colors and shriveled sizes, animals muted to fit their prison environment, the sea had more to show her here. Just then he spotted an octopus holding itself very still, blending in the mottled corals to allude them. Much more to show them, he thought smiling.

An octopus of average size, about two feet in length, clutching a clam tightly with three of its tentacles. The octopus is highly intelligent, and though a shy creature, can be formidable if challenged, especially for food.

Bobby remained on watch, but Warren was able to point the octopus out to Judy Ann and her eeks grew quite loud until he got her subdued. The octopus however, was frightened and emptied its ink sac, eliciting further eeks until Warren feared the invertebrate had slipped away in its camouflage. An octopus sitting on a coral head in broad daylight is a rare sight. They were nocturnal creatures and Warren saw them often on night dives.

The ink dissipated and the octopus remained motionless on the coral. Besides intelligence, octopuses possess keen eyesight, quick reflexes and delicate tactile sensing. Touching an octopus is a threatening, sometimes dangerous business for the shy creature. Warren removed his gloves and with extreme patience, slowly slid one hand toward the soft, saclike body. Its prominent eyes watched and winked but there was no other movement. Index finger extended, he made contact. The octopus responded immediately, spinning a tentacle around the finger - holding tight, then feeling gently with its suckers. The three tentacles holding the clam tightened their grip.

In the flick of an eye Warren's other hand appeared and jerked the clam from the octopus' grasp. The little mollusk drew itself up in surprise but held its ground, staring at Warren in outrage. Or was it playfulness? The eyes seemed expressive and bold to Warren and he chuckled. Judy Ann slid closer and he could see in her eyes and from the wrinkles at the corners of her mouthpiece how amazed she was at what had just happened, and Warren guessed that never before had she had more than faddish passion for the creatures she trapped in her aquariums. He had one more surprise for her.

Slowly, Warren extended the hand holding the clam. Not all the way to where the octopus sat, but a foot away, tight in his grasp. A puff of sand, a whip-like motion and the clam was returned to its owner. Warren laughed at the octopus's strength and coordination, yet neither used against him. Now with its dinner clutched by four tentacles, the octopus puffed itself with obvious pride at defeating the big critter exuding bubbles from its head.

But Warren wasn't giving in so easily and stole the clam a second time. He felt Judy Ann snuggling under his other arm, and when he turned to her, tears glistened in her magnified blue eyes almost like diamonds. She was hooked. Warren played with the octopus at least a dozen times more to convince himself the thing really did have a sense of humor that surpassed its hunger for a clam. And when he finally returned the meal for the last time, the octopus held it lightly with one tentacle and by then he'd convinced himself the little mollusk wanted to play all afternoon.

Judy Ann had managed to bring Bobby into the circle for the last few acts, but his concentration wandered. Divers descend for reasons of their own. Bobby White exhibited little curiosity or sense of discovery, and would most likely never know the true gratification of scuba. No surprise. Warren always thought inner space or outer space must be somewhat the same. If you didn't pay attention, relax and wonder about it, well, you didn't get it. Most everything you saw, touched, or heard - on the moon or underwater - might be virgin. You were likely the first to ever see it. He marveled that such a miracle might be something others found unimpressive.

Warren retrieved his tank pressure gauge and peered at the numbers - 900 psi. Enough air for him for another half hour, but he guessed the Whites would be sucking it down to almost zero by now, so he turned and held up the gauge for them to see. They took the hint and after some fumbling, recovered their own gauges, which were low. Judy Ann with 300 psi and Bobby almost empty at about 100. Warren made the thumbs up signal and they began their ascent.

"Inflate your BCDs and let's snorkel to the boat," Warren ordered them on the surface.

Judy Ann exclaimed, "I'll never forget that as long as I live!" Turning to Bobby she asked, "How cool was that?"

"They're fish, right? Isn't that the kind of thing they do?" He pressed his power inflate button. "But yeah, it's cool."

Warren led the way back to *Esteban* and thought he detected a note of disguised awe in Bobby's voice. As with the rays, Bobby had seen a new and dynamic thing. Just so he didn't want to form an international corporation now for performing octopuses. The Octopus Review, he thought. Oh, no! Octopussy. At least the wreck of *Imperial* had eluded them, as always. For that he was grateful. He'd find it one day, all alone, and with time to honor the dead, maybe recover a jar of sand nearby, hoping a shard of Reggie Wilson's worn bone was mixed in. He'd bury it as a tribute to his bravery and some measure of atonement for the injustice of his death. A self-righteous thought, since Warren hadn't bothered to attend the burial of either his father or mother, and known exactly where to find them both when they were still alive. This thought should've made him ashamed, but instead it just made him angry.

They climbed onto the swim step, tossed their fins aboard and finally finished stowing their gear before Warren began to wonder about the other divers.

He found Rosa and Armando below in the galley drinking Cokes. "Whites are back aboard," he said. "Any sign of the others?"

"Should I climb to the flying bridge and search for their bubbles?" Armando wanted to know. He loved to use the large, expensive binoculars.

"Yeah," Warren said. "Do that, Armando." He needed a moment alone with Rosa.

Several minutes passed before either of them spoke. Rosa was sitting in the booth, arms crossed, eyes on the tabletop.

"We went to dinner Rosa. We hugged and kissed, of course." He thought something close to the truth might be the best course. "I loved her when we were kids, back home. A million years ago."

"But not long enough to go from hugging and kissing to hand shaking," Rosa said.

"Jealousy doesn't become you."

Rosa placed her large hands on the table and spread her long slender fingers. "A handsome black man comes to take me to dinner," she said. "You see us in the restaurant dancing and kissing, and you know we have been lovers before, and that's okay with you?"

The trap was sprung. "Of course not," he said.

"Of course not," she repeated to him. "Of course not."

He retreated to the flying bridge. Armando had sighted the bubbles, pointing them out a few yards astern. They were returning underwater. Freddie still possessed his uncanny sense of direction. In a foreign environment he'd lined them up perfectly with *Esteban*. If he was showing off, Warren decided it had worked. He was impressed. Even the most experienced diver is often fooled on a sand flat, even more so fighting a surge.

Their arrival on the island had been so strange, Rosa's reaction so strong, Warren had said but a few passing words to Freddie, and obviously too many to Ruth. Not that he was anxious for conversation. His old mentor seemed surprisingly unchanged by the years, while Warren felt damaged, even bedraggled by time's passing. His boat needed paint and the services of a first-rate diesel mechanic. He'd shacked up with a black Pentecostal dishwasher who had a son by some other guy. He owed most of his present and future earnings to a fat man plotting to overthrow the government and trap him into smuggling, a serious felony most likely to land him in jail, or worse. Now, one day after their arrival, he was yearning after Freddie's widowed daughter. He worried that he and the old man had way too much to talk about, and once they got started the result was likely to be disastrous.

But it was Myron, not Freddie, who finally climbed the flying bridge ladder. "Just a one-tanker?" Myron questioned.

Warren shrugged. "Didn't think anybody wanted more than that today, but I've got enough air in the system for refills if you want." *Esteban* was equipped with an onboard compressor and storage air enough to fill forty-eight tanks.

"Naw," Myron said. "Ain't much to see really, is there?"

"Sorry. Didn't expect to find it today, did you?"

"Nope." Myron grinned. "Like lookin' though."

"Me too. Rosa's a little pissed with me just now. Want to check and see if she made sandwiches or something for lunch? Save me getting my ass chewed one more time."

"Sure," Myron said, climbing down.

Later, Warren learned Rosa had done more than just make sandwiches. Two loaves of homemade bread and the Pink Sands Hotel's famous lobster filling and crisp lettuce created the best sandwiches any of them could remember. She'd also shaped a fresh fruit medley that spelled *Esteban* on a large, handmade wooden platter. Armando had snorkeled the sand flats for conch, sliced fresh, making hors d'oeuvres to dip in Rosa's highly-regarded hot sauce. Key lime pie for dessert with dark island coffee and whipped cream. A clean white tablecloth hid the chipped paint of the galley table where this feast was presented as nicely as in any fine restaurant. The plates were China, the silverware silver, and the matching serving platters contrasted so sharply with the boat's surroundings it appeared even more lavish than it was.

Warren came to this feast when it was half eaten. Myron hadn't bothered to report back to him that Rosa had made sandwiches.

Ruth was complimenting Rosa. "I've been on a hundred dive boats," she said in a worshipful voice, "and never seen anything like this! It's just incredible, Rosa! Marvelous, just marvelous."

"Sounds like a 7-Up commercial," Myron said, recalling Geoffrey Holder's famous Uncola ads of the 1970s. "Ha! Ha! Ha!" He removed an imaginary hat and threw his head back.

Armando was laughing. Rosa demure. Warren said, "Shut up, Myron."

Warren didn't admit it to himself, but Rosa had impressed Ruth and he didn't like that. A suppressed belief that Ruth was a cut above a black dishwasher with an illegitimate son? He'd settled for Rosa because she was all he deserved as a middle-aged loser - a fellow who spurned his family though they'd supported and loved him since his birth. He wondered, were his viewpoints powered by some twisted sense of self-flagellation? He didn't want to think about it. Face the likelihood that his life had always been about filling the hole left inside him since Stephen's death. His adventures gave him hope. Rosa was part of it.

Freddie had been watching Warren and now led him up to the flying bridge where they might find privacy. The large red dive flag, its diagonal white stripe pointing to the water, snapped in the breeze just above their heads. The old man had quickly found his sea legs and though most of his diving in the past decade had been freshwater, the smell and taste of salt, the motion and embrace of the sea, renewed him. In a flash, he recognized Warren's bitterness though the younger man went to great lengths to hide it behind a bemused expression. He wondered if beneath it all the boy wasn't still the boy he remembered, just scabbed over and scared.

Warren settled in his captain's chair. Freddie on the starboard life jacket locker.

"What in hell's the matter with you?" the old frogman asked.

"Excuse me?"

"You look like some pussy who just got jilted by a B-team cheerleader."

"Pussy? Really?" Warren's temper flared. "Wasn't it that kind of talk landed you in jail ten minutes after you got here? What in hell's the matter with you talking to me like that?"

"You got a woman and boy down below, and you're messing around with my daughter. What do you think? I'm some old geezer with his head up his ass? That what you think? I can't see what's going on? Your woman knows. Boy too, I bet. What I *should* do, is kick your dumb ass."

Warren's surprise was complete. The shock of his first boyhood meeting with Freddie-the-Frogman was duplicated again now. If anything, the distress was deeper, cutting as it did across the years as if they meant nothing. He fumbled for words to express his outrage. All he thought to say was, "It's none of your business."

And that made Freddie laugh.

Several minutes elapsed and they didn't speak. The flag snapped and the breezes fanned Freddie's thinning hair. *Esteban* bobbed at anchor and the murmur of voices below seemed miles away.

Finally Freddie said, "I've gone about this all wrong." He drew his feet up onto the life jacket locker and hugged his knees to his chest, as a much younger man might do. "For some years now I've been corresponding with your mother."

Warren felt betrayed. "You've been writing letters to my mother?"

"Yes."

"Why?"

"You mean what did we say to each other?"

"No," Warren said. "I mean why did you write to each other? You never even met."

Freddie sighed. "We did meet twice, when she was dying of cancer."

"Why, I asked you?"

"She wrote me about you and we became friends." Freddie stood and faced the sea, his profile to Warren. "I think she was the bravest person I ever met. These days they make fun of good Christian ladies like her, you know, church lady, but I doubt any of those assholes could die as beautifully as she did, in pain, suffering every minute. She avoided the painkillers too, until at the end. Disease wasn't the greatest sadness in her life. Do you know what the greatest sadness was?"

"Shut up. It's none of your business."

Freddie turned to face him. "Do you think I came to this crummy little island on vacation?"

"I don't care why you came. It's none of your business."

The old instructor's slate-gray eyes were cold as winter fog, but his voice came softly. "You might be right. Not my business, except your mother was my friend and only asked one thing of me, that I would come here and talk to you."

"Great. Well, you've accomplished it then."

"Not quite." Freddie's eyes were gripping. "She wanted me to pose a question to you."

"Great. Pose it."

"Why didn't you come home? Why did you abandon your parents?"

"That's two questions."

"Don't be a smart-ass."

Warren spun his chair away and stared ahead, across *Esteban's* bow, and refused to answer. Finally he said, "Get off my flying bridge."

"Not yet. Do you know what she told me? She said you turned your back on your mother and father because you were ashamed. Not of them, but yourself. Is that true?"

Warren was furious. So angry it was all he could do not to grab Freddie by the neck and throttle him. He applied every ounce of self-control he possessed and answered in a level tone. "She wrote me. I got the message. She didn't need to send you. Could've saved your money. Travel ain't cheap these days."

"Love like that isn't cheap either," Freddie responded in stronger voice. "Is that true? Are you ashamed of yourself? Do you have some problem so overpowering you can't solve it?"

"Guess you didn't get the part about it's none of your business."

"Sure I did." Freddie's tone was lighter now. "I got it, but then I'd already peeked into your life. Now I've gone out on your boat. Man, what a mess. This boat is dirty. The engine sounds like something in a crummy city bus. The bright work is dull. Paint's peeling off. When you come up from below there's more barnacles on the hull of this craft than on a pier post. It's the kind of boat that's owned by somebody without pride in himself. So I'm going to ask you again what you've got to be so ashamed about. Speak up, boy. You're not fifteen anymore."

It occurred to Warren then that Freddie was baiting him, and that discovery calmed him. "Did my mother tell you she forgave me?"

"Yes, she did."

"Then can't you just leave me alone?"

Freddie heaved another of his heavy, obvious sighs and turned back to the sea. "Let's drop it then, for now," he said. "But keep this in mind. I didn't come down here to fail and I haven't backed off on anything in my life. You think about that." He started for the ladder, then stopped. "Fat man at the hotel told me he owned this boat and that if things didn't happen like he wanted, it might be up for sale pretty soon. Know anything about that?"

Warren stared at the top of Freddie's head as the old man scampered down the ladder, leaving behind a just bearable strain of truth. God and his mother had it in for him. Maybe there was a Heaven. Explained how they got to be in cahoots.

Half an hour passed and Warren didn't go down and see any of them, and by some miracle nobody came up, or even called up to him. He heard their voices and laughter. No one seemed concerned about what had become of the boat's captain.

Awhile later, Judy Ann's pretty head halted chin level with the flying bridge deck, and she said to his feet, "Hi. All alone up here? Get anything to eat? It was great. Your maid is such a fantastic cook. I'm going to hire her away from you and take her to the States with me when we leave. If we aren't going to do another tank, is it okay if we snorkel?"

The woman's face had the most perfect bone structure, like the rare marble sculpture of a goddess. Stone wouldn't talk, of course. "Yes," Warren said. "You can snorkel."

Hiding on the flying bridge wasn't an option. He'd barely spoken to Ruth or Rosa all day, even Armando. He swung down the ladder and smiled pleasantly at everyone. "Breeze might be freshening a little. Often does midday. Anyone besides Judy Ann that wants to snorkel, now's a good time. Sun's high. Good light."

Ruth said, "Judy Ann and I are buddying up. What's out that way?" She pointed at a diagonal toward the right-hand curve of the cliffs that formed the shallow cove where they'd anchored.

Warren saw the white sand surrounding darker sections of low reef underwater. "More of the same, I expect. Never swam in that direction. Surge is light today, but keep your eyes open and stay clear of the cliffs. Force increases close in. Overpowers you. That sharp limestone's a bone grinder. You'll be nothing but a soft sack of mush for those big morays in the caves along the cliff base. Swallow you whole."

Even Judy Ann laughed at that. "Seems like there's a lot to swallow around here. Come on, Ruthie, let's skin dive, baby."

Ruth shrugged and catapulted from the stern just behind Judy Ann.

Myron said to Bobby, "Your wife has the best ass in the Caribbean. I've seen a lot of 'em. That's the best. Muscular but not too muscular, you know? Jiggles like Jell-O, but not Jell-O."

"Damn it, Myron!" Bobby growled. "You wanna shut up about my wife's ass?"

Warren walked forward to see what had become of Rosa and maybe get her to thaw some. He saw she had cleaned up the lunch dishes and trotted down to the galley. Rosa was washing, Armando wiping. "Hey," Warren said.

"Did you eat?" Rosa asked.

"A little."

"I'm sorry," she said.

"For what?"

"I'm jealous."

Warren nodded, "They're tourists, Rosa. They'll be gone. We'll still be here."

"I know," she said and wiped her hands. "You tried not to look at her or talk to her. It made me jealous. I'm sorry."

"Forget it." They hugged and Armando grinned.

From on deck Freddie shouted, "Warren! Judy Ann wants you."

Warren climbed up to the main deck and walked aft to the fantail where Freddie, Myron, and Bobby were all facing out to sea. "What's up?"

"Judy Ann is calling for you," Freddie said.

Warren jumped up onto the gunwale, searching for Judy Ann and Ruth. They were more than a hundred yards apart. Judy Ann the farthest away. He cupped his hands around his mouth. "You okay?" he shouted.

She was bobbing up and down in the water. "Cannons! There are cannons everywhere under the water!"

CHAPTER FIFTEEN

Cannons. Warren heard but doubted his ears. His stomach churned. Hopefully she couldn't tell a cannon from a water-logged palm. Stumbling, he searched for his snorkeling gear. What if she had found *Imperial*? The irony panicked him.

His fin tips struck water and pitched him slap-bellied onto his face. Out of breath, he swam toward her, unnerved by what he suddenly knew was true. Then he saw them. *Imperial* had 120 cannons, one of the most heavily armed, fearsome ships in the world in 1806, and there below, her guns rested where they had fallen long ago, in rows, unmolested.

Warren forgot Judy Ann.

Bent rays of afternoon light flickered across the pitted faces of the guns and he thought them almost too real to be believed. They seemed a commonplace sight, just what one expected, and this made a lie of a lifetime dream. His visions proved to be nothing more than things anyone could see. His faith in them meant nothing. Even so, all he could think to do was reach out and touch it, like putting a hand back into a dream to see if it returns to you bloody.

Warren spit his snorkel and kicked back to the boat. "Armando! Toss me another rope and float ball!" Warren caught and re-coiled it, then turned and swam away. He slowed his approach to the wreck site and tried to take it all in. A coral mound in the shape of a ship, guarded by its decaying cannon, most still pointing outward at the enemy, others lying about in haphazard disarray. *Imperial* was a reef of hard and soft corals, its massive beams, polished decks, noble sails long ago eaten by fire, sea salt, and worms. What remained was a living thing, as a grave is a living thing, where soft and hard corals replicate shrubs and grass above a resting place.

Warren's feet kicked high, straight into the air, driving him down to the bottom. He wrapped the rope twice around the black mouth of a gun that last spoke in battle, made it secure with a bowline, then swam lazily back to the surface. He had claimed *Imperial* with a blazing orange float ball. She was his prize now. Judy Ann White be damned.

The discovery held his full attention as nothing had ever done before. He failed to notice the large man concealed above in the sea grape, watching from a few hundred yards along the headland. Wesley Bens had hidden himself well behind thick foliage and sat cross-legged, steadying his elbows on his knees, binoculars bringing Warren's head into sharp focus. Bens knew they had found something significant and decided to remain until he had the sense of it. At the same time he marveled at how simple it would be to take the head shot. A scoped rifle waited uncased behind the seat of his pickup. Warren's head bobbed like a ripe coconut on the surface. "Pop!" he said aloud. "Pop, you pissant beach bum bastard. Soon now. Oh, soon."

He wondered then about the small blocks of plastic C4 high explosive in the room where he slept. What would it do to an ancient shipwreck? Might it not be like the rays?

Warren felt like a thoroughbred without running room. He had tanks to dive, but remembered now that they were empty. *Esteban* was equipped with an onboard air compressor, but to save fuel he never ran it when the boat was in port or anchored somewhere. He'd have to start the engine, then run it in neutral to fill tanks. He'd never done this because he only turned the air compressor on when the boat was underway, filling tanks with the same fuel used to power the boat. He became enraged, in fact, if anyone tried to fill tanks while the boat was stationary.

Freddie-the-Frogman was already attaching the filler whips to the tank valves, humming a tuneless ditty as he worked. The diesel had not been started, and this at least hinted that Warren might still be in command of his own vessel.

Climbing aboard and tossing his fins on deck, he asked in a stern voice, "Has anyone bothered to check and see if tanks can even be filled while the boat is stationary?"

"What?" Freddie snapped. "Do we look like idiots? Of course they can."

"It's not my policy to do it," Warren replied.

"Your policy? You have a policy? You barely got a boat. Start up the damn eggbeater and let's get these tanks filled. Daylight will be gone and we'll have pissed away our chance to see the wreck close up. What's your problem anyway?"

"My problem is that this is my boat. The engine is not an eggbeater. It's a sophisticated 12-71 Detroit Diesel that burns one gallon of fuel per hour. And I pay for it."

"No," Bobby White jumped in, "I pay for it."

Freddie stood and stared at Warren. "How long to fill these tanks?"

"Half hour at least."

"So, two quarts of gas?"

"Number Two Diesel fuel."

"Right. Well, how about I give you the buck fifty right now? Save all this indecision."

Warren felt trapped and knew Freddie's anger and sarcasm spilled over from what they'd left unsaid earlier on the flying bridge. He needed to regain control, put an end to bickering. "That won't be necessary Mr. Frogman, but don't assume anything aboard my vessel. I make the decisions. You're just another tourist, far as I'm concerned. Keep trying to take charge and I'll give you back to Sergeant Cumberbatch."

Before Freddie could reply, Ruth stepped between them and smiled. "You boys are acting silly. Enough! We came here to dive. Now let's start the boat, fire up the compressor, fill the tanks, and just do it. Okay?"

Warren nodded and climbed up to the controls.

Freddie locked eyes with his daughter and soon lost the stare-down.

Water clarity around the island averaged 100 to 150 feet and water temperatures remained constant between 80 and 82-degrees Fahrenheit. Here in the shallows, a relentless surge fanned the sand and visibility varied. One minute a hundred feet, twenty the next.

Warren armed each of them with hammers and other tools to beat away the hard corals and shovel through the shifting sand. "The British sailors gave these guys time to ferry their goods ashore," Warren reminded them. "We aren't going to find a load of gold bullion. It wasn't a treasure ship anyway. What would be nice is confirmation it's the *Imperial.* A long shot, but keep your eyes open. Nothing looks now like what it was then, so you'll have to pound the hard corals off. See if you can spot things with straight edges and sharp corners - man-made. Don't senselessly beat hell out of the reef. Study things. Use your imagination. There'll be metal but no wood. A rifle or pistol might be there, but just the iron parts." He stared at them since no one had responded. "Understand?"

"Yeah," Bobby White said. "We get it."

A moment later there was nothing left to see on the surface but bubbles, and Wesley Bens stood and stretched behind his cover. The divers were invisible in water made cloudy by swinging hammers and shoveling. Digging at a reef. Some sort of collective hallucination? He saw nothing. Dark shape of a reef. A half dozen like it nearby. It made no sense. His scuba equipment was in his truck. Once they left he'd go down for a closer look.

Warren had used his knife handle to tap a cannon, just for luck, and moved on, away from the others to clearer water. First he'd decided to make a full circuit of the *Imperial* reef and see what, if anything, protruded from the coral mound. Two centuries is a long time underwater, but *Imperial* was a large vessel with many tons of iron, brass, copper and other metals. If iron cannon survived then most likely so had smaller brass ones, copper hull nails and gunport hinge pins, anchors and ammunition for cannon, carronade and muskets. Heavy, dense metals that wouldn't corrode for centuries. There would be hundreds, maybe thousands of iron balls. A man in a hurry snatched sword and pistol, his personal possessions, but there wasn't a means to remove heavy items. And while they might have been gentlemen, the British weren't foolish enough to arm their enemies with heavy weapons after taking such costly efforts to defeat them. He reasoned that there must be thousands of musket balls alone resting in the immediate area. The sea couldn't hide them all.

Warren moved on alone. The sounds of hammering and chipping faded. The spirit of adventure that once powered his childhood dream returned, as it always did, then just as suddenly back-filling his mind with frustration and anger. All Freddie had said, and his mother had written, convicted him as a coward, even a fool. Had he atoned for his brother by making a mess of his life, hiding from his parents, refusing to accept responsibility, even love? Back on board a boy waited to become a son, and a woman waited to become a wife. Another woman waited to fall in love again.

He sank to his knees on the sand and reached out to steady himself, curling a hand around a great ring of iron. Warren closed his eyes and thought of home, the little house in Lake Darling. Like a boy, he might tell this tale to Mom and Dad. He listened again to his mother's voice in the letter. She was gone. Dad too. No one left alive who knew him from the beginning. His second stage diaphragm vibrated with his ragged breathing. Today he had everything he wanted and it meant nothing. He might have wept, but laughed instead.

Warren Wilson discovered that after all, he was a fraud. Hadn't escaped from anything. Just denied the obvious. He was who he was - child, son, brother who let his brother drown in a frozen lake out of fright and cowardice. Shame led him astray, but shame too was a lie. The truth is what it is, and if it convicts you then maybe you should let it. He knew for sure you didn't escape it. It followed you even into the depths of the sea.

He removed his mask and wiped a hand across his forehead, eyes, and down the length of his face, then replaced the mask and cleared it of seawater. When he opened his eyes and blinked away the mild sting of salt, his focus rested where he gripped the iron. He pulled himself up so as not to stir the sand and reduce visibility. The iron he held was a circle so large he could easily have swam through its center. He wondered what such a thing could be. Too large for any part of a sailing vessel's rigging aloft, it was pitted and grooved but almost clear of coral. He slid his hand along as he swam its circumference, feeling the edges.

There was an area, on the downside of where the ring lay on the reef, where the circle entered an even larger block of iron and passed through it, continuing out the other side. What was this thing? Had the British thought to rig a tow and salvage *Imperial* for a prize? Surely she was beyond that. The hull had been ravaged and holed by the rocks. The rigging decimated by shelling and battle fire. No. This was something else.

He inhaled, and pulling himself higher, rising above the thing so he could look down upon it. The ring didn't enter a block, it entered the end of a shank. A massive iron shank that stretched beyond Warren's sight. And then he knew, and swam several feet higher until the flukes materialized in the gloom. There were no flukes like these. Giant iron plows. The weight of such an anchor was beyond calculating and he tried to imagine the naked-chested sailors, laboring like oxen at the windlass to raise this giant iron thing from the bed of the sea and then secure it at *Imperial's* bow. Wooden ships and iron men, Freddie had told him long ago when they'd first talked about sunken ships and the men who'd crewed them. Not like men now, unless, Freddie said, you were a frogman. It struck him that he'd come full circle, and not to fail as he had often thought, but to be fulfilled by achieving what many dismissed as fantasy.

Warren kicked and exhaled. A moment later he knelt between the flukes. They stretched along the reef to the sand flats, and he scooped a handful of white, gold, red, green and amber sand. He pulled open his BC pocket and filled it. Then the other. Uncle David would find this in his mailbox. One day he'd go home and sprinkle a jar of it on his parent's grave, joining the family, past to present. All but him. He'd do something about that too. He would. He'd clean up his act. He was a Wilson. One of a great people. He owed them. He owed Stephen, and his parents. He might even stop drinking. There must've been a smile then because he was drinking seawater, and coughed.

He swam away toward the distant sounds of hammering until he found the others and led them to the anchor. The mass and size of it struck them too, and they shook his hand and touched him. Myron hugged him, with a lot of clanking. Freddie put a hand on his shoulder and nodded. Ruth blew him a kiss and the Whites just stared. And Warren thought, as he watched Bobby gape, that these damn people were barely past their first dive and sitting alongside one of the wonders of the world. Did they have brains enough to know it? But then he smiled and thought maybe they weren't so bad. Everyone is a little foolish, after all, and the sea wasn't their place. Yes, he was going to try and do better. He'd talk to Freddie too, and take his medicine. Why not?

In what seemed like only minutes, their tanks were empty and they drifted to the surface singly or with their buddies. The dive was over. The greatest dive Warren ever imagined was at an end. Or just beginning.

They were surprisingly quiet on deck. No one wanted to be the first to speak, to try and put words to something they all knew was beyond talk. But Rosa and Armando had seen the looks on their faces and finally urged the words from them.

"Awesome," Judy Ann said.

Freddie said, "Come here, boy." When Armando was close, he reached inside the dripping catch bag he carried and withdrew a ten-inch copper nail, thick as rebar. "This is for you because it's your discovery much as ours." Then he went to Rosa, placed a small gold coin in her hand and said, "She isn't a treasure ship but somebody had a buck in his pocket."

Rosa stared at her hand. The coin seemed to shine as if it were just minted. "No," she shook her head.

"I've got two more," Freddie said. "There probably won't be many of them, but before it's over we might all find a few." He glanced at the Whites. "Be a shame though if anybody opened their mouths and tomorrow we couldn't even find a parking spot on the ocean around here."

"Well, I sure ain't going to tell anybody," Bobby promised. "I want a handful of those myself."

Warren dug into his BC pocket for his sand. "That's what I got," he said, walking over and dropping a blob of the wet grains into Freddie's hand. "You find those gold pieces together?"

"No," Freddie said. "Fanned the sand all around and they popped up. Take a look." He handed the two coins to Warren.

Warren thought they appeared very worn. A man's head and the name Napoleon. On the back the number 20 and something written in French. "Well," he said. "This is our confirmation."

"Twenty-franc Napoleons," Freddie said. "Oh, well."

"Oh, well?"

"Not worth much. Couple hundred each maybe. Could be less."

The new Warren smiled at his old mentor. "I'll keep them then?"

"Go ahead. I owe you for the gas." Freddie smiled too, but Warren returned the coins.

The warm winter sun was poised to begin its daily drop into the sea and Warren told Armando to start the engine again while he raised the anchor. "Hold on a minute," he told the boy. "I need to get a mark."

They climbed the flying bridge in single file. He planned to take this mark sitting in the captain's chair so when he returned everything would line up. "You'll take the mark with me," he told the boy and sat him on his lap. "It's good for two of us to know this place. You're the only other person I trust." Armando felt a surge of affection, bowing his head and closing his eyes to receive it. While he was still glowing Warren said, "Are you going to look over here and pay attention?"

"Si, Señor."

"Okay, we're anchored northwest of the wreck. We need anchoring room. So, look up there on the cliffs. See the big rock shaped like a hammer?" They both stared for some time before Warren continued. "Far to the right where the cliff turns back to sea is a hole, almost a cave. If we line them up just like that when we come back we'll be right where we are now. Understand? Gives us a position on the coastline and distance from the cliffs, too. See?" Warren grinned.

"I see them," Armando said sternly.

"Hand me the glasses for one more look, then you can turn this baby over and we'll haul anchor."

The boy gave him the glasses. The sun was behind him now and lit the cliffs like a stage. A stage on which something was moving. A large man bent at the waist, disappearing into the brush. Bens.

He handed the glasses back to the boy. "We can find it again, right?"

"Si, Capitán."

"Don't talk silly. Start the engine and warm it up. Watch me and don't be lollygagging around now. When the anchor line is straight up and down swing her out to sea. Be careful. The current will push you as soon as the flukes are free."

"I know," Armando sighed. He'd done it a thousand times. First he's the one person left on earth that Warren can trust, then he's nothing more than a foolish boy. But he was a patient boy and knew his day was coming.

Esteban was constructed as a sport fishing yacht, and a beauty in her day. Below decks, where Freddie followed Warren, she still was. Five steps down beyond the tarnished door, a passageway led forward. To starboard a large head with a salt water commode, sink and roomy shower. To port, the captain's cabin. Farther forward another door, leading to a V-berth that slept six and a rope locker that occupied all the space beyond, right up to the prow.

These spaces were the responsibility of Rosa and Armando, and they were immaculate. The brass work was polished to a soft, satin gleam. The mahogany trim and white bulkheads gleamed in the manner of the yacht she once was. And in the captain's cabin, where Warren now led Freddie, there was carpeting and soft bedding, cleanliness and order. Shelves lined with good books. It was a man's space, ordered and kept alive by a woman.

Freddie sank into a worn leather chair and said, "I've underestimated Rosa." When he saw how Warren's face held no expression he continued. "Maybe you, too. I'm sorry."

"It's okay. I'm behind on maintenance. Always. Engine needs a thorough overhaul, hull needs scrapping and anti-fouling paint, electronics are outdated, and a hundred other things. Money. There's never enough."

"Well," Freddie smiled again. "She takes the sea well and rests in the water like she was born to it. Can't remember a firmer deck under my feet."

Warren nodded. "We need to talk a minute. There's a bigger problem."

Freddie cocked his head and crossed his arms.

"I have an arrangement, like you mentioned, with this fat guy, Javert. He holds the paper on *Esteban*, and with it, our livelihood."

"Got you by the balls?"

"Exactly."

"Maybe we'll get a few more of those gold coins."

"Might," Warren agreed, "but it goes deeper. I've decided to help Javert bring some weapons in to protect his political ambitions. He'll hold me to it, and he's brought in some muscle to be sure. Just now I saw his main guy, a Brit named Wesley Bens, up on the cliffs. Suppose he was watching us. They say he's a diver, and when we're clear he'll be down for a look."

Freddie stood and walked to the open porthole, gazing at the passing coastline. "What political ambitions?"

"Javert leads an independence movement. It appeals to lots of people here because the Brits still rule the island. The governor is appointed by the British Parliament, and though much of his power is symbolic, sometimes symbols are more important than what's practical." Warren chuckled. "I've stayed out of it. Rosa hasn't. Anyway, you've met Sergeant Cumberbatch and our customs officials. They're islanders, and it's islanders who really run the government. So there's no sensible reason to rebel, but that won't stop Javert. He sees big tourist bucks in his future so he's always busy feeding the freedom machine. Cuban who owns the Tortuga has a group opposing Javert. There are others. Rosa and the damned Pentecostals. It's a mess."

"And now you're going to bring weapons into it?" Freddie's voice was sharp.

Warren slid into the chair Freddie had vacated. "Listen. I know it sounds dumb," he said. "There's a vote coming up and nothing can stop that. On the politics I agree with Javert. These people can care for themselves. Helping him might even keep this place from becoming another Jamaica. I don't think Javert wants violence. He's got the most to lose. He gets guns, or maybe not," Warren grinned. "There's no army here for him to fight anyway. Just cops, and they don't carry firearms. They've never been a violent lot."

Freddie's head had sunk into his shoulders. Finally, when he turned from the porthole, he tried to smile. "You and me been scrapping since I got here," he said. "It's your mom with me. But this thing. Hope you got it figured right. For somebody who's not involved, you sure got yourself smack dab in the middle. When do you go and get these weapons? Where are they?"

"Pointe-a-Pitre in Guadeloupe. And soon."

"Middle of the night? Some deserted beach? We flash a light three times and wait for the answer?"

"Nope. Broad daylight. Commercial pier. Boxes marked as dredging equipment for the fat man's noisy piece of crap there in the harbor."

"Can I sit here?" Freddie asked, sliding into the chair behind Warren's desk. "You going over there alone?"

"Done it many times. Few days."

"When do you sleep?"

"Autopilot. Nod at the wheel or sleep on the life jacket locker. No big deal. I know the way."

"Tiring though. We'll come along. Myron and me. Gun running. Cool." Freddie cocked his thumb and fired his forefinger in the air. "Been awhile since I killed a man with my bare hands." He held both hands up. "Arthritis. Fingers are bent at the knuckles. Weaker too. Get older you got to start using the knife more."

Warren's first instinct was to say no, but he wouldn't mind the sleep and the company. If somebody had got wind of the cargo, well, it was the Caribbean. More pirates here now than in all those swashbuckling days put together. Mostly drugs, but a fat load of weapons was just as juicy a prize. He stared at Freddie and said. "I'm the Captain."

"Hey. No problem. I said I was sorry."

Warren glanced out the porthole. Armando had them miles along the coast already. "So," he asked Freddie, "are you still good with a knife?"

"Knives, guns, garrotes and all manner of explosives. Fists too. I'm old, not dead."

"The reason I'm asking is because I think we should do something about Bens right now, before he's strutting around Edward Town with a pocketful of Napoleons."

"Go back, you mean?"

"Yeah."

"And what is 'do something' in your book?"

Warren knew Freddie had killed when he fought in the Pacific during World War II, and from everything Ruth had told him years ago, he was a fearless adversary. Those frogmen were called SEALs now, and just as lethal. Few military men or women take a life, but the Special Forces train for it daily. He knew they didn't hesitate when the time came. He studied the old man sitting behind the desk and wondered. He might be even more fearless today. "Well," Warren hesitated, "I guess I don't want to kill him. Or anybody."

"Fair enough," Freddie said. "Just remember one thing - if you leave a man like that alive, you watch your back forever."

"Can't he be scared?"

"Sure. For awhile. Then he'll figure a way to get even. With you, or maybe your family."

"I don't have any family."

"Sure you do. Just haven't owned up to them yet." He held his palm up as he said this. "I'm not going to lecture."

Warren walked to a tall cupboard, opened the door and pulled out a long, three rubber speargun that barely fit upright in the room. "I was thinking this might scare him."

Freddie laughed. "Scares me."

"Bens has injured his foot somehow. I saw him limping. Maybe the other foot?"

"You that good a shot?"

"Actually, I am. I once shot a swimming lobster between the eyes with this."

"Was it swimming the other way?"

"Sure."

"This may be a little different then."

Warren shrugged, left Freddie there and went to tell Armando to turn the boat around.

CHAPTER SIXTEEN

They anchored half a mile from the wreck site, hidden by the headland and moored close in. Warren put out two anchors and still he knew Armando would have his hands full making certain they didn't drag. The surge was powerful, carrying all the force of the open sea, rebounding as the island threw it back, and *Esteban* caught between.

The Whites were curious. Warren decided to tell them the truth, or something close to it. Judy Ann spotted the speargun and asked what it was for. Lobster, he told her. Freddie talked privately with Ruth. She didn't like it any more than Rosa did when Warren told her. Myron was eager as a puppy.

They left quickly, swimming on the surface. Three red-tipped snorkels soon lost in the chop. The boat seemed large and empty to the five who remained, watching the snorkels disappear.

Rosa was first to speak. "Two hours," she said. "It will be dark. We turn on the engine and lights before then, so they can find their way back." Her heart beat against her breastbone and she prayed for courage.

"Won't this guy they're after see the lights?" Bobby asked. "What if he's got a whole crew with him?" Warren told him to hang back and protect the women.

They had sought each other's company and gathered together at the stern. Rosa knew Bobby was right about the lights, and maybe the rest of it too. "Can you shoot?" she asked him.

"A' course I can shoot. I'm from Texas. Everybody from Texas can shoot. We invented it almost. Ever hear of the Cheyenne? They were real Indians. They fought us for years. Prairies ran red with blood. My family was in it all the way. Great, great Uncle Toad was scalped by Cheyenne warriors not a hundred yards from where our house stands today. Can I shoot?" He chuckled. "I can shoot."

This was the kind of talk that made Armando smile. Alone, above them on the flying bridge to watch the anchors, he felt as if he were the Captain. "There is a gun," he called down. "In the life jacket locker. We use it to shoot sharks." Of course they had never shot any sharks, or even seen many, but that's what

Captain Will had told him years ago.

"Rifle or pistol?" Bobby wanted to know.

"A British rifle."

"Well, let's see it."

Armando opened the life jacket locker and removed the weapon. Ruth started toward the flying bridge ladder to get it but there was a sucking, slopping noise and a giant man wearing a tiny black bathing suit popped from the water and landed on the swim step only a few feet away.

"Afternoon," he said, kicking away his fins and striding to the ladder. He brushed Ruth aside when he saw Armando with the rifle and took the ladder in three strides. "Well, now," he said, snatching it from the boy. "Quite an antique you have here. .303 British." He examined it more closely. "Made in Australia, and in deplorable condition. Green with corrosion. Tut, tut, tut. What a shame." He tossed it overboard and climbed back down.

During this time no one had moved. No one spoke.

"Boys gone off then, heh?"

The surprise was fading but no one seemed able to speak.

"Sort of a timid lot then, are you?"

Bobby stepped forward and said, "You're just lucky that rifle's over the side or I'd show you who's timid."

Bens smiled warmly. "Well, well. I suppose I did give you a start coming out of the sea that way. But by all means, dive down for the rifle. My scuba gear is tied off on your anchor line. Use that if you don't have anything handy. I'll wait right here until you swim back and shoot me."

Bobby didn't move.

"Are you going in?" They all waited in silence. "Well then, let's get acquainted. I'm Wesley Bens, an employee of Monsieur Javert in the town there, come to see how things are progressing with the treasure hunt. Seems as though you've found something. Delightful. Not gold, by chance?"

Three women, a man, a boy. Five against the one, and Rosa knew the odds favored the one. She glimpsed a quiet madness in the intruder's eyes. He was unafraid. More than that, amused by his power over them. Large boned, muscular, relaxed, standing satisfied as a lion in the blood and bones of its fresh kill. Threats no longer necessary. They all saw it.

Rosa asked, "Is that what you think? We are treasure hunters?"

Bens stepped toward her and stopped just short. Broad-shouldered and lanky, she stood her ground with one leg slightly cocked. Her eyes steady and fearless. "You must be the captain's nigger then."

Rosa endured racial slurs since childhood. Now when people said she was a slut, or a dishwashing slut, it failed to cut her. Often, below a polite white skin there was the name-calling. She'd learned to predict when *nigger* would pop from their mouths. She watched them hold it back, saving it until a few drinks loosened their tongues. Nigger was their ultimate weapon. So she smiled at the big man. "Yes. I am the Captain's nigger. And this is the Captain's boat. A vessel I see you were not brave enough to board until the Captain was gone. Such a big man you are, huh?"

Bens did not expect sass from the mistress. His urge was to strike her, or cut her, but his instincts told him to play it cool. "The little bastard up there? Your son?"

Rosa said nothing but her eyes flicked to see Armando's reaction.

Bens smiled. "Your Captain is a dimwit. I disposed of his stingrays and I may yet dispose of his shipwreck, but do remember that my patience isn't everlasting. Boys are easy to catch." He glanced again at Armando, then turned to smile at her as if they were old friends. "That's better. Keep your mouth shut then."

It wasn't logical, Rosa thought, for such a man to check himself this way. She felt the brutishness and malice in him, and on those rare occasions she'd felt it before, the only thing that kept it leashed was equal force, or the threat of it. She stood her ground in silence.

A second later Ruth was at her side. "You have no business on this boat. You're trespassing. Get off before I call the police."

Bens backhanded the woman with such force she lifted from the deck, skidding several feet, colliding with the flying bridge ladder. "Another mouthy bitch," he said.

It was Judy Ann who bent over her and lifted her head. Blood ran freely from Ruth's torn lip onto Judy Ann's bare legs, dripping in bright red dime-sized pools onto the deck. "You son-of-a-bitch," she said.

Rosa stood still but Bobby started for Bens.

"You," Bens said, pointing a finger. "You I will kill."

Bobby halted.

Bens smiled warmly. "Why don't we all relax? Here's the thing. If the little captain of the Love Boat here has found something, then I want it. Or maybe I break a little boy's neck, smash a nigger, or pop, pop a few American tourists." He aimed a finger at Bobby. "Or the captain will do what he's told, and who knows but we might be sending each other Christmas cards? Tell this to Captain Billy Bob. He has one day - 24 hours - to make a firm commitment to me. And I only want half." He shrugged and grinned. "I'm a reasonable fellow. So, do what I ask. Or else. Do you pissants understand *or else*?"

Above him Armando said, "I understand."

Bens' smile faded as he looked up at the boy. He held some sort of speargun about the size of a long-barreled pistol. "What have you got there, boy?"

Armando held the Scubapro Magnum 45 rock steady in his small hands. He'd shot it accurately for more than two years and when he went hunting he strapped it to his thigh in a snap-away plastic holster. It too had been in the life jacket locker. Armando said, "Do you understand *pneumatic*?"

Bens kept his composure, but it was a double-barbed spear and there was plenty of line to reach him.

"From 30 feet this boy can shoot a grouper in the eye," Rosa suggested. "The spear will come out the back of your skull I think, and then we all pull the string."

Bens gazed up at Armando. "Going to shoot me boy? Huh? Not so easy to shoot a man in the face. To kill him. Not so easy."

"Helps if you call his mother a nigger first," Judy Ann said. "I'd pull the trigger and I'm nothin' but a dumb tourist bitch."

Pneumatic spearguns have a high muzzle velocity and are usually more accurate than rubber sling guns. If the boy was afraid, Bens thought, it didn't show on him. The spear remained pointed at his face and the boy's hands steady, like his eyes. "Calm down now, all of you. Can't a mate drop by for a chat without things becoming violent? My, my. Think I'll just be leaving then." He shrugged his huge shoulders, turned smoothly, snatched his fins from the deck and somersaulted back into the sea.

Ruth sat upright and spit blood after him. "Dirty bastard," she said. Then looking up at Rosa. "Dammit girl. Comes out the back of his skull and we all pull on it? I love you."

"Shush," Judy Ann told her, patting her arm. "Let's get you up." After they were standing she told Bobby, "Get a tank. Go down and fetch that rifle. I think we're going to need it."

Rosa climbed the ladder and drew Armando into her arms. He still held the speargun. "Put it down now. He's gone."

"He is gone to find Captain Will and the viejos (old men)."

"Maybe not. Maybe he had enough."

"No," the boy said. "Not him."

Bobby thought Bens could very well be waiting underwater. After all, he'd told them his tank was tied to an anchor line. He wondered if the boy would give up the speargun.

"Mrs. White," Rosa called down. "There is a first aid box in the pilothouse, behind the red cross, for the lady."

"I'll get it. Call me Judy Ann, please."

"And I'm Ruth," Ruth said, spitting blood. "I'd like to be your friend."

Rosa nodded, close to smiling.

Ten minutes later Judy Ann had a Steri Strip across Ruth's split lip and was lecturing Bobby, now outfitted in scuba and sitting on the swim step, both feet in the water but reluctant to go in alone, unarmed. "Okay," she said. "I'll ask him."

Judy Ann climbed the ladder to where both Armando and Ruth were now watching the anchors and the water. "The speargun," she said. "Do you think Bobby can take it with him? He's never shot one, but it would make him feel better being out there alone."

It was Armando who answered. "I can show him."

Armando proved a fine teacher and Bobby an apt pupil. With the small gun strapped to his thigh, Bobby felt a bit like great, great uncle Toad, though he didn't like to think how that had turned out.

"Shoot high," Armando repeated. "Water bends your eye. What you see is farther away than where you see it."

"If I miss, I can just haul on the string, get the spear back and shoot again, right?"

"Si," Armando said. "If you have time. A red snapper will not wait for you. I think the big man might kill you while you are reloading. It is better not to miss, or cut the line and swim away."

It seemed to Bobby White that he was seeing this boy for the first time. A few days before he had seen him for the first time, and joked with Javert that the boy was like a monkey. It shamed him now. The boy was his ally, and he was surprised to hear no fear in the high, child voice. He was in every way a little man, with more pluck than Bobby felt himself. So he reached his hand out and said, "Give me five."

After he was gone the three women and the boy stood together watching his bubbles until they disappeared beneath the stern.

Rosa tussled the boy's hair. "Can you eat a sandwich?"

"Not tuna."

"Climb up and watch your anchors. I will make something for all of us. Not tuna." She smiled. "Don't forget Mr. White's bubbles. See if he finds the gun."

Bobby sat a long time beneath *Esteban's* stern, kneeling on the sand, the heavy surge sliding him back and forth. Visibility was lousy. Much worse then on the wreck site now that they were closer to the cliffs. He could barely see twenty feet and when one of the larger waves moved overhead it swept sand from the bottom like a giant broom and filled the water with it so he saw nothing at all for a minute or more. Bens could be two feet behind him waiting to cut his throat.

The rifle probably rolled away in the surge, or Bens might've taken it. Why would he leave it there for them to retrieve? He shouldn't have listened to his wife. What did she know? He patted the speargun. It was cool to the touch. The surge lifted and swung him again, upsetting his stomach. He was light-headed and weak.

Bobby felt that a certain amount of bravado was essential to his image as a security consultant. You went in a little heavy, like a cop might. Swaggered even, if the job called for it. Might hint that you'd seen some violence yourself, or dealt some out. What did it hurt? Just part of the game. Now he sat beneath a dive charter boat near an almost forgotten Caribbean island with a nasty pneumatic speargun strapped to his thigh, about to search for a deadly weapon not minutes after a hired killer had threatened his life. How did he get sucked into a thing like this? No wonder his belly was doing flips.

He could always go back aboard and say the rifle was gone, swept away in the surge or taken by the Englishman. Armando's frank, trusting eyes. No sir. He'd look around first. Why would Bens hang around? He wanted the wreck not them.

The light was fading. Bobby exhaled a ragged breath and let himself fall forward, then kicked away toward the boat's starboard side where Bens had tossed the rifle. It wouldn't have gone far. Unless the Englishman took it or hid it somewhere in the reef or nearby rocks. The shadow of the boat covered a large area of underwater landscape, and he knew by its motion how the waves played with it. The shadow was dark and beneath it he saw no sign of the rifle. He swam back and forth, sliding his hands in the sand, peeking into rock crevices and spreading what soft corals grew in the surge to see if they hid the weapon.

His fears remained but taking action was better than sitting and waiting. Swimming, searching, thinking out the problem pushed the fear down, but didn't help him find the rifle. Two possibilities existed, he decided. It was near where it was thrown, or it was moved. Only the surge and Bens could've moved it. The surge a short distance. Bens, who knew?

Again, he settled to the sand on his knees. If Bens moved it, there was no reason to take it with him. You can't fire a rifle underwater. It was a heavy old thing and he'd not want it encumbering him during his swim after Warren, Freddie and the lunatic Myron. But where would he ditch it? Drop it somewhere along the way? Not inshore. Too much surge and chance for a mishap. So, deeper then. Bobby nodded and swam toward the open sea.

Because he had no compass or much sense of direction underwater, Bobby swam to his left, and when he'd equalized pressure twice, began circling to his right again, hoping to make a large loop and end up back at the boat. He didn't want to surface and give anyone a look at him, just in case Bens hadn't gone off like he figured.

The rifle was laying in some short turtle grass and he'd almost swam past before catching it in his peripheral vision. With a mask on, it was a lucky find. But there it was, like a cannon in the grass, large and deadly. When he picked it up its weight forced him to add air to his BC for extra buoyancy. Even so, he was back on the sand again when he exhaled. He was struggling with the rifle in the surge and sat back down again on his knees. Swimming with a heavy rifle wasn't easy so he switched it to his right hand to operate his power inflator with his left and achieve neutral buoyancy. He'd done a fine job underwater. Not even a certified diver and about to complete a dangerous mission, and have a story to tell back home. Judy Ann better take his picture when he got the rifle onboard, like those hunting photos he'd seen where the hunters knelt in the snow and ran their high powered rifles through the racks of dead bucks lying before them.

The first indication that something was wrong came when he heard a crunching noise like car tires on gravel. Then pain pierced his upper back on the right side in the area alongside his shoulder blade. He drew a tortured breath and spun as Bens withdrew the long blade from his back. A winding trail of green blood followed the tip away, then he saw Bens swinging his arm high and away in preparation for another plunge of the blade. The steel tank had protected his spine but Bens aimed the next blow at the soft tissue of his neck, his arteries. A kill shot.

He bowed forward to give Bens the tank again and instinctively brought the rifle up, trying to roll away and fend him off, but Bens moved like a cat, even underwater, and slipped quickly around to face him. The blade was up and Bobby, instead of unholstering the deadly weapon at his thigh, thrust with the empty weapon in his hands.

Underwater motion is slow motion, but blows delivered aren't painless or impotent, and carry the same or greater force. The rifle barrel struck Wesley Bens in his scrotum and the rusted sight ripped through his sack skin like wet crepe paper. The forward edge of the sight caught the ductus deferens and its deferential artery, severing them both in a burst of arterial blood and tissue as if the rifle had been loaded. The pain this produced radiated upward into Bens' lower torso in a manner which might well have sent a lesser man into irretrievable shock. The knife tumbled from his hand and when he looked down at himself and saw the rifle barrel where it entered his lower body and punched through to come out near his anus. A paralytic weakness rushed upward. His bowels squirted like a squeezed grape.

Bobby saw none of this because he had his eyes closed, but drew the rifle back instinctively and ripped the sharp-edged sight a second time through Bens' damaged scrotum. The wailing sound he heard seemed distant as he struggled to right himself and swim away to safety, dragging the rifle. He was marginally aware that Bens no longer threatened him but the pain in his back was so great it made all the decisions for him. First, find the boat. Get help. See what was wrong with his back.

Standing his anchor watch, Armando scanned more than just line and chain. He spotted the rush of bubbles surfacing from seaward, and wondered why the Texas man would make such a display, until he saw one set of bubbles separate from the other and move toward the boat. "Mama!" he screamed, pointing to port.

Rosa saw nothing and climbed the ladder for a better view. Immediately she saw blood in the water, a dark stain. "Something has happened," she told the boy. "I must go down. Watch. Hide if you need to."

Rosa dropped down and snatched a long boat hook. "Ladies," she said. "Trouble comes." She pointed it out in the water.

Ruth's lips were swollen to something the size of a walnut and her voice was thick. "Is that blood in the water?"

"I think so," Rosa said.

Judy Ann arrived last to the portside and said simply, "It's Bobby."

No one spoke as the bubbles weaved to and fro, sometimes halting or circling before finding their way toward *Esteban* once again.

Rosa climbed out onto the swim step with the boat hook as Bobby struggled to find the stern. The dark cloud of blood drifted behind him as if it were part of the energy propelling him forward. He surfaced several feet behind the boat and the waves held him off, threatening to tumble him into the cliffs and shred him. The boat hook dropped behind his neck and caught the slightly inflated shoulder of Bobby's BC. Rosa pulled hard and brought him closer to the swim step. With help from Ruth and Judy Ann they dragged the semi-conscious Bobby first onto the swim step and then aboard. Blood and seawater greased the deck.

"Get his equipment off," Ruth said.

Three pair of hands tore at plastic snaps and stainless steel quick release buckles. The volume of blood running red and bright across their bare toes frightened them. "Hurry," Rosa said.

Judy Ann was crying as she worked.

They saw the knife wound immediately. "Apply pressure," Ruth said, and Judy Ann pressed down, closing the wound with her hands as Rosa and Ruth rolled Bobby from his left side to a full facedown position.

"He's cut a large vein or artery," Ruth said. "We've got to slow it down. Get him to a doctor."

Bobby's face too, was pressed against the greasy deck. His lips were compressed but he said, "Am I bleeding from my mouth?"

"I don't think so," Ruth answered, staring briefly at his mouth. "It's blood from your back wound. Judy Ann's slowing it down. We're going to get you some help."

"I'm dizzy," Bobby said. "It missed my lung."

"Don't worry, Baby," Judy Ann said. "You're okay. Just let us figure what to do."

And for a moment they all seemed overcome by the same hopelessness.

Finally Rosa spoke in a plain voice to supplant indecision. "We don't have time. Two hours or more to the harbor. We must call on the radio and talk to a doctor. He will tell us what to do."

Armando had climbed down from the flying bridge and was standing out of their way on the swim step. Lying across it he saw the rifle, and picked it up. At that moment Bobby said, "I got the rifle." Then passed out.

"He did it," Armando said, holding the weapon out for them to see.

"Clean it then," Rosa said. "Fill it with bullets and when Bens brings his head above the water, do what you were going to do with the speargun. Don't wait. Just shoot."

"Is there a blanket?" Ruth asked Rosa. "We need to cover him. Avoid shock as much as we can."

Rosa nodded. "Below. When you finish, come to the pilothouse in case I need you on the radio. Maybe there is no doctor and we will need another idea."

Ruth saw something fearful in Rosa's eyes, and hugged her shoulders.

Rosa said, "No one has ever been hurt on this boat. The only blood on the deck was the blood of fish."

"We're not going to let Bobby die," Ruth promised. "We'll do whatever it takes, but he's not going to die." She let go and turned back toward the bloody figure sprawled on the deck. "He's one of ours."

CHAPTER SEVENTEEN

Wesley Bens grew up in Putney, in London, the chubby, spoiled child of a neighborhood cobbler. His heavy-bellied and bossy father dominated his mother, and she in turn petted the tubby boy, often kissing his round cheeks and twisting locks of his blond hair in a longing, sensual manner. The affection of his parents collided with the realities of Putney in those days, a tough and unsympathetic urban slum, where bullies and smart-mouths enjoyed Wesley's misery when they nicknamed him "Little Fatty."

Little Fatty took that nickname to heart and even now - a muscular, hard man - Wesley feared physical weakness above anything else. He dwelled on his body until narcissism became both his cancer and his chemo. He demolished Little Fatty, but Little Fatty remained his greatest fear, and in his heart he was still running as he did at seventeen when he joined the Royal Navy and disappeared, he promised, from Putney forever.

Then returned twice, when each of his parents died. He buried them without fanfare and at little expense to himself, then found a tough neighborhood pub, picked a fight and savagely brutalized his victims. But this thing with the rifle was not like a fight. He'd been kicked in that most sensitive spot on various occasions, and like most fighting men, endured the radiating pain and waves of weakness and fought on. This was different. It hurt from the tearing of his outer flesh into his deeper, internal arteries and ligature, connecting to his very core. It left him breathless and stunned, yet somehow he achieved a higher level of consciousness about his predicament.

Bens had taken no notice of the old rifle. Expected no threat from it, nor the silly tourist that held it. The man was stabbed and dying, and purely by accident left Bens in this sorry state, kneeling on the sand with both hands clutching his groin. Blood pumped between his fingers and it was a long swim yet to the tiny crevice he'd found leading down from the cliff top to the churning water below. If he made it there, could he climb the dozen meters or more to where he'd left the truck and then somehow make it to a medical facility?

Little Fatty was destroyed by the determination of a young man who realized one misty London afternoon that he was fat, but big too. His wrists were wide and deep with bone and his shoulders were broad, his heavy legs long below a massive torso. He just needed to lose the fat, and less than a year after he did that, he discovered the power of his own will. Big Ben was born, and now with his scrotum in his hands, he summoned the strength to move toward the cliffs where he would climb or bleed to death or find some quack to sew him up.

At the base of the cliff, Big Ben was tossed about without regard for his will or his injury. The sea picked him up easily, tortured him in merciless disregard for his condition and frailty. He was another insignificant bit of flotsam. Bens expected nothing more, and without fear, endured the pain of his repeated collisions with the sharp limestone cliff face until one powerful arm found a purchase among the crevice rocks and he dragged himself clear enough to drop his scrotum and pull himself above the waves, where he kicked out of his fins and climbed the first few yards upward.

He forgot the 40-pound tank on his back and pressed his nearly naked body against the sharp rock and crabbed his way upward, leaving behind a bright smear of fresh blood. He would have cursed the tourist who caused his pain had he retained enough strength to speak. Instead, he inched his way toward the sea grape and windblown palms rattling above. The ray's spine hole in his foot ached almost more then his scrotum. It had opened, tearing away the scab, the black rock ripping at the tender flesh around it until it too bled freely, causing him to slip.

His legs were powerful, but his arms and shoulders, the breadth of his chest, sinew of his back, hoisted his heavy body with a frightful effortlessness that made it seem he possessed magical powers. A few minutes later he gained the cliff edge and rolled gasping onto solid ground, rested, then finally stumbled to the small station wagon where he tossed the tank, grabbed a towel, wadded it into his groin and sat on it. The engine fired and he was gone.

On board *Esteban*, Ruth and Rosa had stemmed the flow of blood from Bobby's body by applying direct pressure to the wound. Judy Ann, with Armando's assistance, radioed the small hospital in Edward Town and spoke with emergency room physician Conrad Goldberg, a German expat who advised them to treat Bobby for shock and tape the wound closed so direct pressure would be more effective, and transport him to the hospital immediately.

Armando had started the engines, retrieved both anchors and got underway in search of the divers. He feared maneuvering the large boat close in along a shallow and perilous coastline - a difficult task even for an experienced captain, but if he didn't make some attempt, he could never get the divers back aboard in time to save Bobby White. If he struck a rock or coral head, holed the boat or damaged the propeller, then they were all doomed. *Esteban* might find its eternal rest alongside *Imperial*. The boy eased the wheel and steered out to sea.

Armando planned to gain sea room, find the marks Captain Will had showed him and then turn in on them, making a direct course to the wreck without risking a quicker approach along the shallow coastline. It proved a wise decision. He found the marks and as he held a straight course toward the wreck site, Captain Will's head appeared and the boy knew he'd heard the engine and surfaced to see why the boat had returned. Armando waved and blew the horn three times.

Fifteen minutes later everyone was aboard, Captain Will was steering from the flying bridge, and *Esteban* was making 22 knots, something she hadn't done in years. Rosa and Armando stood beside him.

After Rosa finished telling him the story of Bobby's battle with Bens, Warren asked, "What happened to him?"

"The Englishman?"

"Yes."

"We don't know."

Warren glanced down at Armando and saw how the boy's dark hair fanned in the wind, catching reflected sunshine from the sea. "You did a good job, Son," he said. "I'm proud of you."

Armando nodded and turned his head away to hide his stinging eyes. Rosa smiled and told Warren that sometimes he was simpático, then hooked her right arm around a stanchion and said, "I like this Ruth."

Warren, throttles to the stops, took his eyes from the course and said, "What did you say?"

"This Ruth of yours. She is a fine woman. Not like many American women, spoiled and sharp. The Englishman struck her with more force then I have ever seen a man use against a woman and she did not cry out or give in to him. She fought down her fear. I like her. She has, how you say 'valor?'"

"Guts."

"Well, she has them."

"She's Freddie-the-Frogman's daughter."

Rosa stared at the distant bumps on the horizon that were Edward Town. "We will see about this frogman." The growl of the engine and the pounding of the sea against the hull muted her words. "And we see about this daughter too."

Bens made it all the way to the crossroads at Pueblo Puente before he passed out from blood loss. A minute before that he guided the little wagon into Daniel Cabral's front yard and killed a chicken. It was pinned under the tire and squawked for some time before it died, alarming the family and scattering the pigs.

Daniel was harvesting plantain, dragging the heavy bunches into the yard so they could be loaded onto a wagon for the trip to market in Edward Town, several miles away. When he saw the little vehicle veer from the road toward his house, he shouted to warn his family. It wasn't the first time some drunkard had left the road, and since it wasn't much of a road to begin with, they were almost as confused when they were sober.

The unconscious man sat in a puddle of blood and more blood had soaked into the seat. Daniel assumed he was dead until he saw the man's eyes flutter, so the entire family turned out, brought the wagon over by hand, and amid a great deal of grunting and struggling, managed to drag Wesley Bens aboard. The donkey was hitched and Daniel and his oldest boy, Marcel, started for town with the dying man.

After they crossed the single lane Ponce River bridge, Joe Spiro, waiting in the line of traffic on his way home from the early shift in the hospital ER, spotted the body in the wagon bed. "What have you got there?" he called to Daniel.

"A man," Daniel said. "He is bleeding. Maybe dead now."

Spiro turned his pickup, pulled ahead of the wagon and jumped out. It took him less then a minute to discover the source of Bens' blood loss and another to get help from Daniel and Marcel to pull Bens to the back of the wagon and strip him of his bathing suit. When he spread the huge man's legs and viewed the black, swollen scrotum, he realized it was too late to move him. A large vein was steadily pumping blood and the only way to save him was to clamp it off and sew it together. He carried nothing with which to do that.

"How long has he been bleeding like this?" Spiro asked.

Daniel shrugged. "Before he came off the road and killed Carlos, I think."

"Your son?"

"Chicken."

"Do you know him?"

"No."

"It would help to have a name. To call his name. I need to pinch a vein that is severed. Do you have a pliers, or even two? Any kind of small clamping device?"

The group of bystanders had grown to a crowd of a dozen or more. They produced three pair of pliers and several paper clips. An elderly woman handed him one of her hairpins. Without further discussion, Spiro grasped first one severed vein end with a pliers, then a second, closing one with the paper clip and the other with the hairpin. A fisherman contributed a bent needle and they pulled nylon thread from a windbreaker. Spiro sutured in the adept manner of one who had done it many times. The stitches held. A small piece of duct tape was applied to the vein joint since Spiro reckoned a physician would redo the whole works anyway. The important thing now was to get him to the ER quickly to stem the blood loss.

Spiro commandeered most of the group to lift Bens into the bed of his pickup. They'd spread blankets, two boat cushions, a life jacket and pillow to keep him from being jostled too hard by the trip. Daniel had dashed to a nearby store and called the hospital. They would be ready, he said.

Warren eased *Esteban* gently against the pier where an ambulance waited. A dozen willing hands lifted Bobby White's limp form across and into the vehicle. The driver, Chester Ebanks, grinned and cranked up the siren, his first opportunity this year and a sound he dearly loved. Heads snapped to the pulsing noise and the ambulance, lights flashing, lurched up the ramp from the pier and roared toward the hospital four blocks away.

Judy Ann White rode with her husband. The Van Dorens and Myron set off on foot for a drink at the Pink Sands. Ruth refused medical attention. Ice and a stiff drink would do more, she said. Warren urged Rosa to go along but she refused and took Armando home.

Warren backed *Esteban* away from the pier and out to her anchorage in the harbor. His thoughts should have been on the injured Bobby, but wandered instead to the things Freddie-the-Frogman had told him on the flying bridge. He cut the engine and climbed down the ladder. His eyes saw *Esteban* in a new light. The cleats, compass and other brasswork were green with salt corrosion. The decks were pitted, dirty, peeling. One of the salon's starboard side tinted glass windows had broken several years before and been patched with plywood, now splintered and dirty. He knew the head was filthy, but didn't allow Rosa to clean it because he didn't want tourists using it more than necessary. He sniffed the air and could smell it even on deck.

The electronics were a joke. The LORAN had seized years before, but he rarely went far enough from local waters to need it. The weather radio died so long ago he'd forgotten about it. A fixture of corrosion now. Unrepairable. And everything in sight needed painting or polishing.

No pride, Freddie had said. No pride.

Shame, his mother told him from her grave.

Warren went below and halted at the head door. He flushed the foul toilet into the sea and crossed to a portside locker. He found rags and brass polish, took them out and went to work.

The sun fell into the sea before Warren sat on a tank bench to rest. The brasswork gleamed in the twilight like golden nuggets. He should've taken some small pride in that at least, since his fingers were black and sore from rubbing, but instead all he felt was a deepening anger. It is no small thing for a man to discover error in himself. But that discovery is small compared to the monster of recovery.

The darkness deepened. Stars blinked on in a black sky and lights from the small craft waggled in the water like sequins on a black dress. Warren sat motionless, frozen by some cold wind of his past that reached out from a frozen lake, across the years, to stiffen him as though he was made of ice himself. And he saw Stephen again, face upturned, drifting down deeper and deeper into the cold, clear water of the lake. He saw the little body in the casket dressed in a suit bought special for the occasion. He was just a little boy after all. A dead little boy. Rosa told him many times to accept what he had failed to do that night, and accept the grace that followed. Trust Jesus, she said. No excuses, no guilt. It was that easy, Rosa said. He didn't know. Wasn't it too much to polish away? Maybe he didn't want to know. Guilt is often a comfortable burden.

The monotonous sound of Javert's dredge intruded finally and he scowled across the water at the thing, with its cheery lights and purposeful racket. Its festive look at night, hiding the brown water that surrounded it like some rain-swollen river of mud. And where was this Bens? This brute of Javert's?

Dr. Goldberg had his hands full. Two patients, both severely injured and in need of immediate attention. He was only one man, after all, so he moved both patients into the same trauma suite and worked between them. Neither was conscious now. Sedated and quiet. Both had lost copious amounts of blood, some replaced with plasma, but neither patient was sure to survive. Not yet.

The Englishman was especially in a bad way. He'd re-sewn the worst of his leaking veins, marveling at the first aid accomplished by one of his nurses on the road, but the man had succumbed to deep shock, partly because of his scrotum but also his foot which had not healed properly and was infected, oozing puss and poison. He'd fill the man with IV antibiotics as soon as he got a minute, he thought. Then ordered one of his nurses to do it immediately. Smiling to himself, he mumbled, "I'm really getting too old for this crap."

The American was luckier. The knife had severed veins but no major arteries. It isn't easy to stab the human torso without piercing something vital. Dr.

Goldberg was still sewing on him but was optimistic, and with some assurance, would be able to report to his nearly naked wife that her husband was severe, but out of danger. Unless, of course, there were smaller bleeders he hadn't found. Maybe he'd just go out into the waiting room and admire her ass like everyone else. Earlier, he asked an orderly to find Mrs. White a hospital gown, but the man had been in no hurry, and when he did return with it, he insisted on helping her don it, then tied the back, leaving a two-foot gap. The heads of every man and half the women in the waiting room followed her as she paced up and down.

No one had bothered to tell Dr. Goldberg that his two patients had inflicted each other with the wounds he now treated. But then he wasn't an idiot, or blind to the coincidence of two men with such wounds appearing on his tables simultaneously. They seemed mismatched. The American pale and flabby. The giant, a mass of muscle. Yet it was the big man who hovered near death. Well, Goldberg thought, when I'm done with them here, I will have them moved, each to a different floor at opposite ends of the building. The hospital wasn't that large and he didn't need another incident. He'd even thought of imposing restraints, and might yet, after a talk with Sgt. Cumberbatch, who was waiting in his office.

Goldberg stretched his back. Not fast at this kind of work as in his youth, but it felt good to work hard and accomplish a thing worth doing. He grew tired of arthritis complaints, stomach aches and hemorrhoidectomies. This was real medicine. Dr. Goldberg was pleased with himself, and might even stop by the Pink Sands for three fingers of rum before heading home. He just might.

Colour Sergeant Gladstone Cumberbatch was nobody's fool. He knew Javert had hired a goon and was well informed about the Texas tourist with a wife who liked to show her ass. He was impatient with Dr. Goldberg, who provided vague answers to direct questions. Is the man going to live or die? He didn't know. How were the wounds inflicted? A knife for the tourist and who knows for the goon. Did he talk to them? No. Did they mumble anything? Just blubbering. He finally allowed the doctor to go for his drink.

Sgt. Cumberbatch answered solely to the Police Commissioner and the Governor. Both were furious that a tourist had been attacked and were busily covering it up as well as they could, and if it was true that Javert's man had stabbed a tourist then one influential fat man was about to learn a lesson in humility. Cumberbatch favored independence, same as Javert, but this was going too far. He had his orders directly from the Governor and left the hospital to carry them out.

The Sergeant was as powerful a man as Wesley Bens and just as fearless. His presence in the Pink Sands lobby in full uniform and with a scowl on his face forced a silence that spread even to the bar and veranda, where Javert sat before a lavish dinner. Every eye was upon him as he stepped lightly around the tables toward the fat man.

"Good evening, Sergeant," Javert acknowledged.

"Do you employ the man Wesley Bens?"

"Why yes. Is anything wrong?"

The Sergeant's full dark eyes narrowed slightly. "He is in hospital, having attacked a tourist. One Mr. White. And apparently struck another female tourist. There is also a rumor that he slaughtered the stingrays that the divers feed. What do you know of these things?"

"Nothing," Javert said. "Nothing. Well, I suppose I've heard what you have heard, but there are so many stories. I give them as much credence as you yourself, I suppose." He shrugged and smiled.

The look on Cumberbatch's face was pure contempt, but he said nothing for some seconds. Then, "Come with me, please."

"Now look here." Javert's face reddened. "I'm not responsible for the misbehavior of every minion I happen to employ. I employ many people and contribute greatly to the economy here. And I don't appreciate being spoken to in this manner. You will please excuse me now while I finish my dinner." He turned back to his plate.

Sergeant Cumberbatch seemed amused by this outburst. He slid the stick from his armpit and swung it with force onto Javert's plate, shattering it and spraying food across Javert's dinner jacket. What conversation was left in the room evaporated immediately and all eyes were locked on Javert as Cumberbatch popped him on top of the head and repeated, "Your dinner is finished. Come with me."

This time Javert obeyed without comment.

Charming Island was small enough so that very little that went on there was missed by anyone, even Governor Sir Henry Leach, though he was perhaps the most insulated and often disinterested inhabitant. Sir Henry was a kindly man in his mid-40s, who instead of climbing the ladder of diplomatic success, was shuffled off to an unimportant place in the Commonwealth. Charming Island was of little interest to Whitehall, or anyone else for that matter. Governor Leach had no idea why this had happened to him and seldom interfered with the affairs of the place, leaving things to the locals, as he called them.

But this business with Javert had angered and embarrassed him. It was one thing to be shoved off to this forgotten place and quite another to become known as the fool who made a mess of paradise. He was pacing the balcony on the third floor of Government House, where he had residence, and red-faced with a fierce anger never before observed by his aide and friend Reggie Hicks.

"Damn it! Damn it! Damn it to hell! You tell Cumberbatch I want that fat Javert thrown in the basement of the dungeon, and toss the key in the commode!"

Reggie said, with as little amusement as he could manage, "We don't have a dungeon, Sir Henry."

"We have a damn jail, damn it! Throw him in there and when this Bens recovers, throw him in there too, and maybe the filthy bastards will have a go at each other and put an end to our problems." He blew a long sigh. "Bloody hell!"

This wasn't the time, Reggie thought, to explain anything about due process or that there was no proof Javert had anything to do with Bens' actions. Let alone that he shouldn't have shouted at Cumberbatch in the manner he had, ordering him to make an arrest that wouldn't withstand the first legal challenge, not to mention that Sir Henry was creating an even greater public relations mess now by his reactionist response.

"We can be thankful that no one was killed," he said soothingly.

"They could still die," said the governor.

"Not likely," Reggie argued. "I spoke at length with Dr. Goldberg. He's confident, if not prepared to make blanket predictions that might see him looking foolish later. I understand that, and we do the same."

"I suppose."

"We have to consider, too, how much of this is simply part of the general unrest," Reggie went on. "We are the government. Javert is a leader for independence, and Bens his employee - or even goon - but we will now be seen as heavy-handed in dealing with those who believe they justly seek freedom and a better way of life. You don't disagree with that, certainly."

Government House was higher on the hill than the Pink Sands and most of the older buildings of Edward Town. Leach walked to the very edge of the balcony and leaned heavily on the ornate stone railing. "I am sorry, Reggie." He stared out across the rooftops. It was early morning and shadows of the buildings reached out toward the harbor. Sir Henry was an early riser and he felt now that he'd spoilt the day. "It's too early for one to be in a temper. I am sorry. Shall we finish our coffee? I promise to behave."

Reggie handed him the cup and in a less urgent voice said, "You are a good man, Sir Henry. As we've said so often, this is an impossible assignment for you, or anyone. On the one hand the Home Office cares nothing for this place, but nevertheless, doesn't want to lose it. They have learned the lesson of Jamaica and the Cayman Islands. The Jamaicans voted for the freedom to be poor, and accomplished it. Cayman Islanders chose to remain in the Commonwealth and their currency is worth more then the U.S. dollar. And they have less poverty than the U.S. too." Reggie moved to the table. "Come and sit down."

The Governor shrugged and took a chair. He had been at school with Reggie and often thought it would've been better if their roles now were reversed. "So you want to hash it out again, I suppose."

"It's a fine morning." Reggie smiled. "Did you know Cumberbatch favors independence?"

"Yes."

"And others like him," Reggie continued. "But the more I listen and talk to people, the more convinced I am that he's in the minority."

"Really? Why?"

"Religion. Charming Islanders are Pentecostal, and influenced more by what they *believe* is right. Their freedom is offered by their faith, not politics. Their view of independence is not the same as a policeman's, or the business interests of men like Javert, even Captain Will and his tourist enterprise. Religion has more power over the mind than politics, so they have already decided. They are free now. What can 'independence' offer them? Not that some won't vote in favor of it, but it's important for us to understand that most people on this island will approach the debate from a very different angle. I am convinced that Javert, and even fair-minded men like Cumberbatch, fail to understand this."

Sir Henry poured each of them more strong island coffee, dropping two lumps of sugar in his. "And you really think that's enough to swing a vote toward remaining in the Commonwealth?"

"I do."

"And our course then?"

Reggie raised an eyebrow. "Calm. Steady at the helm. Unperturbed by events. No harsh statements from us against independence. We are their allies, and rather then wanting what is good for them, we encourage their right to decide for themselves and promise our support however they choose."

This brought Sir Henry's first large, and genuine smile of the morning. "So, perhaps the governor of this little place should curb his anger, is that it?"

"Yes Sir." Reggie returned the smile. "And release Javert from jail immediately."

The Governor nodded. "Of course. You will see to that after breakfast?"

"I shall. Thank you."

Why, Leach wondered, does doing the right thing so often leave you feeling empty and impotent.

"One more thing before I leave," Reggie said. "That storm to the southeast has been upgraded to Tropical Storm Bernie. Give it a name, might develop into a hurricane. So say the TV meteorologists."

"Perhaps," Sir Henry replied. "It's been a quiet season so far, but run up the flag if you like. Better safe than sorry, huh?"

"Okay, Jefe," Reggie said. The flag was an old custom used in times past, before radar and satellites. It warned residents of foul weather, often about the time the weather was upon them, but on Charming Island such tradition died hard and it amazed Reggie how often he saw people in the streets below gazing up to see if they could spot a flag. It would be only a yellow caution flag today, but create an awareness in ways electronic media never did.

Howard Nevelle was Gladstone Cumberbatch's second in command and carried the rank of Sergeant. He religiously addressed Gladdy as Colour Sergeant when on duty, but since he was Gladdy's brother-in-law, they were informal during their off time. And they were good friends too.

Now Sgt. Nevelle was faced with telling the Colour Sergeant that Government House wanted Javert released from custody, and just as Cumberbatch was enjoying the interrogation so much. But orders were orders, and he knocked on the door.

"Enter!" Cumberbatch shouted.

Nevelle leaned his head through the crack and said, "Would you step out please?"

When they were outside and the door closed, Cumberbatch looked at him crossly. "What? I've got him babbling."

"Mr. Hicks," he began. "He called from Government House. We are to release Javert immediately."

"Am I hearing this?"

"Yes."

"Finally I have a chance to squeeze him and this is what they do? Am I hearing this?"

"Mr. Hicks said to get him out of here before his lawyer showed up."

Cumberbatch grunted. "I haven't let him call a lawyer."

"All the more reason then, don't you think?"

"Oh, reason be damned! Along with all the politicians and every other blithering idiot."

"Colour Sergeant?"

"Fine then. Just fine. I'm not hearing this. I'm going to my office and have coffee. Get him out the door then, and kick him in the ass when you do it." Cumberbatch left the room, shoulders hunched.

A moment later Nevelle heard the office door slam and went in to release Javert.

Javert, whose armpit sweat had created dark circles that encompassed his sagging breasts, strutted from the room, the wounded but innocent man. Nevelle felt like kicking him in the ass but didn't dare. Anyway, they'd got rid of him before any lawyer showed up. Nevelle feared lawyers in the same way he feared snakes, but if you had a nice sharp machete and a snake reared his head at you, you could slice it off in one swing. And it felt good too.

Patriots & Lovers

CHAPTER EIGHTEEN

A storm was coming.

Rosa started to take Armando home where she could sort through the fear and confusion but changed her mind. Violence was not new to her, but since she had been with Captain Will, her confidence returned and she no longer feared for Armando or herself. But now she took her son to church. She sensed wider, more powerful forces threatening them all. A pending upheaval she could not define or confront. Things she must bring before God.

The church was dim and empty. There were no stained glass windows or frescos. No ornate figurines. She led Armando to the simple altar, a rough wooden table, and brought him to his knees beside her and prayed a simple prayer. "Abba. Hear the prayer of Your sinful daughter. We are afraid for ourselves, our people, our Captain. Protect us from the storm that comes. Lead us to a safe place. If You have anything for us to do, make it plain so we know it comes from You. Beside me is a good son. Hear us for the sake of Your son, Jesus. Amen."

Her words died away in the empty church and the prayer was finished, but she remained on the floor and continued in silence, keeping her thoughts from Armando. There was a heavy foreboding gnawing at her, and it went beyond the sinfulness she held against herself and she had seen it in the pitiless eyes of Wesley Bens. Evil. *Don't let them hurt Armando,* she prayed. *Take me. Whatever happens, please protect him and Will.* There, she thought, I've done what I can do.

Rosa was limber and rose quickly to her feet. "Come," she told her son. "We go home."

A more definable, visible storm had threatened the island for several days. There had been ominous weather reports, radar images, but it wasn't classified as a hurricane and no one took the usual storms with more than a passing curiosity, except fishermen and sailors. Rosa took it seriously because their business too depended on good weather. The dive tourists didn't dive even in mild rain showers. Something she always found curious. After all, weren't they planning to get wet anyway?

Rosa picked two plantain before they walked up onto the porch at home and Armando walked behind the house to milk the goat. After the plantain was fried in peanut oil and the goat's milk laced with raw sugar, they snacked together on the wrap-around porch.

"Hijo," she said to Armando between bites. "Hijo."

Armando knew at once what she meant. "Yes," he said, smiling. "I liked it."

"Haven't I said a hundred times that he loves you?"

"No," he said. "Ten thousand times."

"Bocazas. Big mouth. Your poor mama is never right, I suppose. Maybe you are now the captain?"

"Maybe," he said, lifting his chin and narrowing his light brown eyes. The grin returned. "But for now, I will be happy to be the Captain's son."

"When we are married, he will adopt you and give you his name," she said. "You will be Armando Wilson."

The boy had no intention of telling her that he worried Captain Will would never marry her. Other boys told him often that his mother was a puta, a whore, and kept only for sex. No one married a puta. And no man made another man's son his legal son. The Captain liked him, even before he expressed his pride today, but liking, loving even, did not mean marriage and all the dreams of respectability his mother prayed for so often. But Armando's expectations were humble. He lived for the moment, and today there was gladness and his spirits rose to meet it.

After their light supper Rosa told Armando, "I'm going to church again. You are a truant. Read the assignment for school and feed the animals. I won't be gone too long."

Armando groaned. She was back on the school binge again. But it wouldn't last. Rosa threw a light shawl across her shoulders, kissed the top of his head, trotted down the steps and dashed away along the path. She had lied to her son. She was not going to church but to find Reggie Hicks.

It took nearly an hour. Reggie was drinking a coco loco on the veranda of the Pink Sands not two tables away from Myron and the Van Dorens. Rosa had to send someone to fetch Reggie and bring him to the scullery so they wouldn't see her.

"Ah, Rosa," he said when he did see her.

"Come outside," she said, leading him into the narrow alley alongside the hotel.

"Hopefully, this isn't anything tawdry, Rosa," he said in a very British voice.

"Tawdry?"

"Cheap. Sleazy."

"You think I am cheap?"

"No. I just thought we'd been over all this and decided not to speak again." He paced a moment across the alley and back. "It was all settled long ago and I've heard you and Will are having difficulties with Javert. If that's what this is about you must realize that Government House cannot interfere. I'm sorry."

Rosa smiled at him and shook her head. "You British. Do you wonder why you have lost an empire? Because you are an arrogant lot, and I am not so foolish as to ask for anything except that you take a message to Harry. He is still the Governor of this place, though neither he or you act as men in charge of a thing, but as men emasculated. We need no help from you."

"What then?"

"You need help from us. This day I have seen one of Javert's hired killers attempt to butcher a tourist and beat women."

"We know about that," Reggie said. "Javert was arrested."

"And let go again," she responded. "I'm not here about this fat man. But Bens is an Englishman. One of yours. There are more like him. Dangerous men."

"We know about Bens. He's in hospital and might very well die there. He's no threat to anyone." Reggie moved toward the door.

She put out her hand. "You are not safe. Harry is not safe. Do you think you can sit up there in a big house and no one will dare to come near you? To cut your throat or explode a bomb? What is wrong with you? Do you forget Cuba or Jamaica, even the Bahamas?"

Hicks halted and stared at the dishwasher who lectured him. "Most of that is resolved."

"But this is not. I am not sitting in a big house far from the people. I hear what they say and I know what they think. You need to show strength. Tell that to the father of my son. If he cares."

"Rosa," Reggie said sharply. "You are no longer part of the Governor's life."

"No," she said. "This I have been told many times. Now tell him, he has a wife and children. A responsabilidad to these people. What he has done to me I have forgiven him, but what he is failing to do for people he governs, that will never be forgiven. Not from me, not from God and not from those who are robbed of their freedoms. Go now. Finish your drink. Then tell Harry what I said. If you do not, then I will come to his house and tell him myself."

"What exactly do you want, Rosa?"

"Fairness."

"You mean when the vote comes?"

"Yes."

"Every effort will be made to assure a fair referendum."

She shook her head. "This needs more effort. Javert is planning things against you."

"What things?"

"Violent things." If it hadn't been for Warren's part in the plot, she would have told him about the weapons. That was something sure to frighten him.

"Rosa, Rosa. Don't worry. This is not a violent place. You have warned me. Done your duty. I will tell Harry." He smiled.

Frustrated and angry, she turned and walked up the alley. She knew then they would accept no help or listen or even understand until it was too late. Well then, it was up to her and the others.

Reggie watched her until she became part of the darkness. No more than a shadow. Despite what he had told her, his regard for her never diminished. Her beauty was like the islands themselves - raw and mysterious. She was uneducated, even ignorant in some ways, but blessed with a keen mind and an observant nature. He smiled to himself and said aloud, "And a fine figure."

CHAPTER NINETEEN

The swirling center of the tropical storm passed ninety miles north of Charming Island. Its backwash left rivers of muddy water meandering the streets of Edward Town and seriously damaged three porch footings on the Pink Sands Hotel. On the outskirts of town, the St. George River crested four feet above flood stage, sweeping away dozens of poorly built shacks and drowning a three-month-old infant. Throughout the island, electricity was intermittent.

Governor Sir Henry Leach declared a state of emergency and asked Great Britain for assistance. A low echelon official in the Foreign Office said they would take the request under advisement. Not to panic. It wasn't a hurricane, after all. One can hardly expect disaster relief every time there's a little blow.

While the main storm front spun like a comet into the Atlantic farther north, its tail continued to pester the island with torrential rains, wind, and heavy seas. In the empty lunch room of the old abandoned sugarcane refinery miles to the south of Edward Town, Carlos Orizondo and several others sat crowded around a wooden table. Electricity had been disconnected for two decades and Carlos lit a stubby white candle - its light gave the men's faces a menacing, fearful quality. They spoke only in Spanish.

"If they weren't such fools in Government House we'd be having this meeting over cocktails on Sir Henry's patio," a dark-skinned man complained.

"When was the last time you were invited to cocktails with the Governor, Francisco?" said another.

Several of the men laughed at this.

"Beside the point," he shot back. "We're the ruling party, not Javert and his crowd. Why should we cower in this stink hole like rabbits? Answer that!"

"Meeting secretly is not cowering," a new voice joined in. "Javert is a spider with many webs. Why tempt fate?"

"What kind of government is this we're fighting for?" asked Francisco. "What kind of government can't defend itself?"

The circle of dark faces appeared as wood in the candlelight.

"Amigos," Francisco continued. "If we keep the British, maybe they are too weak. Maybe they fall even if we win. Can this be worth our jobs? Our lives?"

Again there was silence.

"You're forgetting something," Carlos reminded them. "We're here to face facts, not debate politics." Carlos paused, looking at each in turn. "Tonight we have one purpose - to rid ourselves of Javert. Expose him before the election. Only we can do this because we alone remember. We alone know what we are. Cubanos!"

"Si," came a low voice. "Men without a country."

"Men with a memory," Carlos responded. "We won't let it happen here. Not again."

"But how, Carlos? How can we stop it?"

"How?" said another.

This brought a smile to Carlos' lips. "We know more than Javert thinks. We know he will create much trouble during the movement for independence, and use it to grab power. We know he's hired an outside agitator - this Englishman they call Big Ben, now in hospital. All this takes money. Does Javert use his own money? No. This big man comes from Castro. His money, and his Russian money. We tell this story and cut off his head!" His hand sliced the air.

"How? How?"

"Expose him!" Carlos, agitated by their hesitancy, spoke more loudly than he'd intended. "Don't you think people want to know Javert is hiring outsiders? Plans to make himself governor, or prime minister, or king? Maybe by force?"

Manny Gomez said, "I think mostly people just don't give a damn."

"Listen to me! My friend Juan from Miami knows of this Bens from his time in the CIA, even from after the Bay of Pigs, and he told me on the phone the man is crazy and that Javert met him on a trip to Cuba last year. Bens is not Cuban and works only for money, and the Cuban communists like him because they can disavow him, and now he works for them and Javert." He stared at Manny. "We expose him as a Cuban communist and Juan said he can make sure the Yankees will take notice."

Manny shook his head. "Notice maybe, action never. This is a small place."

"So is Granada."

Outside, the wind blew in gusts, whipping palm fronds violently against the building. Rain laced the rusted galvanized slates of the windows. Somewhere in the dark the sound of dripping water striking metal. Plunk, plunk. Plunk, plunk.

Slither flattened himself farther against the side of the building, as much to keep dry as to hear the conversation inside. He shifted his feet, aching in the cold. He'd been standing like a statue in the damp ooze under the window since half an hour before the secret meeting began. Whenever he shifted his weight or leaned too heavily against the building, his feet began to slide out from under him. Typical of the jobs he got stuck with. Javert no doubt sat somewhere dry, sipping Tia Maria after a late dinner of prime rib.

His broken fingers itched and throbbed under the tight bandage. The German doctor had cut away the electrical tape and replaced it with a more sanitary-looking white variety, but other than that did little to repair the damage. All we can do is immobilize it, the doctor had told him. About what he'd expected. It made perfect sense to the fat man to send him way out here in the middle of the night, in the rain, to stand for hours and spy on Orizondo and the others. The one with smashed bones should go, of course. That made perfect sense. Bens was out of it now. That pleased him. Even more pleasing, maybe the bastard would die.

Slither could've gone to Lord Nelson's Pub and sat in a warm corner with a pint of ale. Later, make up some story for the fat man. He'd done it before. Would've now but for what he heard inside. This stuff was money in the bank.

Water running off the roof had dug a trench just ahead of his toes. He struggled to maintain a foothold. Inside, the men's voices were loud enough to be heard above the rain. What a careless group of conspirators they'd turned out to be, almost shouting at times. Did they think because they spoke Spanish no one understood?

The next voice he heard spoke English. The voice of Gladstone Cumberbatch, Colour Sergeant of Police, and it caused Slither a sharp intake of breath.

"Do you know how many generations of my family have lived on this island?" Cumberbatch's deep baritone paused, "Ten."

"I didn't mean you when I said people don't care," Gomez assured him.

"Good," he said.

Slither pictured the broad black face, at once both benevolent and threatening. The policeman's eyes, probing and clever. The full mouth perpetually hung with a shrewd grin. A cane cutter's build, amaretto-skinned and towering well over six feet, Cumberbatch spoke like an Englishman and laughed like an islander. Though just a sergeant, higher ranking officers asked his advice. It was said even the governor respected him. He was never overlooked and the very fact that he'd come to this meeting was staggering news. Cumberbatch was black island. Slither had just made a discovery the magnitude of Watergate.

"All of us here," Carlos gestured at the others, "are newcomers to this island. A couple generations at most. But we are not newcomers to this fight. No, Mr. Cumberbatch, we are not. If you met our Fidel you would find him amiable. An interesting, intelligent man with great curiosity. A scuba diver, something like our Captain Will. But he destroyed a culture, ruined a nation, murdered thousands."

"This is not Cuba," Cumberbatch said. "And Javert is no Castro." A branch separated from a nearby banyan tree and smashed against the building. "Perhaps," Cumberbatch went on, "you imagine blacks cannot govern themselves?"

A chorus of protest.

Slither could almost hear the grin spreading across Cumberbatch's face. "We former slaves haven't done so well in Haiti and Jamaica, but we're learning. Is it possible you missed the point here? Perhaps independence isn't the tragedy you fear. Most islanders are good people. They want what you want. What makes you so sure you have the answers? A vote for independence is our chance to be truly free. Don't be so pessimistic about freedom."

When he finished, one by one heads turned toward Carlos. "You're a man of good conscience," he said carefully, resuming his seat to show he didn't mean to dominate. "But you know as well as I that it's more often instant prosperity people expect when they first gain their independence. Let's not forget the lesson of Jamaica and the Cayman Islands."

Several men nodded.

"Remember how the voting went then, my friend?" he continued. "How the Jamaicans, ruled by the British as we are, voted for independence while the Caymanians voted to remain in the Commonwealth? Jamaica was soon communist. Without an economy. Without friends. Without tourist dollars. A beautiful nation, once the seat of power and prestige in the Americas, slid farther and farther into poverty and Rastafarian nonsense while the little, bug-infested Cayman Islands built themselves into a mighty economy. Three scrubby sand spits overrun with mosquitoes became the tourist mecca of the Caribbean, while the big island with unsurpassed natural beauty sank deeper and deeper. Today, Jamaica's recovered some of its losses, but still in more need of missionaries than tourists. The Caymans have a higher standard of living than almost any nation in the Caribbean. Cayman dollars are worth more than U.S. dollars. How many countries can say that?"

Cumberbatch held his tongue.

"This is not North or South America, this is the Caribbean," Carlos said. "The gringos have quit buying our sugarcane. We have agriculture, but no energy resources or industry. What we have is clean air and warm, clear water. We have white sand and palm trees. Americans, Canadians, Europeans will pay us for these, but if we go the way of Javert, it will be all his. Foreign corporations or even communists. You can't want that."

They sat a long time listening to the rain.

Finally Cumberbatch spoke. "Everything you've said is true, Carlos." He paused and Slither heard a chair scrape against the floor. "But this is not Cayman. Why has the British government here been so reluctant to help us while the same British government in Cayman has been a blessing to the people?"

"It is not the same government," Carlos asserted. "Sir Henry isn't even a good politician, let alone a businessman. The British aren't the worst possible governors, unless you're forced to eat their cooking. And you're forgetting scuba. Men like Bob Soto and others saw the underwater potential of Grand Cayman. They promoted the islands to divers."

"Si!" Gomez burst out. "And we have Captain Will. Stingray butcher and drunkard!"

To everyone's surprise, Francisco rose suddenly and shouted, "No! These are lies!"

Carlos defending Captain Will wouldn't be surprising, but Francisco hardly knew him. In fact, Francisco's family were fishermen, in direct competition with Captain Will's tourists for fish and lobster. For years rumors abounded that Will slashed underwater lobster traps.

Almost without thinking, Carlos said, "I'm surprised at you, Francisco."

Francisco glanced from the Cuban to Sergeant Cumberbatch before he spoke. "I am alive today, and my sons are alive, because of Captain Will."

"I've heard nothing of this," said Carlos, skeptical.

"No. You've heard nothing, any of you," he explained softly. "Captain Will insisted we keep quiet. Perhaps it's time to speak."

Francisco, leathery, thin, ill at ease as the focus of attention, planted his feet and stared up at an empty corner of the room. "You know me as the fisherman from Punta Alegre. Cubano. My father, his father before him - fisherman. My boat *Santa Martes*, carried us across to Miami and freedom. 1961." He paused, listening a moment to the rain rushing in the trees outside the window. "What you do not know is that I abandoned the traditions of my family years ago to make myself rich. For money I risked the lives of my sons. Nearly left my wife a widow. Enough to eat, a dry place to sleep, a simple life was not enough for me then. I wanted all those things I had seen during my years in Miami. A car. Color television. Electric, oscillating fan. Javert told me all this could be mine and found in New York, U.S.A., a seafood buyer. You can be rich, he said. Become a vital link in a food chain stretching from Charming Island to hundreds of fast-food restaurants across the United States."

Here Francisco's voice trailed off as if the idea had struck him anew and still had merit. Then he smiled, nodding his head in a wise, absent manner.

"But we could not fish for lobster in the old-fashioned ways of our fathers. We must adopt new methods, Javert explained. Learn scuba. Big lobsters are deep, you see. Down along the great vertical walls of the dark reefs, hiding in the cracks and caves. One hundred feet, one hundred and fifty feet, two hundred feet below the surface. Big lobster. Ten, fifteen pound tails. Our money was earned by the pound.

"Javert spoke the truth. We acquired scuba equipment, learned to hold back the pain in our ears, and dove the deep walls. Giant lobster. Javert bought them and begged for more to fill the bellies of the rich. He was pleased with us. We spent the money in the way we had hoped to spend it - a new engine for the boat, television, electric oscillating fan. It was good.

"A cloudless day. The sea a damp blanket billowing softly in the wind. Felix, the youngest, became ill. His skin erupted in sudden corruption. He lost energy. A few hours, he could barely walk. The German doctor shrugged his shoulders and told us it was some new tropical fever. Wait, he advised. Felix will get better or he will get worse.

"We waited until morning. He grew worse.

"That next day Captain Will came to see him. My wife told Rosa about Felix and told also he was diving deep. Captain Will spoke to him no more than a few minutes, then drew him from the bed and carried him away to his boat. 'Come or not,' he told me, ' I'm taking him to the recompression chamber at Guadeloupe.' A long trip. I didn't believe the boy would survive."

Here Francisco stopped, the skin of his cheeks trembling with the force of his self control. "His bright eyes - he has such eyes - rolled back. White. Dead. Pain so deep he could not speak or cry out. Then you know fear. Then you will give anything. Know you've been a fool for an oscillating fan. You will tell any lie to God. I did this while Captain Will covered the boy's mouth and nose with a plastic cup and fed him oxygen from a small tank. I held his head in my lap. He couldn't be still. Pain from the deep water was in his body like worms squirming to free themselves. Under his legs, Captain Will piled blankets. He ordered me to bathe him in cool water.

"He was still alive when we reached Guadeloupe. They put him in an iron machine. Sealed him inside. I sat on a bench. What would I say to my Isabel? I slept. When I awoke I heard Felix speaking on a radio. Captain Will smiled at me. Much later Felix walked out of the machine and embraced me. The sickness had gone. He must never dive again, the doctor said.

"On the way home, Captain Will explained the sickness and told us many things Javert had not. I don't understand these things, even now, but Captain Will understands them. Now we fish in the old way. No one is sick." Francisco resumed his seat. "The electric oscillating fan had a bad motor," he added.

Carlos seemed most affected by the story. "You were right to defend the Captain," he said. "No man is just one thing."

Outside, Slither, too, listened carefully to the story. It might prove a valuable commodity one day, but it was not something he'd serve the fat man as part of the regular menu. He'd wait for just the right time and just the right price.

Inside, Carlos confided in the others. "I have often asked Captain Will to these meetings. He has always said no, but I believe he loves the island as we do."

"Or at least the water around it," Sergeant Cumberbatch said.

"What does it matter?" asked Francisco. "Captain Will is not a politician."

"No," Carlos agreed. "But he's white in the manner the English are white. Even you, Mr. Cumberbatch, must see this would be helpful."

"Many dislike a white man and a black woman," Cumberbatch said.

"And you?"

He shrugged, smiling suddenly. "I have known white women."

"With some help from us, Captain Will may yet be persuaded to help Charming Island become like Cayman," Carlos reasoned.

"I do not think he will do it." Francisco shook his head. "And we should not ask."

A sudden gust rattled the shutters. Candles flickered, darkening the room instantly.

"There's another way." Carlos spoke deliberately, voice devoid of emotion. "We could go into the streets. Let them count us. See that we are many. Javert, even the governor, can count."

The wind died and light freshened on their faces.

"Such things are not done," Francisco said.

Other voices murmured assent. Charming Island might be multi-cultural and multi-racial, but it was thoroughly British. Demonstrating in the streets was left to Americans and other hotheads.

"I myself would stand against you," Cumberbatch said. "A policeman does not march in the streets. You invite riot."

As Carlos rose from his chair to protest, Slither's feet slid out from under him. He just had time to choke off a scream before landing hard on his rump, overturning an upside-down box that supported a steel pan. The pan clattered loudly.

A moment later he heard shouting and rapid footsteps approaching, but Slither's reputation was well-deserved, and he slipped away in the dark like a wet shadow.

After his departure the meeting broke up. Again, there'd been talk. Carlos blew out the candle. Others feared the gathering storm. Carlos welcomed it.

God granted Charming Island as a refuge for him and his family forever. He knew this as surely as he knew his blood would soak the ground before he ran again. And he knew something else. He knew they possessed a secret weapon in this fight - someone whose power came from within like white heat. For the present, it burned in secret. Soon this power would consume the island and nothing was strong enough to stand against it.

CHAPTER TWENTY

Dr. Goldberg stared down at his patient's heaving chest and thought maybe life still held a few surprises for him. He hadn't yet seen it all. This Englishman should be dead. He'd poured pints of blood into him and did what he could to repair the ripped scrotum, but for days he bled through the stitches, his life ebbing, his skin gray putty, and not a sound came from his mouth. The Englishman was dying, but taking his time about it.

This, of course, was no thanks to Dr. Goldberg. He had given up.

Pouring a large whiskey for himself that evening, he peered through the golden brown liquid and remembered Cindy Moser. Dr. Cindy Moser, urologist. The only female urologist he knew. She loved whiskey, too. They'd shared more then one bottle after various medical functions in Guadeloupe. She was especially fond of bourbon, and he happened to have a few extra bottles in his locked wine cellar. Would she fly over for them? Might she find his strange case of the Englishman interesting? Maybe, he thought, if she wasn't too overloaded.

She arrived the very next day. Her small fingers and the tiny plastic surgery instruments she used, suture so small she wore loupes to see and manipulate it precisely with her long delicate fingers, was a marvel to Goldberg. He had never seen her work, and as he watched he thought maybe all surgeons should be women. His sutures were clumsy and crude. She had removed them but instead of envy, he only felt relief.

A week later, Wesley Bens walked out of the hospital, his face dark with menace and his eyes the unseeing orbs of a crazed and fevered animal. Poisonous thoughts of revenge occupied his mind and he felt both deadened and empowered by them. Bobby White would die slowly enough to regret every moment of struggle and agony Bens endured during his climb from the sea to the cliff above, every ripple of pain and drop of his blood shed in the effort. Before it was over, White would long for his own death. And then the rest of them. Every one, beginning with the little speargun bastard and his mother.

Death had stalked him before, but this clumsy attempt with a useless weapon wielded by a frightened tourist, left him shaken in ways he didn't understand. Some stupid American blowhard, women, children. It was unimaginable, and he couldn't rest until the memory of them was wiped clean with their own blood.

Violent fantasies empowered him while they calmed him. His thoughts often turned to violence and it never failed to cheer him up. Unlike those who thought about it and did nothing, Bens knew he would accomplish the things he imagined, and more. He was calmed by this knowledge. A kind of calm that brought clarity and inner peace. When he seized control of someone else, bringing them to an end or sparing them, it created a new perspective and restored his sense of humor. The darkness of his violent hatreds faded and he believed himself to be quite a charming English gentleman. Others noticed this too, and responded. Women especially.

Bobby White, too, had been released from the hospital, but days before. His knife wound was clean and pierced no vital organs or arteries. He was stiff, thankful to be alive, and according to Judy Ann, a hero. He didn't feel heroic, but lying in a hospital bed with a knife wound in his back, Bobby had time to think. What he thought about was that he had always been afraid. He chose the security business not to be of help to people, to protect them, but because it eased his own fears. Creating a system of security wasn't the same as feeling secure in yourself. Not at all. But strangely enough, now he did. He'd lost his fear somewhere.

The thought of his panic in the water on the day of his first deep dive brought a smile. There was much worse a man could face, and overcome. He knew what he'd done to Bens and that the man lived. He also knew what Bens might still be capable of doing to him. It made him shiver, but that stomach-wrenching hollow fear he'd endured all his life when an argument took a step toward violence, had evaporated. Whatever comes now, he thought, he'd face it like a man.

Judy Ann had taken him back to the hotel by taxi and he had rested three days, listening to the storm beat itself against the window. Each day he grew stronger and on the third day he made love to his wife as he had when they were first married. Her ardor, too, had lost the complacency of repetition. Bobby thought maybe getting stabbed in the back might be the best thing he'd ever accomplished.

Rosa stopped by their room with a flower arrangement she'd made, and both the Whites commented on the change in her. She treated them more like friends than tourists, and her smiles were genuine. Bobby was especially charmed and held her hand and apologized for his earlier behaviors.

"Nothing like this ever happened to me," he told her. "You helped save my life, and I reckon maybe a lesser woman would've just told me to bite it. Judy Ann and me, we talked it over. Our vacation wasn't ruined, it was made better by this. Hell, our lives are better. So I called the office and told them I got hurt and was staying on 'til I was damn good and ready to come home. And they can get along without me, or just stuff it."

"That is exactly what he told them," Judy Ann said proudly. "Bobby gets stabbed and he's never been so happy. Not in years."

Rosa saw the change in Bobby's eyes and knew his apology was genuine. She hugged him and said, "You are part of our island now. Spilling your blood here for us. We speak three languages, English, Spanish, and French, and you are welcome now in them all."

After she released him, Bobby held tightly to her hand. "The Capitan. Will he let me dive?"

"He will do exactly what I tell him." Rosa smiled. "Unless he wishes to sleep with the goat."

They parted as friends and for the first time since she'd met Warren Wilson, Rosa thought she would find a way to claim him. If these tourists, who had no connection to the place, could be changed, then it seemed impossible that her truest love was so mulish he'd abandon her for Ruth, or anyone. This was his place. She was his. Armando would be his son. All that remained now was to save the island from the growing menace of men like Javert and Bens. Lately, she'd been making some plans for that too. As she strolled up High Candle Street, head high, shoulders back, breasts uplifted, she felt like a woman of promise and worth. Let them say what they pleased, the dishwasher was on the march.

Not far away in his opulent hotel suite, Javert had Slither all but pinned to the chair beside his desk, hooded eyes ablaze with anger. In all the time he'd known Javert, Slither had never seen him lose his temper before. Though he was winding down, spittle remained in the corners of his small fleshy mouth and both his chins held a raw red color as if someone had applied a blow torch to them. The fat man was pissed.

"The Englishman," Javert spat. "The filthy eunuch! I'd like to feed him his balls if he hadn't already had them removed."

"Actually," Slither ventured, "he still has them, I think. A woman from Guadeloupe put them back on. That's what I heard."

"Why would she do that?"

"A doctor friend of the German doctor."

"Idiots! All of them. This entire island is inhabited by mindless idiots! And now I've hired one."

Slither made no comment, though he had warned Javert more than once about the Englishman.

"Well, my little friend," Javert continued, "we are in a mess. I did not tell that fool Bens to kill the rays. He was supposed to observe. Report. Keep me informed. And now I have been arrested. Jacques Leon Du Gard Javert has been arrested and dragged to the jail like a common pimp. Half the people in this very hotel saw it. And I certainly did not instruct him to attack women and children. Tourists, for God's sake! Filthy Englishman! You will kill him the very moment I'm finished with him."

"Kill him?"

"You will take that little knife of yours and slit first his femoral artery, then his jugular vein, and then his larynx so he can suck his own blood until he chokes. Filthy Englishman!"

Slither felt a lump growing in his own larynx. "Yes, Monsieur Javert, I understand. But this Englishman is very dangerous. He threw me from the boat and I had the little knife in my hand at the time. He is not afraid of little knives. And you know, he broke my finger like you snap a pencil. Can't we get somebody to maybe shoot him from a distance?"

"You are afraid?"

"No. I am terrified."

Javert considered this a moment, and then he smiled. "Yes. Wisely I think. I too, am afraid of him. Later. We will make a plan for him. Shooting him from a distance is not a bad idea."

Slither exhaled with relief but failed to bring a smile to his face. "And in the meantime?"

"He will not be too eager to fight until his strength is back. We say nothing. Act as if everything is normal. I have another job for him." He grinned in that hungry way of his. "Soon as it can be arranged I want a large public rally for independence. I want bands, singing, marching in the streets, sign-waving islanders, anti-British rock throwers, everything we can imagine to light a fire under this movement. It's languishing with disinterest. What you heard from the Cubans is important. They are an organized group who have support and some money. We need to counter that. Beyond them there is nobody here who can bring a crowd together. If we strike first we achieve the upper hand. A few years from now the British will be gone. I will own this hotel. Bens will be dead and Sergeant Cumberbatch will work for me, like Captain Will. Ha! A new era of prosperity, my little friend."

Slither nodded. Yes, he thought, it will be a new era. One of everything for Javert and nothing much for anybody else. He wondered if maybe he couldn't slip over to Guadeloupe for a few years. Of course, there was the trouble some time back, but maybe that was forgotten by now. Maybe nobody cared. On the other hand, he might land in jail. Even Javert was better then that.

"One more thing," Javert said. "Investigate the polling apparatus. Find out how it will be done and who will be appointed as election judges. Who will count the ballots and so forth. Some of these civil servants are our people but do we have enough? Understand me?"

"Yes. You want me to help you swindle the voters and manipulate the election."

"Mr. Slitter, you are much the sharp-eyed, insightful little fellow. This is why I have you in my employ. But is it a swindle to give people what is best for them?" Javert's slick eyes watched Slither some time before he continued. "Leave the politics to me. Just find me the answers I need. Understand?"

Slither nodded. He never relished Javert's presence for long. The Fat Man could sweat menace and soon Slither was sweating dread. Now would be a fine time to leave.

"Fine. Then I shan't detain you any longer," said Javert. "Find the filthy Englishman. He can help you round up loafers, rummies and any other ne'er-do-wells in the town to act as marchers in the independence parade. Get a band. Fireworks. Drums. Lots of noise and smoke. I want His Excellency Governor Sir Henry Leach to hear it and see it and smell it. His end. The new order. Ha!"

"Oui Monsieur. Adios." Slither started for the door, but paused there. "And the money for all this?"

"Tell them that I, Jacques Leon Du Gard Javert, will pay them handsomely. Handsomely!"

Slither smiled and left. He was working for idiots. Javert had no intention of paying anyone. Bens without balls was more dangerous then Bens with balls. Was he, Todd Slitter, the only person left on Charming Island with all his marbles? He chuckled. I made a joke, he thought.

Several days later they had done the impossible. Slither stood halfway along High Candle Street beside a bedraggled royal palm left wounded by the passing storm. The weather now had become unbearably hot and muggy. The sun beat down on his bare head of sun-bleached hair. The growing bald spot at the back was red and hot. He'd neglected to bring a hat.

Out of sight some blocks away, the band was tooling up. It sounded like an idling diesel. The Englishman would begin the parade and march them down the street, making sure none veered off to the bars or eateries along the route. When he reached Slither they would join forces and escort the marchers the remainder of the way to Edward Charming's statue in the square where they would shoot off the fireworks, play the "Charming Island national anthem", very similar to "Rule Britannia", then Javert would speak. More fireworks, more music, and more rum distributed.

The filthy Englishman had wanted to instigate a fight that would lead to a riot, but Javert had squashed the idea and Slither wondered why Bens acquiesced so mildly. Maybe he really was de-balled.

He shifted his feet. The mid-day sun baked the sidewalk and soaked through the soles of his shoes. The band seemed to be settling into a tune of some kind. There were only eleven of them. Four were the same group who played for the tourists at sidewalk cafes until in desperation they tossed tips into a Bustelo coffee can to be rid of them. Two others were self-taught trumpet players - loud but tuneless. Four were drunks given drums and told to keep the beat. So far they seemed incapable of hitting their drums in unison. That left Harvey Napoléon, who was the only person on the island who knew all seventeen verses of "Palms 'a Sway'n", the national anthem. He possessed an annoying, trembling tenor voice forceful enough to drown out the entire band. His facial expressions were so exaggerated and phony they had become part of the Mexican comic's routine at the Hotel Palace Royale's Turquois Room.

The band finally settled down and came together with John Anderson's country tune "Swingin'" - a big favorite on the island since its release five years earlier. Harvey's voice didn't have the twang of Anderson's, but once again, he knew the lyrics, and could say "Charlotte Johnson" almost as well, which caused a stir in the crowd along the street. Slither heard a spattering of applause.

With the music came more people. Most were locals. The storm had sent some tourists scurrying to quieter beaches on islands without crashing surf and plastic garbage rolling up to form a dump at the high-waterline. Slither soon realized he'd failed to get the marchers to understand that their signs should be spread among the group and face outward so people along the route could read them. Instead, most were swinging them in tune with Harvey's song, and had forgotten to show the onlookers what the march was about.

Well, he supposed it didn't matter. The banner of Sir Henry Leach's head, caricaturized with a pig nose, was leading the procession and seemed to Slither clear enough to give people a sense of the thing. He noticed the editor of the *Charming Guardian* taking a photograph of the sign. He was also the newspaper's only reporter. Even though he would take the British side of things, his covering of the event would in itself be all they needed to draw attention to the cause of independence. It would gain more legitimacy appearing on the front page of the newspaper then anything else they could do. People would be forced to discuss the event and its cause.

Jogging across the street ahead of the sign was Captain Will. Too late, Slither realized the Captain was coming toward him. He pulled the corners of his mouth up in a hurried smile that he hoped would appeal to the Captain.

"Drop the fake grin, Todd," Captain Will said. "I see the Fat Man has you gainfully employed."

"This is not my doing."

"Todd."

Slither sighed. Another thing he liked about Will was he never called him Slither. "What can I do? Javert wants a parade, I make a parade."

"Where's Bens?" Warren's eyes flashed along the throng of marchers.

"Coming behind," Slither said. "We have to escort them to the square. Please don't do anything now."

Captain Will smiled unpleasantly. "Now or later. He survived Bobby White. He won't survive me. He threatened my son, my woman, my friends. I plan to take more than his balls."

"Actually," Slither said, "I think he has his balls. They just got sewed back on or something. A woman doctor from Guadeloupe."

"Is he coming or not?"

"You can't do anything here. Cumberbatch is over there watching and I'm pretty sure somebody from Government House has been sent down to see what's going on. You better leave."

"I think you better shut up. I don't plan to kill him in front of half the island, just give him a preview of what's coming."

Wesley Bens appeared just then over Slither's shoulder. "The brave Captain." He chuckled at Warren. "Come to see the parade, have you then?"

"No. Just knew that where a mob of fools gather, you're no doubt in the midst of them. And I have a message for you - from me - get off this island as quick as you can. You threatened my family and friends. That won't happen again."

Bens grinned. "You will prevent it?"

"Definitely."

Bens stepped around Slither and stood almost on top of Warren. "Harbor scum piece of shit! You threaten me? I kill for money." He grinned again. "You. I'm doing you for nothing. Just for fun. You irritate me, little ponytail scuba boy. I will take you, then your family and friends."

He was gone before Warren could respond.

"Please," Slither begged. "Not now. Be careful of him. He hates you. I fought him. He took my knife and broke my fingers. He moves like something made of steel. Like a piston. Before long the Fat Man will take care of him. Wait. Just wait."

Warren did not answer and the band marched by singing "Little Charlotte, she's as pretty as the angels when they sing...."

The music blared. The crowd joined in the song and Warren walked away toward the harbor.

Fireworks sounded. Smoke rose above the trees and drifted up the hill toward Government House. Javert's voice, echoing from the loudspeaker system, ebbed and flowed like carnival music heard across town. There was shouting and applause. Somebody blew a single blast on a trumpet. Laughter drifted like smoke.

Sir Henry Leach stood frozen. He smelled the smoke, heard the sounds, knew the source. The shock of it gripped him in a seemingly permanent inertia. He thought he might've had a hemorrhage in his brain. Apoplexy maybe. Or was that the same thing?

"Should we go down for a look?" Reggie asked from his side.

"Not hardly."

Reggie smiled. "No. Don't suppose it would be seemly. But in due time your reaction will be necessary, and expected."

"Of course," Sir Henry said. "But I don't even know what it is yet."

Reggie noted his despondency. His friend Henry had always been one of the stiff upper lip set, but that didn't mean he wasn't down in the dumps about it on a personal level. He wasn't much of a governor really, but he was Governor, and took it more seriously than he let on. "You'll find the right thing to say when the time comes," Reggie told him.

Sir Henry nodded, crossed his arms and leaned down heavily on the wrought iron railing. "That would be Javert's voice we are hearing below?"

"Yes."

"Is it my fault because I had him arrested?"

"No Henry. I'm sure he's been planning this for some time," Reggie assured him.

"I can't arrest him now."

"No."

"Well," the Governor said as he turned to face his Chief of Staff and best friend, "this is the politics of the times, but I had hoped we were past it somehow. That CI would be one of those to stay in the Commonwealth. I really believed that."

"It's just beginning, and I have reason to believe we can win this one, though a few weeks ago I would have thought otherwise."

"Oh? Has something happened?"

"Rosa has contacted me."

Sir Henry sighed and shook his head. "I thought you were going to give me some good news."

"I am. She wasn't talking about that. She was calling in a favor."

"She can't want money!"

Reggie poured himself another cup of tea from the server on the table. "You know, if a man in your position has an affair with a woman, everything depends on the woman. She is in control of events then, and later."

"I'm not a fool, Reggie. I know that."

"Well then, be of good cheer because you picked the proper woman to sleep with. The favor is not for her, and most certainly not about money. In fact, she wants what you want. Her favor is that you will help her achieve it."

"What are you saying?"

"I'm saying Rosa is your political ally."

"Fantastic," the Governor said without enthusiasm. "Rosa is a dishwasher with whom I've conceived an illegitimate son. She is now shacked up with a destitute American expat hopelessly indebted to Javert, who is just now speaking about my downfall. Splendid."

Reggie walked to his friend's side and took him by the shoulders. "Come on. Let's sit and talk a minute."

When they were seated at the table, Reggie poured tea but said nothing for awhile.

"Well?" the Governor broke the silence.

"It's important Henry, what I have to tell you." Reggie smiled in a particularly modest manner and went on. "I'm not the proper messenger. You know my views on religion, and they are confused at best. Our Anglican Communion once sent hundreds of missionaries to Africa, and did you know there is now a movement in Africa to send missionaries to England? Our bishops appear to them in need of it. African Christians now believe they must come to darkest England and save our souls. Do you not find this odd?"

"Quite an irony, if true."

"Oh, it's true all right."

"Fine," Sir Henry acknowledged, "but what on earth does it have to do with us?"

"The people here are mostly of African descent and primarily black. Unlike me and most Englishmen of this day, they are religious." Reggie pressed the letter R into the tablecloth with his spoon. "Rosa is black. She is religious. She is Charming Island. We, my friend, are outsiders."

Sir Henry's face was dark. "I told you, Reggie. I am not a fool. I know all this."

"Of course you do, but Rosa can save this island for England, and you can't."

"Now that's ridiculous."

Reggie shook his head. "No. It's just Caribbean politics. The Rosas of this island have the religious cohesion and power, and they will vote against independence because they aren't stupid like Javert thinks. Why would they give up a system of government that rarely interferes with them, never oppresses them, and keeps the economy strong? Javert, and other so-called businessmen, are greedy little men who wish to enrich themselves with the almighty tourist dollar. Do you think Rosa or Cumberbatch or the Cuban who runs the Tortuga are so stupid they don't understand this? They joke about us but they don't hate us. They play a fine game of cricket here, for God's sake. They speak the language and drive on the left side of the road. In some ways I think they are more British then we are, or what we once were. And Rosa comes to me to ask you to do yourself a favor by supporting her with organization and expertise to guarantee a fair election. She will give you this island in return. Can you beat that?"

"Can I believe that?"

Reggie leaned back in his chair and stared hard at his friend. "Can you afford not to?"

They were both silent a long time.

Finally Reggie said, "Henry. Talk to me as a friend for a minute. Off the record? Please?"

Sir Henry sat up straight and knew immediately what his old friend wanted. "You've asked before, you know. Is nothing to be private then?"

"I have no prurient interest. No curiosity of the titillating details. You know that, or I would've asked long ago." Reggie poured himself more tea, mixed in sugar and cream, and stirred it slowly with the spoon. "Damn it, Henry. Some things don't make sense to me. I don't want details, just reasons. I admire you more than anyone I know. Always the beam on, hardy fellow. The very reason you are here is because you refused to compromise your integrity. Refused to bend the rules of decency. Never the expedient choice for you, but the right and just. I'm the politician who kept you - barely - from going over the waterfall. So to me, Rosa never made any sense."

"So, flattery is it?" Sir Henry smiled. "Fine then, I'll answer you. After all, I've left you with the problem and you've handled it well over the years. If nothing else, I'm sure you noticed how little she asked of me, even when Armando was born. I would have given her anything - money, a better job, opportunities for the boy...whatever she asked. She refused it all. How did that make me feel, Reggie? Huh? Yes. Small. Very small. Took me down a peg, she did."

Reggie shrugged. "Whatever she is, she is her own woman. And the most discreet person on this island. There have always been rumors, but never a word from her nor any proof."

"Our Captain Will is almost as responsible for that as Rosa. He took her in when she was pregnant and kept his mouth shut, and like her, asked for nothing. I've doubted, in fact, that she even told him."

Reggie grinned. "How lucky Governor, or you might be missing your front teeth."

"Undoubtedly," he chuckled. A moment passed. His face, slack and expressionless now, he continued. "A decade ago. She was young, maybe nineteen, and Peg, you know, was on another of her six month *vacations* to the UK. I was lonely. Eating dinner by myself at the Pink Sands and some tipsy tourist decided to make my acquaintance, leading to a mess. The scene grew into a troubling thing and Carl, the manager on duty, hustled me out through the kitchen and there she was, outside in the alley smoking. I waited there. We talked. She wasn't like anybody else. She didn't say 'Good evening, Governor,' or anything like that. She just talked to me like a man. Regular guy. I told her things about myself. Personal things. I don't know why. I just said them and she was kind and like someone I'd always known. Even now Reggie, I don't understand it. I can't tell you it without sounding the fool." He stood and walked to the railing again. "We kept seeing each other, just to talk, and then I don't know, over the months it became something else. My God, Reggie, I felt so close to her. And when she got pregnant - we quit. Her idea, not mine. I was in love with her by then. Didn't know what to do..."

"Enough!" Reggie said, following him to the railing. "Enough. I'm sorry. It really wasn't my business. I'm sorry."

"Never mind. What is sad for me is that I want her still. I'd divorce Peg and marry Rosa tomorrow if she didn't hold it all as sin and shame. I learned a lot about myself from her, Reggie. Look at me. I'm white. I'm the Governor. What black dishwasher wouldn't want me? Oh no, Reggie. You don't have to convince me that people on this island answer to a higher power." He sighed and spread his lips in a sad smile. "I learned something about equality too. It's not a political movement. It's inside the people. Inside them, like part of their souls. We judge like fools. By the bank account, social position, skin color. All that crap, Reggie. All crap. You're right. They should be sending us missionaries. They really should."

Reggie stared at him a long while and neither spoke.

Governor Sir Henry Leach draped his arm around his friend's shoulder and said, "You know, we do belong here. We do. We contribute our ability to govern. It's simply too boring for these people and they aren't very good at it. So, what do you say? Shall we get on with it?"

"Yes, Sir. I will see to it we give the dishwasher whatever she wants."

The Governor drew himself up, smiled and said, "The State is pleased."

CHAPTER TWENTY ONE

The decision on independence loomed closer, another dark storm rushing toward the island. The people of Government House scrambled to find fair, impartial election judges but could hardly have them vetted in time. A small contingent of civil service workers had managed these things in past elections and the realization came too late that they were compromised, their ranks infiltrated by Javert's people. The vote for independence was in doubt. It might go either way.

On election eve, Warren and Rosa had invited the Van Dorens, Myron, and the Whites to dinner. The occasion was their first opportunity to discuss possible uses for the *Imperial* wreck. Warren's first instincts were simply to keep quiet and not include the Van Dorens and the Whites, since all would soon be leaving the island, and in this way keep the discovery to himself. He feared that once the thing was common knowledge there would be a rush to exploit it, and in the end it would be destroyed as the rays were destroyed. But Rosa convinced him that no amount of such secrecy was possible on Charming Island. Better to get busy and make a plan for the public use of the wreck site. Like an underwater park, she said, used but not destroyed.

He had no more than accepted this loathsome notion when she went off onto politics again. For crying out loud he could just as well be married to the woman. Three times their dinner was interrupted by someone, mostly church ladies, pounding on the door and babbling about this or that person who didn't show up at some place on time to do something vital to their mission to stop independence. The irony alone was enough to make him ill.

After the third interruption he shouted, "Let the damn people on this sand pit make up their own minds! Who in hell cares anyway?"

"I am one of the damn people!" she shouted back.

The guests stared down at their soup. Silent.

The silence stretched out too long for anyone's comfort, and for once, Freddie-the-Frogman kept his mouth shut. Warren was especially thankful for that. He knew somehow this would all be his fault anyway, since he disagreed with Rosa, and that had lately become a mortal sin.

Warren disliked any kind of public display of emotion. "Listen," he said reasonably. "The vote is tomorrow. It's the eleventh hour. Let it go. You can't change anything now. How about we just finish dinner and talk over our own problems. I got a couple bottles of great French liqueur. Okay?"

Ruth lifted her head. "He's right Rosa. I spent my life married to a politician." She shrugged. "We had nights like this too. At some point, it's up to the voters."

Rosa looked across at her and smiled. "Yes," she said. "But I am so afraid it will all be dishonest. A cheat."

"Shocking," Warren said. "Imagine politics a cheat."

Rosa opened her mouth to speak, but Ruth held up a hand to stop her. "Please," she said. "Let me." She turned to Warren. "I spent my life in politics because I married a politician. In the end I rejected his liberal views but I never rejected the man. He was good and did what he did mostly for the benefit of others. I don't know anything about politics on this island, but Rosa has the same passion for a cause my husband had. If you don't respect the cause, then at least respect her. Anyone can see she loves you. And she loves her home."

"Damn it, lady," Myron said. "You sure talk like a politician." He winked at Warren, assuming he'd done him a favor.

Red-faced, Warren rose to leave.

"Sit down," Bobby White said.

For no reason anyone could understand, Warren sat down.

"Ya know," Bobby began, "In the security business we've done some pretty big shot politician's houses. Like Captain Will I never liked 'em much. But good money usually bought the best. Later, when the calls for help came in, lots were from them politicians."

"Get to the point, Bobby," Judy Ann prodded.

"Sure. Point is that they needed that security because lots of folks don't like politicians and get too over excited about their politics anyway, and come after 'em." He shrugged. "Well, I mean you wouldn't do that - put yourself in harm's way so to speak - if you weren't pretty committed to your cause. Right?"

"Aw, bullshit," Myron said. "Hitler, he was pretty committed too. I know. I fought him."

Freddie-the-Frogman shook his head and grinned. "I think I remember that. Didn't you storm the Fuhrer Bunker all by yourself and throttle him with your bare hands?"

"You know what I mean," Myron said, simply.

"Guess I do, Myron," Freddie answered. "But it's better we don't fight these kind of people in the first place. Take 'em out before they take power. Seems to me that's what Rosa is doing. If she's willing to stick her neck out, then we should have her back."

Warren lifted his head and stared across the table. "Listen here, Freddie. I've had Rosa's back for years. You're a bit late to that party."

Rosa stood and moved to collect the soup bowls. Ruth and Judy Ann joined her. "It's arroz con pollo," she said. "Rice with chicken. In the oven. I will bring it now. More wine?"

"We've had enough," Freddie said.

"I haven't," Myron responded.

Rosa sent them all outside onto the veranda after dinner, refusing any help from Ruth and Judy Ann to wash dishes and clean up. Warren's political attitude wasn't surprising after so many years with him, but the other Americans confused her. She imagined they would be more democratic. It's what she had always heard about them, but they seemed to take it all for granted. Was she naïve or maybe stupid? Without an education she learned what she knew from observation and experience. Ruth had been to college. So had Warren for that matter. And yet, she trusted herself more than she trusted them.

When she finished in the kitchen and joined them on the veranda, the conversation had turned to the shipwreck. She was relieved.

"What makes you think this Governor Leach will even declare something underwater to be a park or even part of one?" Freddie was asking.

"Don't know anything for sure," Warren said. "It just makes sense, more I think about it. Takes the wind out of Javert's sails. He's blowing all the time about tourism and here we have a ready-made tourist attraction. Governor's got no love for Javert. Idea might just put a smile on his face."

"Well," Freddie said, "then we best get out there tomorrow and figure how to put divers down there. I mean, that's a tough dive for some lake diver from Iowa. Not that they have any lakes in Iowa."

"Big surge," Myron added. "Smash their heads in."

Warren sipped his wine, wishing it was rum. "Thought maybe we'd put lines down connecting the cannons and the anchor all around." He shaped his hands like a boat. "You know, outline the wreck so they hold the lines. Pull themselves along. Keep them from kicking up the bottom too."

"Makes sense," Freddie nodded.

"Smash their heads in," Myron said.

Warren wasn't convinced anything would succeed against Javert. Unless it was secret. "Javert can't know," he said. "If these people vote for independence then Javert wins and he'll take power. Once the Brits leave, who can stop him?"

"Yeah," Freddie said. "But either way you got to live with it, or leave, right?"

"Smash their heads in," Myron said.

Freddie glared at him. "Shut up, Myron."

The four men occupied chairs arranged in a semi-circle. Warren on the far end away from the door. The sun gone. The night dark with only a light inland breeze. Three candles flickered on the tables, their light making faces sway and gambol above inert bodies when they talked or tilted their heads. It occurred to Warren that they were becoming friends, and he wondered what he might have to give up for that. Friends were like family - dangerously close to the heart. Close enough to bring disaster.

Warren stared at Freddie a moment before he spoke. "I'm tired of leaving places. Maybe just this once I'll go for broke. We'll see tomorrow what happens."

Tomorrow came with blazing sunshine and long lines at the polls. No one seemed able to decide if a heavy turnout was good for one side or the other. By late afternoon not much had changed. Just under fifty-five hundred people lived on the island and it seemed that every eligible voter among them was lined up. Rosa cast her vote early and Warren escorted her, though he couldn't vote himself, as an American. Frankie Sebastian, whom Warren and Rosa had known for years, scrutinized her ID and asked her to state her name and address. Warren knew Frankie as a Javert crony, and thought it a bad omen to find him as an election judge. He feared Rosa might soon be proven correct. A rigged election.

Governor Leach had declared the day a national holiday and the polls closed at six o'clock that evening except in several mountain villages where people came on foot or by donkey and were forced to travel long distances on trails and over high passes. Government House was optimistic and Leach himself spoke to a sizable crowd earlier that morning before the polls opened, promising to conduct a fair and impartial election and assuring them that Her Majesty's Government would abide by the result and do whatever necessary to help the new government, should one need to be formed afterward. The crowd had seemed much subdued compared to the one surrounding Javert during his recent independence rally. Sir Henry and Reggie thought maybe they had a chance.

The ballots were counted and recounted all during the night. A final result didn't come until after ten o'clock the next morning. It wasn't even close. According to the certified count, only 757 voters cast ballots to remain in the Commonwealth. The rest - 3,241 - chose independence. The total was greater than the number of eligible voters. The election was a fraud. More than half the population was made up of children under voting age so there could have been a vote total of no more then 2,616 on both sides of the issue. However, if they accepted at least the 757 count to remain in the Commonwealth, the independence total was still greater, and this made it difficult to prove fraud. Many decided it was a win for independence either way so why not just accept it?

In the end, the British government decided to take the same position and avoid a world view of the UK as some colonial power past its peak attempting to hold onto a tiny backwater island just to save face. Plans were being made to retire gracefully and help the islanders form a new government of their own. It was over.

That evening Warren, Freddie-the-Frogman and Myron Bose went for drinks and dinner at the Charming Arms, an English pub that had been on the island for at least one hundred years. They did it in honor of the British, who had also packed the place. They planned to dive the following morning and begin creating a diver-friendly shipwreck out of the *Imperial.* Warren also wanted to persuade them to accompany him to Guadeloupe and help load Javert's weapons. The Fat Man had talked to him just after the election results were announced to say that now was the time for the voyage. Warren was perplexed. The election was over why the need for weapons? Javert had won. Nevertheless, he insisted. Warren was eager now to run this needless errand and earn back *Esteban's* mortgage.

Bobby White insisted on taking his wife, Ruth and Rosa to dinner at the Tortuga. He said they had been his saviors and they would find the "man talk" of working on the shipwreck a boring evening.

The Charming Arms was a rather tall two-story building that overlooked the harbor about a half mile around the bay from the Tortuga. The ground floor was taken up by a chandler shop that now sold mostly tourist goods but still managed to stock a few items needed by local fishermen. Upstairs a large window brought the sea and harbor into perfect focus. It was air-conditioned, carpeted, and featured a grand mantel and long L-shaped bar the envy of any English pub in London. Bass Ale and other British brews were fresh on tap, and the pub featured the best fish and chips within a thousand miles.

The three men had just finished their second round and ordered a third when a little man who worked for Orizondo the Cuban appeared at their table. His name was Garcia, and he was missing his left eye, which he said had been hooked from his head when a fishing net was thrown into the sea. With his remaining eye, he claimed to have watched as some kind of mullet swallowed the first one.

"What's up, Garcia?" Warren asked.

"Your woman is in a bar fight."

Freddie and Myron chuckled. Warren said, "What? Rosa? She's not in a bar fight."

"Yes," Garcia insisted. "Señor Orizondo sent me to fetch you because she has already been injured and refuses to stop fighting. She is crazy from drunkenness."

Now Freddie and Myron were wiping their eyes from laughter.

"Idiot!" Warren addressed Garcia. "Rosa hardly ever drinks and even if she did she wouldn't be brawling in some bar. She's having dinner with friends."

"They are all fighting," Garcia said. "Everybody in the bar. Your woman is big and has beaten two men and sent another one to the hospital."

Freddie paused and wiped his eyes. "What about the other women with her? They aren't fighting?"

"Of course they are fighting. Everybody is fighting. I was the only one they could send because I have one eye and when I look at something, like a nose or a chin, it's someplace else than where I see it, so I can't fight anybody."

The barmaid slid three pints of foaming ale onto the table and Warren grabbed her arm. "Bring the tab. I think we need to leave right now."

"You buying this crap?" Myron asked.

Warren shrugged. "Garcia here isn't a genius, but I never knew him to be a liar either."

"Thank you, Captain Will," Garcia said, seriously accepting the compliment. "It is a big fight. I never saw any fight like this."

"What's it about anyway?" Freddie asked.

"Politics," Garcia said. "The church people started it. They came along the street and into the cafes and bars and places shouting '757 we fight!' and then some other ones decided to fight them so now everybody is fighting. The Tortuga is smashed and people are in the street and two cars are burning and the women are meaner than the men."

Warren wondered if maybe Garcia was lying. "What's this '757 we fight' nonsense?"

"I don't understand it," Garcia said. "Are you coming? I have to get back."

"Why?"

"I am the doctor until the doctor comes," he said. "Since I lost my eye I learned a lot about medicine." He ran for the door.

Warren took a long drink of his ale, leaving a foam mustache. "Nobody could make that up. Let's go." He waited while the other two all but drained their glasses. "And if those Pentecostal church ladies are in a fistfight I pity whoever faces them. They're big and black and the Lord God Almighty is with them."

"Jesus Christ!" Freddie said.

"Him too."

Little Garcia had not exaggerated. The Tortuga was a shambles and both intersecting streets were filled to the corner with struggling bodies of combatants. The three men came to a halt across the street and a half block uphill, and stared. One hundred or more normally docile and law-abiding men and women were engaged in such a mêlée of striking and pushing each other that Warren was speechless. His eyes darted among them in search of Rosa, Ruth and the Whites. The whole scene seemed to him like a huge writhing ball of worms. Impossible to distinguish individuals. He suddenly didn't seem to know anyone.

At his elbow, Freddie said, "I was in Roosevelt Roads, Puerto Rico this one time in the Navy and there was a fight like this. Started in the EM club and spilled out onto the greenest, prettiest lawn you ever saw. And before long there was blood everywhere and gouged out eyes, broken arms, you name it. Know what started that fight?" He didn't wait for an answer. "Nobody ever knew. Just started and everybody joined in." He shrugged and glanced at the other two men. "So, here we are."

One of the burning vehicles, a small Toyota sedan, was being extinguished by a man and woman with two buckets. They had tied ropes to the bucket handles and ran periodically to the seawall and dropped them into the sea for another bucketful of water. Warren guessed the car belonged to them or they wouldn't be so faithful in an attempt to put out the flames. He hoped the gas tank had already exploded.

Myron said, "I'm too old for this shit. I'm going back up to the Charming Arms and have another beer." He punched Warren's arm. "Coming?"

Warren shook his head. "No. Rosa's there somewhere."

Myron glanced at Freddie and knew he'd get the same answer so turned and started back up the hill, then stopped. "Say, Captain Will. You ain't got a few extra bucks I could borrow?"

After he'd gone, Freddie said, "Well? We don't have a choice, you know. Not just Ruth and Rosa. We got those goofy Whites down there. Can't have Bobby getting his wound opened up again. For a rube he sure manages to find trouble."

Warren glanced up along the row of houses, businesses and pensions that fronted the Tortuga. People were hanging out the windows, crowding verandas, laughing or cheering. Where in the hell were the cops?

"Let's go around back," he told Freddie. "Come into the Tortuga through the kitchen. Might be safer."

"Or you might get a fourteen-inch cast iron skillet up side your head,"

Freddie said.

But the Tortuga's kitchen was quiet, except for Garcia sitting above a large bucket peeling potatoes. "So, you finally got here," he said.

Warren stared at him. "Why in hell are you peeling potatoes?"

Garcia kept his eye on his peeler and said, "Because, Mr. Captain Know-it-all, these people are going to be hungry when this is over and Carlos the Cuban is going to sell them papas fritas and get some of his money back. You know how much stuff is broke out there? I bet you won't be back here tomorrow to help clean up."

Freddie was chuckling and Warren asked, "What's so funny?"

"This has been one harebrained, rowdy vacation. No wonder you never come home."

"It's never like this," Warren scowled.

Freddie shook his head and gestured toward the swinging kitchen door into the café. "Well? Shall we?"

Warren led the way. The door swung outward and a white nightstick two feet long came out of nowhere, aimed at his skull. "Mr. Cumberbatch!" he shouted. "Hold it!"

The big policeman checked his swing. "I've not known you to be a brawler, Captain Will."

"I'm not. I'm here to find Rosa and the other divers and take them away."

Sergeant Cumberbatch glared at Freddie. "Why do you have this troublemaker with you?"

"He's searching for his daughter." Warren smiled. "And Sergeant, didn't you place him in my charge? I'm keeping him close."

"And you have not been fighting?"

"Look at us. No bumps, no bruises, no bloody knuckles. We were up at the Charming Arms having a beer."

"Hump," the Sergeant said. "Where I'd like to be."

"Can we go?"

Cumberbatch nodded. "Be careful. We are sorting it out but some do not seem interested in abiding by the law. This is what happens when politics comes to a peaceful place."

"I couldn't agree with you more, Mr. Cumberbatch," Warren said. "And you know me. Have I been involved in politics? Ever?"

"Maybe not. But your woman is another matter. Half the arrests we are making now are ladies from one or another Pentecostal church. Tell me, what is happening to my island? To my home, when I am arresting women who minister to the poor, make a joyful noise singing hymns? What is the sense of this?" He wiped sweat from his brow with a bare forearm the size of a small tree trunk. "I have been too long in this work, to see such things."

The big Sergeant turned away and it seemed to Warren there was a slump to his wide shoulders and a hesitancy in his step.

"There they are," Freddie said, pointing to Rosa, who was seated on what was perhaps the last remaining chair in the cafe, with Ruth, Judy Ann and Bobby White bending over her. Judy Ann was cradling Rosa's tilted head while Ruth dabbed at her bleeding mouth with the corner of a tablecloth. The others didn't seem to be bleeding but both had torn clothing and their hair in knots. Bobby stood over them with a club that looked as if it had once been a leg for something. "Reminds me of one of those scenes you see in paintings of the French Revolution," Freddie continued.

"Why didn't I think of that," Warren said.

It took time to make sense of their story, but the ladies from several of the Pentecostal churches in Edward Town had eyewitness evidence that election judges loyal, or bought by Javert, were "losing" independence no votes and doubling the yes votes. Arguments ensued but nothing was done about it. When the final count came out and showed that only 757 islanders had voted to remain in the Commonwealth they coined the phrase - 757 we fight - but didn't mean it literally, just that they were fighting the 757 count. Things got out of hand and a real fight broke out.

Rosa, spitting blood while she talked, said simply, "The Fat Man robbed us of a country."

Ruth told her to shush and looked at Warren. "She'll need a couple stitches or some Steri-Strips. It's a deep cut."

"Jagged," Warren said, peering closely at the wound. "Fist?"

"No," Ruth admitted. "Purse."

"Purse?"

"I think it was a metal hook holding the strap to the purse. Her friend To-John caught her on the backswing. Accident."

"Where's this To-John, then?"

"Jail."

"We were just sitting there in the Charming Arms," Warren said, "having a nice cold beer to commiserate with the poor Brits and it seems like the whole place went nuts." He picked up a three and one half-legged chair. "I think I need to sit down." He slid off but regained his feet. "Damn Cuban! Wrecked his furniture. Where is he anyway?"

"Jail."

Warren cautiously edged up onto the table next to Rosa instead. "How many people did Cumberbatch haul off to that tiny jail? Not room for a dozen in there."

Ruth shrugged. "We were busy, but I saw them dragging away two at a time. Every officer he had was making arrests and off they went. The Sergeant was very cranky."

"I noticed. He usually doesn't arrest church ladies and business owners." Warren swung his legs to test the table's strength. "Brits won't shoot you, but they got nothing against busting your head with a truncheon. Damn Cumberbatch nearly cracked me one when I came through the door."

Rosa, feeling ignored as they talked above her head, said, "My lip." Which came out, "My ip."

"We can't take you to the hospital, Rosa," Ruth explained. "It'll be nuts up there. All I really need is a couple Steri-Strips or even some glue."

"Glue?" Freddie asked, turning from his guard dog posture. "There's a little bookstore just across the street. They've always got glue." He jogged off as a much younger man might do.

"Dad's changed since we got here," Ruth observed. "He's in his element. Feels useful again. Even smiles once in awhile."

Warren was about to agree when Bobby White came around still carrying the large stick. "What is that anyway?" Warren asked.

Bobby grinned. "Stave off a cane wagon." He pointed. "Crashed over there. Damn fine piece of hardwood. See the hair on the end? From one of those Javerites. Came at me with a knife. Couple of his buddies carried him off awhile ago. Never did come to."

Warren shook his head. Guess maybe Bobby had found the Texan inside himself. "Well," Warren said, "maybe time to call it a night, huh? Take Judy Ann back to the hotel?"

Judy Ann said, "Bobby likes the hotel. Don't you Bobby?"

Warren held up his hand. "More than I need to know."

Bobby grinned like a fool and asked, "Are we diving tomorrow?"

Warren had been thinking of leaving the Whites behind but now he nodded. "Let's make it nine o'clock. Everybody needs a good night's sleep. I'll get Armando to stay home and take care of Rosa."

"We go together like always," Rosa said. "I don't need to talk."

"Shut up then," Ruth said, laughing.

Judy Ann kissed the top of Rosa's head and the Whites walked away in the direction of their hotel, with Bobby casually swinging a hardwood stave from a cane wagon. Clutching his other arm, Judy Ann rubbed her hip against him as they walked.

Freddie returned with a bottle of glue large enough to put the café's broken furniture back together. "Only size they had," he said.

Warren held the cut open slightly while Ruth applied the glue inside and out.

Rosa drew a ragged breath but did not cry out. Afterward Ruth said, "We still need some kind of tape."

Freddie handed her a roll of Scotch. "All they had."

She placed a small piece across the wound. "Should be okay until the glue hardens." She turned to Warren. "Might be a scar."

"She's not a very good kisser anyway," he said.

Rosa punched him in the stomach.

After he got her home and instructed Armando on her care and bedtime, he left to find Javert. It seemed as if things had died down in the city. He expected to find the Fat Man enjoying himself with friends at the Pink Sands or at one of the more upscale restaurants further uphill.

He stopped at the Pink Sands first, just in case, and found Javert alone in his customary veranda table.

Uninvited, Warren pulled out a chair and sat down. "Thought I'd find you drinking champagne with your worthless companions after their big success in fixing the election. Don't tell me they've deserted you already. Worthless hirelings, I suppose."

Javert did not seemed annoyed by the interruption. "Not at all," he said. "With one or two exceptions, all is well, my Capitan Friend. Please help yourself to some of the bread and escargot. It's more then I can eat."

"I doubt that. You seem to have a big appetite, especially for things that shouldn't be on your plate."

"Oh my!" Javert tapped his mouth with a white napkin. "Does it have to be like this? Can't we be civil?"

"Well, you greedy bastard," Warren began, "I guess you should be civil since you just stole the entire island. I imagine they're eating humble pie up in Government House tonight."

"Please. I'm imploring you," Javert said with feeling. "Hasn't there been enough violence and trouble? You can say I am the cause of some of it, but not all. Don't be so suspect of my every intention, when you can't know them. I am happy to see you, and wish only for us to have a calm conversation. Is that so much to ask?"

"Javert. You are not even a clever liar. You think that if you tell a lie over enough times, it becomes the truth." Warren shook his head.

"Because it is true." Javert laughed. "If you tell them what they want to hear, no matter how stupendous a falsehood it may be, they embrace it because it is what they want. How can you hold this against me?"

Warren held his temper but said plainly, "I hold everything against you, Javert. The threats your boy Bens has made against my family, and me. This mess. And years of other crap I'm not going to talk about right now."

"What do you want to talk about?"

"Tomorrow."

"Your errand to Guadeloupe."

"Yes."

"There will be no trouble about your money or the mortgage. I will keep my word."

Warren smiled. "Yes," he said. "You will keep your word. If you don't I'll have nothing to lose by killing you. Anyway, this has become sort of a lawless place, if you hadn't noticed. The Brits might not look too closely at whoever removes you from the scene."

The Fat Man chuckled. "Aw, my Capitan. Please. Don't threaten me when we both know you are most unlikely to kill anyone in cold blood." The smile faded. "You are, despite yourself, an honorable man. I may be many things you despise, but a poor judge of character is not one of them."

It was this kind of statement that always seemed to derail his discussions with Javert. "Okay," Warren said. "More to the point, what in the hell do you need guns for, and whatever else, now that you've won the election? The Brits will leave. You have an open field to make this place into a damn bed and breakfast."

Javert passed the bread plate. "Please," he said. "Before it gets cold. It's only bread. I haven't spit on it."

Warren smiled and took a piece. The Pink Sands baked it fresh before every meal. Best bread in town.

"That's better," Javert said. "I will answer your question. Bens and a few others I have. Maybe a dozen or two. Not an army. You can imagine I am not without enemies." He held up a hand. "I know, I know. This is my own doing. To me, a hazard of doing business at the higher levels of enterprise. Anyway, we are experiencing a substantial change now - you must agree - and with it will come uncertainty, maybe even more violence than what we have just witnessed. I will not, and I repeat this, not use these dangerous weapons to harm any innocent person on this island. You have my word. And don't say it isn't worth anything because you know better."

"You think you can control men like Bens? You're naïve, Javert. Childishly naïve."

Javert buttered his bread slowly, cleaning the knife carefully on the edge of the crust. "No details," he said, shaking his flabby head. "I will give you another promise. Bens is finished."

Warren saw the truth of this statement, but said, "Or so you hope. Sometimes, Monsieur Javert, you open the box and the genie comes out and eats you."

Javert shrugged.

"We're diving in the morning," Warren said as he stood to go. "Still need those tourist dollars until our business is concluded. When I bring them back in afterward I will refuel and make the run to Guadeloupe after dark. Depending on weather and seas, I'll be back in a two or three days. If anything should happen to my family when I'm gone, I will make you a promise and I hope you know better than to disregard it. The first round fired from one of those weapons is going to be into your head."

Javert raised an eyebrow as Warren walked away. It was something to consider, this threat, but it didn't curb his appetite. He called his waiter.

CHAPTER TWENTY TWO

Yellow coils of nylon line several hundred feet long were stacked alongside a dozen one-gallon empty milk cartons near the stern on *Esteban's* starboard side. Freddie had inspected them and hoped none of it would be visible from the surface. He didn't like yellow for a line color or big gallon jugs when quart size would've worked just as well, but Warren had told him it was all he could find in a hurry. Anyway, they had more important things to worry about.

On the flying bridge, Warren had the throttles to the stops and *Esteban* blew a cloud of diesel smoke twenty feet astern. The sky above white blue and cloudless. Early morning sunshine painted the hull of the old boat a lively pale yellow and she seemed to gallop across the sea like the thoroughbred she was built to be.

Freddie's head popped into view as he climbed the ladder from the main deck. "Permission to come on the bridge, Captain," he snapped.

Warren shook his head and smiled. "Granted."

"This old girl must be making fifteen, sixteen knots," Freddie said.

"More like twenty," Warren replied. "She was a swank sport fishing yacht before I converted her. Used to get twenty-two when the power plant was at its peak. Could still, I bet, if I had the cash."

"I can tell you one thing. I've ridden some boats in my day but few take the sea like this one does. She cuts deep and can take a beating."

Warren nodded. "Mostly glass these days. More maintenance free but float like corks. Give me an old wooden hull any day."

Freddie was pleased they agreed about something they both had in their blood. For most people the sea is something to look at, or walk along. For those who made a living on, or under it, the sea was life, as soil is life to a farmer. But even the best farmer can't enter the soil as a diver enters the sea to become part of it. A matchless experience too rare for words. At least, Freddie thought, he'd never discussed it with anyone, only felt it as he did now.

He pulled himself onto the bridge and dropped down on the starboard life jacket locker. White spray gushed from the bow cut and a pod of dolphins were taking turns riding the pressure ridge. "Where'd we pick them up?"

"They were waiting outside the harbor," Warren answered. "Not unusual. They know the boat and feel safe about it. Maybe someday it will be the same with the surviving rays on the flats. They knew *Esteban* too. Maybe they'll come back, knowing instinctively that we aren't to blame. Do you think?"

Freddie stared at the peeling deck awhile. "Maybe," he said finally. "But what if they do come back? How vulnerable will that make them?"

"Yeah," Warren said. "Maybe we don't need the answer."

Freddie nodded. "I talked to Rosa. Asked her what in hell was she doing onboard. Know what she told me?"

"Mind your own business?"

"No. Wanted to know if I was making lunch."

"Wasn't going to stay ashore no matter how swollen and sore her mouth was, so I figured better to have them all close today, after all that crap. Myron and I got aboard early. Fueled up and laid in enough stores to get us to Guadeloupe and home again after we mark out the wreck."

Freddie leaned forward. "He going along?"

"Yep."

"How about me?"

Helm in his left hand, Warren swiveled the captain's chair to face his old instructor. "Talked to Javert again last night. Still wants his guns and still promises me my boat back."

"You don't trust him?"

"Hell no." He watched Freddie's thin hair fluff and flip above his head in the wind. "I haven't given him any weapons yet. But in my possession they are more valuable to me than to anyone else. And he will present a satisfaction of mortgage to me from the bank before he's told where they are."

"Unless Bens twists it out of you beforehand."

Warren smiled. "I'll just have Bobby White kick his ass."

"You're not taking White to Guadeloupe?"

"Yep. He asked to go."

Freddie stood and hooked his right arm around the aluminum Bimini stanchions. "Damn. Nobody asked me."

"I'm not taking the women. Somebody has to stay with them. There is nobody else."

There was a long silence before Freddie said, "So, let me get this straight. You're all going on a dangerous night smuggling run to a far island where you will most likely be apprehended by the police, sunk by a gunboat, or murdered by a double-crossing Fat Man capable of anything. And even if you escape all that, a mad Englishman, who has sworn an oath to kill you and everybody you know, is very likely to make his move, since he has a fast boat at his disposal, and probably knows of this scheme. Oh! And is very likely to choose a dark, empty sea for the place to murder you and all your merry crew. But me, Freddie-the-Frogman, the only trained killer in the bunch, you leave behind to watch the women. Is that about right?"

"Pretty close"

"Bullshit!"

Warren adjusted their heading slightly, then told Freddie, "I'd rather have you along than any ten people I know. But what if Bens stays behind? Kills Armando, Rosa, Ruth, Judy Ann? Gets even, and still comes after us? He'd have time for that. He's mean enough. Smart enough too. So tell me, what should we do?"

Several minutes elapsed before Freddie said, "Kill him before we leave."

Warren held Freddie's eyes for a long while before he spoke. And then he said softly, "Is that what a SEAL thinks?"

"That's what this old frogman thinks."

"It's cold."

Esteban found her rhythm now as they took on the steady swells of deep water farther from land and Freddie released his hold on the stanchion and stood with his feet apart to ride the rolling deck. "Dangerous too," he said.

"So far," Warren said, "we've been lucky. Cumberbatch looked at White and Bens as two guys who hurt each other in a fight and let it end there. He won't do that again, even if he does have bigger problems at the moment." Responding to a change in the diesel's pitch, he reached over and adjusted the throttles slightly. "If Bens is killed, White will be the number one suspect, don't you think?"

"Maybe. Unless it looks like an accident or he simply disappears."

Again Warren was silent a long while. "So, I guess you've been thinking about this."

Freddie nodded. "I try and look at all the angles."

"Sea cleans any kind of mess, I suppose. Had to be hundreds of bodies in the water after the old *Imperial* went down." He smiled in an odd way.

Freddie nodded again, waiting for Warren to see all the angles too.

"I don't like it," he said finally. "I'm not even sure we can pull it off."

Freddie held his tongue.

Warren said, "Or have you got that all figured out too?"

"Most of it."

"Tell me."

"There are people," Freddie said, "can just walk up and kill you. Terrorists. Soldiers. Even in war, few soldiers or sailors just walk up to an enemy and kill him in cold blood. Not until they've been at it awhile. Someone shoots at you,

you shoot back. You're scared, of course. But that isn't what I did. Team drops into the sea and swims ashore. If it's supposed to be quiet, we carry knives and kill everybody we meet. There's no battle, just killing. Sudden, unexpected killing. That's why it works. That's why every branch of the service has special forces teams like us."

Warren wasn't looking at Freddie any longer but staring out ahead, watching the bow greet a wide swell of brilliant blue water and climb confidently to the top and slide down the other side. Predictable and reassuring headway through the sea.

"I threatened Bens," Warren said. "Threatened to kill him. But maybe it's just talk. Maybe I wanted to scare him."

"You were a good kid, Warren. Kinda goofy like all you diving kids were, and I can see you didn't change that much." He smiled. "Still kinda goofy. We're talking here about stuff most people never consider. Not seriously anyway. That's a good thing and I didn't expect any different from you. But this Bens is a killer. He didn't hesitate before. He won't now. He'll kill Rosa and your boy. If Ruth or anybody else is in his way, he'll kill them just as quick. You're making judgments based on a different set of rules than he has. You can't do that. It's like trying to persuade a terrorist that killing innocent civilians is different then killing armed soldiers. All people they hate are their enemies. They don't fight by our rules. The Japs didn't fight by our rules so we fought by theirs. And beat 'em. I'm an old man, but I can kill Bens close or far because I won't hesitate even a second. We won't talk. I won't ask him to surrender - or threaten him. I will kill him immediately when I see him. Understand the difference?"

"Just like that?"

"Just like that."

Warren remembered the picture in the scuba folder when he was a kid. Was that what he'd admired in Freddie's eyes then? Deadliness? "Freddie," he said. "They asked me, you know, in the Navy, would I be a SEAL. I was one of the few divers that came already trained in scuba. I wanted to do it. The course was tough and I talked to them about that. I knew it wouldn't be that tough for me. Swimming for miles, that kind of thing. It made me feel special that I knew for sure I'd pass their course." His voice faded. He sighed and shook his head. "I was eighteen. Strong. Nothing could kill me but when I got right down to the heart of it and knew I'd become a SEAL - the SEALs were at war then - and would swim out of the sea one dark night with a knife strapped to my leg and be expected to kill someone I'd never seen, and if I didn't, then I'd get somebody else killed. Well..." He shrugged and gave Freddie-the-Frogman a wistful smile. "No," Warren said. "No. And it was the best decision I ever made in my life."

Freddie moved closer and placed a gnarled hand on his shoulder. "Okay," he said. "Then don't change it now."

They were passing a place called Ocoa, near the halfway point. There was a reef there that stretched some distance from shore and Warren steered to port, giving it a wide berth. He felt the pleasant pressure of Freddie's hand on his shoulder and looked up at the frogman. "What's wrong with me?" he asked him.

"Nothing, boy," Freddie said. "Not one damn thing."

Less then an hour later, they picked up the marks for the *Imperial* wreck and the anchor was dropped. Everyone remained onboard except Freddie and Warren. Freddie had scrounged a pistol for Ruth, and Bobby White stood guard with the 303 British. Armando ran up the ladder to the flying bridge and scanned the cliffs with binoculars. They were a serious crew, determined in their vigilance.

Underwater, Warren and Freddie pounded three dozen two-foot-long heavy rebar into the coral outlining the wreck. They threaded the yellow rope through eye bolts for the safety line to keep divers from injury in the surge. Then they placed the plastic jugs on places of interest like the anchor flukes and pieces of wreckage that had separated from the main portion. Most of the deck cannon collapsed in rows as the ship burned. A few were catapulted a distance away, and lay alone on the sand. The jugs danced and strained at the nylon cord that secured them. Warren and Freddie shrugged at each other, fearing the jugs might very well break loose. In which event, they would need to be replaced with something more resilient.

It was nearly lunch time and Freddie, wiggling his index and middle fingers to indicate the antennae of a lobster, pointed to deeper water. They had just enough air remaining to catch a couple for lunch, and maybe some fresh conch to go with it.

On the surface, about a mile out to sea, a fishing boat passed on a northerly course. Armando watched it through the glasses. He had become suspicious of many things since the bad day, when the big man came out of the sea and frightened him. The days since were like times his mother told him he was going to the doctor for shots. A threat of pain waiting for him.

The boat kept her course and he could see float balls and nets hanging in the rigging. He tried to remember that the shots never hurt as bad as he imagined, but even as the fishing boat passed steadily on north he felt a chill.

"Mama!" he called down. "See the boat?"

Rosa came out from the salon until he could see her. "We are watching, Armando. It is passing."

"Yes."

She strained to see with the naked eye but it was too far. "Don't worry," she told him.

"Okay," he said, and decided if it was the bad man he couldn't swim this far. But like before, Captain Will and the frogman were underwater. He wished they were beside him.

Warren and Freddie surfaced just astern of *Esteban's* swim step, each carrying two lobsters and a conch. Hunting had proven plentiful for daytime, when most lobster are in a dark hole beyond arm's reach.

Warren held up the catch and saw Rosa grinning. Anything fresh from the sea cheered her.

"Ay!" she said, touching her swollen lip. "I told you," she scolded Warren. "I must not smile." But couldn't resist.

When they cooked aboard, the division of labor was structured. Rosa prepared, as Warren said, the S's - seafood, sandwiches and salads. He was in charge of grilling. A rusted Weber was mounted to the portside gunwale just aft of the salon. And Armando, surprisingly, did the complicated, mixed dish cooking. He made casseroles of lobster and various meats, especially chicken and beef. He enjoyed mixing ingredients it didn't seem logical to mix, but somehow came together nicely. A friend's mother taught him spicy Cuban dishes and he created many of his own, including the best chili Warren had ever tasted. The boy's specialty was shrimp stir-fry and he'd bargained with a Chinese cook for a broken wok and used a vice grip as the handle. *Esteban* was a poor boat, lacking maintenance, but the smells at meal times were mouthwatering.

Warren finished stowing his scuba gear beneath the long starboard side thwart and leaned back against the empty tank he'd bungeed into its PVC holder. Freddie had finished and gone to the flying bridge where Armando stood watch. Bobby White bent to position the rifle just inside the salon doorway and around the corner where it would be secure and quickly accessible. All three women were in the galley chatting as if they'd known each other all their lives. A clear, familiar and comforting sound. In the midst of instability and danger he was calm.

He remained motionless so as not to break the spell.

Awhile later, Ruth came out and sat beside him. "Hi," she said. "I've never prepared a lobster fresh from the sea. It's funny how you think there's nothing ahead sometimes and you learn a new thing and it opens so much more. I mean, when we came here I didn't know what I wanted. Didn't think I was looking for anything." She took his hand. "But now it's like I connected the back half of me to the front half. Young to old. Not that I'm that old!" She laughed, interlocking their fingers. "Understand?"

"What is this? Some kind of proposal?"

"No. Just something I needed to share."

"Women."

She released his hand and stood beside him. "I'm helping Rosa boil the lobster now and see how she cooks it fresh. You don't learn a thing like that in Minnesota."

Warren watched her walk away. She had her sea legs and kept a straight course on the slightly rolling deck. Much had changed in a short time.

He thought he too had left part of himself behind in Lake Darling. But which part? Youth, she said. The tragedy of Stephen's death and his determination to breathe underwater had always overshadowed the rest. Had remorse cheated him of happiness? Maybe that was what his mother tried to tell him in her letter. If so, then unlike Ruth he hadn't connected his front half to his back half. Never hauled the full load.

The noonday sun heated the boat as she rode at anchor. Bobby White stepped from the salon, struggled from his T-shirt and pitched it back playfully at Judy Ann, who caught it one-handed and shook her bottom. When he spotted Warren he came over and sat beside him.

Warren looked at the healing knife wound on Bobby's back. It had closed but left a raw ridge of scar tissue larger in size than the blade, and red skin spread from it almost like blood. "Still hurt?" Warren asked.

"Not bad."

"Who knew you were so tough?"

"Yeah. Who knew?"

"Still on for Guadeloupe tonight?"

Bobby turned to face him and hiked one leg up onto the thwart. "Having second thoughts about me?"

Warren shook his head. "No. Not at all, but Freddie isn't too pleased about being left behind with the women."

"Fact is, we could use him. All we got is Myron." He whispered this last remark though Myron was napping in the pilothouse thirty feet away. The old man had an annoying habit of hearing just what he liked, and nothing of what he didn't.

"I agree. Did Freddie mention his solution?"

"No."

"Kill Bens before we leave."

"Shit, man!" Bobby said, wide-eyed. "That's heavy. Just drop him? I mean, there's no love lost, you know. He nearly killed me, but man. I don't know."

Warren shrugged. "He's sworn to kill us all and we can't just sit and wait either. I don't know. If it has to be done, then it's this afternoon when we get back. I was thinking maybe we need to talk about it. All of us."

"The women too?"

"It involves them."

"Man, oh man. Judy Ann's gonna freak."

Warren shrugged.

Lunch was served, but when everything was cleared away Warren called them all back to the table. He looked pointedly at Freddie and said, "We have something all of us need to understand and face together. You agree, Freddie?"

The old frogman's face darkened and it was obvious he wanted no part of sharing. That wasn't the way it was done. These were things that happened in secret and remained secret. Nobody talked about it beforehand, and afterward, it was history. Not worth remembering.

"This is a mistake," Freddie told Warren. "But I'm not in charge here."

"I was thinking all or nothing," Warren answered. "We all agree or it's a no go."

Ruth straightened in her chair. "Enough mystery," she said. "Let's hear it. Dad?"

"Warren has the ball," Freddie said, leaning back in his chair.

Warren noticed Armando standing just outside the salon door trying to look invisible. "Come here," Warren called. "Sit down. You're as much a part of this as anybody."

"Thank you," the boy said formally, then sat on the edge of his mother's chair. She embraced him.

"I made a deal with Javert to smuggle weapons onto the island for clear title to my boat," Warren said simply. "We plan to do that tonight. The weapons will be put ashore someplace where Javert can't find them until I've got the paperwork for *Esteban* and everything is legal. After that we'll see what happens." He raised an eyebrow at Freddie, and the frogman frowned in return.

"But before we go, Freddie thinks we should deal with Bens."

"Deal with him?" Ruth said, glaring at her father.

"Decisively."

"Meaning dead, Dad?"

"How else?"

"Have you lost your mind? This is not war. You can't just go around 'dealing' with the people you don't like!"

"Let me tell you something, girl. By the time you were born I'd killed more then twenty men and people bought me rounds of drinks and the U.S. Navy hung metals on my chest. Now those people I killed, I never knew 'em. Never saw 'em before. They were doing their job just like me. Now this Bens is a killer. If he gets near to any of us he will be decisive. Depend on it." He pointed at Bobby. "Look at Bobby's back. Bens came from behind and stabbed a man just because he was in the way. He's a killer, and he'll kill again as soon as he heals up. Now he's got an even greater motive. Hate. He hates Bobby for surviving." Now he looked at Armando. "Even a child because he had the courage to stop him from killing you and Rosa and Judy Ann. Don't you get it? In the military we'd call it a preemptive strike. But for us it's self-preservation plain and simple."

Ruth shook her head and sighed, too angry to speak.

Bobby looked at her, then Rosa. "Just a few feet from here. On this boat. Both of you helped Judy Ann care for me. Stop the bleeding. You got beat up for it. We'd all be dead now if Bens had his way. All of us, Ruth. Think. What happens if we don't act? The government is in a mess. The cops here don't even carry guns. Who will protect you? Armando? I don't like it any better then you, but Freddie is right. There is no other way."

Rosa had said nothing all this time and sitting next to Ruth her face had shown no emotion as the others spoke. Now she turned to Bobby who sat on her other side and reached for his hand. "Once before I held your hand," she said softly.

"I remember," he said. "In the hotel room."

"Was it the first time?"

"First time?"

"The first time you held a black woman's hand?"

Bobby blushed. "Yes."

"Was it unpleasant for you?" she asked.

"No. No. Of course not. I liked it." He glanced at Judy Ann.

"I liked it too," she said. "We Pentecostals seem odd to many people. We are a religion of miracles not violence. We expect God to come to our aid when times are bad. We expect miracles and pray for them. You and Freddie, and I'm sure Warren too, see no way out with Bens but killing. And maybe none of you are religious. Warren isn't. Faith then is no option for you. But for me, I will take this to a higher power. No killing."

She paused and placed Bobby's hand between both of hers, smiling, stroking as she might a frightened child. "If you can hold hands with a negro woman Bobby, can you trust her? Believe her? Is there nothing beside killing? Can you be so sure, all of you?"

Everyone but Freddie was staring down at the table. "I'm not sure what you want us to do, pray?"

"It wouldn't hurt," she said. "But since you don't believe it, grant me one favor. You will wait one night and one day before you do anything. All of you stay home tonight and if evil comes, defend yourselves. But wait."

"We're scheduled to pick up the weapons in Guadeloupe tonight," Warren reminded her.

"They can wait too," she said. "Are you in such a hurry to hand out these guns?"

Warren shook his head. "We can wait. But we'll end up doing it anyway because I want this boat back and I don't give a damn if I have to go alone to get the price. I'm finished with Javert. Period."

"You are finished, I know," Rosa said. "How many times have I asked you? Finish. But it was not always so. You were his friend, no?" Rosa knew that bringing this up in such a public way would make Warren furious. He often told her such things after they made love.

"Well, that's just great," he said. "Thanks for sharing that with everybody, Rosa. Guess there's nothing in that Bible of yours about ratting out your spouse!"

"Spouse," she said. "Is that like husband? When you marry me then you can be safe from the ratting out."

"Okay," Freddie interrupted. "Let's not have a domestic. Calm down."

"Just a minute," Ruth said. "*Were* you friends with Javert?"

Warren glared at Rosa. No secrets with women around, he thought. "We weren't really friends," he began. "Things were different then. Javert was always greedy and he employed some unsavory guys like Slither, who lots of people here find creepy. But nobody like Bens."

Warren looked from one face to the next. "When I came to this island years ago, Javert was the first person I met. He introduced himself and I recognized the name immediately. Hugo and *Les Misérables* and my family. Was it a coincidence? The day the *Imperial* was sunk" - he glanced out the salon door toward the sea where it lay below them - "February 6, 1806, another Javert, a French sailor, murdered a guy named Reggie Wilson. Or so the story goes, at least in my family. I questioned Javert and we pieced together our family histories and it seemed possible. Then we laughed about it, and strange as it seems now, we became friends of a sort. It was a link and neither of us was interested in retribution for something that may or may not have happened nearly two hundred years ago. So we sometimes joked about it and it became known. One year during Carnival the organizers persuaded us to fight a mock sword duel in French and English costumes."

Myron interrupted. "'Course I knew Warren, Captain Will, pretty well already then. I warned him about that jackass Javert. I never trust a fat man."

"Shut up, Myron," Freddie said.

Judy Ann giggled. "Myron. You're a geek."

"Anyway," Warren continued, "time passed and I came to know Javert better. By then I'd borrowed money from him, mortgaged the boat to the sky. We'd done some deals. There's a fisherman here named Francisco. He was diving with his son Felix for lobster one day and the boy got the bends. Decompression sickness. I took him to the recompression chamber in Guadeloupe and found out the deep diving they were doing was prompted by Javert. Another of his enterprises, selling large lobster from deep, unsafe depths, to a large seafood chain in the States. The boy nearly died. I was pissed and that was the end of our friendship, if we ever had one." Here Warren paused and seemed to lose the will to continue.

"Then what?" Ruth asked.

"I don't know," Warren said finally. "It stuck in my head, that old story. The *Imperial*. Was it really here? Maybe I got obsessed, I don't know, but I started searching and checking old charts and reading up on it again. Wrote the Admiralty in London. Got copies of an account of the battle from the French Archives in Paris. Years of digging around. When I was a kid and first read about it I was all fired up, you know, like kids are." He glanced at Ruth and she smiled sadly. She remembered. "Anyway, I grew up." He shifted his deep brown eyes to Bobby White. "You almost died because of this."

Bobby had been listening with his mouth partially open, fascinated. "Man, that's the best sea story I ever heard." He grinned. "And the sucker's true. Know what? I'm part of it now, right?"

"I'm more a part of it then you are," Myron said.

"Myron," Judy Ann scolded, "you really are a geek."

"Yeah," Freddie said. "Shut up."

"If I'm part of it," Bobby continued, "then I wanna go for broke. What's the best we can do?"

"Finish what we started, I guess," Warren answered. "Make this bit of history an underwater park. Save it from treasure hunters, and Javert, of course. The Netherland Antilles and other islands have wreck sites, but nothing like this. Often they find an old vessel, buy it and sink it for divers to explore. But *Imperial* is the real thing. There's nothing else like it. Nearest I can think of is Truk Lagoon in the South Pacific, but that's World War II. Ships and planes. We've got something here nearly a hundred fifty years older then that. And sail. I'm not sure there's anything left in the world like this."

"Rarer then gold," Bobby said.

"Men kill for gold," Ruth reminded them.

"Yeah," Myron told her. "Just to hang it from some broad's ear."

Freddie opened his mouth to tell Myron to shut up again but Ruth placed a finger on her lips to shush him. "You're right, Myron. Men have no exclusivity on greed. The difference here is that the government likely to approve this plan is on the way out. We are about to import a boatload of deadly weapons for the people least likely to side with us. Correct?"

"I get it," Warren said. "Does everybody want to wait?"

No one looked at him and silence prevailed. Only Rosa had her head up as her eyes moved around the table. In her heart she was joyful and sad at the same time. She had hurt Warren, and though they had fought as any couple does, this seemed to her a betrayal and it would be a long time before he trusted her again.

Warren nodded his acceptance. "Fine. We give Bens a day or two. We'll wait for Rosa's 'higher power' to deliver us from evil." He stood. "Meeting adjourned. Let's go diving. There's plenty of afternoon left."

He walked outside and they could hear him clanging a fresh tank into the rack.

CHAPTER TWENTY THREE

Late that night an aging and weather-beaten freighter with Panama registry stopped her engines about a mile offshore from an isolated beach on the eastern side of Charming Island. Several minutes later a rubber boat splashed into the water near the ship's stern and a six-man team of Cuban commandos descended on knotted ropes. Their leader pulled the starter on the muffled outboard motor and the small craft moved toward shore. The freighter got underway again, heading in the opposite direction away from the island.

The beach was not protected by a reef, bay or lagoon as were many other of the island's beaches. For this reason few people swam here and steady winds discouraged fishermen from building homes where their boats were likely to be damaged in storms or difficult to launch, even in fair weather. When the commandos reached shore and struggled through the surf there was no one to greet them or spy on them. They were alone. Within minutes they had deflated their boat and hidden it, along with the motor, in a dense bamboo thicket. Camouflaged with palm fronds and sand, it was invisible even close up.

Five of the six men spread out along the tree line to scout the area and make certain their landing had been unobserved. Several minutes passed before they regrouped around their commander. He whispered to them in Spanish, "Nada?" Nothing.

Nada, the answers came back.

Their commander was Captain Jorge Pimentel, a stocky man who had led similar raids in Africa and Central America. His devotion to his men and hatred of America and Britain made him a popular commander. Every member of his team preferred to shed someone else's blood, but would gladly shed their own to please Capt. George. This mission had few military risks. There were no combat-ready troops anywhere on Charming Island and the small police force was unarmed. Their main concern was secrecy, and they had just achieved that first objective, arriving unseen and unheard. The landing boded well for the success of the remainder of their mission.

The commandos removed their Viper Night Vision Goggles from their backpacks, stowed their caps and adjusted the lens correctly in front of both eyes. They would travel only by night but it was a long hike from the beach, across the island to Edward Town. In between were thousands of people, mountains, two rivers and several small towns. Their satellite maps were precise but things always look different on the ground and in the dark. Capt. George wanted them moving but they saw his white teeth flash a smile before he signaled for them to move out. This was, after all, everybody's idea of a great time.

Single file, they followed Capt. George at a trot. He led them inland, away from the beach. The smell of salt water faded, replaced by scents of rotting vegetation and stagnant water. Branches and leaves struck their faces. The dense foliage was wet and before they'd gone their first mile all six men were soaked to the skin and sweating.

Nearly an hour went by before the Captain held up his hand for a halt. The men breathed heavily. Each carried an AK-47 and five hundred rounds, two grenades, knife, small radio, flashlight, maps, food, extra socks, field binoculars, spare batteries and personal items. Capt. George only had one rule about over-packing - you pack it, you carry it. Nothing would be discarded, or even buried. No one must ever know they were taking hostile action on the sovereign soil of the United Kingdom. And no one wanted to think of a company of Royal Marines dropping from the sky.

Their intelligence said that no British troops were on the island. However, the Royal Navy operated in the Caribbean, conducting joint exercises with the U.S. Navy, which might include Royal Marines and Navy SEALs. They were unlikely to survive an encounter with either, and were wise enough to know it. Stealth was their only hope. And a little help from their friends.

At just after 0:500 they halted for a second time. Capt. George signaled them to rest and wait while he went on ahead. Fewer than one hundred meters farther along the Captain spotted a blinking amber light. Two short blinks, a pause and a longer blink. He knelt on the donkey trail they had followed and waited until the signal was repeated twice more to be sure it wasn't a coincidence.

Then Capt. George took a deep breath and moved ahead in a crouch, eying the dense jungle and the trail ahead for an ambush. As he moved silently forward, the amber lights repeated yet again. Capt. George stopped.

"Bens?" he called in a hoarse voice.

"Come ahead," Bens replied. "The truck is nearby. Been a long time, Jorge."

Capt. George had flipped his Vipers up and studied Bens before he spoke. "Mira. You look pretty good. Thought you had your balls cut off?"

Bens laughed and hugged his old friend. "Don't believe everything you hear, Amigo. I actually had them caught in a rifle sight. A woman sewed them up."

"Of course she did. Ha! You haven't changed," the Captain said. "My men are just behind us on the trail. Follow me." They moved off single file. Jorge thought maybe he'd seen Bens looking better but decided to take his word for the health issues, though Bens was a key part of what was to come and when he had contacted Cuba by radio and reported his injuries, there was talk about abandoning the mission. Now it would fall to the Captain to decide. They had much to do before they were in position and he had time to assess Bens and reassure himself he was able to carry out his part of the plan. If not, they could fade back into the hills until they were picked up. There was enough room in the rubber boat to take Bens away too, if he wished to leave with them.

They regrouped with the other five commandos and Jorge introduced them. One of the older men was familiar to Bens but he'd never seen the rest of the younger troopers before. They seemed fit and eager. He hoped they were also smart. Wesley Bens had thought this an easy assignment too, not so long ago. It had proved anything but. Sometimes when things begin to fall apart, they continue that way. He wanted to turn it around.

In his soft tenor voice he related what was to come. "I've a small truck hidden up near the road and tomorrow night I will transport you across the larger of this central range of hills. Some are steep. We have no choice but to move slowly. There are no regular police patrols or anything like that." He grinned at them. "The coppers here don't even have vehicles. But it's a small island. Large families who talk to each other often. They would soon pass the word if six armed men were seen. Once I transport you over the hills, you lie up another day and begin down the next. Questions?"

"Si." It was Lopez, the soldier Bens knew from his years in Cuba. "If these people are so weak, why can't we just drive into Edward Town and be done with it?"

"Not weak. Unarmed. There's a difference." Bens narrowed his eyes to slits. "Listen to me. In the time I have been here a little man has attacked me with a little knife. A dive boat captain has threatened me. Tourists have tried to shoot me underwater, and succeeded in mutilating me. I've had a speargun leveled at me by a boy no more than nine or ten years old. Even a fish has tried to kill me by driving a poisonous barb through my foot." He opened his eyes and stared at Lopez. "Remember Africa? Six weeks of struggle against man, animal, jungle. There I missed a couple meals. Here I came near to death. So, be careful. Don't underestimate the unarmed."

"Thank you for the warning, Wesley," Capt. George said. "Any special place you want us to bed down for the day? It's getting light."

"There is a clearing off to the west about two hundred meters back along the trail," Bens said. "It gets used as an overnight camp sometimes when coffee beans are taken to market but no one should be there now. Just take off camo, packs, anything military. Hide them for the day, along with your weapons. If anyone comes say you are Boy Scouts, camping."

"Very amusing," Jorge said. "Do we look like Boy Scouts?"

Bens grinned. "You are almost young enough, except for you, Jorge."

"We are not Boy Scouts or tourists. We look like what we are."

"Many Argentinean hikers come here." He shrugged. "I don't understand it, but maybe you could pass for a small group if someone comes along. Most likely just farmers and local merchants. Remain calm. It will be fine."

"Where will you be?" the Captain asked.

"Napping in the bed of the truck with one ear open." He turned away, then stopped and addressed them again. "I know you were briefed in Cuba, but after lunch I will come back and give you the details. Much has changed here since those briefings were given."

Captain George nodded. "Excellent. The most dangerous things are those that are not expected. None of us like surprises."

"Fine," Bens said, and walked away into the pre-dawn gloom.

He returned at just after two o'clock that afternoon and found them waiting in the clearing. They didn't look anything like Boy Scouts.

"You are armed and in military camo." He scowled at Captain George. "Jorge, what are you thinking?"

"We decided to sleep among the trees and brush. For that we use camo. This is foreign soil. We feel more comfortable with a military posture, regular sentries and proper procedures. Tonight we can change clothes if you insist, but we are more comfortable being what we are."

Bens had spent a difficult night in the truck. He was taking a strong antibiotic for the stingray wound, but the infection around the injury was slow to heal. While his scrotum seemed to feel steadily better, the damn fish had left enough poison inside his body that some days he felt as if he'd taken some mind-bending drug that grew inside him, like the onset of a deadly illness. He didn't have the strength or mental agility to argue with Jorge.

"I will not insist," Bens said. "The risk is low in the dark, but remember, Jorge, it's your risk, and if the mission fails that responsibility is yours also. The next few days will be critical. Maybe deadly."

The Captain's greatest strength was his cool head. Unlike some of the other commando officers, who loved to fight more than to think and plan, Jorge was all the more deadly for his calm demeanor and deliberate planning and execution of his missions. So he nodded at Bens and said simply, "Understood."

"Marvelous," Bens acknowledged. "Shall we move back away from the clearing into the shade near that large banyan tree?"

They obeyed without comment.

When they were away from the clearing Bens felt less exposed. But he was tired and sat down on a giant exposed tree root. "Gather close so we can speak softly," he told them.

Jorge moved in to sit beside Bens and the rest knelt or sat on the scattered leaves surrounding the massive trunk. "Snakes?" Jorge asked.

"Yes," Bens said. "But none poisonous."

"Just the fish," Jorge chuckled.

"Rays," Bens corrected. "Now, listen carefully. Jorge, you will remain in command of your force but will report to me. Clear?" Bens said this so all would hear and know who was overall commander. He stared openly at Capt. George.

"Of course," Jorge said.

"Your force is small for a reason," Bens went on. "This little country just voted to become independent from Great Britain and is in a period of transition and volatility. We are going to exploit that. Quietly. You are the muscle. No heavy-handed tactics. What we do will be clandestine, not overt or careless in any way." He looked them each in the eye before he went on. "This is very important. The world cannot notice us. If they do, we will be dead as soon as the Royal Marines or U.S. Navy SEALs hit the ground. No place to run on a small island. And, of course, our mission will fail. Cuba will be embarrassed, and I doubt Fidel will be happy either."

They glanced at one another and said nothing.

Bens continued. "There is a man here - Jacques Javert - in position to assume power when the British depart. He has been part of the independence movement but is not aligned with the Americans or anyone else. He wants power for his own selfish reasons and we are going to give it to him. You are his enforcers. Not that he knows this, but that too will become apparent very soon. The election was a sham and enough people here are suspicious of Javert anyway, so the whole thing may soon unravel. Discreetly, we will then prop him up and install him as president or emperor or whatever he wishes to be. By discreetly, I mean we will seek out any leaders who oppose Javert and kill them quietly. If it seems they died accidentally, all the better. We keep things in a state of flux for awhile, then in a year or so make the island a communist state aligned with Cuba. We ask for economic and military assistance. And it will be too late for the Americans or British to act."

"Wasn't too late for Reagan in Grenada," Jorge said. "I witnessed my comrades stacked like cord wood along the fence lines into St. Georges. American Marines, Rangers, Delta Force, Navy SEALs, even the 82nd

Airborne killed them quickly. And that is a small island just like this."

"There will be a new president in the United States in a few months. We won't declare ourselves until then, and if a liberal is elected we have nothing to fear. They are fellow socialists."

Jorge chuckled at this. "Maybe," he said. "Today in Grenada they celebrate October 25, 1983, the date of the invasion by U.S. Forces, as Thanksgiving Day. Don't assume anything, my friend. It was the liberal John Kennedy who began the Vietnam mess. The liberal *socialist* Lyndon Johnson who expanded it until he finally ran away from it. I never trust North Americans to do anything we wish them to do. Who cares what political party they use to gain power? They are unpredictable. If any are socialists, they are not fellow socialists with us or anyone else. No. I don't accept this."

Bens' scrotum was aching and he pushed himself up to stand beside Jorge. "Fine. Don't trust them. My point is that if they act slowly, hesitantly, then we can get Charming Island firmly into our hands in a humane way that doesn't invite invasion or retaliation. Maybe we can do here what we failed to do in Grenada. The British gave independence to Grenada just as they will here, and were quite irate with the Americans for their invasion."

"I know this," Jorge said. "But do the Americans?"

"Rest. Eat something. After dark we move. Politics is not our problem." Bens adjusted his khaki shorts to give himself a bit more room. "We have Javert. He's not communist and we will have him declare himself a friend of the United States. They have never heard of him and he won't offend them. I will be back before it is full dark."

Jorge and his troops watched Bens pick his way out of the bush and into the clearing. No one spoke.

Less then a half mile from where Bens had hidden his truck, Bonnie Loca was in the yard feeding her chickens. Since Loca wasn't just her name, but her condition, she lived alone and talked to herself at great length, sometimes loudly, but mostly in a soft and reasonable voice. She dressed well whenever she went into town and if you struck up a conversation with her in a store she might be wearing the latest fashion - a ribbon or colorful scarf in her long auburn hair, and crisply ironed blouse of good material over a new skirt. On her feet, heeled sandals. Her toes red and carefully trimmed. But then you might notice a splash of gravy over one breast and while you spoke she might be looking at you, or the ceiling. While her speech was proper, clear and pleasant to hear, it may or may not be related to the subject at hand.

Bonnie Loca had been abducted by aliens from another solar system and could relate calmly the experiences of having copulated with them and been delivered of their offspring. Childbearing was the primary reason for them taking her away in the first place, she'd told her neighbors. Something none of her three husbands had remained with her long enough to accomplish. All three saw her beauty - and she was beautiful - and married her without thinking. In the surrounding area, most people liked Bonnie and thought her beauty came from her lineage, that of a British sailor and his French wife. One of the older neighbors thought her real name was Packer, but no one was certain, and it didn't seem to matter since she was well-known and as much a part of the community as anyone else.

But that afternoon her mind became even less focused then usual. For one thing, she was feeding the chickens at the wrong time of day. They ate in the evening.

"Chick, chick, chick!" she called, scattering seed by hand from a plastic bucket. The chickens greeted the mistake with enthusiasm and ran in circles pecking the ground.

Afterward, she wandered along the path from her humble clapboard home to the road not far from where Wesley Bens was taking a somewhat painful leak. She spotted him there and decided he was one of them that had taken her before - they often feigned human form - and the time had come for her to copulate and deliver another green, six-legged child. "They really are green, you know," she told her neighbors. But when she greeted Bens in the manner of the far-away planet - Bazanka! meaning friend in their language - he thought she said bazooka and spun around and exposed himself.

Focused on the business at hand and in the military mindset of his mission, bazooka was an easy mistake. They had no such weapons, of course, or any need for them. This was momentarily lost on Bens and he screamed, "What in hell are you doing here?"

He realized then where she was looking and zipped his pants. She was a fine looking woman, barefoot and otherwise dressed properly in matching pink blouse and skirt. After he covered himself she smiled pleasantly and said, "I'm sorry to have frightened you. I just finished feeding my chickens."

Bens looked left to right and saw no chickens. "Sorry," he said. "Just stopped here to relieve myself."

"Are we leaving now?" she asked.

"We?"

"You know," she grinned, fluffing her skirt. "To make babies."

Now Bens was a man of the world and she wasn't the first woman to proposition him, but he couldn't remember one coming on to him in exactly this manner, asking him to make babies. "Well, you're a handsome bird, I'll give you that, but the timing isn't good. I've some medical difficulties and I just got here."

"From Ovindim?" she inquired. "You are an Ovinden? Was it a hazardous flight? I had one once, too. My ears nearly burst. Probably from the pressure."

Still confused, Bens asked, "Do you live near here?"

"Of course," she said, smiling shyly. "You know that."

"I've never seen you before."

She shrugged. "I guess you don't look like the others, but they are different every time. How am I supposed to know? Anyway, it's never painful or anything, except that time with my ears, and I do enjoy it. You aren't teasing me? I believe the Ovinden sense of humor is different from ours."

Bens took several steps toward Bonnie Loca, but she only smiled and waited for him to speak. He said, "What's this Ovenden?"

"Ov*i*nden," she corrected. "With *i's*. Ovindens are the creatures who live on Ovindim."

"Fine. What is it?"

"Are you testing me?"

He approached her closely now and glared down at her as if she were something someone had heaved up. "Yes," he said. "I'm testing you."

Bonnie Loca smiled. "Well then, Ovindim is the third planet in revolution around the small sun of the Arauma System seventy-five thousand light years from here."

"Well, that explains it then."

Bonnie's grin widened. "I passed the test?"

"Yes," he said. "Can you remain here a moment while I go and check something?"

"I will," she promised.

Bens walked several yards into the brush toward his truck and stopped there to consider the problem. She had seen him and talked to him and he felt she was reasonable enough to be a good witness, and if she saw the commando team she would remember them as well. On the other hand, she might be likely to explain them away as aliens, which probably meant no one would believe a story of commandos anyway. But if they did, everything might be in jeopardy. He could simply snap her neck and bury her in the bush and most likely people would think she wandered off or was back on Ovindim making babies. People round the area had no doubt heard it all a hundred times. But if he killed her, and the body was discovered, someone would certainly get curious. It occurred to Bens that Charming Island was a very odd place indeed, and once again he faced a dilemma seldom anticipated in operational planning sessions. Who supposed you might meet an attractive woman who was willing to accompany you to an alien world, where she had traveled extensively to copulate with the inhabitants? It just never came up, like fish attacks or deadly underwater tourists. No amount of training can prepare you for this, he thought.

Bens walked back to face Bonnie, who stood patiently in the shade. "Well," he said. "I didn't get your name."

"Bonnie."

"Listen here, Bonnie," said Bens in a soothing voice. "Can we maybe take a rain check? I'm not at my best just now and what I really need is to go home and rest awhile. I'm not inconveniencing you, am I?"

"Oh no," she said. "But sir, I do so enjoy my trips to Ovindim, and I'm still young enough to bear more children."

"Of course you are," he assured her. "And very beautiful, too. Can I come back for you later?"

"When?" she asked.

"Shall we say two Ovindim years?"

"Oh, wonderful! So I will see you Friday."

Bens thought he might be cursed. "Did I say two? Sorry. I meant two hundred Ovindim years."

"Well," she sighed. "It's not so long, I guess."

"Go home and wait now," he said.

"I will," Bonnie assured him, and smiled slyly again. "Will you be coming yourself?"

"Oh yes. You can count on that. Wouldn't miss it for the world. Any world," he said and strolled off into the thick jungle of a very strange island and disappeared.

Later, after dark, Bens led the commando unit to the truck where they loaded their equipment and began the night journey through the mountains. He kept quiet about Bonnie and his decision to spare her life. Surely, Capt. George would have silenced her, but the more Bens considered the notion, the more he feared the risk of what seemed an obvious military decision. What could she report to anyone now? That she had once again conversed with an alien and he was returning for her? Even if anyone believed that, he would be gone and there was no evidence he had ever been there in the first place. She might be a problem dead, but alive she had no complaint, and no story to tell much different than what she had no doubt been saying for years. Anyway, Bens thought he just might go back one day when he was healed up and give her a ride to Ovindim.

Capt. George sat in the cab with Bens and the other five commandos crowded in the bed with their gear. There was no moon but the stars were bright whenever the narrow road looped out from the trees to expose itself as it switched to escape the valley and gain height on the mountainside. Bens drove carefully, shifting down when the grade steepened. At times their progress was at speeds less then a jog. The first hour no one spoke.

"Now I see why it's going to take so long to get there," the Captain said. "Roads are even worse than at home."

"This is nothing," Bens answered. "If we were on this road during the day it would be crowded with old diesel trucks, buses and donkey carts. Meet someone on the way and you spend half an hour with two wheels hanging over the drop while you attempt to get past them. This isn't the Malecón in Habana."

"How far will we get tonight?"

"Most of the way through the mountains. I have selected a secure spot where we can spend the day tomorrow." He glanced at his companion. "No rush, Jorge. For once there is no deadline. No rendezvous. We move at our own pace and everything depends on us. We will manage most of what happens from now on, with maybe one exception."

Jorge stared at his old friend without enthusiasm and complained, "Exception? I'm hearing this now?"

"Relax. It's unlikely."

"Can I be the judge of that?"

Bens chuckled. "Well, you haven't changed. Fine then. It's Javert. He's imagining himself a kind of king or something. I don't know. But he's a resourceful fat thing and located a cache of arms in Guadeloupe that he has blackmailed a scuba man to fetch for him. I say it's an unlikely problem since he has no army to arm. Besides, I'm not so sure the scuba man will do exactly as Javert imagines. The payoff, I was told, is the man's dive charter boat. If he has any brains he won't give the weapons up until he has legal possession. I wouldn't. Javert seems to trust this Captain Will, and they have some sort of history, I'm sure, but it doesn't appear to me this will affect any of our plans."

"Unless this Javert *does* have someone to arm with automatic weapons, they *can* shoot, and we are outnumbered twenty to one."

Bens shifted once again to a lower gear and the engine labored against the grade. "When did you become such an optimist, Jorge?"

Capt. George stretched his legs in the cramped space. "Think, Wesley. Think of all those times we escaped death, not because we were brave or well-equipped, not even because we fought in a righteous cause, but because of luck. Just luck."

This stirred Bens' memory and unsettled him. Lately, his luck had been nothing but bad. Those dive people had changed his luck, but soon that would be over. Thoughts of killing them were never far from his mind and he toyed with the idea in the manner a shark will sometimes nibble a victim and even push him before ripping the flesh, separating bone and ligament, feasting on blood-soaked tissue. These thoughts fed his hatred, and the deeper he drew them in, the more satisfying they were to him. Anticipation. Sweet delay, drawing forth the juice and flavor until it remained long afterward so he could drink of it again and again.

"I have been encouraging the scuba man with a poke or two," Bens continued. "That way I will know who is in possession of the weapons. The scuba man is no fool. I doubt he will turn them over to Javert until all their business is settled. I plan to keep close watch on him, his people and his boat. It's a small island."

Jorge shrugged. "It's just the luck thing. Worries me."

Bens slapped his friend's shoulder. "We are together. Our luck will improve."

CHAPTER TWENTY FOUR

"Bens is gone." The words came out of Freddie's mouth almost in a whisper.

"Gone where?" Warren asked.

Esteban was moored to the town dock, loading more supplies for the voyage to Guadeloupe. Their plans were made. Freddie had just returned with extra line, a gun cleaning kit for the rifle and spare flashlights.

"Did you hear me? Gone where?"

Freddie stepped back aboard. "Nobody knows."

"Well, how do you know?"

"Cornered that little Slither person. What a creep. But he spilled his guts in a hurry. Said Bens had disappeared. Asked *me* where he was. Javert is having a fit, he said."

Warren glared at his old scuba instructor. "You *don't* know where he is, right?"

"Hey! I keep my word. Didn't touch him."

"Okay," Warren said. "Get aboard. We'll store the rest of that stuff below, then figure this out before Myron gets back and we have to listen to all his crap."

Ten minutes later they were drinking coffee in the Captain's Cabin.

"You don't think it's a trick, do you?" Freddie asked, leaning back and throwing one leg over the arm of his chair.

Warren shrugged. "Who knows? Doesn't smell like it. Todd isn't a very good liar anyway. Overacts."

"Yeah," Freddie nodded. "Can't say why, but I believed him."

Warren sipped his leftover tepid coffee. "If we leave in an hour or so we'll be in Guadeloupe by dark. Load and be gone. Make a night passage back here, off-load at a remote spot I know, then anchor out as usual here by dawn. Four guys. Plenty helmsmen and watch-standers. Women should be safe until morning if Bens has really gone off somewhere."

"Damn!" Freddie said. "If only I was sure."

"There's risk even if someone guards them. Bens is a nasty piece of work. But this just might take him by surprise. He's arrogant. We're nothing to him, and that's his weakness. So we move fast and get back before he knows we're gone."

Freddie grinned. "You're becoming quite the little frogman. Maybe you could've made it in the UDT."

"I just want this to be over." He stood and tossed the remainder of his tepid coffee out the open porthole. "And I'll tell you something," he said, turning. "No matter what happens, nothing here will ever be the same again."

"Is that bad?"

"Don't know yet."

"Sometimes," Freddie said, "change is a good thing." He grinned. "Man, when things change around here they happen fast, but I'm glad to be going along, and that's a fact."

"Yeah. That's what worries me."

"Let's play it safe then with thc women and kids, huh? Move them to a hotel away from town so if Bens does come back he can't find 'em so easy."

Warren nodded his agreement. "I'll give Sergeant Cumberbatch a heads up too. He's not exactly a friend but we respect each other and he's an honest man."

Freddie rolled his eyes.

"Just don't piss him off," Warren laughed. "Don't beat up any more immigration agents and you'll get along with the good Sergeant."

"Thanks for the advice," Freddie said, standing. "I'll round up White and his missus, then fetch Ruth. What about Rosa and Armando? Are they at home?"

"They'll be here in a few minutes. She's bringing some canned goods I forgot about. Let's take them to the Satisfaction Bay Club instead of a regular hotel. It's mostly a golf club with rooms and good security. The Queen of England stayed there once. Security isn't armed, but they got some big boys working. If Bens clashes with them he'll have his work cut out for him, though I doubt he'd look there. If he does, well, he stands out in a crowd. Mention that when you check them in. Be handy if we can talk those women into staying in their rooms instead of lounging by the pool or shopping. They can eat room service."

"Right," Freddie said. "You tell 'em."

The boat rocked slightly and they heard shuffling footsteps on deck above their heads. Warren slid open a desk drawer and withdrew a small silver automatic. He stood up and slipped it into the waistband at the small of his back. "Can't be too careful," he told Freddie, who nodded approval.

Warren walked quietly along the passageway aft, past the head and storage locker across from it. The sound of footsteps had faded. He paused at the foot of the stairs leading to the main deck and listened. Not a sound. Freddie moved up behind him. He put up his hand, signaling for them to wait. They were expecting Myron, but Myron was anything but quiet and stealthy.

Both stood silently at the bottom of the stairs, but still no sound from above. Warren knew someone had come aboard, and whoever it was remained onboard, making not the slightest noise. Not an easy thing to do on an old boat moored in calm waters. A friend should have hailed them, or a stranger requested permission to come aboard.

The longer they waited, the more suspicious he became. A head poking up through the deck hatch was the perfect target for a fist or a fid swung by a strong arm. Not to mention knives and guns. Warren shrugged at Freddie, and got the same in return.

Maybe he was over-reacting, he thought. He placed his foot on the first riser, keeping his back pressed against the bulkhead. There were only eight steps and after the first three he could view a larger portion of the after deck and see to both sides somewhat. The blind spot was forward and above. He could see nothing there.

He felt a tugging on his pants and turned to see Freddie pointing frantically toward the pistol in his belt. Warren nodded and drew the gun, clicking the safety to the firing position. He forced himself to draw a deep breath, crouched and moved up one more step to the halfway point, then halted again and listened. Now he heard the mooring lines creaking softly and the slapping sound of *Esteban's* gentle wash against the pier pilings. Natural sounds, but were they louder than they should be on such a calm day? He exhaled and rested his back against the bulkhead. If he took one more step he might be able to peek on deck and see forward.

What the hell, he thought. This is my own boat and I'm done creeping around. There was another sound he separated now from the creaking mooring lines and the water lapping against the pilings, like a small faucet running.

"Damn it all," he mumbled, and walked up on deck. "What in hell are you doing? Trying to scare us to death?"

"I'm taking a piss," Myron said, staring at the pistol over his shoulder as he finished urinating into the water. "You're gonna scare yourself creeping around on deck with a little pistol like that. Where the hell's Freddie?"

The frogman's head came up past the cowling. "Damn you, Myron! Why you sneaking around up here?"

Myron zipped his fly. "You guys got some kind of pre-voyage heebie-jeebies, or what? Get up here and lend a hand with my gear before you shoot somebody. Put that gun away. I got two tanks and gear bag up on the pier.

Gonna give me a hand or not?"

Warren slid the pistol into the small of his back again and climbed to the surface of the pier where Myron had left his pile of scuba equipment. He yelled back down, "Why do you have all this gear? We're not going diving, we're going to Guadeloupe."

"Holler a little louder so the whole island can hear you," Myron answered. "Anyway, I'm always going diving, and sure as hell ain't goin' off to sea with my gear onshore."

"Myron. You're a pain in the ass," Freddie said, turning to Warren. "I'll get the women moved over and bring White back with me. What are you thinking? Two rooms in that place?"

Warren shook his head. "Get a suite so they stay together."

"How much does this joint cost?"

"Ain't cheap," he smiled. "I'll just add it to Javert's bill."

"Works for me." Freddie climbed the ladder and strolled off along the pier.

"What's going on?" Myron asked.

"Tell you later."

Less than two hours later Rosa and Armando, Ruth and Judy Ann White unpacked their belongings in the Honeymoon Suite of the Satisfaction Bay Club. Only Armando was at the sixth-floor window to see *Esteban* clear Edward Town harbor and set its course for Guadeloupe. He brushed a tear from his cheek but his mouth was set in a determined line. Warren had told him he was the man of the house now and should protect the women, but he knew better. Warren left him behind because he was a child and belonged with the women.

Armando watched until the boat was no more then a white smudge on the horizon. They better not look for the little pneumatic speargun, he thought. That was safely in his duffle under the bed. He hadn't forgotten the look on Bens' face when he saw the speargun pointed at him. That moment he was a man, not a helpless boy. Bens knew it, too. Even his mother knew it.

He didn't know Warren was squinting back across the water, watching Charming Island blur to a green cloud of loveliness, rising from the sea with the allure and mystery that only land endows to a sailor. Leaving, he thought, was akin to homecoming. The melancholy joy of exchanging one world for another. He felt the purposeful motion of the boat as it conquered the sea and it wasn't so different from swimming underwater where his body was the boat and his fins the power. Things on land tired him, but under the water or on it, he was truly free.

The captain's chair swung back to face the empty sea ahead and his hands rested easily on the helm. They moved with unconscious intent, correcting the course a degree or two and the steering gear groaned quietly in mechanical response. Warren leaned back and rested his bare feet up on the console beside the compass. He thought what a fine cloudless day it was with a fresh breeze and a gentle, rolling sea. A thin smile lifted his lips and he marveled once again at the fickle nature of this massive body of water capable of taking him around the world or to the depths of discovery. No wonder sailors embraced it as a woman. He prayed that for the next twenty-four hours she would be submissive.

For some reason that day, he had stuffed the folded letter from his mother into a front pocket and now he patted it to be sure it was still there. He knew it was wrinkled, creased, and some of the writing smeared. He was undeserving of the letter. He was undeserving of the sentiments she had expressed when she wrote it. The mother, he thought, was a far better human being than the son. But unlike before, now it depressed him. Rosa was right to condemn him, and when he had first come to accept that, he silently conceded to regret. But was that the first step to recovery? Or self-pity? We repent for the good of our souls, she told him. Well, she had just as much to repent about as he did. That, however, was not a comfort.

A small flock of seagulls had followed them out from the harbor, diving and squawking in the wake. They were gone when he glanced back and the boat's long path left a churning white smear in the surrounding deep blue of the sea.

He heard voices from below.

One by one, Freddie, Myron, and Bobby White climbed the ladder and sat down silently on the port and starboard life jacket lockers. He knew they had something on their minds. They'd been huddled below talking since putting the harbor far astern.

"What is this?" he asked. "Some kind of mutiny?"

No one looked at him.

Warren gave them another minute or two but they held their tongues. He shrugged and the chair squeaked on its pedestal as he swung back and faced forward again.

He felt their eyes on the back of his head and thought they must be working up to something unpleasant and unlikely to please him. He smiled inwardly. Like that ever bothered any of them before.

Surprisingly, Bobby White broke the silence. "Listen, Captain Will. Warren. We've been talking." White's voice drifted off.

"And?" Warren said.

"Well," Bobby responded. "It's just that I don't - we don't - want to piss you off. Know what I mean?"

"Not really."

"So, we've been talking..." His voice drifted off.

"Yes," Warren said.

Bobby stood up and grabbed a stanchion to balance closer to Warren. "Okay. Can we turn around and go back?"

"Are you seasick or something?" He didn't think Bobby had been this far out to sea before.

"No. I'm fine. But see, the thing is we been talking, and what if Slither or somebody was watching for us to leave harbor? A Javert spy, or somebody. Just waiting for us to leave and right now they're already at the golf club after the women. The boy. If they're smart, that's what they'd do. Wouldn't they?"

Freddie and Myron offered no support to Bobby. Warren guessed they were less convinced of the need to turn back.

"You might be right, Bobby," Warren admitted. "I can't know that. The risk is there. But Slither won't harm them and Javert won't order it, from Bens or anyone else. Javert's a snake, no doubt. But unless we step on his tail and trap him, he won't bite. Javert hates violence. Loves intrigue. His satisfaction doesn't come from hurting people physically but from deceiving them or taking something from them to prove what fools they are. I've watched him for years. This is why I thought I could safely borrow money from him and beat him at his own game. That's up in the air yet, I guess, but this I know: if Bens brings harm to our families it will be his idea. Javert might threaten violence to scare someone but fancies himself a genius, achieving his ends by deception. What really does piss me off, Bobby, is that he's damn good at it."

Bobby stood awhile gazing out to sea across Warren's head. "I just had to say that. I'm scared."

"No, you're not," Warren answered. "You're concerned for your family. That just makes you a man. You help me do everything I can to get us there and back quickly. We lessen the risk."

"Okay," he said. "Okay."

Warren swung his chair suddenly and faced the two aging frogmen. "And what did you geniuses have to say to Bobby about this?"

Freddie stared at the deck and Myron said, "Guess we should a told him what you told him."

"Truth is," Freddie spoke. "I'm scared for them too. Besides Marilyn, still the love of my life, Ruth's all I got. Marilyn had hip surgery awhile before we left but made us go without her."

"You want to go back, too?"

Freddie shook his head. "No. I'm just telling you I feel this in a different way because it's family. Not like a military mission." He glanced quickly at Myron. "Hard to explain. It's a bitch, that's all. I was a tough young sailor in the war but that didn't include family." Freddie frowned. "Maybe it's all psychobabble bullshit, I don't know."

Warren knew that the young Freddie-the-Frogman never admitted to such feelings, but he was older now. More thoughtful. "We're all older," he told Freddie. "But you don't think old. Maybe that's enough."

Freddie grinned. "Unless I have to jump too high or swim too far. Still have the will, but might need an equalizer these days."

"We'll have a boatload of them equalizers by tonight," Myron promised. "See what Javert bought with his money. Nice little M-16 would suit me. No sneaking around. Just walk up and blow 'em all away."

"A crew of cutthroats," Warren chuckled.

"Lead on, Captain Ahab," Freddie said.

Bobby White asked, "Does that mean we're not turning back?"

"That's what it means, Bobby," Warren said. "But it'll be okay."

The land was far astern now, beyond the horizon. Flying fish launched themselves from the wake curls and glided long distances across the surface of the deep and disappeared as suddenly as they appeared. The sun was gaining on the day and Warren squeezed a few more RPMs from the ancient diesel. They were going to make it. This was going to work.

"Let's have a beer," Myron said.

"Don't think there is any," Warren answered. "Wasn't time."

"Yeah? Well then, what's in them coolers right there behind the lockers?"

"Whatever Rosa brought us, I guess."

"Rosa's stuff's in the galley," Myron said. "I brought those two coolers aboard last night. There's a case of Union in one and a case of Antilles Amstel in the other. That's what happens when you don't have women to bother with."

"Didn't know you had enough money for two cases of beer," Warren said.

"Well, I didn't, but this is an official trip. You know, work. I put it on your tab at Etlie's. He was fine about it."

Warren gave Myron the finger and the old man grinned proudly, flipping his loose upper bridge with his tongue. The dislodged teeth protruded between his lips like those of a snarling dog.

CHAPTER TWENTY FIVE

Back along the island coastline, Bacon Hornfisher and his son Martin trolled parallel to shore directly above the wreck of the French man-o-war *Imperial*. Their fishing lines were set to a depth of thirty-three feet and this was their last pass before swinging the nose of their flat-bottomed lloyla out to sea and away from the ceaseless surf crashing against the black cliffs. Martin was hungry and they were forced to eat at sea because the coastline contained no suitable beach or bay where they might go ashore.

The eighteen-foot open boats were termed scows by many, but proved more seaworthy than seemed likely. Bacon pushed the outboard motor throttle handle to starboard and the lloyla they had named *Hillary*, in honor of Bacon's common-law wife, responded in a lively manner and swung to port and seaward. They began to reel in when Martin's line snapped taut and he set the hook.

"Strike," he told his father, and Bacon throttled back to neutral so Martin could work the fish.

Martin gained less then two feet of line before he realized something held him fast. It was not a fish.

"Hook's down in the rocks," Bacon said.

"Don't think so," Martin answered. "Line's got give to it, but no fight like a fish. Can you get me over the top of it?"

Bacon turned sharply to give Martin the best angle on the line he could, then moved ahead slowly until the line stood almost vertical. "Can you jerk it loose?"

Martin, standing now and jerking the rod up and down and sideways, shook his head. "It's really stuck, Papa."

"Well," Bacon said. "Best hand me the rod and put your mask, fins and snorkel on. Not that deep. You can easily dive down and free it." Neither of them mentioned cutting the line and abandoning the tackle. That was done only as a last resort.

Martin's first dive was unsuccessful, but he got a better breath on the second and came up with hook and bait in his hand. He spit out the snorkel and shouted, "I found more than this!"

The Hornfishers forgot their lunch and while Bacon kept the boat on site Martin dived the wreck again and again. His fishing line had been caught on the yellow tourist rope Freddie and Warren had rigged to guide their future customers along *Imperial's* boundary. Martin spent an hour snorkeling the wreck until he'd seen most of it twice, including the giant anchor.

Then finally, after marking the spot well, they started for Parson's Bay.

It was late afternoon before they motored into the calm waters of the bay and pulled the boat beyond the high water mark, tying it to a beach palm. From the beach they walked directly to Toady's, a ramshackle beach café that catered to fishermen thirsty for a cold beer and the fresh catch of the day. Toady herself waited on them. She noticed their excitement.

"You caught something big?" she asked.

Bacon glanced at Martin and answered, "You might say that."

Toady was a heavy woman with thick upper arms and a voice that rumbled like surf. "You might say it? Why don't you really say it?"

"Because it might be a secret," Martin told her.

Toady grinned. "Young Hornfisher, if you got a secret, don't tell me you got a secret unless you want me to ask about it. Now spit it out."

"Give us a couple beers first," Bacon said. "We're thirsty and we missed lunch."

Toady complied but said, "It ain't on the house."

After guzzling a half bottle each, the Hornfishers felt compelled to tell their story. When they finished, they both saw Toady was impressed. "I got some fried plantain, fresh French bread and squirrel fish. Sit tight. I'll fetch it. Then we need to talk about this before the word gets out. You tell anybody else?"

Both men shook their heads.

"Good," she said. "I'll be right back."

Toady's little café had no kitchen and she cooked everything outside under the palms where she lit a fire beneath a giant black kettle alongside a wooden table. The kettle contained peanut oil and the wood fire kept it bubbling. Fish, plantain, potatoes, pork, and chicken were lowered into the hot oil in a wire basket and deep fried. The bread she baked in a nearby concrete and brick oven. What the preparation lacked in hygiene it made up for in taste. While tourists seldom wandered this far from Edward Town, those who did, and had the courage to try Toady's fare, found themselves well rewarded.

Toady, barefoot and sweating from the fire, returned with their brimming plates. "Eat. Then we talk," she told them. As they ate she bought them each another beer.

* * *

An hour's drive away, Wesley Bens and the six Cuban commandos were stirring from a good day's rest in the foothills just north of Edward Town. Their mission was unfolding as planned and no one they passed on the dark journey over the mountains took any notice of them. Some guys in a pickup. A common enough sight anywhere on the island.

Bens moved silently from one commando to the next, shaking them gently as one would a sleeping child. "Upsy-daisy," he whispered in his lilting British voice. "Upsy-daisy."

"Up your ass," Capt. George told him when Bens shook him.

"I'm sure you meant that in a humorous way, Jorge, no?"

"Naturally," he replied.

"Good. We've been lucky so far and ahead of schedule. It wouldn't do now to have any kind of a falling out." Bens smiled. "Before morning you will be in position on the outskirts of the town and I will leave you for awhile to make certain nothing has changed with our mission. I'm feeling somewhat stronger as well and must attend to some overdue business I let go until my health was improved. I may be gone as much as a day or two. All your needs will be provided for but you must remain undercover until I come back for you. Is that understood?"

Capt. George nodded.

"I said, Jorge. Is that understood?" Bens voice had lost its lilt.

"Si, mi general!"

Bens sat down next to his old comrade in arms. "Listen to me, Jorge. I have everything in my life riding on this mission and so far nothing has gone right except these last couple days. I can't afford mistakes now. This has to work the first time or it fails totally. Understand that. Live that." He paused and softened his voice. "This looks so simple, but so far I've barely stayed alive and not from any organized resistance like is usually the case, but from one foolish mishap after the next. This has been a minefield of uncertainty. What I'm asking is for you to move cautiously, thinking every step before you take it. Comprende?"

"Si, si." Jorge gave Bens a weak smile. "I understand your caution, but it does seem a bit too conservative."

"I hope so," Bens replied. "I do hope so, Jorge."

That night they didn't break camp until after midnight, when they were loaded into the truck again and driven the remainder of the distance into Edward Town. The city was asleep. Most of the bars and restaurants had closed. Just enough traffic moved to cover their arrival at a warehouse near the docks. Jorge jumped out of the passenger seat and slid aside a large metal door and Bens pulled the truck inside. Jorge closed the door and they all stood in silence until Bens turned on a small wattage light above a workbench.

"This is one of Javert's," Bens told them. "He's too cheap to employ a night watchman so we're alone." He pointed to a worn wooden stairway leading up into the darkness. "Follow me," he said, leading the way.

At the head of the stairs Bens snapped on another pale, metal-shaded light and pointed to a closed door. "In there," he directed.

Jorge opened the door and the commandos followed them inside. When Jorge found the light switch Bens shut off the other light.

They found themselves in a windowless room. The air smelled of dust and disuse, as if it had been bottled, heated and stored until they came to consume it.

"First class," Jorge told Bens.

"Best I can do," replied the big man. "Most important, it's safe. The boxes in the corner contain canned goods."

"Latrine?"

"Take the stairs down and turn beneath them. Small door into the WC."

Captain George was not pleased, but he supposed it was better than sleeping another night in the open. "What happens here during the day?" he asked.

Bens shrugged. "Depends. Javert's activities tend to ebb and flow. I've seen this place sit unused for weeks, then suddenly there's nothing but activity. It's impossible to predict the affairs of the Fat Man."

Jorge gestured at the small space. "There's no room here for even elementary exercises," he said. "We've got to be able to stay fit and ready. We can't just lie around in the dark, in some breathless room for days until you come for us. This is a highly-trained unit and we need activity. Daily activity."

Bens' face darkened. "Are your weak little muscles going to shrivel in a couple days? Are you so out of shape you can't be still and quiet for awhile? Jorge, are you maybe trying to make trouble for me instead of cooperating?"

Capt. George's patience came to an end. "Screw you," he said. "I was sent here to accomplish a mission that involves more than just sneaking around and hiding. Our mission is to help disrupt the government, coerce these simpleminded islanders into seeking protection from Cuba. We can't do that without taking physical action. We have explosives in those packs, grenades and machine guns. Not for show, but force. Now I'm here, with my men, and I decide how and when this operation will commence. Your job is nearly finished. You were instructed to provide intelligence after we arrived but not take command of my team. That falls to me, and me alone."

Tension in the small, close room became almost unbearable before Bens spoke. "Fine," he said in his usual pleasant voice. "Go ahead. Dance around the rafters if you've a mind to. You have grenades and machine guns. You are invincible. I had a machine gun and a fish took it away. But you have been here a couple days and already know more than me. So do as you please and see what it gets you."

Bens turned and left the room, closing the door behind him.

Jorge swept sweat from his brow. "What has happened to the man? A fish attacked him? I'm tired of this fish. If I didn't want to break radio silence, I would call in for someone to come and take him home for a rest. Wesley Bens, one of the toughest commandos in Cuba, is an old lady."

When Bens reached the street he saw no one and no traffic moved on the streets. The boats alongside the dock were dark and the only sounds were those made by the lapping water and squeaking mooring lines. The last thing he had expected was trouble with Jorge. Capt. George had been a comrade in the truest sense and their time in combat together had been exciting and rewarding. They had covered each other as good soldiers do, drank and whored together. Now it was as if those times were gone completely. Jorge treated him almost as a stranger, or worse, a has-been. He couldn't help but wonder now if it came from Jorge alone, or from higher up. He had been unwise in reporting his injuries and seeming weak. In the army of the revolution there was no room for weakness. No concept of failure. Bens was a mercenary. Jorge was a true communist and a Cuban. They were not equal.

Bens walked slowly along the dock. In the harbor, the usual boats swung at anchor, their lights shimmering on the water. He felt strong. Cuba was a job to him, and maybe it was time to make some changes. He'd taken care of himself most of his life. There was no loss of work for a killer. He wondered if he could jump rope. Might tear something loose. The water of the bay sloshed against the pilings. He stopped and stared at the boats again. All the usual craft, except *Esteban*. Where *Esteban* usually anchored there was only a dark hole. They had gone already then. Bens smiled and hurried back into the town. Now might be the time to punish those who had raised their hands against him. Chills dried his skin and he felt cool in the humid night air. He thought of Rosa in his grasp. Then the boy.

Less than a mile away Rosa slept soundly in the Satisfaction Bay Club, Armando by her side. That evening she had made a decision which had been a long time coming and in the morning her life was to change forever.

CHAPTER TWENTY SIX

They had skirted wide out of sight of Basse-Terre Island, one of the two largest of the Guadeloupe Archipelago, then straight in from seaward to a small bay south of the town of Marigot. The darkness was complete and the depth finder showed nearly twenty feet of water beneath the keel. They had avoided Pointe-A-Pitre and Grande-Terre itself with its airports and larger population centers. Warren ordered the anchor dropped. All lights were dark and now they waited.

Warren decided to cut even the flying bridge instrument lighting, though it was red and unlikely to be visible from any distance. Javert had given him a radio contact in case anything went wrong. He'd used it to fake a mechanical breakdown, saying he would arrive too late to make the Pointe-A-Pitre docks before customs and immigration offices closed. Any arrivals or movement of goods off the docks after that would raise suspicion. A new, last-minute, rendezvous was arranged and now they waited for a signal from the deep line of palms and forest beyond an abandoned deep-water concrete pier used briefly during World War II. They planned to sail in, load quickly and disappear.

"Think we made the right decision?" Freddie asked again in a hushed voice. The carbine lay across his lap.

All four men had gathered on the flying bridge. Warren had armed himself again with the small automatic. "Anybody's guess," he answered. "Thing is, more I think about it, more I dislike doing anything predictable when Javert is calling the shots. If they get down here on time we can still be back in the CI harbor before sunrise. This might be the smartest decision I ever made, or a waste of time, but if it comes off whoever we meet here will tell Javert, if they haven't already, and he won't be able to predict where we are or what we're doing. Should mean we're free to drop the boxes anywhere on CI, and I know just the place."

"Or he sends his own boat out looking for us," Myron said.

"It's a big ocean."

"Yeah," Myron said. "But he knows where we're going to end up."

"True," Warren agreed. "But that won't help him until after we've off-loaded the weapons and show up in the harbor. That gives us the leverage. He isn't going to have time to search the whole island, and for all he knows, it's hidden underwater someplace."

Freddie nodded. "Risk either way we play it. Better to hold the cards."

"Man," Bobby said. "I hope you're right."

Headlights appeared on the old pier, went out, flashed twice, paused and flashed a third time.

"That's it," Warren said. "I'm going straight in, starboard side to. Freddie. Keep the rifle on them. Myron. You and Bobby climb down and get the anchor up then help load when we get alongside. Don't take any shit from them, whoever they are. No money changes hands. That's all been done by Javert, so we need no discussion. We take the weapons. We're gone. Okay?"

"What if they ask for ID or something?" Bobby wondered.

"Tell 'em to kiss your ass," Freddie said. "How many stinking boats are meeting them by an isolated dock in the dark of night?"

In the darkness Warren saw a flash of white as Bobby smiled. "Sheit!" he said. "I'm a smuggler. Gun runner. Damn! Like the movies. What an awesome vacation! Secret signals in the middle of the night."

"It's only 8:15 there, Indiana Jones," Myron told him. "Let's get down and meet the bit players."

Minutes later they had the anchor up.

Esteban was a single screw vessel and hard to maneuver to and from a dock even in daylight if there was a swift current, wind, or both. Warren eased the helm and backed off on the throttle to creep ahead alongside with effortless efficiency. "Tell them to throw some fenders over the side," he whispered to Freddie.

Freddie relayed the message to Myron and Bobby. To Warren he said, "Don't want to damage this *yacht's* mahogany rub rail." But there was no malice in the remark and Warren only shook his head.

The distance between *Esteban* and the pier closed quickly enough and they saw three shadows standing spaced apart to catch the mooring lines. Warren reversed the throttles and the propeller bit the water, slowing the boat to a walk alongside the pier. Myron tossed the stern line and Bobby the bow line. Warren cut the engine and there was silence.

The shadow in the center jumped across the narrowing gap between the boat and the pier. Without invitation or word of greeting, he scampered up the ladder to the flying bridge. Freddie swung the rifle to cover him and the man stopped short.

"Don't let's get nervous, Grandpa. Be cool, mon."

Warren smiled. "Grandpa might not be a guy to piss off. Who are you?"

"Who were you expecting? Jacques Cousteau?"

Warren lost his smile. "We're ready to leave now, with or without cargo. Our job is transport, not guessing games. Are you loading or not?"

The Frenchman grinned. "You are afraid, maybe, eh?"

"Not really." Warren drew the automatic from his waistband and pointed it at the man, then reached around and started the engine. "Don't want to load? Fine. Explain it to Javert. Now, get off my boat." His smile returned. "Or I can shoot you."

"What is the matter with you? Are you crazy?" The man held up both hands. "Be calm. We will load." He motioned to the others and they moved toward the small van parked on the pier.

There were six large cases in all. They took less then ten minutes to load. Warren held the pistol steady, then called down to Myron. "Open one. Let's make sure it's not coconut juice."

Myron slid his Kbar from his leg sheath and pried the cover from one of the cases. "I need some light," he said.

Warren drew the bridge flashlight from its holder and tossed it down.

Myron played the light across the inside of the box. "M-16s," he said.

"Do one more," Warren said. "From the bottom row. I don't trust this bastard."

The Frenchman smiled. "Mon ami."

Myron shrugged. "More M-16s."

"Off the boat," Warren ordered the man.

"You seem a suspicious man," said the Frenchman. "Relax. There are also a dozen smaller boxes of ammunition. Do you want them, or are you in too much hurry?"

"Fine," Warren said. "But you stay with me. Have the dock boys do the loading."

He shrugged and told them to load the remaining twelve boxes. Myron spot checked. They were the correct .223 caliber rounds.

"I feel better now," Warren said. "Get ashore."

"Remember," the Frenchman answered. "You were late so we had to do this here. At night. You are a very nervous fellow, I think. I will be glad to see the end of you."

"Then go quickly."

He shrugged again and started down the ladder. With his head still above the deck he said, "Give my regards to the Fat Man."

"I'll do that."

The man dropped down on deck and jumped quickly to the pier.

Almost before he landed safely, Warren reversed the engine, spun the helm and *Esteban's* stern began to swing away. The two dock boys tossed the mooring lines aboard and made a gesture Warren knew was less than polite. A minute later they were well clear and the van was leaving the dock. Warren drew his first full breath and Freddie grinned.

When *Esteban's* bow cleared the end of the pier a good distance, Warren slammed the throttles forward and spun the wheel. The old yacht's propeller churned water astern and the distance between boat and dock widened rapidly. "Uffda," Freddie said in perfect Minnesotan. "Had my attention there for a minute or two. Hope he's not already talking to Javert on his car phone."

"Won't matter if he does," Warren said. "Nobody knows where we're going."

"Including me."

"You'll find out soon enough. We are going to have to make all possible speed to get there before sunup. The rest of this night better go as well as this did. Are they getting that stuff below?"

"I'll check," Freddie said, sliding down the ladder.

Warren grinned. Their little adventures had wrought a noticeable change in Freddie. For that matter, in all of them. But then, Warren reckoned, that was always the case. Adversity made you stronger or exposed your weakness. His little crew of misfits proving themselves more than capable. He recognized, too, they had accepted his authority. Even Freddie. And he drew strength from that. Many years had passed since he regarded himself as anything but a failure.

Esteban cleared the bay and dashed into the open sea, quickly leaving the dark land behind. To starboard, the lights of Marigot glowed in the distance. They were safe. Once out of sight of land he would change course for Charming Island and with any luck they would make the sugarcane refinery at Prince Henry before dawn, unload quickly and return to their anchorage in Edward Town Harbor before they had been missed. There was plenty of fuel, but Warren knew he must push the old boat beyond her limits.

He smiled to himself at the thought of Prince Henry. While the growing of sugarcane still existed on Charming Island, it no longer supported the two refineries that had been there since colonial times. Prince Henry closed at the end of the 1970s. The perimeter fence was rusty but in reasonably good repair, and if someone squeezed inside it was usually curiosity, not vandalism. Kids mostly. Metal equipment rusts quickly in tropical air. Nothing of value remained. But there were two deep water docks. Both designed for ships, not boats, and constructed higher above the water. But because Warren had made several dives there, he knew that if a boat such as *Esteban* nosed in close to the rocky shoreline, the distance from the surface of the water to the top of the pier was less at high tide. A rusted metal grid served as a ladder. He planned to tie *Esteban* securely to the pier, manhandle the weapons and ammunition up and see if he could find a dolly to get the boxes inside one of the warehouse buildings and hide them.

Freddie's head reappeared from below. He climbed up and withdrew a cold beer from each rear pocket. "Dutch or German?" he asked.

"German," Warren said, reaching for the Union.

Freddie gave voice to Warren's thoughts. "Damn! I haven't felt this alive in years."

"How many of those have you had?" Warren asked.

Freddie grinned. "Think if it was only that easy."

"Everything stowed below?"

"Safe and secure, Captain."

"Going to be a long night."

Freddie drank deeply of his Amstel, then stared awhile at the bottle. "They make this from desalinated water in the Netherlands Antilles, he said. I was there once years ago, and always believed I could taste the difference. Beer made from seawater." He shook his head at the memory.

"I've got a few course corrections to make over the next couple hours then it's pretty straight forward after that," Warren said. "Should be able to stand two-hour watches so everybody gets some sleep."

Freddie nodded. "Good. I'll pass that along. Turns out Bobby White can cook, and if Myron can keep from driving him nuts, we'll have some supper before long. Want yours up here or coming down for it?"

"I'll come down after I make the next turn. Stretch my legs."

After Freddie had gone, Warren leaned out beyond the canopy and stared up at the clear night sky. He counted silently the stars and constellations he knew, recalling how LORAN was rendering his sextant superfluous. A novelty now instead of a necessity. And from what he'd read about GPS, LORAN would soon be redundant itself. Then what, he wondered? The stars appeared the same. Their names and positions didn't change. He smiled. Except some of them light-years away might've gone out already.

Warren returned to the captain's chair, resting his bare feet on the console. Only human nature remained unchanged. Technology had no effect on love or hate. Wesley Bens might've been just as much at home two thousand years before Christ as he was today. But then, like now, there were Rosas.

His thoughts wandered. Something was changing inside and again he reached down and patted the pocket containing his mother's ripped and soiled letter. A tide of confidence washed over him and he hoped it was real.

Awhile later he had made the course corrections and engaged the autopilot. He'd keep an eye out from below for traffic while he ate something. The automatic steering device had been a large purchase for Warren, but inter-island travel by private boat was more efficient than the intermittent ferry and he made these trips often enough to justify the cost, he'd reasoned. But that cost added to his mortgage and his dependency on Javert. It seemed no matter what he did, the Fat Man's grip tightened. He shrugged to himself. At least the damn thing worked, and probably did a better job of holding a course then he did at the helm, just so you kept a sharp lookout and didn't forget it was on.

Inside the salon, the crew had switched from beer to rum.

"Hail the Captain!" Bobby White said, raising his glass. His face flushed.

Warren placed both hands on his hips and growled, "So, while the poor captain is working to keep the ship on course, the crew is drinking."

They laughed and Freddie asked, "Well then Captain, who's driving the damn thing now?"

"Autopilot."

"No shit? You got autopilot?"

Myron answered. "We got all the latest stuff here. Freddie, you gonna sit on that damn bottle or pass it around?"

As Freddie handed it over, Warren snatched it. Holding it to the light he said, "Was this full when you started?" The rum level was below the halfway mark.

"'Course not," Freddie said. "It was something we found in Myron's dive bag. I mean, can you imagine Myron with a full bottle? We're just having a few snorts to ward off the cold when we go up to stand watches."

Warren shook his head. "Any food left?" The salon smelled of bacon.

"I made some BLTOs," Bobby said. "Two left on the stove. Should be warm yet."

"What's the 'o' for?" he asked.

"Onion."

Warren reached down a paper plate from the cupboard, took an exploratory bite before loading it, then crowded into the booth with the others. He preferred milk, but settled for a slug of the warm rum. It tasted like strong honey and warmed his insides.

"How we going to work this watch standing?" Freddie asked.

Warren said between bites, "Simple. Four guys, two hours each and we'll be home."

"Home, or wherever you're taking us?"

"Old sugar refinery," he said. "Abandoned for years. Been there a dozen times. Never anybody around and the perfect spot to store the weapons. And, it's on the way to the harbor, just at the other end of the island. Be in and out of there in less than an hour."

"In the dark?"

"We got lights," Warren said.

"Who takes the first watch?" Bobby wanted to know.

"Suit yourselves."

"Me," Bobby said, grinning. "There's nothing around to run into, is there?"

"Big ships," Myron said. "Big islands. Frog's Head."

"Frog's Head?"

"Nasty lookin' rock three stories high surrounded by a couple miles of sand flats. Like a fat frog squatting right in the middle of the ocean taking a shit," Myron explained. "One time Captain Will and me - Warren, I mean - got off course in this squall when the damn bow hook handle flipped out of the overhead and smashed the compass and we were steering best we could after that but couldn't see nothin' and then it started raining in damn sheets and we got screwed up and came almost alongside the friggin' frog so close I coulda kissed the bastard as we went by. Gimme that bottle back. I'm telling you, when I looked up and saw that big ugly sucker, I figured we was gone. Done for, man." He drank deeply.

Freddie rolled his eyes and looked at Warren. "Any part of that true?"

"I might not have related the event in just that way, but yeah, it's true enough," Warren said. "Afterward we remembered the other compass down below so the whole thing was just dumb on our part."

"Your part," Myron said. "You're the captain."

"If you're going to bad-mouth me, Myron, pass the bottle."

Warren drank from the bottle and the warm rum tasted even better than before, but he handed it back, got up and went out on deck. Instead of climbing to the flying bridge, he swung up along the gunwale, moving forward, past the salon windows and up to the bow. He flew the American flag and heard it snapping in the breeze. The boat's pitch was even and gentle. The sea vacant. A perfect night. He could see by the position of the stars that the autopilot was holding a true course. He smiled. And miles from Myron's frog rock.

When he returned to the salon awhile later, Freddie was saying, "That was in 1944, and a sub dropped us near this atoll where we were going to station a spotter. By then we'd given the Japs a good lickin' or two but they still had some deadly fleets at sea in the South Pacific. We were hunting one of the biggest but even with planes up, subs, surface craft, it seemed swallowed by the sea." He paused, drinking beer again. "So our job was to get a guy on this atoll in the middle of nothing where they had no eyes because it was mostly out of range for aircraft. He was going to stay there a week, set up a large telescope and radio anything that looked like a fleet of Japs."

He drank again.

"Anyway, the sub surfaced and we took the guy in by rubber boat, unloaded all his gear. So dark you couldn't even see the white surf line. I was in the same team as him - John McAllen his name was - and we said goodbye, see you in a week or so. On the way back into the water one of our guys was bit by a sea snake and died before we got him back onboard the sub. Corpsman said those snakes were deadlier then a cobra. One he told about had enough venom to kill a thousand people.

"We surfaced out to sea and buried our guy there. Sewed him in canvas with a bunch of busted engine parts and slid him into the sea. Short service because of enemy aircraft in the area. Never saw a sub skipper who'd leave his boat on the surface with planes around. Didn't surface again for three days, and then at night to do our radio check. Damned if we didn't get orders back to the island again. They never heard from McAllen and figured he had a bad radio, though we'd checked it twenty times.

"So, back we went. On the way there the planes found the Jap convoy, all hell was breaking loose so they told us to go in during daylight, snatch McAllen and close down the operation since it was all a waste of time now.

"Sun was shining that day and the sea was glass. Japs were busy elsewhere so the skipper said once we got McAllen and all his gear back aboard we'd have a beach party. Somehow the supply geeks had acquired twenty-four cases of beer and the skipper decided it was crowding the boat anyway, so why not drink some of it up. Guy wasn't too dumb for a pig boat captain so everybody was in a pretty good mood.

"When we got the boat launched and were closing on the atoll I smelled something rotten. I hollered for McAllen but he didn't answer. The only trees there were toward the middle of this narrow strip of land where we'd put him. Beyond that was a kind of lagoon with brackish seawater that must've been trapped there. From the beach to the lagoon wasn't more than a hundred yards or so. Besides the scraggly trees nothing grew there but bushes and rocks.

"Closer we got we didn't even see the telescope he was supposed to set up or the radio antenna. It got real quiet in the boat and I knew we all had that same feeling, like before a mission. When you know the next time you sit together there won't be so many of you." Freddie took his turn with the bottle.

"We were in our swimsuits. Knives. No other weapons since we needed our hands free to carry the gear. The bow scraped the sand and we jumped out, grabbed the painter and pulled her free of the water. Then I smelled it again, but stronger.

"Nobody said anything and we heard the palm fronds scratching in the light breeze. There was something under the trees and we ran toward it.

"McAllen. His body was alive with snakes. He'd already been partially eaten by them or birds or crabs or something. The flesh was black in places. His eyes were gone. A small snake was living inside his cheek, poking its head out a hole he'd made.

"We'd all seen some shit by then, but two guys puked right there beside the body and then we all ran away. First Class in charge said we couldn't leave him like that but nobody wanted to see it again or get near the snakes again. Finally sent two guys to loop ropes around his ankles and we dragged him back to the beach, tied him to the boat, pushed off and towed the poor bastard out to the sub. Snakes kept coming out of him like spaghetti with black tongues as we pulled him along the surface. When we got alongside the sub and the Exec saw it, he wouldn't let us bring McAllen any closer then a few yards. We just left him tied to the rope, floating. The Skipper came topside with a Bible, said the burial at sea service, we tied some heavy nuts, broken tools and crap to the ropes, then let him go." Freddie's voice petered out.

"After that," he said, "I was never the same. Fly walked across my face at night and I'd wake up sucking air and crying."

The men in the salon were silent.

Finally Freddie said, "There are some things, you know, worse than war."

An hour earlier in Edward Town, Rosa slipped unseen from the Satisfaction Bay Club's kitchen door and disappeared into the night.

Sometimes, at the height of the hurricane season, the weather on Charming Island was fickle. This warm night a chill mist slid down from the forested mountains, filtering into the narrow streets, cloaking the incandescent street lighting and neon signs of restaurants and bars. The mist was cool and drifted steadily in fast moving clouds until it blanketed the entire town and harbor.

Above the flatland portion of Edward Town that comprised the commercial section of the small city, the streets were less planned and poorly maintained. The city had no choice but to grow up the hillsides and into the adjacent valleys where restaurants with a view clung next to a gully crowded with the shacks of the poor. It was a steep climb and diners, when they ventured here, arrived by taxi. Rosa knew these streets well and made her way diagonally across the face of one foothill after the next, angling upward toward her Pentecostal church.

The meeting was set for eight o'clock, but she wanted to be early and get back to the hotel before anyone missed her. She lied to Ruth, Judy Ann, and her son, saying she was suffering cramps from her period and needed to lie down for an hour or two and rest. The women were sympathetic and even Armando, after a mild protest, left her alone in their room. She had to be back before they missed her.

Despite the faithfulness of the island's Pentecostal community, the illegal drug trade that swept the Caribbean had not neglected Charming Island. There were fewer drug dealers and users on the island than in other places, and though there was seldom street peddlers or junkies in doorways or addicts who disturbed visitors as they did in the Bahamas and elsewhere, an alley street named Clarence was the exception. Rosa's preacher thundered from the pulpit that misery loved company. But even so, the church organized many outreach missions for the Clarence Street addicts, welcoming them into the church, feeding and caring for them. The church janitor, who slept in a room there hardly bigger then a closet, was an ex-junkie and once every year gave his testimony before the congregation. And so Rosa was not fearful of walking along Clarence Street after dark and in a mist.

Rosa's thin cotton dress offered little protection from the damp air and she clung to her purse, hugging it to her chest as she walked. Barefooted in sandals she shivered and kept a brisk pace, eying the ground to avoid the pools of vomit, dog feces, and sometimes human feces that were common obstacles to pedestrians.

A voice called from the darkness, "Mama! Here, mama. Spare a dollar."

Another night she might've stopped, heeding a call for help. She often carried a few extra dollars for this. Warren scolded her. "Don't be stupid," he said. "They're just going to buy more drugs with your money. You're part of the problem, Rosa."

He was right. She knew he was. They bought drugs with the money, or wine, or rum. But sometimes they had to eat too, and she prayed for them to get a meal and be strengthened for the time when Jesus would come and lift them from the gutter, as He had lifted her.

Tiny mud-packed paths twisted uphill in between the shabby buildings. It was from one of these dark passages that the man had called to her, and now as she passed another dark path, a new voice came clearly, "Mama, come to me."

It was a higher voice, masculine and oddly familiar. She stopped and turned toward it. The darkness was complete and the foggy air hung in the dark shadows of the place where the voice had spoken.

"What do you need?" she asked the darkness.

"I hurt," the voice said.

"Come out," she said, struggling between her instinct to help and her growing fear.

"I can't move."

Rosa's feet felt nailed to the damp roadway with unexplained dread. Never before had she been so hesitant. Maybe the murky night that seemed so unnatural and oppressive. Maybe recent events unsettling her heart. She shook it off. "I'm coming," she said, and crossed into the shadows.

She saw nothing at first but felt a presence - invisible and oppressive at once. A fetid odor of garlic. Sounds of breathing. She raised her head and felt the warmth of tainted breath, as two arms crushed her body against a massive naked chest.

Bens chuckled. "Now, I have you."

"Englishman," she gasped into the rank sweat of his muscled breast.

"I told you I would come for you. Where were you hiding? Where is your captain?"

She was so crushed against him that her breathing came only in wheezing gulps. "He's coming behind me," she said.

Bens laughed. "Bitch," he said. "You are a religious bitch, I'm told, but still a liar. The boat is not in harbor. Where is it?"

Rosa couldn't remember if Bens knew about the weapons or not. She tried to calm herself and think clearly. If Bens had meant to kill her would he be asking questions? "Working for Javert," she said, hoping this might give her a chance.

"Ah," he said. "The guns. I was sure of it. A mistake to leave you alone, I think."

She said nothing.

"Convenient then for me," he said. "No one is about tonight. Filthy weather, I'm sure. I was going to impregnate you, you black bitch, but you left me with yet unhealed injuries, so what I said to you is true. I am hurt. You could heal me. You might have enjoyed me, but now," he panted, "I will get right to the killing." He squeezed her even more tightly, flattening her face into his breast until her mouth gaped and her jaw muscles stretched. Her ribs flexed against her lungs and the air escaped in sharp gasps as the pressure mounted and she knew in a moment that her strength would be gone along with any chance of escape.

She forced the fear to the back of her consciousness and found one desperate chance for survival.

Slowly, she drew in a painful breath of air. It cleared her head and gave her hope. Pressing her ample breasts against Bens' stomach she was able to swivel her head enough to plant her teeth upward where she found his erect nipple and bit down upon it deeply, closing her teeth together until his blood squirted warm and salty along her tongue, nearly choking her as both rows of teeth came together.

Bens howled like a wounded beast and pushed her away enough for her knee to spring up into his groin, connecting with the thunk of a coconut striking the sand. She spat a generous chunk of his flesh, including the nipple, into the mud, swiveled and ran.

Biting out a chunk of Bens' flesh would not have stopped him, but his injured scrotum was tender and her blow there rendered him immobile. His knees turned to water. He struck the mucky ground with a loud oath and complete loss of strength, disabled and bewildered. It had happened to him again.

Rosa's long young legs stretched their full length as she fled up Clarence Street, crossing Claypoole and Stanley until she reached the church, exhausted but giddy. If Warren ever found out she left the hotel, she might be safer with Bens. She collapsed on the front steps and smelled something foul. Her shoes. She kicked them off and carried them by the straps to the hand pump in the churchyard. Once the water began to flow she washed her feet first, then the sandals.

At sea, Bobby White was excited to stand the first watch. Now, an hour later, he was bored. The other three men were sleeping below and he was alone on the flying bridge looking out at a black night. *Esteban's* running lights were on, and the instrument lighting made a warm glow, but that only served to render the night even darker, he thought. Warren had said he might see the Frog's Head lights off to starboard.

"Starboard," he'd asked Warren, "is the right. Right?"

"If you're facing forward. Facing the bow. The pointy end. Then it's right. But if you're facing aft. The back of the boat. Then it's left. In other words, it's always the same side," Warren had explained.

Bobby had nodded his understanding but it really made no sense to him. Was it left or right? Sailor talk seemed needlessly complicated and foreign. Why didn't they just speak English? Warren had explained the electronics to him as well, but Bobby thought most of the equipment - LORAN, autopilot, ship to shore radio, RPMs, weather radio - wasn't anything he needed to know. He wasn't going to drive the boat. The autopilot did that. His job was simple. Watch the compass to make sure the autopilot was on course and keep an eye out for shipping. If a ship or something showed up he'd wake Warren and let him deal with it. But it was boring just sitting there staring out into the blackness. He'd watched the wake for awhile, marveling at the phosphorescence. They were moving fast through the water and the bow wake also contained the bright green phosphorescent sparkles, and some even glided alongside. But after the first hour that too became routine and familiar.

Beneath the console Warren stored a number of tools and instruments. Bobby withdrew a large wrench so heavy it took two hands. The jaws and handle were rusted and for awhile he played with it until he freed the adjusting wheel and moved the jaws an inch or more, then that too became boring and he laid it on the console until later. Above him another radio, a standard AM/FM, was mounted to the hard canopy. He managed to find several stations but only one in English and that was a religious station. He snapped it off.

Then he remembered the binoculars. Warren had said to keep a sharp lookout for ships and small craft. He hung them around his neck and searched the horizon. Nothing. Darkness. Don't look at the horizon, Warren had said. Look just above it and use your peripheral vision to see pinpoints of light. There was no light.

He leaned back in the captain's chair and placed his feet on the console as he'd seen Warren do, shoving the wrench toward the compass.

Three beer cans were left on the console too, on the other side, and Bobby White, well lubricated, dozed in the chair.

A quarter hour later his back hurt and he awoke. He climbed down to the head and took a leak, then went back up to resume his watch. Making a sweep with the glasses he spotted a light to the left. That was port, he thought. Warren had said their course was west of the islands, far enough out to sea that if he saw anything there it was most likely a ship. But Bobby didn't think it was a ship. It looked more like one of the warning lights you saw in channels or the inland waterways of his native Texas. And the light bobbed gently up and down with the sea. Except for one that was higher above the water.

His watch was nearly over and he wondered if he should wake Myron a few minutes early and ask him.

He studied the higher light and thought he saw something dark beneath it. The hull of a ship? Best to be safe, he decided, and started down the ladder. The boat shuddered and there was a scraping sound like that a boat makes when it's dragged onto a sandy beach and suddenly Bobby was flung against the ladder, cutting his lower lip on one of the steel rungs. The engine roared but *Esteban* had stopped dead and was held fast.

Bobby screamed, "Wake up!"

And later, after Warren had stopped the engine and they shined lights in the water it was obvious they'd run aground on the sand flats east of Frog's Head. No one had said a word to him about being off course by miles or that he was somehow responsible, but Warren had found the old iron wrench next to the compass. "A magnetic compass," he'd said to no one in particular, "is corrupted if you put metal next to it." But it seemed to Bobby the remark was meant for him alone.

"I'm sorry," he'd said.

A careful check below found no more water then usual in the bilges but Warren started the pump to be sure.

"We're screwed anyway," Myron said. "Won't be high tide for hours. Even then we might not get off here without a tow."

They had gathered first on the bow then moved to the fantail and Warren had used a boat hook to see if they had clearance for the prop. They did. Move everything back to the stern, he thought. Get the heavy boxes and anything else they could carry and see if the bow could be lightened enough to slide her off in reverse.

He put them to work but it was no use. The propeller produced a cloud of sand and mud but *Esteban* remained imbedded in the sand as if it were cemented there.

"No use," Warren said, shutting down the engine. "Grab my gear and an underwater light," Warren told Myron. "I'm going down for a look."

Fifteen minutes later he crawled back onto the swim step and sat there awhile staring off into the darkness.

"Well?" Freddie finally asked.

Warren slipped his fins off and tossed them on deck. "At least twenty five feet of keel is in the sand. Half the boat on the bottom." He unbuckled his BC and Freddie lifted the tank from his back and laid it on deck. Warren stood and flipped his mask and snorkel carelessly after it. "Myron's right. We're screwed."

CHAPTER TWENTY SEVEN

A cloud of despair hung above them in the darkness. They sat around the table in the salon drinking coffee. No one spoke. Bobby White blamed himself for the wrench and the rest, and sat head down, staring at the tabletop. He'd refused the coffee. Bobby was no sailor, Warren told himself. Learning took time. It was just that they didn't have any.

"It's okay, Bobby," he said. "Not as bad as it could be."

"No. It's worse," Myron said.

"Shut up, Myron," Freddie told him.

Myron stood up and started to the door. "We're not going to get there. Understand? We aren't going to make it. We'll be lucky if we get off this sandbar in a week." He stomped out on deck.

"He might be right at that," Freddie said.

"I'm so sorry," Bobby said again.

"Shut up, Bobby," Freddie said.

Warren rose slowly to his feet and refilled his cup. At least the grounding had sobered them up. Nothing like danger to clear your head. "Only grounded once before," he said. "Crewed for a guy on the West Coast awhile, years back, learning the ropes before I took the captain's test. Smaller boat but we kedged it off a sandbar. Just the two of us did it in an hour."

"Kedging?" Freddie asked.

Warren nodded. "Unlikely in the Navy, I suppose. Get stuck and usually there's another boat around to pull you off. Or hell, you just leave the damn thing and transfer. But civilian sailors got their own money in a boat and do what they can. And they're alone, mostly, you know?"

"So what is it?"

"Old-fashioned thing, kind of. About all you need is an anchor and some rope."

"Got another anchor?" Freddie asked.

"Two," Warren said. "One big enough to do this, I think."

"Can you explain it?"

Warren grabbed a small notebook from the sideboard. "Grab that pencil behind you."

Freddie was skeptical but complied.

Bobby lifted his head and watched.

Warren drew the outline of a boat in sand. "That's us," he said needlessly. Then he drew a line from the stern out some distance and angling starboard. At the end of the line he drew a crude anchor. "That's the kedge anchor." Further alone he drew an arrow to indicate current, also coming from starboard. "Current isn't strong here but moves slightly offshore. We got no wind."

Freddie studied the crude drawing. "How far from the boat is that kedge?"

"Yeah," Warren smiled. "That's the problem. It's got to be out there as far as we can get it."

"How much does this anchor weigh?"

"About a hundred and fifty pounds." He shrugged. "Got it free. Never used it for anything but ballast."

Freddie shook his head. "We got no boat or dinghy to carry it. Can't swim it. Might as well be a thousand pounds."

"I know," Warren said. "Might just lift it over and drop it to the bottom. Put our gear on. Leave the fins. Couple guys down there lift it up by the flukes and drag it."

"You mean walk on the bottom?"

"Well, you learned hardhat in the Navy, no?"

"Sure. We had brass helmets and lead boots and air pumping in from a surface compressor so the suits had buoyancy. This ain't the same."

"I know," Warren said. "We got to work with what's here. Inflate our BCs maybe."

Freddie thought for awhile. "Okay," he granted. "We walk this kedge anchor out to starboard like you drew it here. Then what?"

"*Esteban* has a right hand prop, so when we put her in reverse the kedge should keep the boat straight and help us use the trough we created coming onto the bar." He shrugged. "And maybe we can wiggle it. Reverse and ahead, reverse and ahead."

"Lotta ifs."

"While I'm working the engine you guys can heave around on the kedging line. If the anchor is well into the bottom, should be some leverage. Tie it off to both stern cleats. They're heavy cleats and even if we can gain an inch or two we might be able to shake her loose."

"Okay," Freddie said. "But you can't think we'll do this in an hour."

"No." Warren shook his head. "Damn lucky if it doesn't take all night."

Afraid to speak, Bobby raised his hand.

"Speak," Freddie said.

"Well, what if we run back and forth?"

"What?"

Bobby swallowed the lump in his throat. "Run together from one side of the boat to the other. I mean if we can shake it loose. Even an inch, right?"

Myron, who had come back to stand in the doorway, said, "Run back and forth? You crazy?"

Warren held up his hand. "He's got something. Strap on a couple weight belts each, loaded with thirty or forty pounds of lead. Maybe even carry a couple tanks. You'd have half a ton moving side to side. Bound to make a difference."

"We can't carry that much weight," Myron said.

"We can for a little while," Freddie said. "It rocks the boat or it doesn't. Worth a try."

"I think so too," Warren said. He grinned at Bobby and saw the relief on his face.

"Damn glad it's the middle of the night," Myron complained. "Somebody sees us running from side to side on the back of this here boat and we'll all end up in the friggin' funny farm."

"Aw, Myron," Freddie said, grinning. "You're half gone anyway."

"Well, least I'd like time enough to get laid once more before I die."

"Now there's a disgusting prospect. Just shut up, Myron."

Warren placed his cup in the sink. "Let's get the anchor out of the rope locker."

Half an hour later the kedge anchor was on the bottom, and the two youngest, Warren and Bobby, were suited up standing on the swim step.

Warren had wedged a small underwater light beneath his mask strap. "When we get down there, Bobby, I'll turn the light on and we crawl to the anchor. Each grab a fluke. Up on our knees, then stand. Okay? We walk as far as we can. Kneel. Put it down and rest. Then repeat. Okay?"

"Can I ask you one thing?"

"Sure."

"I never been underwater at night." He shivered. "Ain't there like sharks and stuff feeding then? That's when all the big fish eat, isn't it?"

"Well, not this shallow," Warren lied. "They're way out on the deep side of the reefs."

"Oh. Good."

Wasn't worth worrying about anyway, Warren thought. If something came in to feed they wouldn't know it until they'd been eaten.

Warren dropped feet first into the water, settled to the bottom and turned on the light. Bobby followed, guided by its glow. They crawled awkwardly forward without their fins until they reached the anchor. Each man required to lift about seventy-five pounds and carry it along the bottom.

Already the bubbles from their exhalations sounded loud in their ears as they lifted the flukes, cradling one apiece in their arms. Everything weighs less in water, but anchors were dense iron and offered small advantage as they tried to stand. The anchor teetered and they fell. A second time they were close, but fell again.

Warren held up his hand. Stop. They rested.

They tried again a third time and both stood, staggering. The sand was uneven and their efforts had stirred up such a cloud of silt and muck the light was useless, giving back nothing but reflections of back-scatter like headlights in a thick fog.

Warren stepped forward and Bobby did the same. After a dozen steps they cleared the silt cloud and the light revealed the bottom clearly enough for Warren to distinguish a gentle slopping of the sand to their right. He angled deeper, but always moving left. Bobby staggered but kept his side of the anchor in his arms. Their bubbles roared from the regulator exhaust ports and Warren knew they were consuming air at an alarming rate. They had an abundance of rope and he wanted to move the kedge as far as possible so they gained enough leverage to break *Esteban* loose from the slot it had dug itself into.

The thick curled flukes of the Bruce anchor they carried pressed their flesh against their bones and it seemed to Warren each step they took would be their last. The Bruce came to him years ago when a Brit he knew put his boat on the rocks during a storm, but this was the first time he'd taken it out of the rope locker, content with his old Danforth, which was so much lighter and easier for one man to handle.

He swung his head to see Bobby.

The mask hid Bobby's nose, eyes and part of his forehead. The regulator and its endless stream of exhaust bubbles obscured his head and Warren was unable to see if Bobby was nearing panic as he had on the dive when the shark came, or was strong and calm enough to go farther along the bottom and plant the anchor a good distance from the boat so kedging had a chance. The weight they carried included their own lead weight belts, forty-pound tanks, and Warren had clipped 2-pound lead ankle weights to each ankle to keep his feet planted. That had seemed like a good idea, but now he knew it was foolish. The anchor provided all the negative buoyancy he needed and plenty extra. His legs ached. Sharp rocks in the sand cut his feet. They couldn't see where they were walking, only the patch of sand ahead. He concentrated on the slope of the bottom, hoping it fell away in a logical way, from shallow to deep, but he knew from years underwater that sand might easily be in drifts not much different from the sands of a desert. Water acted on sand much the same as wind. If they made wrong choices now, he doubted they would have the strength to move the heavy anchor this far again. It had to be the right direction.

He closed his eyes and staggered forward. Their inflated BCs were of little help.

Alongside him, Bobby White was crying bitterly. Not long ago he'd been in the hospital, stabbed in the back. He'd been scared out of his wits and plunged into one frightful event after the next. When he disembarked from the Charming Island ferry with Judy Ann it wasn't much different than any other Caribbean vacation they'd taken over the past dozen years. There was an abundance of good travel deals to be had in Texas and this was one of them. A nice little two-week package - hotel and ferryboat ride. Now he was ankle deep in cutting rock and sand, cradling a heavy anchor ten feet below the surface of the water. His legs as wobbly as a child's. Knife wound throbbing. Bare feet bleeding. And his arms. He prayed for his arms. Too many years behind a desk. His muscle tone was gone and his belly sagged. He could drop the anchor and relieve the pain or cry out in frustration. The difference now, since Bens tried to kill him, was that he'd rather cry than give in, strain than rest. So he sucked at his compressed air, swore under his breath and let the tears flow.

Before the kedge anchor was dropped over the side, Freddie had tied their longest piece of rope to it. One hundred and fifty feet of strong nylon line. They'd decided a hundred feet was a good distance, leaving them fifty feet of line to tie securely to the large fantail cleats. Freddie had already tied the rope off so that when they reached one hundred feet it would come taut and their struggles with the anchor would be finished.

That happened just seconds before Bobby collapsed with fatigue. At first he didn't understand what was holding him back. But as the realization came to him so did an overwhelming sense of relief, and not a little bit of pride. He'd done it, and with Warren, fell to his knees and planted the burden in the sand. They both deflated their BCs now that the burden was gone.

Warren's exhaustion diminished, and as his strength returned he repositioned his head to shine the light on Bobby. He saw the bubbles streaming from his exhaust ports, head bowed, both arms resting on the anchor. Minutes ticked by before Bobby turned to the light, removed his regulator mouthpiece and smiled like a fool. Weak from his injury and fatigued, Bobby astonished Warren once again. Lately, it seemed everything he'd once believed now left him dazed, dumbfounded. He hated tourists; now they were becoming heroic.

The Bruce was laying in the correct position for it to dig into the sand when a strain was put on the line. Warren had arranged beforehand with Freddie that when the anchor was in position he would signal with three hard pulls on the rope. Then those onboard could pull while he and Bobby watched below to be certain the flukes dug the kedge anchor deep into the sand.

He gave the signal and shortly afterward the rope came taut and the kedge was set.

Warren signaled Bobby to follow the line back to the boat. This would have to work, but even if it did their arrival back home was dangerously delayed.

On Clarence Street, no one observed Wesley Bens stagger from the dark alley, face gray with pain, eyes brimming with hatred. He had not seen which direction she ran, but instinct told him uphill. The church was uphill and she might imagine that a refuge. He bit hard into his lower lip until his teeth split it like the skin of an apple and he tasted the blood. The warm flavor and pain moved him forward toward the prey. Rosa, rose. She would soon feel the deadly prick of his steel thorn, his fingers stroking the ivory handle.

He was unable to run but kept a steady pace, no more than minutes behind her. She might seek refuge in the church and he was aroused by thoughts of tearing the door from its hinges, smashing windows, cornering the bitch at the altar and hanging her mangled body on the cross. They always had an empty cross in these Pentecostal houses of worship. Cheap wooden crosses made by some campesino in the congregation. Bens was overcome by exhilaration and he moved even more rapidly forward.

Before she entered the church, Rosa rinsed the taste of Bens from her mouth at the pump, straightened her dress and carried her wet sandals to the wooden steps leading up to the sanctuary. She left her sandals on the top step and entered barefoot by the unlocked door.

She crossed the threshold, moving silently into the small narthex where she bowed her head and asked God to accept her presence though she was a sinner, undeserving of His grace. It was humility that gave her courage. Through the ages God had endured every manner of sin, but as she read her Bible daily, she knew it was arrogance He disliked most.

The double doors ahead were open to the sanctuary and her bare feet made no sound as she walked to the altar and knelt there. As Bens thought, a tall, crude wooden cross hung from chains, the sanctuary's only ornamentation beside the simple altar itself. Rosa prayed silently, asking first for forgiveness at doing violence to the Englishman. She was too quick to fight, she told God. If she might learn patience, then when dangers came He could show her another way. A way that came from the Holy Spirit because she never knew any other way. Always the same. Battle before self-control. But it was the puzzle of her nature. It had preserved her and her son. Or did God preserve her in spite of her recklessness? So much was yet a mystery, and this thought brought a smile to her lips. Wasn't it the mystery that drew her closer at times such as these?

Rosa pushed herself upright, head still bowed, when the floor creaked behind her. She turned and faced Wesley Bens. He had ripped his shirt into strips and tied them around his chest to staunch his bleeding left breast, with its missing nipple. It looked as though he wore a blue brassiere.

The knotted sleeve of his shirt hung from his left hand and Rosa saw the flash of a silver blade in his right hand. He planned to tie and cut her. Had she not just prayed for self-control? The gruesome smile on Bens' face, the vile breath he heaved as he stepped forward was unbearable and she felt bile rise in her stomach and adrenaline flow, strengthening her muscles.

Everything inside her screamed for action. Terror gripped her, but unlike the first attack in the alley, she felt no panic. The prayer had barely fallen from her lips before the test had presented itself. Faith that isn't tested may be only imagined, she thought. Time seemed suspended as she decided. No urgency. The moment waited for her with the assurance of a planned event - pregnancy, birth, death. She smiled at Bens and said, "I have eternal life."

She watched the frightful smile fade from his lips and the malice in his eyes seemed muted with curiosity. But there was no pity when he spoke. "There is only eternal death." And he stepped close to give it to her.

To-John was a large woman and often carried a cane. Her knees were bad. The cane was a gift from the former addict who lived in the church. He'd carved it from a horse's foreleg and ground out the top joint to insert a granite ball about the size of those used in tennis. He was vague about the source of these items but the granite was smooth to the touch and To-John loved the cane, though she found it a little top-heavy.

Now when she swung it, the granite collided with the right side of Wesley Bens' head just above and slightly behind his ear. The sound it made was like the crack of one well-hit croquet ball against another. Hollow and hard.

It was the only sound in the room and Bens crumpled at Rosa's feet and was still.

Behind To-John stood a crowd of Pentecostal sisters. Rosa had called them from the hotel. A decision had been made. Government House had promised its furtive support. More than one thousand parishioners pledged to march the following day, and every day until a new, fair election was held. This would give Sir Henry his authority to intervene. He had already vetted new election judges that had proven honest, and sworn an oath to make a fair count.

To-John said, "So this is the Englishman we hear so much talk about."

"I think you killed him," Rosa said quietly.

"Yes," one of the sisters said. "He's gone to the Lord."

To-John disagreed. "To hell, more like."

Rosa knelt beside him, and placed two fingers on his jugular vein. She felt a slight pulse and bent her ear to his foul mouth. "He breathes."

They turned him onto his back, straightened his legs, and someone found a pillow for his head.

"What is that he is wearing to cover his breasts?" To-John asked.

"A bandage made of his shirt," Rosa answered. "I bit off one of his nipples earlier."

The sisters had all gathered round to stare down at him.

"Hump," To-John said. "Is this not the same Englishman who the woman doctor from Guadeloupe came here to sew his manliness back onto his crotch?"

"Yes," Rosa nodded.

"The same that was in the story of the big fish who nailed his foot to a boat awhile back?"

"The same."

"I see," she concluded. "We will care for him. God must have a plan to keep this man alive in spite of so much adversity. But keep him quiet. The cane broke his skull, I think."

Rosa found Jerome, the addict, outside smoking behind the tool shed, and together with the church ladies they moved Bens into the shed and placed his inert form on Jerome's workbench.

"It's a good height," To-John said. "We won't have to bend to wash or feed him."

Rosa brought water from the pump and they washed the hematoma above his ear. They noticed the ear itself had been split and after it was cleaned To-John found needle and thread, stitching it neatly together. Bens maintained regular breathing but his pulse was weak and difficult to find at times, leading them to conclude he was near death.

"When he dies," To-John said, "I will go to see Mr. Cumberbatch and confess my sin to him. We must talk to the brothers so he has a Christian burial on our own ground where he met his Maker."

"I will pray for him," Rosa said. "My enemy."

"Pray for those who persecute you," To-John reminded them. "It is late now. But if he lives until morning I will bring the German doctor here. He knows him."

"Or we could leave it in God's hands," Rosa suggested, thinking of the consequences To-John would face.

To-John smiled. "Thank you, Rosa, but I have nothing to fear. The Lord is with me, and I did nothing I wouldn't do again." She shrugged her heavy shoulders. "Maybe not hit him quite so hard."

Onboard *Esteban* four men were sprinting across the fantail, port and starboard, port and starboard, in what appeared to be a peculiar race to see who could carry the most scuba equipment from side to side. The engine was running and the deck lights shown brightly, cutting a hole in the darkness. Their faces were red and sweaty. The boat stayed fast in the sandbank.

Warren held up his hand and unbuckled both weight belts, swinging them to the deck. "Enough," he gasped. "Enough. I don't feel any movement. She's stuck fast."

Freddie-the-Frogman pulled a large handkerchief from the back pocket of his khaki shorts and mopped his face and neck. "It was worth a try," he said.

Bobby collapsed alongside Myron on the tank bench. "When I get home I'm going to join a health club. Shoot! I'm beat."

Myron was wheezing so loudly Warren and Freddie were casting furtive glances at him. His lungs were shot anyway, and the men had told him to sit this one out but that had only made him more determined. They could all see now he was too tired to speak.

Warren crossed his legs and flopped down next to his weight belts. "Yeah. It was worth a try. Who knows? Maybe we pushed a little sand away from the hull or wiggled the keel enough so she'll come loose when we heave on the kedge line."

"We rest first, right?" Bobby said.

Warren nodded. "Rest and water. We'll need to put everything we've got into the kedge or we're here until the next hurricane blows us off."

"I'm sorry, guys," Bobby said. "I wasn't thinking. I should've known that wrench could mess with the compass. I should've known."

Myron stuck an elbow in his ribs. "Quit beating yourself up about it. We all screw up. I've even done it myself."

Freddie stared at him. "No," he said. "Not you, Myron."

Myron dislodged his upper bridge and tongued it out between his teeth. "Thee dat?" he asked.

For no particular reason they all laughed.

Fifteen minutes later all four of them were on the kedge line.

"This works two ways," Warren instructed. "We pull and the anchor gives us leverage. When we've done as much as we can we hold fast and loop the rope around both the big bits on the stern. Rest and do it again. Once we've got a good strain on that line, the current pushing and sea lifting, we don't have to work so hard. Our big job is to maintain the strain and not let the line go slack. I'm guessing several hours, if it moves at all."

"When's it get light?" Freddie asked.

"Around five, five thirty."

"Shit! It's almost two a.m. now."

Warren sighed. "Maybe we get lucky. Doesn't matter now. We go with the hand we're dealt and hope we can land this stuff at the refinery without anybody seeing us."

"In full daylight?"

"It's not a tourist attraction. We could get lucky."

"Yeah," Freddie said. "We've been so lucky this far."

An hour later they were still waiting. They had heaved on the line, gaining a few inches, and linked arms, running back and forth, port to starboard, at least a dozen times. Everything they could carry was now at the stern but still *Esteban* adhered to the bottom like it had grown from the sandbar instead of plowed into it. As time passed, Bobby became more and more despondent.

"This is all my fault," he confessed once again.

They were sitting along the portside bench. Warren realized he didn't have to lean out and see the expression on Bobby's face or appreciate the true remorse the man felt at his mistake. "Fault," Warren said. "My fault for putting us here in the first place. Javert's fault for being a greedy bastard. Freddie and Myron's fault for helping me when they probably knew it was a fool's errand. There's always plenty of fault to go around. I think we should make another pot of coffee and eat some sandwiches. Right after we haul around on the line one more time and see if we can gain an inch or two."

He stood and walked to the coil of line and tossed the end to Freddie, then loosened the portions held tightly in the cleats. They assumed their positions along the line and began to heave without a word. The line grew taut again and they felt the familiar strain in their arms, backs and legs as they pulled and pressed their bare feet against the deck for leverage. They had attached plastic tie wraps to the line at two-inch intervals and they watched to see if they gained an inch or two with their effort. The line made a squeaking noise. All eyes on the next tie wrap, and when it crossed the transom Warren moved forward, then began to bring the line first around one cleat, then the next, until they could slack off and rest.

It didn't seem that the boat had moved but the tie wrap said it had, so they went below to brew coffee and make sandwiches.

When they all gathered around the table with Warren's crude sandwiches - ham, cheese and mayo on hamburger buns - Freddie said, "That radio of yours. Can it reach Edward Town?"

"Most likely," Warren said. "But who would we call?"

"Some proper authority or other. Warn the women."

Warren shook his head. "The police have a night guy, and a radio. Even if we got them anybody listening could hear us. If Bens heard, he'd know right where to find them."

"So we do nothing."

"We get off this damn sandbar."

Freddie took a bite of his sandwich. "I hate mayo," he said.

Myron grinned. "Shut up, Freddie."

Bobby stood and poured more coffee. He was trembling and the coffee in his cup rippled.

"Feel that?" Myron said.

"Thought it was me," Bobby answered.

"Hell no! We're moving!" Myron ran up the steps and onto the fantail. The kedge line was slack. He untied it from the cleats and began to heave. "Come here! We're loose!"

They weren't free of the sandbar but the wind had freshened slightly and rocked the boat, while the constant pressure from the kedge had gained several inches. They began to heave with fresh energy and when they all pulled together the boat moved again and they gained several more inches. Frightfully slow it seemed to them, but again they brought the line taut and again they gained on it. Then finally there were no more tie wraps. *Esteban* floated free.

Warren did not engage the engine and back off toward the kedge anchor for fear of fouling the prop. They hauled the boat back by hand but it seemed easy work compared to the hopelessness of pulling on what before seemed like dead weight. Minutes later they had the kedge anchor back aboard. The weapons were stored below again and Warren stationed Bobby on the bow with their most powerful dive light. "Shine it about ten feet or so in front as I try to maneuver out of here," Warren told him. "Freddie! Come up here and watch the depth finder. Myron! Douse all the other lights so I get some night vision and see where the hell I'm going."

They were a crew again, and while they would never make Charming Island by sunrise, every minute closed the gap between them and those they held dear.

Warren put the bow out to sea and the Frog's Head Light was soon far astern. He turned north again. "Come up!" he shouted down.

When they had lined up grinning on the life jacket lockers, Warren said, "One more thing to do. Get four of those M-16s out and plenty of clips to test them. Fire a clip through each one, then hand them out and each of you take some practice shots. Nothing to see, I know, but you need to be familiar with the weapon enough to work it without thinking. I'm sure the Fat Man will appreciate our testing of his equipment. I won't even charge him extra."

"You know," Freddie said. "Always wanted to fire an M-16. Heard so much about 'em, but they came so long after my time, ya know?"

"My generation," Warren said. "Haven't fired one since Vietnam, but some things you don't forget, so if you need help bring them up here."

The M-16 is a fairly user friendly weapon and twenty minutes later four of them were firing from the fantail. After several bursts let off almost overhead, he heard Myron yelling, "Keep the damn things off full auto. Just pull one round off at a time. We ain't got anything against the moon!"

If there had been one, Warren thought. But even without a moon the bow wake blew across the water, white and urgent. He had both throttles wide open and *Esteban* seemed more responsive than he ever remembered, though he had retrieved the Bruce kedge and left the sandbank without taking time to inspect the hull for damage. A reckless move, but he didn't want to know if the hull was damaged because he had no time to repair it. Lives were at stake, and if *Esteban* was sacrificed, then that was their luck.

CHAPTER TWENTY EIGHT

Wesley Bens was lying unconscious on the tool shed bench of a Pentecostal church, he lived in a dreamy world of uncleanliness, reliving again and again base and foul acts until his subconscious mind became a squalid, horrifying place where he could not dwell without boundless pain and fear. His sweat-soaked body writhed in protest, while a lifetime of evil gripped him down. And he found no escape. His past upon him.

When he was unconscious these visions ruled him. When he awoke to a semiconscious state the blinding pain behind his eyes and the realization of his own acts of violence and evil filled him with dread so profound he begged for sleep again.

Hour after hour he remained in this state and exhausted himself. Before daybreak he became too weak to cry out.

Rosa stood alongside him and from time to time dipped a soft cloth into a cool bowl of water, bathing Bens' face and neck. She did not speak and her eyes were far more watchful then sympathetic. She feared him even though he was incapacitated. She felt the terror of his dreams almost as if they were open to her. She read them on his face and smelled them in his sweat. This was as close to evil as she ever hoped to be.

She blinked as To-John pulled open the door. "Daylight," she said.

"He lives."

To-John heaved her large shoulders. "The ways of the Lord are mysterious."

"I have to get back to the hotel. Armando and the others will be awake soon. They will miss me and come looking."

"There is nothing to fear now," To-John said, glancing at Bens. "Even if he lives there is a crack in his skull. I will have the German doctor come to look at him when the hospital opens. I will also report this matter to the police. Mr. Cumberbatch will not be happy."

"And today we begin our protest of the dishonest election?"

"Yes." To-John stared down at Bens. "Every congregation on the island has promised to send as many members as are willing. There will be more than one thousand, and with the Cubans we will fill the town with protest."

"And what from Government House?"

"The ears there are listening and the back doors open, but they say nothing in public."

Rosa nodded. "It's for the best. They replaced the corrupt election judges and tomorrow will be a new day. We will win a fair election."

To-John's eyes flicked from her face to Bens. "It is possible," she said. "But Javert has made no move yet. He will. He will."

Rosa smiled. "You still have your cane."

The older woman stared openly at the restless form of Wesley Bens. "Love has the power, Daughter. I did wrong to strike this evil man down, but there was no choice. Perhaps the Lord will forgive me, but even so, I will answer to Him. Violence is not our way." She kept her eyes on the Englishman. "If this one recovers, he will never be the same. The cane," she said, "I threw into a fire and when the coals died I took the ball of granite, so smooth and comforting, and dropped it into a blow hole along the sea."

"I'm sorry."

To-John looked up and smiled. "Rosa. We are sinners. All of us. Not just you. All." She reached out a pudgy hand and stroked Rosa's cheek. "It's an incurable disease." She looked back at Bens. "We are alike. He is us. We are him." She tossed her head and reached back to pull her hair tight under the scarf she used to keep it away from her face. "I will pray for this Englishman."

Jacques Leon Du Gard Javert watched daylight creep across the harbor and light the white pillars of the Pink Sands Hotel with soft pink, deepening the dawn around the veranda restaurant and blazing in the white tablecloths and silver. Even Javert's coffee cup was aglow. He sat alone with Todd Slitter. The restaurant had not yet opened for business but the two cooks were at work preparing for a large breakfast crowd. And naturally, they had accommodated Monsieur Javert. Who dared to do otherwise?

"Feel it?" Javert asked.

"What?" Slither was often at a loss with the Fat Man and rarely trusted himself to venture answers to anything that might seem to him oblique, but obvious to Javert. A safe strategy.

"The water is breaking." Javert smiled in a particularly satisfied manner. "The birth of a nation is at hand, and you and I my little friend, will catch the slimy, wiggling infant and put it to right. Make it ours."

This analogy seemed naïve to Slither. Had he not just told Javert that Bens was still missing and no one had seen him for days? His pickup truck was discovered abandoned in a narrow alley behind Clarence Street where all the dopers and hookers lived. Did the Fat Man expect to soil his own hands in the birthing process? How would he accomplish it without the muscle of Bens?

"So," Slither began submissively, "you have found the Englishman then?"

"Of course I have not found him! Imbécil! You were supposed to find him and what have I heard from you? Excuses, excuses, excuses." Javert belched. "He's the biggest hunk of flesh on this island but can you see him? No. No."

Slither cursed himself for bringing it up. "No one has seen him Monsieur. No one. I have asked and searched everywhere. The Englishman has vanished. Puff!"

"Puff! Puff! Everyone knows the crazy black Christians and pathetic Cubans will rally in the streets within hours, and where is Wesley Bens? Disappeared. And who is paying him? Javert is paying him! I pay people, like you, to do nothing. To wander about the town saying puff! Puff!"

"If you have any idea where he might be I will look there. I will search."

"You have ruined my morning. My coffee is cold. Don't tell me what you will do, where you will search. Go away! Search. Go puff yourself!"

Slither was only too pleased to comply, and all but ran from the Pink Sands.

The second cook swung through the kitchen door and noticed Javert was red-faced and disturbed about something. He brought more coffee and a fresh plate of pineapple and golden papaya, sliced thick and soaking in sugared juice. "I'm sorry to have waited so long to attend to you," he apologized.

"Nothing," Javert said. "Nothing. I think it will be a long day."

"Ah," the cook observed. "Most of them are."

Sergeant Gladstone Cumberbatch had ordered every policeman on the force to report early that morning and they had formed into two tight ranks in the small parade ground near the flagpole. They had been told to don their full dress uniforms with starched white shirts, Sam Brownies and truncheons. Their gleaming white bucks were freshly polished, worn below knee-high white, gartered stockings and pleated Bermuda shorts. The black skin of their knees, arms and serious faces in deep contrast, below the bills of their distinctive red baseball caps with the Charming Island Police insignia sewn on their fronts.

Citizens passing by that morning sensed a more serious determination in the ranks of the policemen. People knew them all by their first names, but this morning no one called out to them or remarked on why they stood so straight and looked so official.

"Attention!" Staff Sergeant Moss called as Cumberbatch stepped from the small office and into the yard.

Normally now, he would let them stand easy. But not today. Instead he came to attention himself and allowed time for his serious dark eyes to travel along the ranks and rest a moment on each face. The eyes of every man was unfocused and still.

"Officers," Cumberbatch began. "This day is one you will tell of to your grandchildren and one you will remember until death. This is a day of decision. Tomorrow we vote. Today we keep the peace. We citizens who lived peacefully in this place since our slavery were recently deceived in a dishonest referendum on that same freedom. And we, the officers of the law in this place, are empowered and responsible to see it does not happen again."

Cumberbatch's voice faded as thunder across an endless sea. The ranks remained still. When he spoke again his voice had softened and the men strained to hear his words. "Our people will be in the streets today, and we will march before them to keep the peace. Hold your heads up. Be serious. No skylarking or posing for pictures. Tend to your duty at all times. Be prepared for trouble." Again he paused. "We've all heard rumors of violence, strikes and marches by various groups. Do your duty wherever you are assigned today. However, should the situation become grave, I will sound the emergency siren there." He pointed needlessly to the high pole on which the device was mounted. "If you hear it, stop whatever you are doing and come here at the double. And I don't care if you're fighting a fire or a league of Pentecostal church ladies, come immediately. Is that understood?"

Cumberbatch waited. The ranks remained silent. "I said!" he boomed. "Is that understood?"

"Yes Sir!"

Cumberbatch smiled. "Better. Much better." He turned to Sgt. Moss. "Give them their assignments."

Cumberbatch executed a perfect about-face, and marched stiffly back inside.

Captain Jorge cracked the warehouse door and stepped out into the dawn. Torn ribbons of cloud near the horizon were all that stood in the way of an oddly benign pink light, painting sky, pier, and warehouse. He drew in a fresh breath and made a fateful decision. One he had postponed too long, he thought, and backed inside, closing the door gently behind him.

Upstairs, he addressed the commando team in a light tone of decision. "We are done waiting for Bens," he said. "There is a mission to accomplish and I'm afraid he has lost focus since his injuries. Or he may even have been apprehended. The town seems peaceful enough and according to our earlier information, this is the day before the repeat independence referendum. I'm going now to find this Javert and see what he knows. Wait for me. When I return, we are done with this dark hole one way or the other. We were sent here to disrupt this election by whatever means we deem appropriate and that we will do in a few hours whether Bens, or this Javert, or anyone else is involved."

"Si, Señor!" the men shouted. They were tired of waiting.

"Muy bien," Jorge responded. "Now get your gear ready. We move with full packs. Leave nothing behind and make sure you have plenty of clips handy so you can reload quickly. Our intent will be to keep civilian casualties to a minimum but destroy any police presence with deadly force. Kill anything in uniform. The rest will run and hide."

Capt. George threw them a casual salute and dashed out the door and down the wooden stairs. For the first time since he'd landed on Charming Island he felt completely confident about the mission. He'd always respected Bens - a brave man - but one he thought unpredictable, even deranged in the manner of a killer not a comrade in arms. Jorge was a soldier and Bens was a freak.

Jorge had left his AK-47 behind but wore his uniform and sidearm. He was not afraid of Javert or anyone else on this backwater island. Let them see how a soldier went into harm's way. Let them see what was in store for them if they failed to obey or step aside. We are Cubans. He smiled within. The only true communists left in the world. The Russians had eaten themselves up with corruption. The Chinese sold out for money. And the North Koreans, the damned NKs, were simply nuts. A half dozen American subs loaded with nukes sat even now at the bottom of the Sea of Japan waiting to turn North Korea into uninhabitable desert for a million years. Idiots. And these people on Charming Island, these ex-slaves his Spanish ancestors brought here to tend their crops and do the heavy work, would learn how a true communist state does its business. And if they had any sense they would fall into line and reap the benefits of socialism.

He wasn't entirely sure where to find Javert, a fat man Bens had described more as a greedy manipulator than a politician. All well and good. Let him be as inept as Bens himself. He smiled. A fish nailed him to his own boat. A tourist clipped his balls. Could a fat man be dangerous?

The map of Edward Town Jorge had studied did not include the names of most of the buildings, but the Pink Sands Hotel was marked and Jorge decided to begin there. He strolled up the broad steps to the veranda and halted to get his bearings.

A commando in full camo wasn't too astonishing a sight in some cities of the world, but on Charming Island it was akin to a unicorn galloping through the streets carrying a naked lady riding side-saddle. Long before Captain Jorge mounted the hotel steps every wakeful eye in Edward Town was upon him.

The Captain marched into the hotel and up to the registration desk and confronted Nelson Forsythe, the day manager. "I'm looking for a fat man," he said in heavily accented English.

Mr. Forsythe - he was always addressed as Mr. Forsythe, even by his wife - took a dim view of camo-man, and after glancing briefly at him, returned to his task of entering upcoming guest names into the computer.

Jorge had little experience with being ignored and raised his voice. "I said, I'm looking for a fat man!"

For his part, Mr. Forsythe had little experience with rudeness. "Keep a civil tongue in your head, laddie, or you will be asked to leave the premises."

There was a pause.

The only sound being the clicking of the keys as Mr. Forsythe went on with his work.

Jorge was clever enough to know that the next move was his and if he made it a violent one it might not be wise. On the other hand, this hotel clerk needed a lesson in humility. You simply did not talk to a captain in the Revolutionary Army of Cuba in this manner.

Capt. George withdrew his sidearm and slammed it onto the desk with enough force to echo throughout the lobby and leave a deep gouge in the polished mahogany.

Mr. Forsythe's voice trembled. "Are you some kind of lunatic?"

"I am asking you a question. I want a fat man."

Mr. Forsythe, who had never seen a pistol close up, studied it for a moment. An ugly thing, he thought. But most likely efficient. "We have as many fat men here as anywhere," he answered.

The Cuban captain was astonished that this frail old functionary seemed unaware of the threat of arms and without fear, answering once again with evasions instead of compliance. He lifted the pistol and placed its barrel on the bridge Mr. Forsythe's nose. "You can die for this fat man," he said.

Mr. Forsythe brushed the pistol aside as if it were a buzzing fly and went on typing.

Foolish bravery, Jorge wondered? Or was the guy simply an idiot?

Again there was a long silence.

Jorge wanted to shoot the bastard. His blood was up. Why not just begin the revolution right now with a hotel clerk? However, Jorge kept his cool, pivoted on the heel of his combat boot and marched back outside. Later he would hang this clerk.

During the time Jorge had been addressing Mr. Forsythe, Farley Sander was watching. Farley was the first policeman in his family, who were among the original slaves brought to the island. He had married a mulatto girl of eighteen and together they produced seven children - four boys and three girls. Farley was proud of the boys but loved his daughters with a passion he never knew he possessed. Like most people acquainted with Mr. Forsythe, he disliked the man. But nobody carrying a firearm and with a foreign accent was to threaten Mr. Forsythe or anyone else while Farley Sander was in the vicinity. Standing behind rose bushes near the bottom step of the hotel, Farley waited until the commando passed by.

Without a sound, or any preamble, Farley stepped quietly out behind Captain Jorge, and gripping his truncheon two-handed, swung toward the Cuban's lower spine at the small of his back. Though not intending any fatal injury, there was a sound similar to train cars coupling, and Jorge crumpled in the dirt. He had been replacing his pistol in its holster at the time and it spun from his hand, landing several inches away. By some miracle of palsy, or involuntary tremor, the hand twitched in the direction of the gun and Farley delivered a second two-handed truncheon blow, this time to Jorge's head. Witnesses later described that sound as wet or squishy.

Captain Jorge Pimentel was killed in action, subduing the native forces of the British Commonwealth nation of Charming Island. He was the first casualty, if you didn't count Wesley Bens, who was also bludgeoned in the head by an islander.

Less than an hour later, Mr. Forsythe informed Javert that the dead Cuban commando had been asking for him. Javert asked Mr. Forsythe to keep this information to himself, which elicited a shrug of indifference. Anyway, plenty of people knew about it already.

Javert then quickly called a meeting with his staff of regular troublemakers, part-time troublemakers and those who he paid only on occasion. They met in the office of his suite, where he had cautioned them to keep off the furniture and stand quietly.

After listing some of their sins and appealing to their poverty and his past benevolences, he instructed them on the day's activities, the center point of which would be the ten o'clock "March for Freedom" that he had outlined for the police and given as a press release to the newspaper, hoping for in-depth coverage with accompanying photographs. He'd suggested that his new and original speech before the statue of Sir Edward Charming would be worthy of quoting, and had enclosed the complete text with the news release, together with an 8x10 glossy of his smiling face. He tagged the photo "Jacques Javert, Author of Island Freedom."

He told his followers about the Pentecostals, who also had permission to march, and said he would not be disappointed if there was some unfortunate clash between the two groups, suggesting in a mild way a certain level of injury might be expected against over-wrought females much given to religious hysterics.

This revelation was received with trepidation by the rank and file, since some had already encountered the hysterics of Pentecostal females in the Tortuga bar fight and come away with injuries still unhealed. Javert did not seem to hear their quiet sighs or see the pairs of rolling eyes. They were dismissed.

Slither remained.

"Still no sign of Bens?" Javert inquired.

"Vanished."

Uncharacteristically, Javert stood and came forward around his massive desk and placed a porkish hand on Slither's shoulder. "You then," he announced, "are in command."

"In command?"

"Yes." He smiled in a menacing way. "Don't disappoint me. We need raucous behavior that turns to chaos. And you must watch for *Esteban*. She has gone to Guadeloupe to fetch my arsenal and I've been notified that the transfer went without incident there last night. She should have been in port by now. Send someone to me the moment she arrives. I do not trust Captain Will, and it's only too probable he will attempt some kind of skullduggery."

"The Capitan is no fool," Slither allowed.

Javert removed his hand, brushing Slither's cheek in a rough manner. "Perhaps so," he said. "That means you better be smarter. Understand?"

"Of course, Monsieur. Of course."

"Go then. Make no mistakes. We can have no mistakes today."

Slither turned to flee but stopped short of the door. "Monsieur Javert. What if Bens does show up?"

Javert's face darkened. "What makes you think he will come now?"

"I don't think it. I only know that he has a habit of appearing when he wishes to appear and disappearing when he wishes to disappear. There is little I can do against him. You want no mistakes. I want no mistakes. Bens is an evil and powerful man. What will I do?"

Javert swore under his breath and lumbered to the window, overlooking the harbor. After awhile he said, "Do you have a relationship with this Cuban who owns the Tortuga?"

"A relationship?"

"Idiot! Good speaking terms. Bad speaking terms. Will he hug you or kill you on sight?"

Slither disliked being called an idiot and said without thinking. "I work for you. That answers the question."

Instead of anger, Slither was rewarded with a rare chuckle. "I suppose that is true," Javert said in a mild tone, then turned to face the little man. "But could you speak to him about Bens? Give him what you know and maybe explain that I, and others, would not deem it a misdeed if the Englishman met with an accident. Understand?"

"Yes."

"Orizondo has weapons. The Cubans have been hoarding them for years. One more reason for me to wait impatiently for Captain Will. However, he might be tempted to take care of Bens for us should he suddenly appear. Understand?"

"Yes, Monsieur."

"Fine. Then tell him and perhaps we will all be safer, huh?"

Slither nodded and left the suite. On the stairs to the ground floor he drew his first deep breath. Now he was to arrange Bens' death. Well, it didn't make him too depressed. Somebody had to kill the bastard.

Rosa had managed the impossible, slipping into the Satisfaction Bay Club suite without waking Judy Ann, Ruth, or even Armando, who was a light sleeper. Her long, slim fingers warmed themselves around a cup of café con leche on the balcony as day broke and the sea was transformed from dark silver to pink and then dancing aquamarine. She watched the fishing boats leave harbor and had even been allowed to carry her own tray of coffee, hot milk and cups to the room. While the waiter was determined, she explained that her roommates needed to sleep awhile longer, especially her exhausted son who was recovering from a cold. A little white lie to protect him, she thought. But even that pricked at her conscience.

The day was upon them. All they had set in motion would be in motion. All they feared loomed just ahead, and somewhere - her gaze swept the sea - Warren was lost in the emptiness. She sipped her coffee and prayed he would arrive in time. Bens was incapacitated but it did nothing for the enigmatic fears hidden in the shadows.

Always she saved a private piece of herself. The inner place where no one came and no one was invited, even Warren. If he left her or rejected Armando, she might retreat there and heal herself until she went on without him. But that place seemed gone this morning and she wanted more than anything to see a white speck on the horizon and know that *Esteban* carried him back to her.

Inside she heard a door open and bare feet on marble.

She turned to see the sleepy eyes of her son. He awakened easily but came fully awake at a measured pace. "Good morning," she said.

He climbed onto her lap and curled his knees. Again his eyes closed and she felt his warm breath on her breast. A rare moment, she thought. When Warren was away the boy was more likely to act his age, without posturing to prove his manhood to the man he wanted as a father. Rosa kissed the back of his head and inhaled the musty smell of boy and wished she could turn back the clock and repeat his infancy. Or, she thought, have another baby. One of Warren's. Never, he had said. She smiled. Never say never, she had heard a diver say once on the boat. It was a good thought. There was wisdom in it. Never say never.

"I'm thirsty," Armando said.

"Well, there is coffee or water," she answered. "I can call room service for juice, or breakfast if you're hungry."

"Yes."

"Yes what?"

"Yes, all of it." He snuggled closer.

"Then you have to let me up."

"No. I'm comfortable."

She relaxed and held him, prolonging their closeness, dissipating more and more with each passing year. The past weeks had drawn deeply on her strength, more than anytime in her life. The darkest day came when she first saw Ruth Van Doren. She was beautiful and carried her age with such careless ease. Rosa saw immediately what Warren felt for her. And it went so much deeper as she began to know the woman. A woman of stature, she'd thought. One who could stand up to a monster like Bens, and yet, be a lady - educated, experienced in powerful things in powerful places like the United States, where Rosa had never been. Next to Ruth, Rosa felt humbled and weakened, like a dark dandelion in a row of orchids.

Even worse, she had come to admire the woman and to see the goodness and longing in her. She was lonely since the death of her husband and Rosa immediately saw the sensible solution Warren offered. Rekindle the youthful love they'd had. Such a thing happened often enough and Rosa found no wrong in it, except for her and Armando.

Since Ruth arrived, she'd noticed a change in Warren. His laziness and insensitivity were less obvious. He dressed better and seemed to remember his manners more often. The men around him - Freddie and Myron especially - were more likely to ask his advice and listen to it when given. And he treated Armando more like a son, allowing him privileges on the boat and giving him responsibility he'd begged to have for a long while.

He even seemed content with the Whites, tourists he'd so often scorned, mocking them before they even boarded the boat. Now they came to the house and seemed to share everything. And in a rare moment of self-pity she thought the only one he scorned was her. The very one who loved him beyond endurance and life itself.

She fought back tears. Never, she thought, never will I cry for him. I love him, and the only thing that can take it away is if he rejects Armando. Grant me peace, she prayed.

"What, Mother?" Armando lifted his head.

"Nothing," she said. "Stand up now and I will order your breakfast. See if the others are awake."

Armando walked toward Ruth and Judy Ann's bedroom just as they opened the door and filed out. He turned back and said, "They are awake."

Rosa ordered a large breakfast for all four of them. Half an hour later they ate mostly in silence, and afterward Judy Ann donned her bikini and started to leave for the pool. "They can't possibly have meant that we can't bask," she said.

"Of course they did," Ruth replied.

"Look at me," Judy Ann said. "I spent a week in the pink stage. Now I'm just becoming golden, perfectly done, like a properly toasted muffin. I'll regress if I can't keep it up."

Ruth said, "Yes. You are perfectly cooked, like a grilled pancake."

"A fine roasted chicken breast," Rosa added with rare levity.

"I think Myron is right," Armando chimed in. "You do have the perfect ass."

The laughter drowned out Rosa's scolding, and Armando smiled at his own wit.

Judy Ann shrugged. "How do they get started so young?"

"They don't," Rosa said, glaring at the boy, "if their mothers get hold of them."

Judy Ann snatched her colorful tote and started for the door.

"Wait," Ruth said, turning to Rosa. "What's happening today?"

"The vote is tomorrow," Rosa explained again. "We have new election judges and now the government will supervise every ballot place. It will be honest. Today is the day to show our support for them and keep things here as they are, not as Javert and others want them. We are happy. We are free. Independence has nothing to offer us but men like those who want only to exploit us. We began here as slaves. We are not going back."

"I understand," Ruth said. "But if you have independence, you have better freedom, don't you?"

"I have never been to your country," Rosa said. "I only know what people say that come here from the United States. It's more than just a sun tan or to get away from working for awhile that brings them. They talk of a different kind of freedom than independence. Maybe I'm not the one to explain it but they talk about the way things are, like they want to be away from things we are free from here." She began to clean the room by gathering cups and plates, stacking them on the room service trolley. "I don't know how to say it. Their talk is about taxes, laws, unfairness they feel. Like their government is against them. Always they say how they need to get away, and so often they want to stay where life is more simple." She paused. "But they go home."

"Don't you think that's just their need to get away from the pressures of modern life? Experience something different? Have fun?"

Rosa smiled. "I don't need to go somewhere for that. I'm happy here."

Ruth began to open her mouth and then decided to say nothing.

"I will be in the march today against this new independence," Rosa said. "*Esteban* has not returned. All of you must remain here in the hotel until it does."

"Not me," Ruth said. "I'm going with you."

Just as suddenly Judy Ann said, "Me too."

"No. No. Who will stay with Armando?" Rosa asked.

"No one," Armando said. "I'm going with you."

So it was decided, though Rosa felt the old fear again in her stomach.

CHAPTER TWENTY NINE

Martha Ebanks discovered a dusty bass drum in the basement of High Candle Pentecostal. As they marched from the church down High Candle Street, joined by nearly one thousand members of other congregations from across the island, it sounded more like a funeral procession than an anti-independence rally.

They were almost two hours late. It had taken much longer than expected for the church members from outlying districts to gather and be transported to Edward Town. Some came by bus, others by the pickup loads, and those without motorized transport rode donkeys or walked. Yet they had remained patient, waiting until all were present and their assembly was strong and united in spirit.

Rosa's role in the organization of the rally, and her surreptitious strategies with Governor Sir Henry Leach, were known to many, but spoken of only in whispers. As they prepared to march, Rosa, Ruth, Judy Ann and Armando were ushered to the forefront of the crowd. Rosa would lead them. Her protests against this honor were useless.

Behind stood the largest assembly of Charming Islanders ever gathered, waving the British Union Jack and a sea of swinging banners and signs. Independence No! God Save the Queen! Vote No! For God and Country! Javert Sucks! This last was held by one of Orizondo's Cubans, who was told to go back to his own group and not mix in with Pentecostals. To-John, who had forgotten her pledge of peacefulness in the excitement, threatened to shove his sign somewhere uncomfortable, and he retreated.

The plan was to move down High Candle toward the statue of Sir Edward Charming and surround the platform from which Javert would speak. It was too late for that. Javert had been speaking for more than a half hour and thunderous applause had reached them and much of the city. From time to time Javert's paid crowd got the signal to cheer, whistle, scream, and the sound of it echoed throughout the commercial district and could be heard quite clearly from Sir Henry's balcony, where he seemed to have spent a great deal of time lately. Now he stood silent beside Reggie and several others. They were relieved when the Pentecostals finally moved.

"My word!" Sir Henry exclaimed when he saw them. "They *are* a mob."

Reggie grinned. "Our mob."

"I've never seen them carrying the Union Jack. Where did they find them all?"

"Some appear handmade," Reggie said. "God bless them."

"But will it be enough? Can it translate into no votes tomorrow?"

Reggie shrugged. They could only hope. A second election so soon was deemed a significant risk by the local Political Section and by Whitehall.

Below, the Pentecostals had nearly reached the park. Javert, it seemed, had no sense of restraint or timing and continued to harangue the boughten crowd. He was an animated speaker for such a large man, pounding the podium to make his pleas for freedom, liberty, and independence from the heavy yoke of British imperialism. And American imperialism, coming by way of the same language. One of Javert's issues was the use of English as the island's official language, and though most spoke it well, French and Spanish should be equal with English so Charming Island became more like Canada with multiple native languages. Someone had even suggested an Indian dialect used by the Caribs, who inhabited the island before its "discovery" by European sailors not long after Columbus. Problem was, there weren't any Caribs left.

Even one of the Pentecostal signs read: Vote No! Votéis No! Votas No!

Martha's drum beat a quicker rhythm. The people quickened their step, surrounding Javert's assembly, marching in place, slamming one foot hard on the ground each time the drum sounded, and as it grew louder the stomping increased to match. Voices rose in unison, "Vote No! Vote No!" until Javert's voice disappeared and the loudspeaker system failed to compete. "Vote No! Vote No!"

The drum. The feet. The voices. The rhythm itself took hold of the people until it became a rolling thunder of synchronized sound, overpowering everything in the town. Cars pulled to the side of the road and small packet boats blew their whistles, people came to their windows and screamed soundlessly into the racket. Cafés emptied of patrons and within less than fifteen minutes the streets were crowded curb to curb and many were cheering or stamping their feet with the Pentecostals.

Rosa, Ruth, Judy Ann and Armando had linked arms and stomped together and felt the thrill of the crowd, now of one mind, unified and dedicated to "Vote No!"

Capt. Jorge had left his commandos in the warehouse. Sergeant Eduardo Lara was in charge of them until he returned. But Jorge hadn't reckoned on Mr. Forsythe or Officer Farley Sander and his deadly truncheon. His body was removed to the hospital morgue long before Sgt. Lara had begun to worry about his delayed return.

When Lara did finally worry, he realized the Capitan had left no orders. Even worse, all hell seemed to be breaking loose outside. They had no windows but finally Lara could resist no longer. Remain hidden, was Jorge's last order, but did that hold even if it sounded like thousands of people were tearing the city apart?

Lara left the remaining four men in the closed room and slipped down the stairs to crack the door and peer at the scene outside.

Lara was shocked. The civilian population seemed to be in riot. Lawlessness and even violence had spread into the streets. All manner of noise, disorder and wild behavior ruled surging crowds of sign-waving demonstrators. At a large park about a quarter mile from the docks, Lara spotted a fat man screaming into a microphone, completely surrounded by mobs of women waving banners, signs, and British flags.

Sgt. Lara closed and locked the door, then returned to his men.

"Women?" Jose Santos asked.

"Not your kind of woman," Lara said. "Older. Fatter."

"What's the matter with them?"

Sgt. Lara shrugged. "Part of the referendum? I don't know. Any more than I know what happened to Capt. George."

"Maybe he was trapped somewhere behind the crowd or they took him hostage," Joaquin Noceda suggested.

"Don't be stupid. The Captain was armed. He's not the hostage of fat women."

"I know one thing," Santos said. "Capt. George wouldn't give up without a fight or leave us for long. Something has happened to him."

Faint sounds of the riot seeped into the room like the sound of a party drifting across water. "I suppose you are right," he said. "And if he is in danger, we must go and look for him."

The men began to shuffle back into their gear.

"No," Lara said. "Leave everything here but weapons, plenty of ammo and a couple grenades apiece. Five of us are enough. We need to be able to move fast." He grinned. "Comrades! We are Cubanos! For the revolución!"

Dust stirred around their feet as they made for the door.

In the tool shed Bens came to himself and sat upright. His mind cleared as if it had traveled far away. He felt like himself and remembered everything, but viewed it differently. It seemed to have happened long ago, losing much of its passion and fervor. This new clarity brought him a sense of well-being, even peace. His spirit, so often troubled and wrathful, was pacified and soothed, bathed in the coolness of peace. This came in a peculiar way he had never experienced, like everything he knew before was the nightmare and this day was the reality. Bens sat on his bench pain-free and smiling.

He swung his legs down and stood. There was no pain inside his head. There was no pain in his groin. Even his foot seemed more flexible and strong. He wiggled his toes and then hopped around the room, laughing.

Bens tried to remember what brought him here. He did remember. He remembered too, the Cuban commandos. What day was it? He had no way of knowing. The churchyard was deserted when he peered out of the door. He walked to the church. It was empty. He stood awhile on the front porch and then heard the roaring sound of a thousand voices.

For a moment he stood silent, listening, his mind sluggish to the sound. Then he smiled again. Of course, the referendum on independence. The pieces fell into place and Bens remembered everything. "Perhaps," he said, glancing down at himself, "I shouldn't go to the party naked." He threw back his head and the old church porch resounded with his laughter. When he came again to himself he strolled off down the street toward the noise, secure in his newfound clarity and nakedness. It was good to be alive, to smell the sea breeze, the smoke of charcoal fires, the rich volcanic soil on the path as it curled above his bare feet. He gained strength with each step.

Colour Sergeant Gladstone Cumberbatch was much troubled by the body of the soldier. He had questioned Officer Farley Sander at length but his answers gave no clue as to the soldier's identity and he had no identity papers on him, nor did anyone but Mr. Forsythe spend time in conversation with him. And Forsythe was little help. "Spanish accent?" was all he could offer. An incident he chose to forget, except that he credited Sander with taking action and removing this dangerous renegade soldier before he terrorized the innocent citizens of Edward Town.

Cumberbatch said nothing to Sander, but felt the officer had acted hastily. On the other hand, it seemed he handled himself well against an armed adversary who appeared hostile, threatening a hotel clerk and making demands. Sander hadn't set out to kill the man, only render him harmless. That's a policeman's job, but death should not be the result. It was disquieting, and left no opportunity to question the man and learn his mission.

Because it was a time when Cuban commandos were much in the news and there was a large anti-Castro Cuban expat community on Charming Island, the assumption was made that the soldier was Cuban and that his presence here was no accident and very possibly part of some communist plot or even an invasion by Castro's horde. Cumberbatch didn't discount this possibility. It was, after all, the Caribbean and African strategy employed by the communist dictator of Cuba for some years. Its failure didn't impress the persistent Fidel, who kept exporting his disastrous ideology to other nations where it flopped even more miserably than it did in Cuba. Granada had stalled things for Castro but most believed this to be temporary.

Nevertheless, Cumberbatch was a policeman. He measured the logic of a situation against the facts. And several facts bothered him - one man does not make an army, and who was there on Charming Island to support such an incursion? Javert? Bens? A secret communist organization? He doubted all these possibilities. Something was missing.

But all that must come later. The situation in Edward Town had once again become frenzied. Self-control subverted by furor. His immediate concern was to restore order. The streets were awash with chanting masses and there had been several altercations between small groups but no destruction of property as before. Now was the time to break it up and send everyone home to rest before tomorrow's voting. His small police force would be on full alert then to prevent any tampering with the process.

Cumberbatch voted for independence in the previous referendum, but now he was unsure. His wife's argument was beginning to sway him as she pointed out the tactics of Javert and the independence movement, which seemed driven more by monetary gain than freedom. And freedom from what, she'd asked. Weren't they already in charge of almost everything on the island? Was there a single British policeman? Were British soldiers stationed on the island? Did the government in the UK level unfair taxes or create laws in opposition to time-held freedoms? No, she said. So what's to gain by throwing the Brits out?

Cumberbatch had listened to these arguments before and his objections to them were never that they were foolish, but that they left out the idea of independence. He wanted his people to be the ultimate authority in all things. This brought a smile to his wife's face. "Gladdy," she said. "Nobody is ever that free. We answer to God, to the law, and to our neighbors. We can't vote away responsibility." So now, he wasn't sure. He might even vote against independence.

He did, however, have an immediate responsibility - restore order.

He had blown the whistle and every officer in the Charming Island Colonial Police Force stood before him once again.

He spoke to them in a level tone.

"If this were another country," he began, "we would face these crowds with riot helmets, tear gas, shields, even deadly weapons. But this is Charming Island. We will face our neighbors with our own bodies and remind them that we are their brothers, not their superiors or oppressors."

He allowed himself a slight smile before he continued, "We want what is best for them. Now it is best they return home and come back tomorrow for the referendum to determine our future. In this spirit I want you to act. Do not contribute to the violence. Just send them home. One at a time if necessary. Talk sense to them, but be serious. You are policemen. You enforce the law. Our duty is not to harm but protect. We will wish them well, and at the same time wish them goodbye until morning. Are there any questions?"

Farley Sander had not been scolded by Cumberbatch but felt the need to justify his action against the soldier. "I regret what happened at the Pink Sands, Colour Sergeant," he began. "I was afraid. Did not mean to kill him. Please accept my apology." He paused. "All of you. Please."

A few heads nodded. Cumberbatch said, "No need to worry about that, Farley. Most of us might very well have done the same in your place. No one has used a firearm in anger on this island in my lifetime. Maybe not since the time of the pirates. A soldier with a weapon is not a common sight and what happened to him at the Pink Sands was brought about by his own belligerence. Think no more about it."

There was a shuffling of feet and grunts of approval.

"Now," Cumberbatch continued, "listen carefully. We will act as a unit. Move together. Stay together. Talk to our neighbors. Tell them to go home now. The issue will be decided by rule of law tomorrow at the ballot boxes, not in the streets. Listen for my orders. No matter what happens, even more violence or gunfire, we will not be turned from our mission to disperse the crowds and end the disorder. Clear?"

"Yes, Sergeant!"

"Very well. I have decided we will remain in close formation, four abreast. Listen for orders. I will call the cadence myself. I wish to hear each foot striking in unison as if you are on parade. Eyes front. Truncheons at the cross chest for defense only unless you hear an order from me to the contrary. This is important. You understand?"

"Yes, Sergeant!"

"Very well. Form up."

In the town, chaos.

More than one thousand Pentecostals had mixed with several hundred Javertistas, fizzing and exploding like sodium in water.

In the beginning the Pentecostals had maintained calm, chanting their "Vote No!" refrain, but one of Javert's worthless fellows struck a woman on the mouth, split her lip and broke off two of her front teeth. Another of his friends drew a knife, slashing like a madman he cut his way into the crowd of Pentecostals, who had no place to go and in the press no hope of avoiding the long blade. Blood splattered the faces of a dozen or more, arms flailed and it seemed to be raining blood. The chants turned to screams of agony.

Judy Ann was down and Armando held her there until the main thrust of the crowd passed. Her knees were skinned raw, her clothing torn and dirty, but she sustained no lethal wounds. Armando himself was injured only when someone stepped on his hand and broke his little finger with a stomach-wrenching snap. He'd cried out but stayed with Judy Ann until Rosa and Ruth finally made their way to them. Ruth's face was covered in blood, but not her own. She fumbled to use an emery board to make a splint for Armando's finger.

They pulled Judy Ann and Armando to their feet. "Come quickly!" Rosa said. "There are foreign soldiers."

Few in the milling crowd had noticed the small commando unit. Sergeant Lara had them form a wedge, and with rifles at the ready, plowed through the crowd toward the podium where Javert stood staring aghast at the mêlée. He was in the best position to observe the entire scene and when he spotted the troops his first thought was that they must be British, but their commander was shouting orders in Spanish.

The small disciplined unit sliced the crowd with vicious force, like the bow of a speeding boat knifes the sea. Javert was fascinated and at the same time frightened. They were moving toward him. The screeching crowd was so loud he had to shout in Slither's ear. "See the soldiers?"

Slither nodded. He had seen them and had not mistaken them for British troops. "Cubans!" he bellowed.

Javert's face paled at the word. How could this be? "Bens!" he roared at Slither.

Slither shrugged. "We must get out of here."

Wherever he looked, Javert saw only pandemonium. There was no way out. In fact, they were better off here above the madness. "Wait until there is a chance," he said.

"The soldiers!" Slither barked, kicking a skinny podium climber in the teeth.

"Maybe they are coming to rescue us."

"Maybe they are coming to kill us!"

Sgt. Lara and his men moved with precision toward the platform. Javert and Slither could do little more than watch their measured approach. Faces came clear now and Javert marveled at the lack of emotion and eyes front precision of trained soldiers. It unnerved him, and the crowd as well, it seemed. They separated, peeling away before them.

When they reached the platform, the three soldiers in the rear turned and faced the crowd. Lara stared up at Javert. "Are you the man Javert?" he asked.

"Si," Javert said, hoping to ingratiate himself by using Spanish.

"I am Sergeant Eduardo Lara of the Revolutionary Army of Cuba under direct orders of El Presidente for Life His Excellency Fidel Castro. You are now installed as the leader of this nation. Please come with me."

"Where are we going?"

"To the seat of government where we will install you as El Presidente and kill the imperialistic English dogs who oppress the nation."

"Are you crazy?" Slither said before thinking.

Lara glanced at Slither, then addressed Javert. "Who is this hijo de puta?"

"My associate, an employee. Mr. Slitter." Javert stared at Slither. "Who needs to shut his mouth."

Sgt. Lara grinned. "We will handle that for you."

In an effort to extricate himself, Slither made it worse. "I didn't mean 'crazy' in the sense of mental illness but only that a takeover of the legitimate government, especially a move on Government House, would be pretty stupid since British ships are never far away and with a helicopter loaded with Royal Marines it seems the five of you might be exaggerating your military capabilities." He paused and tried to smile. "That's all I'm saying."

Lara's English wasn't polished but he understood this speech well enough. He withdrew his pistol and pointed it at Slither's chest. "You have a big mouth. Shut it."

Slither needed no further convincing and stood silent for several seconds while Lara seemed to be making up his mind about shooting him now, or later.

Javert sought to defuse the confrontation. "Sgt. Lara," he said. "We are an unarmed population. Weapons were supposed to have been delivered to us last night or earlier this morning but there's been a delay." He spread his arms out above the crowd. "None of these people have weapons and you can maintain order without violence. Mr. Slitter's speech is not very diplomatic, but I think he does have a point. Why risk yourselves and invite failure when you, shall I say we, are the only armed force on the island? We can disqualify the vote tomorrow if it goes against us and take power during the confusion. Isn't that better? Wouldn't that have been closer to your orders, however they came about?"

"They came from Cuba, from our Captain and some British soldier of fortune, Wesley Bens."

"Bens!" Javert blurted.

"He disappeared," Lara said. "Our captain, Jorge, is also missing."

Javert glanced quickly at Slither to assure his silence. "I think you should know Sergeant that your Captain was killed by the police."

"I don't think so," Lara said.

"His body is in the hospital morgue if you would like to claim it."

For the first time Lara's troops turned their heads and stared at Javert. The fat man held their gaze.

"No," Lara said. "Impossible."

"Sergeant," Javert continued. "I am not in the habit of making up stories. This Jorge went into the hotel, in search of me, I believe, and became involved with the reservation clerk in some manner and drew his pistol. He didn't harm the man but a policeman outside later clubbed him with a truncheon. He died." Javert shrugged. "That is what people are saying. I wasn't there at the time."

"Truncheon? What is this?"

"In America I believe they are called billy clubs."

"Do you speak Spanish?" Lara asked.

"Si Señor, but I don't know this word in Spanish. It's just a stick - club - used by police."

"Ah, cachiporra. Why didn't you say so?"

"I'm sorry."

Lara stared hard at Javert. "You are telling me that my Captain, a highly trained guerrilla fighter, was attacked and killed by an unarmed native policeman?"

"Yes, but he wasn't unarmed. He had the truncheon," Javert persisted.

For a second Javert thought perhaps he would be the one shot.

The crowd was pressing, milling, some individuals nearby listening to this exchange. Lara turned his men back to face them. Finally Lara asked, "Are you ready to leave, Señor Javert?"

"Yes," the fat man said. "Let us go quickly."

The crowd had quieted down but as Javert was helped to the ground by Slither and one of Lara's men, they fell silent. Into this vacuum came the high, tenor voice of Wesley Bens. "By the authority of the High Council of Ovindim I command you to disperse. Put violence and disorder behind you or answer to Bonnie Loca. Return to your homes or be damned!"

Bens was no more then fifty yards away, astride an underfed horse that stood splay-footed at the edge of the square where High Candle street ended. Lara recognized him immediately and said, "Bens. Naked and talking crazy."

"He must've found Jesus," Slither said.

"Don't be an idiot," Javert told him. "The man is Satan's first cousin."

"Brothers and sisters," Bens began a second time, his clarity expanding inside his mind to include all mankind and the universe itself. "Harken to my voice and put aside your differences. Do not give in to hate. Go home."

Rosa was barely a half block from Bens. Close enough to read the expression on his face. She turned to the others and said, "Look at him. He has come to himself."

"No," Judy Ann said. "He's bonkers. Who's Bonnie Loca?"

"Let's get out of here," Ruth said. "This is creepy."

But Rosa stood her ground and kept her eyes on Bens. Finally she said to Armando, "Go to Ruth and Judy Ann. Stay with them."

Armando shook his head no.

"Now!" Rosa barked. "Go."

Armando obeyed and she stared at the other women. "Take him. I have to know this. I will be back soon."

"Don't Rosa," Ruth said.

Rosa smiled at her and pushed through the crowd toward the mounted Englishman.

The crowd was milling now, having lost its focus with Javert down from his platform, the arrival of the soldiers and this naked Englishman on a horse. They allowed Rosa to pass but one of Javert's people had the presence of mind to slap her across the ear as she came close. She did not recognize him, covered her ear and moved on.

Wesley Bens watched Rosa's form materialize before him out of the crowd. At first he didn't seem to recognize her. But a moment later he began to cry.

Rosa took hold of the bridle and looked up into Bens' eyes and whatever fear remained, left her. It wasn't the tears but the shame she recognized. "Do you remember me, Mr. Bens?" she asked.

Bens bowed his head. "Forgive me," he said. "I met a woman from Ovindim in the mountains." His mouth opened to speak again but he faltered.

With her free hand, Rosa reached out to touch his bare leg. "What happened to you?"

Bens sank farther down in the saddle and his voice, which seemed to deepen as he spoke, was soft but clear. "On the bench in the tool shed," he began. "I saw a woman and thought it part of my dreaming except the dreams were terrifying and this woman was gentle. She spoke softly. Her words weren't words we speak. Like touching, but on the inside too. I can't explain it. Do you know what she said to me?" He lifted his head and his eyes pleaded with her. "Do you know?"

She smiled. "Only you can know. It was for you."

He struggled to sit straighter in the saddle. "She said, 'I grant you peace. The peace of Ovindim.'"

"Did you understand that?" she asked. "What the woman said?"

"Yes." He smiled. "It was Bonnie Loca. Soon we will be lovers."

"And what will you do now?"

"I don't know. I feel strange. Different. What happened to me?"

"A large woman with a cane hit you in the head. We thought she killed you."

He smiled. "No," he said, shaking his head. "She saved my life."

Rosa saw that the smile was genuine and spread across his face and settled like luster in his eyes. In her heart she knew Wesley Bens was a changed man. "Would you like to come with us?" she asked.

"No. I must make amends. Do you know the man Javert?"

"Yes."

"Where did he go?"

"He was just here, near the podium. But there are soldiers. Cubans, I think, and they are heavily armed. Why don't you come with us? You can rest awhile and have something to eat and drink. You need clothing and you're still weak."

Rosa was tall, but Bens on a horse dwarfed her. He bent down and took both her hands. A most natural gesture, she thought. These same hands had not long ago seemed terrifying and filthy. "When I have done what I need to do here, then I must see all of you. The boy too. I mean no harm to anyone." He dropped her hands and smiled again. "I think now you should get the hell out of here."

She watched as he and the skinny horse walked toward the crowd, the Englishman's eyes scanning for Javert. The horse angled to the right side of the crushing crowd and shied away from those who were pushing, fighting or shouting. Bens pulled steadily on the reins.

Rosa glanced away, seeking the two women with Armando, but at that moment the Cuban soldiers pushed out from the mob and faced her, Javert at their center. Sergeant Lara shoved her with his rifle butt and she tripped backwards and fell. A second later there was gunfire and Sergeant Lara fell beside her, bleeding from a series of holes in his chest and one in the leg. She rolled away and glanced up. Carlos Orizondo and at least a dozen others were standing or kneeling some yards away and had fired the shots. Before she could think what to do the commandos returned fire and three of Orizondo's Cuban expats crumpled to the ground.

It had taken a moment for those in the crowd to realize what was happening, and where, but once they did they fell silent and let their feet react. Banners flew skyward and everyone seemed to be running in opposite directions, including some who ran toward the groups who had just opened fire.

Rosa remained on the ground, but so many people were now fleeing in panic that the combatants were in danger of being trampled, and so were forced to retreat. The four remaining commandos picked up Lara's body and dashed across the square toward the Café Renaissance, the Sergeant's head jerking at the end of his slack, elongated neck. Orizondo's free Cubans dragged their friends away in the opposite direction toward the Public Dock, where there were stacks of boxes, barrels and coils of plastic pipe to offer cover.

Rosa scrambled to her feet and ran back toward the podium where she'd left Armando, Ruth and Judy Ann. The crowd was thinning but they were gone.

She heard a new sound.

The chest-thumping rhythm of Colour Sergeant Gladstone Cumberbatch's baritone as he called the cadence for his marching force of Charming Island Police. "You'r lef, you'r lef, you'r lef right lef!"

In perfect unison their white bucks pounded the pavement. Their lines were straight, eyes front, hands gripping their truncheons. The sharp white of their starched uniforms caught the sunlight like the sails of a schooner and their movement was magical - stern black faces above the crisp white shirts, strong arms holding truncheons across their chests and black knees above knee-high white stockings lifting and falling in precise measure to Cumberbatch's booming voice.

Even those running away stopped. There was silence. The riot seemed forgotten. As the police contingent moved closer, down the street almost to the square, Rosa's heart pounded in her chest. This was the pride of her people. They needed no votes to declare their independence. No politician had ordered these brave men into the streets unarmed. They marched to their own cadence in order to do their duty to their people in a time of need, and she felt then that all she had wanted was achieved in a moment.

There was a flash in the doorway of the Café Renaissance and the sharp crack of a rifle. Sergeant Cumberbatch flinched but he did not lose step and his voice caught momentarily and then began again as strong as before. Then a second crack and one of the officers in the front rank crumpled. Those in the rear stepped over him and continued on without pause.

Rosa gasped and shouted, "No! No!" She began running toward the café to shield the policemen with her body, spoil the Cubans' line of fire and make them stop.

Then came the sound of hoof beats and Bens, bent over the neck of the emaciated horse, howled like he led a cavalry regiment. The horse's hooves sparked on the hard surface of the square and the poor beast's eyes were wide with fear. Its nostrils flared but it ran like a true warhorse of times past when men fought on horseback.

Horse and rider swept past Rosa so close she smelled saddle leather, but like the policemen, Bens was unarmed. If he only had a sword, she thought.

Again muzzle flashes from the café. A stuttering sound. The remaining commandos fired a burst, and every round caught Wesley Bens full in the chest, and had he been another man he might have toppled from his horse and fallen dead on the street. But Bens was a new man and held the reins and kicked his heels into the old steed's rib cage so that it galloped straight toward the doorway of the café.

There was a sustained burst of firing then and bullets tore into the horse's nose, neck and chest where they seemed to discover a reservoir of bright blood that fountained from the wounds and ran in rivers down the forelegs and blew spume-like sideways into the air. The horse screeched and tumbled forward toward the doorway, unseating the bullet-ridden body of its rider and sending him like a soft projectile into the soldiers crowding inside the door.

The firing stopped.

Rosa watched in horror and when she realized both horse and rider were destroyed she fell to the ground, covered her face and wept.

When she looked up the square was empty. The people seemed to have vanished without a sound.

And then she heard Cumberbatch's voice as clearly as before. Had they not taken cover? She saw them then, marching toward the café from the opposite direction. The square was empty because they had cleared it, moving people to safety before they confronted the commandos. And now they were the only remaining targets. Had they learned nothing from their previous skirmish with the heavily armed soldiers? Had they missed Bens' hopeless ride?

Undeterred and determined to finish the fight, the remaining Cuban commandos filed from the café and stood in line facing the closing squad of policemen. Their rifles were at their shoulders and they were quiet. This would finish it.

As the policemen closed in the same unhurried march, feet striking the hard surface of the square, shrinking the distance between them and the waiting soldiers, Rosa noticed the right side of Cumberbatch's white shirt was bright with blood. He had been wounded.

They marched on, correcting their line slightly, each man in column facing death in perfect order.

Rosa's knees were so weak she could not regain her feet or find her voice. They would all die, and for nothing. It was over now. Why finish it with this one last desperate act? The pointlessness seemed to surpass even the horror.

"Rosa! Stay down!" The voice was Warren's, and came loud from a bullhorn. "Cumberbatch! Right turn! March!"

For some reason no one could determine even later, Sergeant Cumberbatch issued the order and the Charming Island Police executed a sharp and precise right turn, taking themselves out of the line of fire between *Esteban*, now holding position on the water near the square, and the commandos. Onboard, Bobby White, a tourist from Texas, aimed an M-16 at the Cubans. Alongside him an old ex-Navy UDT member named Myron did likewise. On the flying bridge Freddie-the-Frogman hung out into space, ready to fire on command.

"Drop your weapons!" Warren demanded.

And also for no reason anyone could determine later, the Cubans fired.

Three rounds struck the boat. Dozens responded and Bobby, Myron, and Freddie emptied their magazines into the doomed commandos.

A few seconds later all was quiet except for the deep voice of Gladstone Cumberbatch calling cadence and turning his men back again toward the center of the square.

CHAPTER THIRTY

The following day, Charming Island became one of only a handful of British possessions that voted to remain in the Commonwealth. This pleased the Queen of England and she immediately scheduled a visit, though she couldn't remember having been there before.

She telephoned Governor Sir Henry Leach, whom she had knighted some years past. She didn't remember him either, but he was terribly flattered by the call. His prestige at Whitehall was boosted. After all, an independence vote usually went the other way, and the man must have some hidden diplomatic and political skill to pull this off. No one knew he owed his success and new prestige to a dishwasher with whom he'd conceived an illegitimate child.

For his part, Sir Henry was content to bask in the limelight awhile, but knew it was temporary and concluded that he had come off rather well in spite of poor odds. The worst that could befall him now was to remain on Charming Island for the remainder of his career and then be retired to the UK. Or he might get lucky and be posted to Paris.

The next day when election results were first released and they realized the victory was overwhelming, he shared a whiskey with Reggie on his beloved balcony overlooking the town, harbor, and sea.

"To your success, Sir," Reggie had toasted rather formally, lifting his glass above his head.

"Our success," the Governor answered. "And the wisdom of the people." He drank deeply.

After a few moments enjoying the smoothness of the whiskey, Reggie asked, "What now, I wonder?"

Sir Henry grinned. "Now, Reggie, a party."

"Party?"

"A celebration to surpass any celebration in the history of this island. We will empty the treasury and hire musicians and marching bands, jugglers, build extravagant floats, cook tons of food and set kegs of the best English ales at every street corner." His grin turned into laughter. "We will dance in the streets and fix this date in history so that whoever comes here knows that Charming

Island is part of the United Kingdom, by choice, not circumstance. We will fix that star in this heaven of the Caribbean."

Reggie thought this over for a minute, marveling at his boss's rhetoric, which was usually more taciturn. "Need I mention that people were just killed and injured to bring this about? Mightn't this be better postponed until some later time?"

"Absolutely not! The time is now. We need to heal. We won't leave the dead and injured out of this party. It belongs to them too, but celebration is needed now more than mourning. We will memorialize the dead Reggie, and celebrate their sacrifices, but if we don't throw this party we might yet lose this island. Dwelling on the past, let alone death, is no way to build a nation. Our own nation, like so many European powers, too often glorifies what it accomplished centuries ago instead of making something great happen now." He grinned. "Guess I've said that once too often for good politic."

Reggie retrieved the twenty-six-year-old bottle and poured each of them a generous amount. "Well Sir, thankfully you remain Governor of this place." He bowed. "And I bow to your judgment."

They drank together.

The very next day a small group of Pentecostals gathered in what was known as The Mango Cemetery, on a rounded knoll above one of the churches, overlooking the Caribbean to the west. They came to bury Wesley Bens, an Englishman. Most in attendance were native islanders, but Rosa had invited Warren, Myron, the Van Dorens and the Whites. Armando stood beside his mother, studying the rough coffin built by Chester Smythe, an elderly woodworker who built church pews, altars and crosses. What he lacked in skill he made up for in billing leniencies.

Only To-John had red eyes. The rest of the mourners weren't mourning. Since Bens was English they persuaded the Anglican priest to conduct the burial service in that tradition, which he did, and most people thought he did a nice funeral. The rich red volcanic soil that he'd drizzled to form the cross on the coffin lid glittered in the sunshine and Rosa, elected to say a final word, rested her hand nearby on the rough wood.

"We hated this man," she began in a soft voice. "I hated him. Little did we know that he hated himself. In the final moments of his life he saved us. Hate collapses in the face of love. He was an Englishman but deserves a place among us. Who will remember him if not us? Many years from now maybe someone will sit under these old mangos and read his name and wonder." She smiled at To-John. "Our sister has suggested we place a stone here with his name, and under it - Englishman, Friend. That seems appropriate." She glanced up at the four men standing ready to lower Bens into the ground. "God grant his soul peace," she said and walked away.

Wesley Bens was lowered into the warm earth of Charming Island, a place he had come to conquer, now claiming him until he was dust.

Warren disappeared after the funeral. Only Rosa knew where he'd gone but kept it to herself. She had been unusually quiet since the excitement ended, feeling she had arrived at a place where she must decide about herself and her son. People recognized her in the street and even those she didn't know, or who overlooked her before, now nodded politely, spoke a cheery good morning or how are you. For the first time in her life she had standing in the community. She was known, even respected, and decided it felt good. And because it did, everything in her life was about to change under the force of her own will, rather than some capricious wind of chance.

Warren knew nothing of this, intent instead on his mission to rid himself of one Monsieur Jacques Javert. Like Rosa, he decided the status quo was no longer acceptable.

Javert was at his usual table when Warren arrived at the Pink Sands. Unlike most visits they'd had over the years, Warren felt confident, almost fearless.

"Good day, Monsieur," Warren began pleasantly. "Is that café con leche there you are drinking? I think I'll join you." He waved at Javert's waiter, who was always close at hand.

"You seem quite pleased with yourself today, Captain," Javert said in a neutral voice. "Could it be the unfortunate defeat of the independence referendum?"

Warren pulled a robusto from his shirt pocket and indicated to the waiter he should clip it, light it, and then be off to fetch his coffee.

"I think Monsieur, that many things are pleasing me today." He drew deeply on the freshly lighted cigar and blew a fragrant cloud of blue-white smoke into the light breeze. "Most of all, I am pleased that you and I are about to end our long partnership. I have your merchandise ready aboard *Esteban*, and once you have turned over my mortgage papers, we can go our separate ways." He grinned. "To be honest, I had planned to hide it." He shrugged. "But we were in a hurry to get here. Luckily, made it just in time. So, let's finish this."

Javert nodded and sipped his coffee daintily before responding. "Yes, Captain Will. Yes. We have certainly enjoyed a long, and I think often misunderstood, partnership." The Fat Man smiled in his hungry manner. "I am sorry you are so eager to end things between us, since it isn't going to be easy. I no longer have any need for your 'merchandise,' I'm afraid."

This announcement did not have the effect Javert intended. Warren expected it and only smiled now that it was on the table. "Of course, I understand that," he said. "What good is a load of weapons unless you plan to use them? You don't, do you?"

"Of course not," Javert said. "I am not a man of violence. It might even have been better had I ordered them without ammunition in the first place and saved quite a few thousand dollars, not a penny of which I will now recover. You are not the only loser in this transaction."

Warren smiled. "However, Javert, I am not any kind of a loser. You ordered. I delivered. I don't give a damn about your intentions or political ambitions. It was a simple business transaction - the boat for the guns. You got them. I want clear title."

"Captain Will!" Javert threw his arms in the air. "You can't believe there is any way for me to recover even one dollar of all that I've lost. Since what you have brought me is useless, how can I pay?"

"Not my problem. Just do it."

Javert noticed something in the Captain's expression and voice that suggested a refusal was anticipated, and safeguarded against, either by some defensive strategy or even a more dangerous overt maneuver. Too many extraordinary events had taken place lately. Dishwashers were leading political rallies. Hired mercenaries leading cavalry charges on borrowed horses. The damn tourists killing the trained commandos of foreign powers. For once Javert feared he may be an unwilling participant in the Captain's plan. A change in tactics was in order. The Fat Man smiled. "Captain Will, my old colleague. Should we be at each other like this? Two men of the world who have shared so much." He held up a chubby hand. "Don't say it. I know our association is much more a trial for you than for me. I am sorry for that. Unless you are drinking heavily, I enjoy your company. And be truthful. There was a time, not so very long ago, when we were friends, after a fashion. What can we achieve now if we begin to fight?"

Warren signaled for more coffee and continued to smoke, the smile easy on his face. Finally he said, "There will be no fight. I possess the weapons. They are more valuable than the remaining mortgage on the boat. I can sell them anywhere and make a nice profit, while you, who already paid for them in cash, now receive nothing. So then I simply buy back the mortgage with your money." His smile persisted. "You can't know how much pleasure this transaction gives me."

Javert had but one card left to play. "I can refuse to give you the mortgage even for cash."

"You are a son-of-a-bitch Javert, but you aren't stupid. Do that, and you must know you are finished here. It's a small island and you live by a code that includes trust. Even if your debtors hate you, they believe in your perverse kind of integrity. They borrow, you rape them, but they can eventually pay the debt. Start defaulting and see how long you last." Warren rolled a long ash into a convenient flower pot. "And you know what? I'll probably get the boat in the end anyway. It is in my possession."

Javert sat stoic for a long while. Then, beginning deep in his belly, a tremble grew like the first tremors of an earthquake and the Fat Man threw back his head and bellowed with mirth. His laughter shook the table and slopped his coffee. The waiter started forward, then froze. No one had ever witnessed the Fat Man laugh in such a manner. What did it mean?

Captain Will and Monsieur Javert remained there at the table for more then another hour, chatting together and enjoying the fine day and ocean breezes. It was decided that Javert would take delivery as promised and sell the weapons to recover his losses. If the amount was equal to or greater than *Esteban's* mortgage, then all was well. But if Javert could not sell the dangerous cargo for such an amount, then Warren must make up the difference by commissions to Javert on all future dive charters until all bills were paid. As an act of good faith the Fat Man would present the boat's mortgage to the good captain in advance and they would go forward on trust, as they had once in the past.

Neither Javert or Warren believed this for a moment, but both seemed to like the idea of it, and why not? Nobody had a better idea. Now that they understood each other, maybe they would become friends again. After a fashion.

Esteban was moored out in the harbor with Myron and Freddie sleeping onboard to guard the weapons until Warren's confrontation with Javert. An hour after leaving Javert, Warren swam out to the boat fully clothed and climbed onto the swim step.

"Prepare to repel boarders!" Myron shouted to Freddie.

"Wait one," he heard Freddie reply. "Maybe he brought beer."

Warren stood and stepped over the gate onto the fantail. "We got beer," he said. "How could I swim with a case of beer anyway?"

"Buy a dinghy," Myron said.

Warren peeled off his shirt and pants. Kicked his deck shoes, and stood dripping in only his underwear.

"Yeah," Freddie said. "Buy yourself a nice dinghy."

"What do I need a dinghy for? We got cold beer."

"No, we don't," Myron said.

Warren grinned. "Did you look in the small electric cooler under my desk in the office?"

"How dumb you think I am?" he asked. "I knew you had that little hidey hole a long time ago. We checked there. Cooler's gone."

Warren's grin widened. "Not gone. Moved."

Freddie shook his head. "You know, Myron, you're a lot of damn trouble. Guy's got to play a shell game with his own goods just to keep you from pilfering. Ought to be a law."

"There is," Warren said. "We just don't enforce it in his case."

"Okay then!" Myron said. "Where's the flippin' beer?"

"Flying bridge. Bottom of the life jacket locker."

"So it's warm."

"No. I plugged it in."

"Ain't no plug-in there," Myron persisted.

Warren draped his soaking shirt and pants over the starboard tank rack and climbed the ladder to the flying bridge. Freddie and Myron followed close behind. "See?" Warren lifted the life jacket lid, moved several jackets aside to reveal a fire extinguisher and a Man Overboard Buoy next to a blue and white cooler. "Buoy needs juice to recharge, so there's a plug-in." He lifted the lid on the cooler and drew out three iced bottles of Union."

"Damn," Myron said. "I'll know next time."

Warren chuckled, "Won't be there next time."

Freddie hadn't said much, and now after taking a long pull on his beer, added, "Well, guess I won't be around to see where it is."

Warren said nothing.

"You ain't heading back to the States already?" Myron asked.

Freddie dropped onto the portside seat and stretched his legs. "Hell, Myron, been here too long already. You know that."

"Well, Sir," Myron said. "Been one hell of a trip. By time you get on back to Minnesota and make up all manner of shit how you saved this two-bit island from a army of commie commandos and discovered treasure ships, well, hell, rest of us be just small-time characters in your great heroic adventure. If we get mentioned at all amongst the topless native babes hanging onto your ass."

Freddie shook his head. "Sounds more like your kind of story. Tourists will eat it up."

They fell silent awhile, drinking and enjoying the growing heat of the day. Below, the breezes were already beginning to dry Warren's clothing.

"You could stay another week," Myron said.

Freddie shook his head. "Ruth needs to get back anyway. Won't send her alone, plus I got stuff to do."

Warren smiled at him. "We did make a fine team, though, didn't we?"

"Damn straight!" Myron said.

Freddie nodded. "We did that."

Again they fell silent.

"Wouldn't mind another dive on the wreck before I leave," Freddie said. "Think we can manage it?"

"Of course," Warren said. "First thing tomorrow."

"Thanks."

"I ain't goin'," Myron said.

Judy Ann and Bobby White had returned to their own hotel from the Satisfaction Bay Club and packed their bags. Their departure was delayed two days by a mechanical mishap with the Guadeloupe Ferry.

Ruth also returned to her hotel and packed. When Freddie told her about the chance to dive the wreck once more she refused, then began to cry. "I just want to go home," she insisted.

"Don't you even want to say goodbye?" he'd asked.

"No. Just go."

And later when Warren told Rosa they would dive in the morning, she only shrugged and said she needed to go out for awhile. He should stay with Armando. Didn't they have work to do? Was there fuel in the boat? Had he got anything ready, or was he just waiting around for her to do it?

She left their cottage and walked away.

Rosa crossed High Candle Street, jaywalking toward the Tortuga. She spotted Ruth there alone at a table on the sea side of the small café. The midmorning crowd was light, but as she made her way between the tables she encountered Slither, also alone. On impulse she stopped.

"Todd," she said politely, "I hope there is no bitterness between us." She held out her hand to him.

His expression seemed to hover between hope and fear. Her hand might be poised to strike him. "Guess you're happy now," he said. "You won."

"Are you afraid to take my hand, Todd?" She kept it stretched out toward him.

A bit of the sullenness seemed to fade from his eyes. "I ain't afraid," and shook it firmly.

"We all won," she told him. "This is a good place. Not too rich, not too poor. And not too popular. Just right. Now it stays that way. That may hurt some like Javert, but most will be better off and we are left to live as we have learned to live. Not to become waiters and hotel maids, but true islanders who enjoy visitors but don't live for them. Is that so bad for you? Does Javert not still have work for you?"

He shrugged. "Yes. He has things for me."

"I am happy for you," she said, smiling. "I hope they are legal."

He smiled too. "Oh yes. We will exploit this shipwreck Captain Will has found."

Rosa stood silent awhile. "You know about it?"

"Everyone knows. I took the first boatload of locals out on Javert's boat this morning to snorkel it while the water was calm." He shook his head. "An amazing sight. Be sure and tell Captain Will we are all thankful to him."

"But we didn't tell anybody."

"Bacon Hornfisher and Martin found it too, and they took the first few people there in a fishing boat, but more wanted to go so Javert filled his boat a couple of times. He's making a fine profit and has given me a raise in pay." He sighed. "That Captain Will of yours, he's quite a man. We were wondering, did he build the rope ring too? Handy, that. Javert wants me to ask Captain Will if he can construct an underwater mooring pin with a surface float so the boats can tie up without dragging anchors on the reef or tie ropes to the cannon. We need to preserve it. And if you have any influence with the Governor," he said, keeping his face expressionless, "Javert thinks it should be designated a national underwater park."

Rosa knew she might get blamed for Javert's interference. Her attention lately had been on the referendum, Bens and other things, not on their diving charters. But then neither had Warren paid much attention. What would he say? She didn't want to know.

She stared down at Slither and couldn't decide if she wanted to laugh or cry. "I will pass all this on to Captain Will. He will be diving there himself in the morning." She started to turn away, then turned back. "You might mention to the Fat Man that it would be better if he didn't send a boatload of tourists, or anyone else, there in the morning."

Slither nodded. "Yes," he agreed. "It might be better."

Rosa moved on toward Ruth's table. "May I sit down with you a moment?" she asked.

Ruth looked up and Rosa could tell she'd been crying.

Carlos Orizondo had seen her come in and arrived with cuts on his cheek and his left arm in a sling. "A privilege to have you in my café," he told Rosa. "A privilege."

"You are at work?"

"Aw, these?" He lifted his injured arm. "Nothing. Nothing at all. We have our little part of this world back again. These small hurts are nothing. No, nada."

"And your family?"

"All well. I have not seen your Captain."

"Well also," she said.

"Bueno. What will you drink?"

"Coffee," she said.

When he was out of earshot, Rosa turned to Ruth. "Can we talk?"

"Do we have to?" Ruth asked. "I think I know what you're going to say."

Rosa reached across the table and took her hand. "Maybe not," she said. "I know you love him. Your Captain."

"And you?"

Ruth shrugged. "I don't know." Then she smiled. "Maybe I'm just lonely. The world seems empty sometimes, though I have plenty of everything. People who love me. My husband was a good man, Rosa. A fine man. Slow to anger, as they say. Soft-spoken, considerate." She sighed.

"And his death leaves you free," Rosa pointed out needlessly.

"Yes," she nodded. "And I'm sure Warren told you about us long ago." She did not avoid Rosa's eyes. "We were each other's first love, I guess. It lasts. And it matters, I think. But maybe not enough to build on."

Rosa nodded. "All love matters."

"Well, I'm leaving."

Rosa nodded again. "Yes. I'm leaving too."

"What?"

"This is what I came to tell you. Captain Will or Warren Wilson, or whatever he calls himself will marry me now, or never see me or my son again." Her eyes narrowed. "When Bens died I saw it clearly. Bens changed - maybe the hit on the head - but he changed. Afterward his life became a meaningful thing, when before he was evil. I have delayed like Bens, keeping to my old ways so Warren could be pleased with me. No more. I will talk to him. He will marry me and adopt Armando or he will not see me again."

"When will you do it?"

"Before you leave this island. I give him that chance."

Ruth squeezed her hand and dropped it. "I'm not sure I want him either. He's sort of a love speculator. A true buccaneer."

Rosa grinned. "All men are freebooters. They take what they can get for nothing, and then, once they have it, they hold it casually."

"Maybe because we let them," Ruth said.

"Not this man," Rosa promised. "Not one day longer."

The next morning they made their final wreck dive together. Rosa hadn't found an opportunity to prepare Warren for what Slither had told her and she was alone on the boat with Armando when she remembered. Oh well, she thought, she had more important things to tell him and it wouldn't matter if she waited another day to see him upset about Javert stealing his tourist trade.

But she was wrong.

Five minutes after he drifted down onto the *Imperial*, Warren knew the site had been violated. Sea fans were uprooted or ripped, hard corals smashed, cannons scraped with knife blades, soft sponges plucked from their bases, and under the anchor, he even found signs of digging. How could anyone have come here with shovels, prepared for a search? A search for what? Did they think a man-o-war carried treasure? Who were these fools?

The others noticed too, even Ruth, who had come along reluctantly and was acting very odd. Withdrawn and haughty, he thought. Rosa was quiet too, and hadn't bothered to speak to him except in short bursts. She and Armando had slept with "friends" the night before. No explanation. Warren thought they should all be happy now that everything turned out exactly as they wanted, but instead there seemed to be tension everywhere he turned. On the refueling pier that morning he'd bumped into Slither refueling Javert's boat. The little creep was even more mawkish then usual, praising "Captain Will" for all he'd done for the island. He hadn't done a thing and was just glad it was over. He even got to take a couple shots at the bad guys and make some points with Cumberbatch, which was bound to come in handy one day.

Why were they all acting so weird now?

And who in the hell had been on his shipwreck?

Some of these questions would be answered sooner then he imagined.

Meanwhile, after consuming half his air supply flitting from one rapacious rape to the next, he calmed down enough to look around and be amazed once again at his good fortune, beholding something marvelous and rare. The most adventurous of men spent a lifetime seeking a thing this fine, and even if it was no longer secret, it was real, and it was here.

Judy Ann White felt almost as possessive as Warren, and with good reason, since she had actually been the first to find *Imperial*. She wasn't prepared for the emotions it drew from her this day when she realized she didn't belong here. She would soon be back in Texas, telling her friends this incredible story, but even if she returned here next year, nothing would ever match that moment of discovery. And in a flash of insight, she knew this was it. Only that first moment and this was all she would get. It was impossible to tell this. Hopeless.

She reached down a naked hand, diamond wedding ring glittering in the shafted sunlight, and scooped a handful of sand. She remembered what Warren had said, that it wasn't just sand, but history. And while she had spent so many hours snorkeling and gathering things from the ocean, now she was part of it. She was the first in this place to connect men of a distant time to her own experience. It brought tears to her eyes.

This moment might be her last here. It might fade when they were among their family and friends, in their familiar house. She would go shopping, rush from place to place and then one day this would all be a dream, a thing that happened once long ago.

With her other hand she moved the grains of sand and saw the flash of reds, greens, ambers, blacks and browns. It was not enough to look and remember. She wanted something to take, and began desperately filling her BCD pockets with handfuls of sand. When they were overflowing she stopped. No, she thought. Something more tangible.

Warren felt a tugging at his right fin. He turned to see Judy Ann giving him the ascent sign. He followed her to the surface.

"Please," she begged. "Please. Can't I have something to take home to remember I found this ship? I don't mean like gold or anything, just a real piece of something so I won't think later it's all been just a dream."

Warren's first reactions were tinged with anger, but he saw the tears in her eyes and realized she wasn't souvenir hunting but begging for proof of this miraculous event and her vital part in it. "We can look," he said. "Follow me back down."

Warren guessed the most likely possibilities were musket balls, hull nails or maybe even a cannon ball. But the sea was shallow and a thousand storms had battered this wreck over the years, lifting and drifting the sand so that much of what was, is no more, or buried deep. They would need some luck.

He pointed to an area a very short distance on the seaward side of the coral mound that was now the *Imperial.* He reasoned that here the sea might cover and uncover its treasures, and if they got lucky, relinquish a memento for her. He fanned the sand and it billowed, making a small hole. Then he moved and repeated the fanning. Judy Ann watched and then immediately did the same. They worked like this for about twenty minutes until Warren heard a sharp intake of breath and muffled scream.

He swam to Judy Ann. She was on her knees, weeping. In her hand she held a small gold coin. Almost as if it were hot, she thrust it at him.

A minute later he was shaking his head. It was indeed gold. A forty franc Napoléon, with the Emperor's bare-headed likeness on its face: *Bonaparte - Premier Consul.* A thing of no great dollar value unless you possessed a chest filled with them, but of incalculable value to one Texas tourist who was first to find this shipwreck and now the proof of it. He immediately pictured it set in white gold, attached to a thick chain and hung proudly around her neck. If anyone dared to question her shipwreck tale, she carried the proof.

Warren placed the coin in her hand and closed her fingers over it. When they surfaced he would tell her about her luck. Judy Ann had what she wanted most - a bit of antiquity. They might search this wreck for years and never see another gold coin. And Warren guessed this bit wasn't for sale at any price.

When they did surface awhile later, Judy Ann couldn't bear to hold her tongue and Warren had to take hold of her to stop the babbling. "Listen!" he said. "Be quiet about this. No shouting. You and Freddie have the proof and I'm glad you're taking it back to the States. Others know about this site now, and if you don't keep this bit of gold a secret, *Imperial* will be destroyed. Understand?"

She nodded. "But it's not theirs. How can they take it?"

"You just took it."

"But the government."

"Did the government stop you?"

She stared at him, uncomprehending.

"Listen," he said. "If anybody thinks there's gold here, salvage ships will descend on this place like a pack of hyenas, dynamite this reef to pieces, suck them up, grind, sift and sluice them until all that remains here is a memory. Do you want that? Are you listening? This is not an opinion. This is what will happen immediately if one whisper of what's in your hand gets out." They were treading water fifty yards from the boat. "Judy Ann. You need to hide that Napoleon from U.S. Customs when you go home and from anyone else until you are home, and even then, I wouldn't go showing it around just anywhere. It's not the value of the thing but the greed it spawns."

"Don't you want me to have it?" she asked miserably.

"I very much want you to have it. This is your proof and your reward, but if you want others to get the same feeling you had that day when you looked down and saw rows of cannon and knew what this was, then keep quiet. I need months to turn this site into a manageable place for divers. The alternative is destruction. Already people have been here."

"But you want me to keep it?"

"Absolutely. You were the first, and I believe it came to you. Just save something for posterity. Okay?"

They began the surface swim back to the boat when a moment later Judy Ann clutched Warren's arm and stopped him in the water. "What about Bobby? The others?"

"We'll tell them. They'll understand, and help you. Anyway, they deserve to see it. They were here too."

Seeing them two days later waiting on the dock for the Guadeloupe Ferry, they seemed nothing more then a small group of tourists and friends saying goodbye. They were undistinguishable from scores of others who waited, nervous before the farewells. Their talk was meaningless and shallow. They looked down or out to sea, avoiding each other's eyes.

Warren's mood bordered on sullenness. The night before Rosa told him she was leaving. He had never imagined such a thing and assumed they would go on as before. Something had come over Ruth too, and he found her all but aloof this morning, shaking his damn hand and thanking him for the nice trip like he was just a good little boat captain that had taken her money and shown her a fine time. Maybe she didn't still love him like before, but now she seemed cold and distant. He wanted to hug her and didn't dare.

Myron was equally glum. He stood around shuffling his feet on the dock and rolling his loose upper plate until his upper lip became a precipice. His roaming eyes avoided Freddie, who was himself silent and shy. The two old frogmen were toughing it out, Warren realized. Their affection for each other held them captive, and they waited for the moment of separation as a child might anticipate a painful injection. They just wanted to get past it.

Rosa was there to see them off, chatting now with the Whites, who were the most animated of the group, her big white smile in evidence while Warren stood by feeling like a cold lump of leftover mashed plantain. He hadn't realized the enormity of what had happened to him in the weeks since Freddie-the-Frogman came back into his life and what he had told him about his mother and how for the first time in memory he felt like he had friends. Not drinking buddies. Friends. The kind who might even be loyal, and think well of you.

A moment later Judy Ann left the others and came toward him.

"Hi," she said, flinging her arms around his neck. She was, of course, dressed like a slut. "I love you. This wasn't the best vacation of my life, it was the best thing that ever happened to me and Bobby. We're coming back here every year whether you want us or not."

"I want you," he stammered into the top of her head.

She nestled against him, whispering. "When I get my Napoleon polished and set, every time I wear it I'll think of you." Her silent tears wet his shirt. Then she said, "Marry the girl, Warren. You can never find a truer love." She pushed back and left him.

Then Ruth came and hugged him. Her eyes were dry. "I'll miss you. Again. Doubt I'll ever be back here, so think well of me."

"You'd be welcome if you came."

She shook her head. "It's too hard."

He noticed how her hair was fluffed and hanging to her shoulders as he remembered it from long ago. "Hard for me too."

"I know. Sometimes we need to do what's right instead of what's pleasing. I need to leave you alone and you need to try and get Rosa back." She ran her hand along his side and ignited a gentle charge of remorse.

"I wouldn't mind kissing you right now."

"Don't."

He smiled. "I won't, but you don't know what you're missing."

"Beer breath," she said, returning his smile.

Then Bobby White came and hugged him and tried to stammer a thank you. He seemed exhausted by the goodbyes. Behind him came Freddie, who hugged him too. He smelled of Aqua Velva.

"Damn it," Freddie said. "Myron invited me back next year and offered to let me sleep on your boat. Nice of him, huh?"

"True too," Warren said. "My boat, my house. Take your pick, but please come back. No more gun running or politics, just diving."

Freddie grinned. "Well, let's keep it a little interesting. Might be another shipwreck around this island somewhere, you know."

"There's supposed to be more than one hundred. I won't look until you get here."

"Yeah. I believe that."

The ferry blew its whistle. They retrieved their baggage and moved slowly to join the line of passengers headed toward the brow. Myron, who remained beside him, turned and threw his arms around Warren's shoulders in a bear hug.

"What in the hell are you doing, Myron? You aren't going anywhere."

"I know. I just wanted to hug you."

"Give me a break."

Myron let go and strolled away down the pier toward Edward Town, never looking back.

Warren stood alone with Rosa.

When he looked at her she seemed changed, like someone he'd only just met. Her great black eyes were oblique, unwelcoming. Before he'd always imagined a longing in them. Now he saw something more like indifference, and it frightened him. She meant what she had said, the ultimatum stood - marry her or lose her. How many men before him had been given such a choice, and capitulated? Maybe not as many as should have. But it angered him. He didn't like ultimatums. She wasn't exactly Snow White herself.

"I've got to talk to Javert and straighten out who does what on that wreck," he told her.

She nodded.

"This is important."

"Would you like me to talk with Sir Henry for you?"

He scowled.

She nodded again, the same indifference in her eyes.

Warren was a second away from turning away, but told her instead, "We'll talk about this later."

"There's been enough talk," she said, and strolled up the pier toward the town, leaving him there alone.

CHAPTER THIRTY ONE

Light from above patterned the waves below, warm patches on a sand quilt. Prone on the bottom, Warren was unable to rise even to his knees and shake off the melancholy gripping him since the fight with Rosa. He had come to Sting Ray Flats in a last attempt to find all that seemed to be slipping away from him, but instead found the same emptiness that lingered inside him.

The rays were gone, the flats empty - a barren landscape of worm eels swaying from their holes like deadly vipers in a nightmare. One conch made its way slowly across the bottom. Nothing else but sand and clumps of sea grass. The motionless bottom bereft even of a single reef fish to add color.

The sand heated his bare thighs and he dug his fingers deep into it, clinging to the warm seabed. He held on and closed his eyes. The world was slipping away beneath him in disinterest. And deceit, he thought.

Deceit was the word now after she brought the ultimatum to him - marry her or live without her. They had never spoken to each other like that, and never about what was between them. No one should talk about that. Talk destroys the true feelings that must be kept secret and whole.

It was over now with Rosa. She couldn't stop herself, confessing everything to him about Leach - Armando's true father. But now Warren was given an ultimatum - marry her, take Leach's bastard and like it.

Well, no thanks. No thanks.

He lived without her before and he could do it again.

Sting Ray Flats was composed of more than one thousand acres of protected shallow water over white sand. The colorless water appeared aquamarine from above but below it was like looking through clear thick glass, and you could see laterally for a long distance until the water found its color again. There it was extreme blue and grew dark and mysterious, like staring into deep space and the emptiness stretching away forever.

Yes, Warren thought, he could live without her.

But his sternness with Armando was always a sham that the boy recognized even quicker than his mother. The feelings they had were of father and son and ran too deep for pretending it didn't matter. The boy would soon know who his biological father was, if he didn't already, and then he would need a real one. A man to help him make sense of it when the moment came to the boy and there was nothing in his experience to salve the hurt and begin the healing. Rosa thought she would be the one to do that but Warren knew better. This was a man's job. Mothers were too loving and deflective of pain. The boy would seek a more practical truth only Warren could provide. What could he do about that?

He pushed off the bottom and sat up on his knees. Thinking about Armando rekindled his anger against Rosa. She had no right to make him choose. The boy would come to him regardless. Who else did he have? Maybe his anger should be directed at Leach but it wasn't. The Governor and the dishwasher. Oddly enough, he found it nearly comic, like some poorly written play where the author failed to decide if it was a tragedy or a comedy and left it to the audience to laugh or cry.

Three spadefish, thin, flat, silver-and-gray striped, glided by and made a circle around him to see what he was. He reached out one hand and wiggled his fingers. They fled. He followed them a few seconds later, heading in the direction of the barrier reef where the deep water was held back and the waves broke white and died, leaving the flats in peace.

Warren disliked confrontation. If a conversation turned to politics, he turned away. Religion the same. He cherished his privacy and wished others would cherish theirs. But now he was trapped by circumstances, and by love, so he turned his body to the delights he had always found beneath the sea and swam toward a place without ultimatums.

It was around eleven o'clock when he reached the inner side of the reef and there was a fine surf crashing just beyond, stirring the water where he paused fifteen feet below the surface. He had planned to see if a spiny lobster might be showing its antennae in one of the dark shallow-side holes.

He edged along, poking his head in each crevice and cave large enough, but saw nothing except powdered sand and a few wrasses. After a while he wondered how much water was coming across the reef and if there was enough for the larger fish to cross. It was risky diving this close with heavy surf breaking, but he didn't care. Secretly perhaps, he sought something dangerous and all-consuming to clear his mind.

There was a surge now, a sucking force created by the expended power of the receding water. It swayed his body and fanned the sand into swirling clouds. He allowed it to take him in its hand and he rolled to and fro in the sand, delighted with the captivity, enslaved by a force greater then a man can resist.

With casual indifference he swam to the surface and the water drew him onto the reef and back again until the greater force of the next receding wave lifted him clear and swept him tumbling and flailing out to sea.

He received no injury or damage to his equipment, only the sudden realization that there was no way back. Fear replaced his earlier bravado and he thought how typical that he allowed himself to slip so easily from safety to peril. The sea beneath him was forty feet deep or more, and a short distance farther out it dropped to unimagined depths. In itself, not dangerous. But except for the flats, black limestone cliffs comprised the coastline for miles in either direction. Jagged, towering and deadly. There was only one way out of the water, and that was back across the reef.

In order to swim the twenty yards or so back to the flats he needed to cross the reef safely once again. This seemed almost as unlikely as safely scaling a high cliff of razor-sharp rock. He inflated his BCD and inspected himself carefully. No apparent injury other then some scuffing on one of his Jet Fins. A small miracle. He rolled onto his stomach, bit down on the mouthpiece of his snorkel and cleared the water with a sharp blast of air, then swam steadily out to sea. If he put some distance between himself and the reef, then caught a large enough wave, maybe he could bodysurf back over the reef without serious injury. Fat chance, but his only one.

The reef was rooted in rock, and even the cut where they brought *Esteban* across was deep enough for a safe passage only at high tide. The rest of the time, it was just as treacherous as any place along the expanse of coral covered rock. All of it constantly battered by waves, especially during heavy weather. Hard corals rarely reached the surface. But just below, elkhorn and staghorn grew in profusion, their arms broken and sharp, able to rip the bottom from a boat with ease. Warren knew what they did to a human body wasn't worth contemplating. He had suffered enough coral cuts to know his failure to clear the reef promised painful injury, even death.

For a while he just watched, counting the sets and calculating when the largest waves appeared. From the backside it seemed even the tallest of them barely cleared corals and rock. Unless he was in a prone position his legs and feet would be dragged across the reef. He could only imagine what damage that might do.

He had come out across from the flats so quickly he had no time for fear. He did it wearing his full scuba equipment and five pounds of lead weight around his waist. It seemed impossible that he could repeat such a lucky passage unless he ditched all his equipment to lighten himself and went over on just mask, fins and snorkel. Nine hundred dollars' worth of equipment would sink and most likely be lost forever, including his new Scubapro Mark V regulator. Like that first one he had purchased so long ago from his idol Freddie-the-Frogman, it was his pride and joy. He didn't want to lose it even if it meant risking his life in the bargain.

The day was clear except for a few high thin clouds drifting from sea to land. Sea conditions were moderate and inside the reef on the flats the water barely rippled. Warren swam farther out to sea, away from danger. He adjusted his buoyancy, paddling slowly away on his back. His pressure gauge read just under one thousand psi, enough for a quick trip to deeper water where he might still find a lobster, which had been what led him into this predicament in the first place.

He dumped BCD air and descended, arms and legs spread, elbows and knees bent, fins pressing the water left and right, steering him into the depths. He drifted down along the vertical outside wall of the reef and with near perfect visibility saw it clearly. Within minutes he spotted a lobster antennae and kicked sharply to close the distance. The crustacean was hidden inside a narrow crack in the coral until Warren slipped his hand gently into the crack and clasped it by the carapace, pressing to pin it against the hard coral floor of the opening. Carefully, he drew it out. Before its tail was clear he caught it in his other hand and gripped it so the large tail muscle couldn't flex and swim the lobster to safety.

Warren's diving attire always included large-pocketed combat pants. He shoved the lobster inside his left expanded pocket. He had him, but could he keep him during the risky swim across the reef?

He surfaced.

He began counting wave sets again. He readied himself and felt his heart begin to race, pounding the inside of his rib cage. He fought down the mounting fear that held him stationary in the water, still some distance from the reef and crashing waves.

Another man in similar circumstances might offer a prayer for his safety, but Warren had given up on God when Stephen drowned. He fought with Rosa about this more than anything else - this loving God of hers who stood by that icy night and allowed Stephen to die. A little boy, giving his life for his brother. Warren's life burdened with everlasting guilt.

Again, he dredged it all up, remembering clearly the moment when he killed his brother. Felt Stephen's strong little child hands pushing him back onto the ice, but it wasn't enough and Warren thrust his feet against his brother's skull and shoved himself to safety, pushing Stephen down into the black water. Water so cold it filled his lungs and froze him, and God watched it all and did nothing. And every day since, Warren could do nothing to ease the pain but drink himself senseless.

He blamed his parents in the same way. They mourned Stephen and packed him away, but they did nothing for Warren. Were they too stupid to know how he felt? Much later, off-handedly, his mother mentioned that Stephen's death wasn't Warren's fault. It came almost as an afterthought and he resented it more than anything his mother ever did. And now, at the end of her life, what had she done? Written him a letter to lay upon him even more guilt to carry. He wanted to rip her letter again and again and again.

The wave sets seemed smaller now and most of them broke in foaming white water this side of the reef, and only the foam itself made it across into the flats. He wondered if the tide was ebbing and he would be stranded here until it changed in the middle of the night sometime. He couldn't wait that long or swim the many miles along the cliffs to a safe exit point. He shouldn't have left *Esteban* in Edward Town Harbor and driven Orizondo's truck to the flats, but feared to moor the boat, filled with weapons, anywhere but the harbor until Javert had collected them. Slither and Myron were both aboard standing watch. So his choice now was simple - swim across the reef or die trying.

As he watched, the waves decreased in size even more until most were breaking on the deep side of the reef and swimming across would be suicide. He considered walking across but knew his soft neoprene boots would be cut in shreds long before he reached safety, and along with them his feet.

It was safe now, though, to move closer. The waves no longer held enough power to pick him up and thrust him onto the sharp corals. Maybe he could see a place that did look safe enough to walk across.

He swam first to the shallow cut where they crossed the reef by boat at high tide, but wasn't surprised to find it no more accessible now at low tide than anywhere else. The larger rocks were above water. So for more than two hours he swam up and down the face of the reef, searching. Hope kept alive by supposing that he'd missed a spot somewhere. Maybe he had looked down or turned his head at the exact moment a smooth rock ledge or stretch of flat coral slipped by unnoticed. Easy enough to do, and he was feeling the stress of failure and the beginnings of exhaustion. After years in the water, he knew rest was an important defense against panic, and panic led to death.

He might scramble onto the reef and slip or be knocked down by a wave. Not that death was anything to fear, he supposed, but the suffering beforehand - ripped flesh, severed veins and arteries, crushed bones - might be a disadvantage.

He rested, reviewing the possibilities, postponing the decision a little longer.

He must be tired. More exhausted than he imagined. He inflated his BCD and rested back on the soft air collar, reminding himself to breathe regularly, slowing the rate to normal. Relax, he told himself. "Relax," he said aloud. That made him laugh. "Hey, God!" he shouted. "One more chance. I'm going for it. Just give me a minute."

But he didn't take it. Instead, he stifled his laughter, stuffed his regulator into his mouth and turned toward the reef for his final swim.

His fins churned the water and he tasted the rubber as he clamped down hard on the mouthpiece. Muscles in his strong legs propelled him faster and faster toward the foaming reef but he didn't slacken his pace, and pushed harder still until his legs drew the fins up and down, up and down.

His speed increased.

He began to lift like a speedboat planing at full power, rising so fast his stomach felt hollow and light.

All fear left him and he thought instead of Rosa. He heard her clearly and she said, "I love you, Warren, but the cost is too high." He cursed her because she made no sense.

The water was stirring beneath him. He felt it swelling, assembling its forces like a swollen river straining behind a weakened dam, about to explode and carry him away. He was lifted higher and higher, light as air, like he wasn't in the water at all. The foaming reef was far below. He saw it in its entirety, stretched out like something you fly over. Beyond, he saw the calm waters of the flats. Aquamarine color sparkling with sunshine. He saw the white sand, beach palms, and cool shadows.

Then the force that had entrapped him trembled. Trembled again, and rolled forward. He was submerged and blue beams of brilliant water blinded him, yet he was swift as a wet wind. Nothing could hold him back. He flew across the reef and it was effortless. He saw the golden and rust red of the staghorn and elkhorn and waving purple of the broken, shredded sea fans, bright oranges of the tattered clinging soft corals and the black urchins wedged in holes and between rocks. His eyes were those of a raven and missed nothing. He saw deep into the sea, rock, sand and foam.

He felt blissful, like a diver seized by rapture of the deep. This strong sense of well-being removed fear and doubt, leaving him at peace.

A moment later it was gone.

The water lowered him, a gentle giant hand, into the calmness of the flats, surrounded by a soapy froth of foam, and then it too, was gone.

He swam on steadily toward shallow water, afraid to think or look around, and in his pocket the lobster wiggled.

Finally he was able to stand. The firmness of the bottom reassured him. He had come across from death to life, from uncertainty to solid ground, and by no power of his own. The wave had come out of nowhere. He knew it happened. There were freak waves at sea, but usually far from land, but he guessed they had to come ashore somewhere. Didn't they? What an incredible stroke of luck.

He swung out of his scuba gear, inflated his BCD enough so it floated the tank and regulator, then removed his mask, fins, and snorkel, piling them on top. He left the weight belt in place, towed the floating gear to the beach and sat down beside it in shallow water to rest. The gentle waves bathed his legs and rocked the tank against the sand. It felt good to be so lucky.

The high sun beamed hot, soothing his skin, warming away the fear and tight muscles of his struggle. The beach was empty. The sky, too, had cleared. He saw no signs that a giant wave had crashed ashore, and the palms rattled their soft song in quiet whispers, murmuring in careless disinterest. Only minutes had passed since Warren faced the likelihood of death. Now he lounged unhurt and free in warm sunshine, secure as he'd ever been.

And so he passed an hour there resting, clearing his mind, until he remembered to check his pressure gauge and realized more then 500 psi remained. Enough for one more dive. He felt no movement from the lobster in his pocket. Why had he taken it anyway? Who would prepare it for him?

Warren donned his equipment again and swam the lobster back along the quiet inside of the reef and released it. Disoriented, it sat on the sand, unable to move. He fell forward again onto the warm sand and watched. He might have to eat it yet.

But finally the lobster found its legs and staggered off toward the reef, kicking up sand and flailing its antennae. Warren crossed his arms and rested his chin on them. The excitement of the past few weeks was fading and while he may have lost Rosa, Ruth, even Armando, he had this. A perfect place of peace and solitude. Underwater he knew himself and there was no phoniness or pretention. He was free of that other world where things never seemed to go right for him.

His pressure gauge read 300 psi. Time to swim back and see what he'd thrown in the truck cooler, besides beer, then stow his gear and go home.

He inhaled deeply and the increased lung volume lifted him easily from the bottom, and with the effortlessness born of practice, he kicked gently and propelled himself ahead like a human submarine at slow speed.

The bubbles of his regulator exhaust ports flowed musically along his ears. The familiar sound cheered him as he arched his back and swung his body toward the beach.

Before he had gone a dozen yards, a wide shadow fell over him and when he looked up, there was a brown stingray. Warren stopped swimming and knelt on the sand. The ray responded immediately and set a course for his head.

Warren raised his hand and the ray came steadily on toward it and Warren stroked his cool silk underside. A lobster's antennae protruded from the ray's mouth, and Warren heard the sound of grinding teeth. It seemed his catch had filled a stomach after all.

The ray glided to the sand several yards away and finished eating. Warren studied him. A large male - he had spotted the two claspers when he soared overhead - but was he one of the old group with Darth Vader and Elmo? Could he recognize Warren without the boat sounds? The ray seemed as before, unafraid and willing to be fed, though Warren had nothing else to feed him.

Many of the rays were not recognizable because they had come to the flats intermittently or resembled others too closely and never named. Vader was black. Elmo huge. Often there were females even larger. Warren grinned and mumbled into his regulator, "I'm going to call you Wesley." Why not? He'd outlived the bastard. Warren attended Bens' funeral, but only to please Rosa. He doubted Bens had any kind of conversion, just a severe blow to the head that left him confused. Had he lived, he might have come out of it.

Wesley stayed close by, but Warren's tank was nearly dry and he had to swim ashore. He grinned. The rays were back. At least one.

Well, he thought, I'll never tell another living soul or exploit them again. No one will ever know and when he was alone, as he was very likely to be, he could come here as before and feed them.

He rinsed out his equipment in the shallows and lugged it to Orizondo's pickup. The beer was still cool and he spotted half a sandwich left in the cooler. He dropped the tailgate, sat and ate, guzzling beer between bites. It was cool in the shade and it felt good to be alone in an isolated spot - nothing to interrupt him and no one making demands. This is the way men should live, he decided. Solitary creatures without schedules or people interfering with the flow of their lives. Yes, men were like the lonely rays, descending to the depths, exploring the unknown and returning to the warmth of the flats to eat, mate, and rest. No obligations, only peace.

A profound observation, he decided. If he had been saddled with a family he doubted that such profundity would have been possible. No. Of course not.

He finished the first bottle of beer and opened another.

"Warren."

Rosa's voice.

He turned slowly to face her. "How did you get here?"

She moved almost leisurely from deep shadow into the sunlight and across to him. "That is what you say to me? 'How did you get here?'"

"Well, you don't drive."

She came closer. "The chicken bus."

"It doesn't stop here."

"I walked the last few miles."

"You aren't wearing any shoes."

"I left them in the shade."

"Always have an answer for everything," he said.

Now she stood facing him and he made no effort to stand.

"Okay then," he said. "What are you doing here?"

"Armando sent me."

"Armando sent you. What does that mean?"

"He told me to come and see you. Get you back so we could be happy again. I said no and he became angry and called me a whore."

Warren sighed. "Well, you should've kept your mouth shut."

"It didn't matter." She shook her head. "He's known all along. The children have been teasing him most of his life."

"And he never told anybody?"

She shook her head again. "He has you and me. Don't you think we would be the last two people on earth he could confide in? The whore and her lover?"

Warren felt sweat beading on his forehead and jumped down from the tailgate, then walked away farther into the shade. Rosa followed a minute later.

"I'm not really sure I want to have this conversation," he said.

"Nor I," she said.

"Well then."

She came very close, almost as tall as he, but did not touch him. Instead she dropped to her knees and said, "I promised him I would ask you again. Beg if necessary. He loves you like a father and I love you like a husband." She bowed her head. "Look at me so that you can know I will do anything to save the one chance for us. Not just Armando and me, but you. Of the three of us you are the most lost, and you won't know it until some night when you are drunk or alone in the water, and the melancholy comes upon you. Then you will know it, too late. Now there is still time."

"Get up, Rosa."

"No. I'm embarrassing you? A black woman on her knees, begging you. Is it too much? Are you too white to be human?"

He felt too weak to lift her up and sank down beside her. "You're trying to force me," he whispered.

"No. Just force you to decide with your heart instead of your ego. If I believed you didn't love me or it wouldn't work for us or that you are too small a man to love another man's son, then Armando could call me a whore for the rest of his life before I came to you. But I am sure in my heart and my head about this. And I am sure about you. Ruth knew it. She told me. Her youth is gone and she still has feeling for you, but it's obvious, she said, that we are family. She didn't say lovers. Family."

Warren sat a long time on his knees, until the sand hurt and the waiting hurt even more. Finally he stood up and extended a hand to Rosa.

They were so close her breasts rested against him. He leaned forward and kissed her lightly on the lips.

"What is this?" she asked.

"A proposal."

Acknowledgments

Books are seldom the work of one person. Authors rely on many others to polish their work. I wish to especially thank St. Cloud artist R.C. McCoy, who faithfully sketched Charming Island, employing great patience in extracting it from my imagination.

George Ernest Weiland, my British dive partner, shared the discovery of *Imperial* with me, and we later worked under near impossible conditions diving an oil rig miles off the coast of the Dominican Republic.

The first scuba dive was made by French naval officer Jacques Cousteau in 1943. Today millions of people around the world are certified divers. It is one of the safest and most exciting sports of our time and those of us who became the first recreational divers after World War II, count ourselves fortunate to have grown up with the sport. Thanks to diving educational organizations for making it safe, and the innovation of scuba equipment manufacturers making it cool.

Author Jimmy Olsen on the anchor ring of the *Imperial* shipwreck, circa 1973